C000197265

UNEQUALLED
16

# SPEDAN'S PARTNERSHIP

*The Story of John Lewis and Waitrose*

PETER COX

Published by Labatie Books
www.spedanspartnership.co.uk



Project management by Cambridge Editorial Ltd., Building 9, Michael Young Centre, Purbeck Road, Cambridge CB2 8QL. www.camedit.com

Design by Paul Barrett Book Production, Cambridge. www.pbbp.co.uk

Printed by in Great Britain by the MPG Books Group, Bodmin and King's Lynn

ISBN 978-0-9551877-2-8

By the same author:
*Sixty Summers – English Cricket since World War 2*
*Set into Song – Ewan MacColl, Charles Parker, Peggy Seeger and the Radio Ballads*

For all John Lewis Partners and customers, past, present and future.

# Contents

# Prologue

At intervals the effects of capitalism are called into question. A hundred years ago ruthless exploitation of labour led to the Russian revolution and the rise of communism as an alternative way to run society. Fifty years ago the world seemed permanently split into capitalist and communist blocs. Twenty years ago, when the Berlin Wall crumbled, the capitalist approach seemed to have triumphed. Now, the recent domino collapse of national banks the world over has reminded us that it hasn't. At best it's still work-in-progress, and still vulnerable to abuse on a colossal scale. That abuse can exist because the theoretical stakeholders in companies rarely have any practical power to check excesses, as indeed they couldn't in communist societies either. But what alternative is there?

Recently, attention in Britain has begun to focus on a form of employee participation that grew up in a small London department store after the end of the 1914–18 War. That company has now expanded to become a retail chain employing over 70,000 employees. It continues to make a decent profit, distributed as a bonus to its employees rather than as dividends to shareholders. It can still raise money when it needs to expand. It regularly wins awards for its customer service. It must be doing something right. Can it be emulated? Politicians of all shades have started to talk of modifying the way public services are run along the lines of the 'John Lewis model'. What does that really mean? How does it work, and how did it come about?

It began as an idealistic concept in the mind's eye of a young man in his early twenties. He was not called John Lewis – that was his father. The son was Spedan, and in 1905, on his twenty-first birthday, he was given, as his brother was two years later, a quarter share of John Lewis's business, a department store that had expanded and expanded from a single shopfront on the north side of London's Oxford Street. His father was nearly seventy now, so Spedan Lewis had the prospect of soon becoming extremely rich. But what he found at first sight of his father's accounts gave him pause for thought, especially when he realised how much he was earning in relation to the employees. Very nearly everyone in his position would be simply content to enjoy what that disparity gave him – a magnificent standard of living for the rest of his life. Spedan was not a socialist – if anything he was a traditional liberal – but he was far from content with this state of affairs, and, during a protracted and painful illness in 1909 and 10 he turned over and over in his mind how he might make life fairer for his workforce. Moreover, how could he help them enjoy work rather than endure it, and in the process make it – *their* – enterprise more successful? And could he do it while still safeguarding the family business?

In Britain there were no organisations to use as a model, but by October of 1910, exactly 100 years before this book was published, he'd worked out how to do it. He would give the employees a financial share in its success. He knew his father would be obdurately opposed to such a revolutionary plan, so he bided his time. Had he waited till his father retired, it would have taken nearly twenty years, for John retained ownership in Oxford Street until the day he died in 1928, at ninety-two. By then an exasperated Spedan would have switched career, probably into politics, had his father not decided in 1906 to buy the ailing Peter Jones store, further west in Chelsea. In 1914, after a series of family clashes, Spedan traded his quarter share in the solid family business for the right to run Peter Jones, now in a parlous state. To run it on his own.

The little continental skirmish due to be 'over by Christmas' was on its way to becoming the Great War, and almost every business (except armaments and uniform suppliers) was in a bad way. That was the background when Spedan took over Peter Jones, having exchanged a certain fortune for the chance to test what even his friends thought was a lunatic idea. Eventually, after a long struggle to overcome a series of setbacks, he succeeded in turning his Big Idea into reality. What happened to that idea is what I set out to explore in this book.

The book came about following a conversation in 2008 with an old John Lewis friend, who remarked that it was a pity that new John Lewis and Waitrose Partners had little to explain to them how this unique and somewhat eccentric business had came about. He and I had joined it at a time when people who still remembered Spedan talked about him, warts and all, but he has been dead now for nearly fifty years and memories have faded. A few weeks after that conversation I got the go-ahead from the new Chairman, Charlie Mayfield, to write the story. The Partnership has not commissioned the book, but has given me full access to anyone I wanted to speak to, and to its extensive archive. It has not attempted to influence the contents in any way, and I have been scrupulous to be as unbiased as I possibly can. However, I accept that someone who worked for the business for thirty-five years, and admired it – but hardly uncritically – cannot be truly objective.

With that caveat, then, here it is. It has been aimed at the reader who starts with no knowledge of the Partnership or retailing at all. The first eighteen chapters tell the narrative chronologically; the last two sum up the business as it operates today, both as a retailer and a co-owned business. The story begins on a spring day in 1864 when a young man from Somerset, orphaned at the age of seven, branches out on his own to sell silk fabrics from a little converted tobacconist's shop in Oxford Street.

1 From Gross Profit only Pref. & A Cum Div. is deducted ∴ B Cum. Div. at all events on first £60.000 should be met out of saving of interest now payable to J.L. & Co., Bank, in loss of Discounts & Debentures

According to these figures full Dividend would be paid to Pref. & Ord. A in respect of next year & thenceforward;

the Staff would receive in respect of next year £1,125 Ord. B:
of the year after next £5,625 Ord. B.
& thenceforward £5,963 " "
every year:

by the end of 1921 the Dividend Reserve would mean that the whole cum. div. for the coming year would be in hand at the beginning of each year, £298 being added yearly to provide for each annual distribution of £5,963 as above:

Ord. A would get their first non-cum.

An extract from Spedan Lewis's notebook in which he works out how to distribute the first Partnership 'Benefit' to all the employees of Peter Jones, in the form of non-voting shares. This was in early 1920. From then on all the employees were known as Partners.

CHAPTER 1

# An Orphan in Oxford Street

John Lewis in his thirties.

Eliza Baker in her twenties.

His was a fine store and did a remarkable trade. Most drapers work to a 33% profit on selling price, which is 50% on cost. John Lewis worked to 25% on selling price and insisted that the public should get the advantage of a good purchase by his buyers ... John Lewis saved on his overheads and he did not advertise. He was a remarkable man ... who stood there like a gnarled old oak, representing much of the worst type of employer in the rugged, rather shameless, individualist past of the Victorian and Edwardian era.

PHILIP HOFFMAN, IN HIS AUTOBIOGRAPHY *THEY ALSO SERVE*, 1948

The business that eventually developed into the John Lewis Partnership started slowly. On its first day in April 1864 John Lewis's rented shop at 132 Oxford Street made just 16s 4d, worth about £75 today: sixteen shillings and four pence in the old British currency, whose addition and subtraction caused such misery to a nation of school children. John, now twenty-eight, had been earning about that sum each day as a buyer of silk fabrics for the draper Peter Robinson on the other side of Oxford Circus. His old employer was now his rival. For a time the newly independent John Lewis struggled, but after a few months he decided to buy a job lot of silks, and sell it at a seductively low price. Customers arrived, returned with their friends, and the word went round. John Lewis's name was made. So who was he?

## A Family of Orphans

John Lewis was born in 1836 in Shepton Mallet, the sleepy Somerset market town whose steadily diminishing wealth had originally been built on wool. Near the market square his father John ran a bakery, and John junior was the fifth of six children born to the baker and his wife Elizabeth Speed. The Speeds were an extended Shepton family of shopkeepers, of grocers and brewers, basket makers and milliners, and their support was called on when the mother of the Lewis family died, followed two years later by the father. The six Lewis children were in desperate need of help. In 1843 when they were orphaned Elizabeth was seventeen, probably at home with her four sisters – Maria was thirteen, Ann eleven, Mary nine, and Eliza five. John was the single boy, the only one who could be expected to earn a reasonable income, and he was seven.

What happened next is clear, if uncertain in detail, and typical for the lives of orphaned Victorian children. Those old enough to work were farmed out as apprentices or domestic servants, while the youngest were taken in by relatives with space and – you hoped – a kindly disposition. The alternative was the grim reality of the Shepton workhouse, which loomed nearby as a constant reminder of the dangers of penury. In fact the town's workhouse was rebuilt in 1848 because it was too small, such were the effects of the economic hardship brought about by the rapid decline of its wool trade in the face of the new mechanised competition from up north. The Lewis children did manage to avoid the workhouse, and, although there are no family stories describing what immediately happened to them, we can deduce what must have taken place. By the time of the 1851 census Maria, Ann and John are with a draper in Glastonbury, Mary is working in a shop in Wells, and thirteen-year-old Eliza is with her aunt Christian in Shepton. The much older Elizabeth is a servant in the substantial household of the rector of a Somerset village. The orphan family has been spread around the towns and villages of Somerset.

It is largely to their Aunt Christian that the Lewises were indebted. The eldest of six Speed aunts, she was single and independent. For many years she made and sold hats in the same street as the Lewis bakery, an occupation she maintained until the death of John's mother early in 1841. Around that time she moved into the Lewis household, and the next year made a late marriage to one James Clark. She was then forty-eight and he several years older, the quaintly named 'Principal Turnkey' of the House of Correction in Shepton. In other words he was the gaoler of an already ancient prison, one still in use today, though without the great exhausting treadwheel used for that 'correction'. Christian married the town gaoler between the deaths of John's parents, and as a consequence was perhaps better equipped to support the orphaned Lewises – and not just them, for she soon had another niece with her, the daughter of her widowed sister Ann. It is tempting, if a guess too far, to see her marriage as one of convenience, undertaken to secure the future of her newly acquired dependents. By the end of the 1850s, now widowed herself and in her late sixties, she had set up in the increasingly popular Somerset seaside resort of Weston-super-Mare, running a drapery shop in the High Street and sheltering under her wing three of John's sisters – Elizabeth, Mary and Eliza. John's aunt and sisters were to be of crucial importance to young John, who was born in the year Dickens was writing about another orphan, Oliver Twist.

What happened to John at first is uncertain, but we know that enough money was found to send him at the age of eleven in 1847 to the grammar school at Shepton. He was probably there till he was fifteen, when in early 1851 he went to work for a draper in Glastonbury, Peter Marquand, already employing his sisters Maria and Ann. But Marquand soon died, and John went to work at the linen and drapery shop of Joseph Tasker, close to Wells Cathedral, where he was apprenticed for three years. At eighteen he moved on to the Bridgwater drapery shop of Henry Nicholls. Shepton Mallet, Glastonbury, Wells, Bridgwater – he seemed set for the life of a provincial West Country draper: one that might content his sisters, perhaps, but he clearly had wider horizons, and he soon upped and went to the city.

## Liverpool and London

In 1855 John Lewis arrived in the seething port city of Liverpool. Why Liverpool? If he wanted the greater opportunities that a big city afforded, Bristol was much closer. Bristol had been Britain's foremost port in the previous century, but Liverpool had recently eclipsed it. Perhaps he was encouraged to come by another Speed aunt, Margaret Godfrey, whose husband had spent time there working for a lawyer. Twenty years earlier, before the railway came, such a move would have been rare. But England was shrinking at what must have seemed a dizzying speed. John was born even before

Queen Victoria was on the throne. When he began his apprenticeship, travel for most people was on foot or by horse-drawn cart: Brunel's Irish navvies were only just starting to move from the canals to carve out the railway lines of England, and indeed they wouldn't arrive in Shepton till 1858. But Bridgwater was already on Brunel's new Great Western line, so a journey to Liverpool was feasible. Once there he worked for a draper called Carmichael in Church Street, where he earned £3 10s a month, the equivalent of about £80 a week today. Board and lodging were provided, and he eked out the rest carefully, keeping meticulous records in his diary of what he spent. (His 1856 diary is the only one that remains.) By that April, however, less than a year after he'd arrived in Liverpool, he was getting restless, looking for other jobs and badgering his employer for a rise. He had just succeeded in getting one when he was sacked for fighting.

Sacked for fighting? Those who only know of Old John Lewis as a venerable man with a ruddy face and a bushy white beard may find that hard to credit. (Later in life this pugilism would move from the shop floor to the courts.) We don't know why they'd fought, but his opponent's bloodied face could not be disguised, and both had to go. What now? He made his mind up swiftly. He borrowed a gold sovereign from a Frenchman he'd been working with, and three days later, on 6 May 1856, he took the train to London. There two of his Speed aunts were living, as well as his cousin Percy Godfrey, who became a companion and showed him the city sights. For six months he lived-in and worked in a Regent Street shop, then at the end of October was taken on by Peter Robinson, a highly successful draper with a store extending east along Oxford Street from the north-east corner of Oxford Circus: a prime location and the position now occupied by Top Shop. Robinson seems to have spotted John's abilities immediately, and was soon entrusting him with buying silks in the City. After four years Robinson formally appointed him his buyer of silks and woollen dress materials. That sounds promising, but in 1861 he was still living with fifty-four others above Peter Robinson's shop, which stretched from 103 to 108 Oxford Street.

Though John Lewis was successful and comparatively well paid, with six people working for him, he was clearly determined to be his own master, and the story goes that a Mrs Morrison, widow of a hugely successful wholesale draper, one who 'bought cheap and sold cheap', encouraged him to set up on his own. He was twenty-eight. He oversaw in person the conversion of the Oxford Street tobacconist's he rented, and there's a story that, when he was having plate glass installed, one evening it was only half-finished. He decided despite a hard day's work that he'd sit in a chair in the window and guard it. But he dozed off, only to be woken at two in the morning by a patrolling policeman, who ticked off the presumed night watchman: 'If you can't keep awake I shall have to tell your master.'

The shop was rented, but he needed money for stock. Early in 1864 he had deposited nearly £800 (about £75,000 today) in a bank in Cavendish Square. That's an extraordinarily large amount for a man who, thriftily as he might have saved, cannot have provided much more than a quarter of it. The remainder was almost certainly supplied by his sisters, most from his elder sister Maria, and possibly his aunt. Maria was thirty-four and had been selling in a draper's shop for well over twenty years, most recently in Bath. Her contribution must have been her life savings, and perhaps some of her aunt's and sisters' as well (for it seems inconceivable that she can have saved that much on her own). Perhaps it had always been the sisters' intention to set their only brother up in business, and Maria supported him more than just financially: she looked after the selling area of the shop for the next six years and continued to help until at least the 1870s. Thereupon she left to join her sisters in Weston-super-Mare. If the money was in effect a loan, as seems probable, then young John Lewis would pay his sisters back handsomely. His farsighted trading principles made him a fortune.

As his son Spedan was to say with admiration, his father had a clear and unwavering policy. He would give excellent value. He would be entirely honest at a time when retailers frequently weren't. He would keep in stock an extremely wide assortment. And the last of these was the most important. John Lewis was convinced that if you had a reputation for keeping in stock, say, colours of ribbon that were rarely in demand, you would gradually build in your customers an unconscious conviction that if you couldn't get it at John Lewis you couldn't get it anywhere. It wasn't worth trying anywhere else, not least because you'd only get it cheaper if it was of a poorer quality. Needless to say, the shopkeeper carried an extra cost if he didn't manage his stocks carefully, and when he came into the business many years later Spedan was horrified to discover how 'stale' some of that stock was, how long it had been clogging up the shop. But his father's wide assortment policy worked. Of course it needed space, and John certainly used every half inch of his, even scraping the plaster off the walls of 132 Oxford Street to gain a little more storage fixture depth. That's a measure of his intensity of will, an innate ability to take simple truths and drive them far further than most others would.

## 132 Oxford Street

The engraving overleaf shows the position of the original rented shop, anonymous now in the whole block it occupies in 2010. Note that the street's numbering has completely changed. What became number 286 Oxford Street was originally number 132, the fourth shop frontage west of the junction with Holles Street, which runs northwards to the south-east corner of Cavendish Square, where the grand houses begin. It was part, then as now, of the Portland Estate. That puts the first shop about 250 yards west of Oxford Circus, where Regent Street crossed Oxford Street on its way up to Regent's Park. Oxford Street was not then quite the great shopping street it is now. It was the westward artery from the heart of London, the City, towards Oxford, lined almost entirely with individual shops. In the early 1860s number 132 was hemmed in at different times by a shoe shop, a brushmaker, a bookseller, a florist, a jeweller, an optician, a dentist, a 'hair draper', a hosier, and a staymaker. All had single narrow frontages, little more than twenty feet wide. The drapers Peter Robinson and Marshall & Snelgrove each had six in a row, but they were exceptions. Regent Street had begun to be fashionable, and contained several 'mourning houses', catering to that necessary and prolonged Victorian exhibition of formulaic grief, that led, in one fanciful account, to John Lewis having in stock 100 different shades of black (leading to some imaginative naming, one can only assume). Regent Street also contained the Lewis and Allenby store, a prior claim to the name which led to John being called 'Little' Lewis. But the most important shopping areas then were in Tottenham Court Road and east to St Paul's. It's to the east that young John Lewis, accompanied by a porter with a barrow, went each morning to buy his fabrics wholesale.

Apparently for several years John Lewis did most of the crucial work of the business himself, buying usually in the City but often in Paris, now readily accessible by a regular train and ferry service. He was determined to look beyond the easiest sources of supply, later going to Lyon for his silk, and Calais for his lace, claiming that he was the first to persuade the Calais manufacturers to bypass wholesalers and sell to retailers direct. (If Shepton Grammar School had taught him anything useful beyond the essentials, it was French, for that was the language in which he wrote the first few months of his 1856 diary, presumably to make it safe from prying eyes.) Sales in his first year of 1864 were an impressive £5,000, which had risen to £25,000 within six years. They topped £100,000 in the 1880s, just under £1m today.

Clearly John Lewis needed far more space than scraped plaster could give him. He bought a shop further down Oxford Street, but he wasn't temperamentally suited to 'branch' trading. He would prove that, for the benefit of

The block in Oxford Street that John Lewis occupies today, as it was in the mid 19th century. Holles Street is at the right edge, and the original shop was no. 132, the fourth from the end.

his son and this story if not for himself, at Peter Jones in Sloane Square nearly fifty years later. But as soon as he could, he bought up nearby shops. He had the money – he didn't spend lavishly, he was extremely tight on expenses (and on what he paid his staff) – and he just needed the opportunity. It took a while, for it was only in 1875 that he was able to buy two unconnected shops in Holles Street. By 1881 he'd got his nearest neighbours on each side. One of them had been occupied by a fruiterer who held the exclusive contract to import and sell that exotic fruit the banana, brought in green and hung together in great bunches in a heated basement in order to ripen properly. Lewis gradually picked off the shops in Holles Street (in one of which a hero of his had been born, the poet Byron) and his determination to get them can be seen from a story his son Spedan told that illustrated his combative nature. One of the shops, he'd discovered, had already been bought by Peter Robinson's son John. Lewis asked John Robinson to come and see him, gripped him by the neck and apparently banged his head against the wall. He got that house, but it wasn't until 1892 that he'd bridged the all-important gap to the Holles Street corner. Even then, his landlord wouldn't allow him to connect them behind the frontage, so he was constantly darting in and out of individual shops.

But, awkward as those arrangements were, he had enough space to diversify, as his rivals were increasingly doing. Drapers thrived because not until the late nineteenth century did you buy clothes ready-made: you bought the material and either made it yourself or paid a dressmaker to do it for you. So he began essentially as a purveyor of silk and woollen dress materials, though unusually he sold ribbons and haberdashery as well – everything you needed to make a garment. He made a good living that way, but the expansion of purchasing power in 1870s Britain, fuelled by its empire, brought new opportunities and approaches for the traditional draper or silk 'mercer', which is how John Lewis described himself: a man who trades in textiles (see Plate 1). He was not alone: many of the great London drapers were expanding even more rapidly at this time, men such as William Whiteley, Tom Ponting, Charles Harrod and Arthur Liberty, as well as a man we'll meet in the next chapter, Peter Jones. Lewis's competitors had been expanding their merchandise from dressing the person to dressing the home, into what was becoming called the 'department' store.

## The Birth of the Department Store – in Newcastle

Back in 1830 a boy of thirteen had begun his drapery apprenticeship in Newcastle. Eight years later that boy, endowed with the sonorous name of Emerson Muschamp Bainbridge, opened a shop in partnership in Market Street, Newcastle. His tenet, too, was honesty: his first advertisements were headed 'A Reform In the Woollen and Linen Drapery Trade', a reform which included the innovation of posting set prices for goods. In 1841, branching out with a cousin, he announced that they 'would not be undersold by any branch in the Kingdom': wording which bears more than a passing resemblance to a slogan that would be coined by John Lewis's son in the next century. But the key innovation gradually emerged in that decade. Because his success allowed him to expand rapidly into new areas of business, Bainbridge by 1849 was meticulously recording his weekly takings by 'department'. Hence together with the Bon Marché in Paris it can claim to be the first European 'Department Store'. The departments Bainbridge analysed separately back then were Furs, French Fancy, Shawls, Cloaks, Fancy Dress Materials, Mercery, Haberdashery, Trimmings, Hosiery, Gloves, Prints, Drapery, Ribbons, Bonnets, Laces, Stuffs, Linens, Flannels, Furnishing and Carpets. Those last two were the only kinds of merchandise that couldn't be worn. A little over 100 years later Bainbridges, unable to sustain its independence, would join the business begun by John Lewis on almost identical principles.

## Property and Marriage

Frustrated by his inability to form his collection of Oxford Street and Holles Street frontages into a properly connected shop as his competitors could, John Lewis was at first unable to expand into such a wide range of departments. He was frugal and his wants were small, and he put almost all the spare money he accumulated into property, particularly in the area between Oxford Street and the Marylebone Road. He kept in constant touch with his sisters down in Weston-super-Mare, visiting them regularly and more than repaying the initial loan. After Aunt Christian died in 1875 he bought for them a house he called Spedan Ham. He had a fondness for coining new words, and it's notable that the name was conceived before his son was. Spedan's brother Oswald appears in a later Weston house of theirs, called Oswaldene. (Later Partnership myth assumed that the word 'Spedan' was a reversal of another aunt, Ann Speed, but she was long dead and seems to have had nothing to do with his upbringing.)

John's sisters did not marry, and neither, did it appear, would he. Although around the time he was starting out John Lewis had formed a close friendship with the niece of one of his suppliers, there seems not to have been a whiff of a further attachment until he was in his late forties. In 1880 he had taken a rare holiday, cruising on the spectacular Caledonian Canal in Scotland, where he met a successful Bristol draper of the same age, one Mills Baker. With Baker was a much younger half-sister and ward, Eliza, known as Ellie. She had been one of the first women graduates from Girton College in Cambridge. Whether there was any initial attraction between the draper aged forty-four and that woman of twenty-six is unknown. It wasn't until four years later that she found herself sitting next to him on an Oxford Street omnibus. She introduced herself – and he allegedly didn't recall her immediately. But he clearly made up for that, and for lost time, and they were married only a few weeks later, in November 1884. The next year Spedan was born and in 1887 Oswald. Suddenly the single-minded draper with nothing in his head but his business and his almost obsessive purchase of property now had two young sons to whom he could envisage passing on that business. That would turn out to be a painful process.

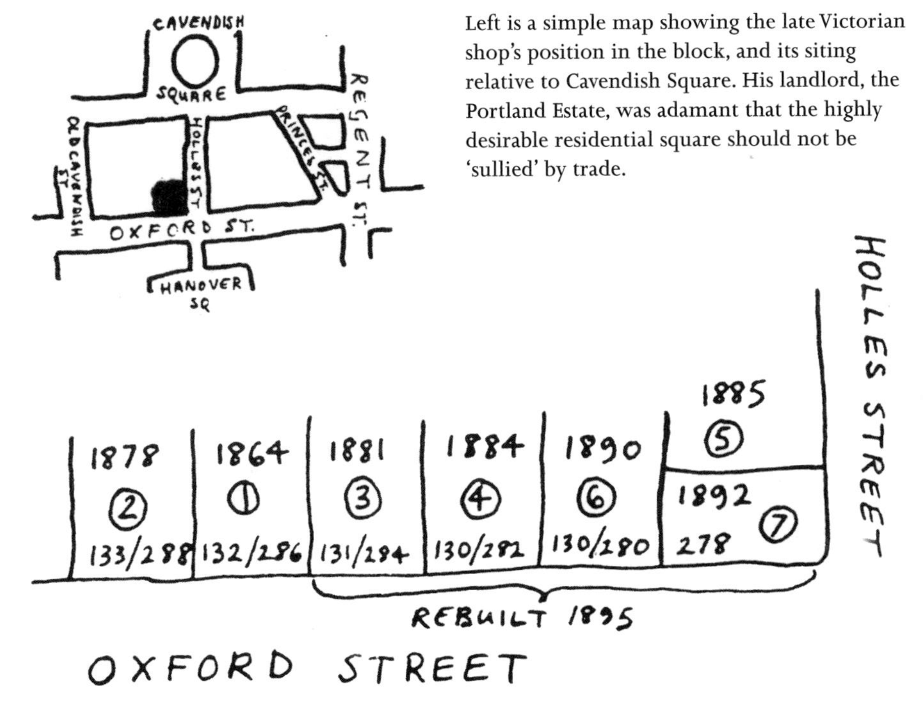


Left is a simple map showing the late Victorian shop's position in the block, and its siting relative to Cavendish Square. His landlord, the Portland Estate, was adamant that the highly desirable residential square should not be 'sullied' by trade.

A sketch map showing the dates at which John Lewis acquired the nearby properties, across the north side of Oxford Street. You can see that he didn't bridge it to the Holles Street junction until 1892, and that when the street numbering was changed it switched direction.

CHAPTER 2

# Growing Pains

**John Lewis and his two sons Spedan and Oswald, probably in the mid 1890s.**

Like so many others, John Lewis, who had fought for his own rights for so long, overlooked the fact that anyone else had any.

PHILIP HOFFMAN, IN HIS AUTOBIOGRAPHY
*THEY ALSO SERVE*, 1948

For the first ten years of my working life one of the most important of my occupations was an effort to see where my father had been right and where he had been wrong. I came to the conclusion that his ideas were sound. I think so still. But the practice was a very different matter.

SPEDAN LEWIS, IN *PARTNERSHIP FOR ALL*, 1948

## Eliza Baker

John Lewis and Eliza Baker seem an ill-assorted couple. Other than coming from retailing families and losing their fathers young, they appear to have had little in common. Eliza's father was a draper from Bristol who had gone bankrupt and died when she was three years old. She was luckier than John: her much older half-brother Mills Baker managed to retrieve the business and make an impressive success of it. He had become Eliza's guardian and was able (and, more to the point, willing) to pay for her education, an advantage that none of John Lewis's sisters had, in an age when educating women for anything other than running a household was decidedly unusual. But she was evidently highly intelligent, and in 1872 when she was eighteen her brother generously decided she should go to the North London Collegiate Girls' School of Frances Mary Buss, a pioneer of women's education, with a view to going on to university. Within a year she had come top of the entrance exam to Bedford College, London. That gained her a scholarship she didn't take up, because she had come second in the entrance exam to Girton College, Cambridge, behind a woman in her thirties. It's said that she danced the normally restrained Miss Buss down the school corridor at the news of her success.

The first Cambridge college for women (though the university refused to award them degrees) had moved to the Cambridge village of Girton from Hitchin in Hertfordshire. It had been set up there by two more of that indomitable band of educated Victorian feminists determined to gain access for women to fields long preserved for men. Emily Davies and Barbara Bodichon had opened the college in 1869, and Eliza Baker was among the first intake when it moved to Girton in 1873. She came top of the roll for the Pass degree in History and Political Economy in 1877. She was clearly remarkably able, and a capable pianist as well. After Cambridge she became a teacher, was then appointed Second Mistress of Bedford High School in 1882, and would perhaps have lived and died a spinster headmistress had she not met John Lewis on that bus. Mills Baker, though no longer her guardian, came up to London to inspect the shop of the man she'd agreed to marry, because he couldn't believe John Lewis was actually taking as much as he claimed from so small a space. Once he saw the stream of customers, though, he was in no doubt.

It was a well educated – if reticent – woman who brought up the two boys Spedan and Oswald. Spedan later described her as a woman with 'a large, strong mind and very little intellectual appetite', a curiously dismissive caveat which suggests that she was not entirely attuned to his ideas. Oswald called her 'one of the sweetest and most unselfish women that ever lived'. The family now lived in a substantial house John Lewis renamed Spedan Tower in a splendid location at the top of Hampstead Hill. Its four acres of grounds lay close to the extensive parkland of Hampstead Heath and Kenwood House. Thus he could live the life of a country gentleman, but with the advantage that he could be at his Oxford Street store in about twenty minutes, initially by carriage and pair but later driven in a Rolls Royce with magnificent brass lamps. (And with an imperious bell, which he rang himself to warn pedestrians of his approach, until his chauffeur refused to drive him any more until it was removed.) He set his own peculiar stamp on the garden, preferring evergreens to flowering plants because he reputedly had little sense of smell, or even colour, which seems something of drawback in a draper. He kept pigs and chickens, and bred rabbits, building a warren for them with drainpipes – the neighbouring gardeners must have been thrilled. He built a rockery with his own hands, using large flints that Eliza collected from Cromer beach and smuggled into their guest house, before transporting them back home in barrels. Before he married, holidays were rare, and he doesn't seem to have enjoyed them much, but once he had a family he allowed Eliza to book at an east coast resort, often in Margate or Ramsgate, so he could nip back to the shop at intervals on the paddle-steamer that plied the Kent coast.

## Growing Up

The Hampstead house must have been an idyllic place for the boys to grow up – and for Spedan to nourish a curiosity about wildlife that became a passion throughout his life. They didn't go to school till they were eight because Eliza was able to teach them herself at home, where they got a first class grounding in the basics, including religion. John Lewis thought religious belief 'childish' – his only faith, Eliza once observed drily, 'was in the Divine Right of Employers'. But Eliza was a Christian and uneasy because the boys hadn't been baptised as babies, so when they were in their teens, in 1900, she had them surreptitiously christened while on holiday in Whitby. It was soon clear that Spedan in particular was precociously clever, and perhaps his mother's early teaching had left him streets ahead of the other boys, because he was sent home from his first school as a result of being 'scandalously idle and insolent'. Doubtless he was bored and unchallenged there, but the headmaster at his second school kept him up to the mark so that he won a scholarship to Westminster School at the age of fourteen. Later Oswald followed him there, and both were day boys. Spedan later recounted that both his classics master at Westminster and the headmaster at his second prep school had said that he was the cleverest boy they had ever taught. Spedan added frankly that he was inclined to laziness, to do only what was essential, and rued that he wasn't sufficiently criticised for it at Westminster, where he had to see others take the prizes.

The question sure to arise was whether the two brothers should go to university, enter a profession, or join their father in the business. You might expect that Eliza would rather they went to university, while John would like at least one of them to learn and subsequently take over his department store under an approving parental eye. Interestingly, it seems it was the other way round. Their father would have been happy and proud for the boys to go to Oxford or Cambridge and then enter a profession, but Eliza was uneasy about the strain the business was imposing on her husband. When Spedan left school their father was approaching seventy, often in poor health, and had been talking of getting a business partner or becoming a public company, as so many other successful store owners were doing. Eliza was apparently keen that the boys should join the business as soon as possible in case John did something rash or fell seriously ill, and Spedan had no objection to foregoing a university career. So he joined the business in 1904, Oswald a year later. Neither can have imagined that their father would live on until he was ninety-two, gripping the reins of the Oxford Street business tightly in his own hands well into the mid-1920s, and going into the shop virtually every working day.

## Expansion at Last

We left the story of the Oxford Street business in 1892, when John Lewis had finally acquired the shops that took him to the corner of Holles Street. By 1895 he had all the units in Holles Street back to the south-west corner of Cavendish Square, so he now had a rectangular block, perhaps about a third of the shop as it is today. His timing was propitious because his landlord, the Portland Estate, decided at last to allow him to knock down the internal walls – a change of policy explained by the fact that the leases were coming up for renewal. A proper department store on the site would enable them to raise the rent substantially, a fact which rankled with their tenant, because it was the massive improvements that John was paying for which enabled the landowner to raise the rents and extract yet more money from him, the man *creating* his landlord's wealth.

In the following year a major rebuilding was complete: there were now long display windows instead of separate poky shop fronts, showrooms on three floors, the whole floor above them fitted out for wholesale trading, and the major innovation of lifts at each end of the new store. John Lewis, increasingly eccentric, was inclined to stop people entering a lift if he felt they were young and fit enough, and insist that they took the stairs, reserving the lift for those who genuinely needed it. The two great staircases were of oak and like everything else were made to last. He penny-pinched obsessively in many areas, but never when it came to shop fitting. As a retired shop worker later recalled: 'The fixtures were made of the finest oak or mahogany, the lino on the ground floor and basement was extremely thick and made to stand years of wear, and the carpets were of the best and most lasting quality.' This enlargement and complete makeover led to a doubling of sales to nearly £200,000 a year by the time both sons had joined the business in 1907. That's the equivalent of close to £20m in 2010, when today's larger shop took over £300m. The shop had become a genuine department store: although still heavily based on dress and furnishing fabrics, it was now selling household goods and fashion accessories in the same way as his competitors' great stores.

His annoyance with his landlord is probably what encouraged John Lewis to go into local politics. From 1888 and for over thirty years he was a Liberal councillor in Marylebone, and was a member of the new London County Council for several years after it was formed in 1900. Some of his employees were his constituents, because he housed about 100 girls in a hostel near the shop in Weymouth Street. Women had votes in local elections, though not, as the Suffragists had begun to demand, in national elections. To gain his hostel-lodgers' votes in the 1901 election for Marylebone he promised them Saturday afternoon off, although he had at first refused to follow his competitors in any reduction in opening hours. He was trying to bolster Liberal Party support to amend the property laws, which he thought iniquitous.

There was a feud brewing with his landlord. In 1897 he had been able to rent Cavendish Buildings, a residential property next to his shops at that end of Holles Street, numbers 16 and 17, and he set about connecting them. This alarmed the trustees of the Portland Estate, acting on behalf of the seventeen-year-old heir to the old Lord Howard de Walden, who were aghast at the spread of Trade towards their desirable residences in Cavendish Square and beyond. They owned an estate bordered by Oxford Street, Marylebone High Street, Marylebone Road and Portland Place, a rectangle of substantial properties which gave them a huge income. In 1901, by which time the younger de Walden had succeeded to ownership of the estate, the trustees issued an injunction to prevent John Lewis from developing the frontages that bordered Cavendish Square, a stipulation he had been obliged to accept under the long lease agreement. They wanted to keep a 'residential' façade, while he needed to replace domestic fittings like fireplaces to turn the space into a modern showroom. Lewis argued that he'd been given a verbal agreement, and carried on regardless – he believed passionately that a landlord should not be able to obstruct a solidly reliable tenant from improving his property to everybody's ultimate benefit. All attempts at mediation failed, Lewis went ahead, and the landlord obtained a formal court order requiring him to undo what he'd changed. Lewis refused, and was inevitably found to be in contempt of court. A reluctant Mr Justice Swinfen Eady was left with only one option.

## Prison

On the afternoon of 17 June 1903 a large crowd cheered John Lewis as he set off from Oxford Street in his own carriage and pair and was driven to

Brixton Prison, where he would have to stay until he had apologised. Prison, for an upstanding citizen like John Lewis? At that time, as Spedan said, 'the Suffragettes had not yet made the imprisonment of respectable people a commonplace.' He was treated as any other prisoner, put in a cell twelve foot by six with a bed somewhat less comfortable than the one he was now accustomed to, though perhaps no worse than those he'd slept on as an apprentice. It amused him that on being asked his religion and replying 'none', the prison governor said: 'Oh, we call that Church of England.' The governor told him prisoners were normally allowed visitors and letters every two weeks, but in his case he could have them weekly. To someone used to reading *The Times* as a daily ritual this would have been vexing, but Lewis must have known what he was letting himself in for, and he settled down to read Freeman's *History of the Norman Conquest*. He at least had the privilege of having his meals brought in by a caterer each day: 'salmon and peas and other such viands', in Spedan's words.

The whole charade was an embarrassment for everyone involved – the prisoner, his family, the judge, the landlord. And for the Liberal Party, whose councillor he was, but who could apply no pressure in a civil case like this. Only a formal apology to the judge would get him back home. His solicitor urged him to offer it but for three weeks he adamantly refused. On 3 July young Oswald reported that his father had 'a frightful row with the governor of the prison'. Eliza's nerves were becoming increasingly shredded, but a week later a friend managed to persuade him that it didn't help his party to continue in jail. So to Eliza's relief he finally 'purged' his contempt and walked out on 10 July. Back in Cavendish Square there was a diplomatic stand-off: Lewis didn't reinstate the inside of the buildings as required by the injunction, but he didn't open them for trade, and Lord Howard de Walden heeded advice to let the sleeping dog lie. And so it would repose for a few years – before waking with an ominous growl...

That was in 1903. Four years later both of his sons were in the business, one which had been yielding a handsome profit of well over £10,000 a year. Intelligent, well-educated sons, eager to learn, arriving in a business run by a father approaching seventy, on tried and trusted principles he'd stuck to successfully all his life. Spedan in particular was intellectually curious and not inclined to accept a dogma without query, while John was unused to being challenged. Both Spedan and Oswald towered over him physically. An explosive brew was fermenting.

## John Lewis the Man

What do we know of the seventy-year-old John Lewis? He stuck firmly to his tenets of fair trading, good value and a wide assortment of stock. He couldn't possibly supervise all the buying decisions as he'd used to, but he was seen about the shop all day and was a figure partly revered, partly feared. Spedan later recalled: 'He constantly preached the doctrine of Praise in public and Blame in private. In practice he blamed in public at the top of his voice and hardly ever praised at all.'

In 1951 Albert Sherring, who had worked as a porter, lift attendant and odd-job man at the start of the century, recalled the Old Man's daily habits:

> He would arrive at the main door in Holles Street almost to the minute and he made a point of making his first job of the day a trip to the marking-off room to inspect the goods his buyers had bought, and woe to the buyer if he did not approve of their quality and price. Back they would have to go to the warehouse they had come from. I remember passing and hearing Mr John Lewis saying to Mr Yearsley (who was one of the biggest silk buyers in the trade), 'You have paid a farthing too much for this silk...'

Yearsley was for many years the John Lewis buyer of silk, and probably the most experienced in the country. He was regarded as one of the few who could stand up to his proprietor. On one occasion an assistant had been sacked for 'making too much money'. When Lewis came to dole out the pay packets on Friday, a job he would entrust to no one else, he discovered the young man had £15 in his packet, and sacked him on the spot as a thief. He gave the assistant no time to explain how he'd come by it. In fact several fixtures of soft silks had been damaged by water running down the wall behind them. Yearsley told the man to sell them among his dressmaker contacts for what he could get, and he'd give him a penny a yard. There were thousands of yards and he sold the lot. Yearsley was away in Paris, but by Monday he was back and went to plead his case with Lewis. He found him in his shirtsleeves, 'dressing' out the shop – preparing it for customers – which he always helped with first thing. Lewis refused to reinstate the man, whereupon Yearsley said: 'Very well, sir, when you want me you'd better send for me.' He put on his hat and coat and walked out. When the shop opened the assistants in the long silk room stood in a line behind the counters, folded their arms, and refused to serve any customers. Yearsley was soon called back and the man reinstated.

Old John knew the cost of everything – he told the young Sherring when he was lift attendant that it cost a penny-farthing every time the lift went up or down. He would never employ a specialist window-dresser: each buyer had one window and a free hand to decide what to put (or cram) into it, which led to a real hotch-potch. Such a creature of habit was he that Oswald observed in 1964:

> When I started work in Oxford Street, an elderly man used to put the day's takings into a large black bag with which he then walked to Oxford Circus,

> took a bus to Trafalgar Square and then walked down the Strand to Coutts Bank who then handled our business. He did this at the same time every day so that to anyone interested it was quite obvious what he was doing, and yet no one thought it at all a rash proceeding.

Old Mr Lewis had set ideas about almost everything. Sherring said he often saw him showing assistants how to 'block' silk, and Spedan said that his father never employed women in the silk room because they could never block silk to his satisfaction. (Whereas today fabrics arrive on stiff cardboard rolls, then they came on wooden boards. When silk arrived it was unrolled and checked for imperfections, then rolled – blocked – back onto its board.) He was notoriously pernickety, too, about his female employees' dress. Young women had to have black dresses without a trace of colour, black shoes and stockings, and high collars kept up by wire supports. These were most uncomfortable, especially if you had a short neck, so many kept the collars tucked down. When the shop's bush telegraph whispered that the owner was on the prowl there would be a frenzied pulling up of collars. What's more, he reputedly disliked blond curly hair to be visible (let alone anyone with red hair) and one old pensioner recalled that some girls used to bolt to the stockroom whenever they knew he was coming.

Alice Cook, who was a housemaid-waitress at the shop before she married in 1891, told her daughter that she was criticised by Mr Lewis once when she waited on him at mealtimes. She'd just had her hair done in the curled fringe currently fashionable. 'You know, Alice, there are only two kinds of women who wear the fringe, those on the stage and those on the streets. Don't let me see you wearing your hair in a fringe again.' At that time, before the Weymouth Street hostel was set up, Alice Cook lived-in above one of the units in Holles Street, run by a martinet of a housekeeper. She said that Mr Lewis provided the best of food, but that it was often spoilt in the cooking and sometimes inedible. The considerable waste was sent up to Spedan Tower to feed the pigs, who did not object. To be fair, by the time Albert Sherring arrived some years later, the breakfast on his first day was more memorable: 'Porridge with as much milk and sugar as you wanted, followed by bacon and eggs, fish or boiled eggs, two each, with slabs of real butter, marmalade and jam served on a help-yourself principle.' That recollection comes over as somewhat wistful, written as it was in 1951 after years of rationing.

John Lewis was happy to spend money when he felt it important, as he knew from his own apprenticeship how vital that breakfast fuelling was, but this generosity Spedan discovered did not extend to his staff's pay. Robert Bichan, who joined Spedan at Peter Jones early in 1915, and whose memories of him we'll hear later, recalled the Edwardian period as one in which drapery was very poorly paid. There were plenty of single men in their twenties who, after completing their apprenticeships locally, largely from

Devon, Cornwall and Wales, would flock to London. There they would earn between £25 and £30 a year, little more than ten shillings a week (less than £50 today), and John Lewis probably paid at the lower end of that scale. Bichan was warned to avoid John Lewis: 'they're rotten payers', and told that the owner preferred married men because they were less likely to jump ship. This reluctance to pay any more than he could get away with affected the entire staff, said Spedan later. 'In theory he was perfectly willing to pay enough to get the right worker for a given post. In practice he could never believe that any particular post was worth more than a very small figure.' Spedan discovered that his father filled the key jobs, such as buyerships, almost entirely from within, from the selling floor, 'because the weakness of their bargaining position made that by far the cheapest way'. He then hemmed them in with a five-year contract with power to terminate at three months' notice, and a clause restricting them from moving to a competitor within a radius of three miles. That ruled out all his major London competitors. One silk buyer was enticed away by his rival William Whiteley, and John Lewis promptly took the hapless buyer to court and won. The poor man, who had built up almost single-handedly a trade which was one of Lewis's major sources of profit, was effectively forced to return to him. He died in harness in his fifties, when he was earning £1,000 a year, and after telling Spedan that he 'reckoned he was the worst paid man in the trade'. Spedan felt all such 'radius' agreements were unjust.

## The Sons Arrive

What else did Spedan find when he entered his father's business? Much later he wrote:

> At home we regarded him as a superman, virtually infallible in matters of business. I had not expected ... to find that the business was in fact no more than a second-rate success achieved in a first-rate opportunity. But that is what I did find. Fate had given my father an occupation that did not suit him.

Although his father was fond of saying that failure to keep adequate accounts was the most common reason for business failure, this was precisely where he fell down. The junior partner of the company auditors confided to Spedan that he was relieved another family member was coming into the business because when he audited the accounts every year John Lewis would lock them in a drawer, start to complain to him (once more) about the land laws, and show no sign of ever looking at the figures. He worried that there might be something wrong – and there was. Spedan said that the head of the post order department and the head of the counting house had been robbing his father for years – one got eighteen months' hard labour and the other avoided it by disappearing to New Zealand. Soon after Oswald joined the business he found appalling inefficiency in the counting house – what we would now called the accounts department – which one day he found himself unexpectedly in sole charge of because its department head had 'suddenly departed with someone else's wife'. Lewis's two sons were particularly struck by the slovenly way the profits were being invested. Almost everything would be sunk in purchases of houses and small shops. Once Lewis had bought them – often at auction, usually when he was made aware he had too much in the bank – he then promptly forgot about them. Oswald discovered there were over 100, and that the total interest they yielded was only 3%, far less than their father imagined. But when Oswald told him and proposed a change of policy he was immediately slapped down for intruding on matters that didn't concern him. Though the last thing his sons wanted was to anger their father needlessly, battle lines were being drawn.

Spedan was not slow to discover that there was an 'astonishing' accumulation of stale stock. His father had an elaborate system for registering every item to show when, where and for what price it had been bought. Spedan: 'I actually found a vest for a very small baby that had been bought in the year before I was born.' He discovered a shocking waste of floor space, and that the third floor, expensively kitted out as a trading floor, was used only for storing stock. He calculated that two of the second floor rooms and the whole of the basement ran at a loss. He described his father as having become 'the captain of a big ship much under-engined and with those engines much under-fuelled'. Not that he maligned his father's achievement. He had made his money without resort to trickery, and he looked after his customers by providing them with merchandise whose value and variety could not be matched elsewhere. He still made a handsome profit from the (comparatively few) departments on the ground floor and part of the first. 'What did it matter', asked Spedan rhetorically, 'if a good part of his capital and of the floor-space of the business had been in a real sense wastefully idle?' He answered his own question – 'It mattered to his staff, and to them it mattered terribly.'

By 1908 both brothers were part-owners of the business. For all his cantankerous independence, their father had given them each a quarter share of his business on their twenty-first birthdays, a gesture Spedan later conceded to be most handsome. He may have done it out of a genuine desire to harness his sons to the business, or to reduce future estate duty, or because his wife pressed him, or a combination of all three. Whatever the motive, the business now had three part-owners of widely different outlooks and personalities. One domineering and unused to being questioned, one dynamic and original, one steady and conservative, all living in the same house with an acutely intelligent woman, not assertive but trying all she could to pour oil on the troubled waters that soon began to bubble furiously. But what caused the final explosion was entirely unexpected. Spedan decided to marry his secretary.

This announcement, at the breakfast table one morning late in 1908, provoked John Lewis into a fury. He told his son it was impossible. What kind of marriage he did envisage for his son is unclear. Did he think Spedan too young, less than half the age he had married at? The lady was the independently minded daughter of a once-successful Welsh solicitor who had come to London, failed, and had returned to Wales close to bankruptcy. The daughter, four years older than Spedan, who at twenty-three was entirely entitled to make up his own mind, stayed in London and found herself a job. Whatever the reason (and perhaps the taint of bankruptcy was too close to home) it blew the old man's top, and Spedan backed down early in 1909 and broke off the engagement. But the family damage didn't end there. Arguments spilled over into other areas. John Lewis decided to kick Spedan out of the business and, perhaps because Oswald had taken Spedan's side, he decided to be rid of Oswald too. So poisonous was the atmosphere at this point that it affected Eliza's health, and her sons spirited her away for a spell to a flat in London. A letter she wrote to her husband refers to their 'many painful discussions in the past few weeks'. The effect of her absence was salutary, and John Lewis soon invited the sons back home and into the business. Eliza came home, and Spedan returned to work at the shop but found his own place to live.

Oswald had had enough of both home and business. He asked for his £50,000 share in the business in cash, his father refused point blank, and Oswald took legal advice from Sir Edward Carson, KC, a formidable figure. He advised Oswald to sue, and for a higher figure, moreover, because the business was then valued at considerably more than £200,000. That had the required effect, Oswald was happy in practice to settle for £50,000 (a little over £4m today), the lawyers moved fast, and by April 1909 the money was paid over and Oswald moved out to a flat in Baker Street. For six years he had nothing to do with the business, and when he and his father met at Marylebone council meetings – Oswald had been voted onto the council as well – not a word was exchanged. He stayed in close touch, though, with his mother and with Spedan, who wrote him a deeply touching letter affirming his friendship and ending 'I shall miss you and miss you. In my daily life I may perhaps have good friends ... but never another brother, and such a brother.'

So Spedan remained, but Oswald had gone. Would peace break out? No.

CHAPTER 3

# The Edwardian Department Store

A 1911 view of a thronged Oxford Street looking west. John Lewis's shop is the far block with the awnings visible. No. 254 and beyond is TJ Harries, which Spedan would buy in 1928.

Kipps was taught how to tie up parcels… to block, fold and measure material of all sorts… and to practise a servile obedience to a large number of people. He had to… hold up curtains till his hands ached. The use of half the things he sold he did not understand… they were to him first and last no more than things, heavy and difficult to handle in bulk, that one folded up, unfolded, cut into lengths, and saw dwindle and pass away into that mysterious happy world in which the Customer dwells.

HG WELLS, IN *KIPPS*, 1905

> Many more people than formerly come to London and to city centres to do their shopping; they prefer to make their purchases where they can concentrate their forces and diminish fatigue. What an amount of fatigue and trouble is avoided where one can order one's mutton downstairs, buy one's carpet on the ground floor, and deck oneself out in the glory of Worth or La Ferrier on the top floor, to all of which one is borne on the wings of a lift, silent and swift.

By the end of the nineteenth century there were over 200 department stores in Britain. The quote above is from the journalist and society hostess Mary Lady Jeune. The Edwardian era was the great heyday of the department store, both from the viewpoint of the draper and his (and it's almost always *his*) customer, but also from the shop floor. What was it like to work there? Who were the people who slaved away in the shops of the great entrepreneurs and helped create their wealth? The second half of the nineteenth century had been a bonanza for the energetic retailer. The population of England and Wales increased between 1861 and 1901 from 20 million to 32.5 million. Rural mechanisation and poverty led to migration to the towns, which accelerated the growth of town centres and major shopping streets. The majority of the population enjoyed a rise in real income of around 40% from 1880 to 1900, particularly among an expanding white-collar professional and clerical middle class. Moreover, Britain's world dominance encouraged a greater confidence that people could afford to spend money rather than save it. And every day there was more to buy. The country itself was opened up by railways; historical trade tariffs and barriers had been largely swept away by the 1860s, and the switch to the steamship brought more goods into the country faster, and they cost less when they arrived. More of the imports were now manufactured rather than raw materials, and the rise in mass manufacture made it hard for the small specialists, like shoemakers for example, to survive. The United States increasingly led the way with new ideas in both manufacturing and retailing, and their exports weren't just goods, but ideas – and a retailer.

## Gordon Selfridge Arrives

In the middle of the Lewis family's implosion, six days after John Lewis signed his settlement with Oswald, a new competitor opened at the west end of Oxford Street, one who had found British stores 'curiously backward', and who determined to bring in some real competition. And the competition he brought shook the complacency of the London department store magnates. It had been widely anticipated ever since the American Gordon Selfridge had arrived with an entourage in London three years earlier and bought a row of shops at the quieter western end of Oxford Street. He acquired them much more quickly than John Lewis had done, doubtless by paying the owners a price they couldn't refuse. Though some of his building designs, such as a dome a hundred feet high, didn't pass the planners, he put on the site a temple to retailing which provoked an architect on seeing the plans to exclaim: 'Has the Parthenon pupped?' Steel girders were employed on a scale new to Britain, needing concrete foundation walls twenty-seven feet deep to fill what was dubbed Selfridge's 'million pound hole'. He employed musicians (apparently successfully) to speed up work on the site, and tried every advertising trick in the book – and out of it, such as proposing a tunnel to the store from Bond Street station, which would have been renamed Selfridges. After a massive campaign in which he took the front page of major national newspapers for a fortnight, he opened the doors on 15 March 1909. He offered to pay the return rail fare of every customer – any family of four in fact – 'from any part of the Kingdom', provided they spent five pounds in the shop.

Imagine the impact of that: 80,000 customers arrived on the first day. Selfridges brought over the louche American concept of shopping as pleasure and entertainment, and Londoners were ready for it. Customers were greeted with music (if not muzak, yet). Women could for the first time in England buy make-up and perfume easily – Selfridge was the first in England to position perfumery next to an entrance, as an enticement. The original Selfridges included a library, a post and telegraph office, a savings bank, reading and writing rooms, reception rooms for different nationalities, and a luxurious 'silence' room, with a sign enjoining ladies to 'refrain from conversation'. These, and restaurants with expensive décor but without their usual price tag, were designed to entice customers in and keep them there, bringing to London the idea of a store as a destination in itself, its advertising asking, 'Why not spend the day at Selfridges?'

Disconcerted at first, John Lewis soon realised that this brash rival was bringing new customers to Oxford Street and to his own store, where the thrifty and prudent saw the benefits of his prices and policies after the razzmatazz of the new Selfridge store. He was not dismayed at looking old-fashioned, choosing not to attempt to emulate the typical Gordon Selfridge PR coup such as displaying all the pictures rejected by the Royal Academy summer exhibition. Or allowing a French aviator, renowned until then more for his crashes and his bankruptcy than any success, to display his aeroplane in the shop. If, that is, Monsieur Blériot succeeded in his unlikely venture of crossing the English channel without ditching in the drink. And he did, was instantly famous, and so it was displayed – and was seen by 150,000 people in four days. But department store owners in other parts of London were much less happy with Selfridge. At a time when publicly quoted store chains were booming, with dividends often well over 15%, other competitors dreaded his much-trumpeted arrival. Harrods made their Diamond Jubilee celebration coincide with Selfridges' opening, but overreached themselves by announcing that the Secretary for War Richard Haldane would open a

Territorial Army promotion: Haldane was forced to withdraw after a fusillade of complaints. Some store owners felt forced to up their advertising budget dramatically, an expenditure which, of course, once incurred was hard to reduce, though Old John was never going to go down the pernicious advertising road. Nor would his successors for nigh on another hundred years...

## The Great Store Owners

The arrival of Selfridges cemented the place of Oxford Street, Bond Street and Regent Street as one of the two prime shopping destinations for Londoners, but it hadn't always been so. It had begun further east. In the middle of the nineteenth century the power and the money was in the wholesale trade, established in the City of London, close enough to the docks which brought in the foreign merchandise. They sold to small retailers dotted all over London and the suburbs, as did their counterparts in places like Liverpool, Newcastle and Manchester, Bristol and Southampton. They held the power of size, but it didn't last, as successful retailers began to expand at an increasing rate. This was the era of the great entrepreneurial shop-owner, usually a draper, whose initial success had encouraged him to magnify and diversify, to supply all a customer's wants under one roof.

William Whiteley was perhaps the archetype. The son of a Yorkshire corn dealer, apprenticed to a draper in Wakefield, he was so deeply impressed by the astounding range of manufactured goods on display at the Great Exhibition of 1851 at Hyde Park that the day his apprenticeship ended he decided to come to London and save for his own shop. Starting with the £10 he brought with him – about £900 today – it took him twelve years of ascetic living (which he would make up for) to amass enough to start a little fancy goods shop in the newly fashionable Westbourne Grove, out west in Bayswater, just after the new Metropolitan railway had opened up the area. Four years later in 1867 he seized the chance to buy a row of shops further along the street, lost no opportunity to diversify, most successfully into the unusual field of building and decorating, and by the end of the 1880s had over 6,000 employees.

'Everything from a pin to an elephant', was the claim of the self-appointed 'Universal Provider', and he shamelessly extolled his store by getting fake letters of commendation sent to the newspapers. His success attracted others – Tom Ponting of Gloucester arrived there in Westbourne Grove in 1873, and Messrs Bourne and Hollingsworth in 1894, though they moved to Oxford Street in 1902. Whiteley carried on trading despite a massive fire that severely damaged the shop complex in 1897. The shop was being reconstructed when he was murdered on the shop floor during his January sale of 1907 by an illegitimate son. The boy's mother was the sister of a shop assistant who had become his mistress, which had led to a messy court case, reported with typical late Victorian relish. In his will Whiteley left the then extraordinary sum of a million pounds to be set aside to buy land and build a village of homes for 'aged poor persons'. The immaculate Whiteley Village was eventually built in Surrey, and today still houses 500 people in delightful surroundings.

The 1851 Exhibition had been a stimulus to another enterprising retailer. Charles Harrod had begun as a grocer in the East End at Stepney in 1834, and saw the chance to supply the waves of people coming to the Exhibition by opening a shop in Knightsbridge. His son expanded it during the 1880s, when it became increasingly popular with the famous and with royalty. Another casualty of fire, the shop was rebuilt in 1888 by Harrod junior, who went on to float the business on the stock exchange. The 1888 Harrods included the first escalator in Britain, with a one-legged man going up and down all day to show it was safe (unless customers assumed that's how he'd lost his leg) and they provided smelling salts at the top to settle the nerves. The great landmark Harrods of today was completed in 1905.

Kensington became a magnet for the big retailers, and London's other major shopping centre. Derry & Toms was begun by Joseph Toms and his sister's husband Charles Derry; Pontings later relocated there; and William Whiteley's manager John Barker left to start his own business in Kensington in 1889. Not far away, at the corner of Knightsbridge and Sloane Street, was Harvey Nichols. The linen shop of Benjamin Harvey had passed to his daughter on his death in 1820, provided she went into partnership with one Colonel Nichols, who added oriental goods and silks to a mix which formed the basis of the store when it moved to its current position in Knightsbridge by 1890. Nearby was the Army & Navy, originally the 'Army and Navy Co-operative Society', a middle-class consumer co-operative set up by a group of army officers in 1872 – originally as a wine club – following the success of the Civil Service Supply Association in the Strand, and at that stage reserved for army officers and their widows. It burgeoned rapidly into a department store with guns. In Piccadilly, Swan & Edgar started to expand in 1866 after fifty years of happily trading there in a small way. That was the pattern: Dickins & Jones had been in Oxford Street since 1803, moved to Regent Street in 1835 and grew into a department store in the 1890s.

Debenhams began under that sole name in 1905. It had started as a draper's shop called Flint and Clark way back in 1778 in Wigmore Street, just north of Oxford Street and parallel to it. It became Clark and Debenham in 1813 when William Debenham joined, and Debenham and Freebody in 1851. In the same year James Marshall and John Snelgrove moved their high-class drapery business from Vere Street to a run of shops from 334 to 348 Oxford Street, a job lot acquired with a speed that John Lewis would have died for twenty years later. The upmarket nature of the business was such that budding apprentices had to lodge a deposit of sixty guineas, a sum beyond the resources of most at a time when to be a shop assistant (and indeed a shop *owner*, as we shall see) was to be a distinctly lower form of life in the class-stratified England of the early twentieth century. What was it like for those shop assistants?

## Life on the Selling Floor

The famous author HG Wells was a lifelong member of the shop assistants' union, continuing long after he became a professional writer. He left a vivid account of the life of an apprentice in a draper's shop in *Kipps*, published in 1905 but referring to the early 1880s when Wells was sent to be apprenticed, first in Windsor, and then to the south coast backwater of Southsea. After two years, he said, he ran home to his mother. She was a domestic servant; his father was unsuccessful at most things he tried, from shopkeeping to professional cricket. Wells cordially loathed his time as a shop worker, when 'the great stupid machine of retail trade caught his life into its wheels, a vast irresistible force'. He describes Kipps being met on arrival for his apprenticeship at fourteen by a shabby man who silently held out a small book 'mainly devoted to a voracious system of fines'.

> The indentures that bound Kipps to Mr Shalford were antique and complex; they insisted on the latter's parental privileges, they forbade Kipps to dice and game, they made him over body and soul to Mr Shalford for seven long years, the crucial years of his life. In return there were vague stipulations about teaching the whole art and mystery of the trade to him, but … Mr Shalford considered this a mere rhetorical flourish, and set himself assiduously to get as much out of Kipps and put as little into him as he could … What he put into Kipps was chiefly bread and margarine, infusions of chicory and tea-dust, colonial meat by contract at threepence a pound, potatoes by the sack, and watered beer … He was also allowed to share a bedroom with eight other young men, and to sleep in a bed which, except in very severe weather, could be made, with the help of his overcoat and personal underlinen, not to mention newspapers, quite sufficiently warm for any reasonable soul.
>
> His round began at half-past six in the morning, when he would descend, unwashed and shirtless, in old clothes and a scarf, and dust boxes, and yawn, and take down wrappers and clean the windows till eight. An austere breakfast, with what only an Imperial Englishman would admit to be coffee … then into the shop, a vast interminable place … with unending counters and innumerable faultlessly dressed young men and, presently, houri-like women staring at him. All day … he plumbed an abyss of boredom, or stood a mere carcass with his mind far away, fighting the enemies of Empire … At half-past seven – except on late nights – a feverish activity of 'straightening up' began, and when the last

> shutter was up outside, Kipps ... would start hanging wrappers over the fixtures and over the piles of wares upon the counters, preparatory to a vigorous scattering of wet sawdust and the sweeping out of the shop. Rarely much later than nine, a supper of bread and cheese awaited him ... The front door was locked at half-past ten, and the dormitory light extinguished at eleven.

Working hours were horrendous by today's standards. While the Shop Hours Act of 1886 restricted working hours of women and children under eighteen in shops to seventy-four hours a week – nearly double today's standard – the new law was poorly enforced. Moreover, there was *no limit at all* on the hours worked by men over eighteen. Ten years later Sir Charles Dilke proposed a Bill that would effectively limit every shop's weekly opening hours to sixty, although the long opening and closing processes extended that to seventy for most shop workers. It failed, and many assistants went on working more than ninety hours. A 1912 Bill at least introduced half-day closing, but its proposed restriction of hours to Dilke's sixty provoked such bitter opposition from shop owners that the Liberal Home Secretary, Winston Churchill, dropped the clause to get through a Bill as watered down as Kipps' beer. (Look at the cartoons on Plate 2.)

The living-in system described by Wells was subject to much abuse. He campaigned against it, as did George Bernard Shaw. Philip Hoffman, orphaned at nine and apprenticed not long after Wells in 1894 – sleeping on the floor and sobbing through his first hostel night – was one of many who experienced it and then campaigned against it. In this he was helped by a remarkable series of articles published in 1898 in the *Daily Chronicle* anonymously, but researched by an apprentice draper, Margaret Bondfield, one of the eleven children of a Somerset textile worker. After joining Hoffman's shop assistants' union she had been commissioned to take employment with various companies so she could test the hostels. From the moment the first article appeared shop workers began to send in their own experiences: cracking bedbugs with their shoes, stuffing soap to fill cracks in the wall, heavy deductions and unjust fines, cold baths, dreadful food. One employer, summoned for selling meat unfit for consumption, got off because it was for his apprentices, and thus he wasn't *actually* putting it on sale. This man had thirty young women in his hostel and no bathroom. They were locked in (or out) at night, and on Sundays, when women would often walk the streets if they had nowhere to go, getting a reputation whether they deserved it or not. The articles by Bondfield – who was to become Britain's first woman cabinet minister – didn't lead to legislation, but the publicity forced the gradual curbing of the grossest abuses. There is no suggestion that John Lewis's hostel was among the worst, although he too had a severe fining system.

Robert Bichan, a shop assistant recruited by Spedan Lewis in 1915, recalled in the 1960s what it was like to work in a London store in the

Edwardian period. Eager immigrants from outside London usually began in one of the wholesale houses in the City of London, sleeping in dreary doss-houses or living in hostels often worse than those of the retailers. Many, as he did, would inexorably gravitate to the bright retailing lights of the West End. Describing how he and his friends would go 'cribbing', Bichan talks of walking west, starting with Thomas Wallis in Holborn and moving on to Oxford Street, waiting with others in a draughty corridor.

> A door would open and a hatchet-faced female call out 'No more today!' and we were out on the street again with our solitary top hat which was, in those days, part of one's set up and which seemingly fitted anyone but was seldom worn, merely carried.

It was an employer's market, and Bichan, who would later battle with, yet revere, Spedan Lewis, paints a harsher picture of the father. Having described John Lewis as preferring married men, who he could hold on to longer – not paying enough to acquire loyalty by that means alone – he continued:

> Thus it was that John Lewis had a high proportion of married men, especially in the silk department, all hanging on to their jobs like grim death, afraid to leave, afraid to complain about conditions, very poorly paid. For example, married men with two kids, catching the early workman's train from an outlying suburb to arrive at Oxford Street by 8.30 a.m., got 37s 6d a week. Moreover they were required to present themselves for work wearing a frock coat, starched wing collar and cuffs and a black tie. I must tell of the agility of these men who could make a 'dicky' shirt front and a pair of cuffs, from the stiff linen-finished paper which the rolls of silk came wrapped in … Every evening, around the punch time-clocks near the staff exit, the floor would be littered with these discarded dickies and cuffs, and the first job the next morning was the making of a new set … Many many times a male assistant could be seen skilfully soling his shoes during the three-quarters of an hour luncheon break with sample cuts of thick brown linoleum …
>
> The payment of such meagre wages monthly would often make it necessary for a man to ask for a 'sub' on account, but this was dreaded because the application had to be put before Old John himself, who would question why it was that the applicant could not live within his means, which resulted in men borrowing from each other a few shillings here and there to tide things over.

Oxford Street stores of that period operated a strict 'door' policy, not least to make sure that only desirable customers came in. Bichan describes how so-called shopwalkers patrolled the doorways of stores all over Britain, happy to show to the door those they thought inappropriate – usually a simple judgement based on appearance – or those who weren't buying, for whom the expression 'tabby' was coined. An American retailing journalist bitterly complained of the absence of 'walk-around' stores, and being pressured by overbearing shopwalkers and assistants into buying unsuitable goods. Indeed customers were often steered towards slow-moving stock. Back then very little stock was on display, and it had to be brought out for the customer. On one reconnoitring shopping mission, Selfridge himself was even ejected from a store after confirming that he wasn't aiming to buy, with the classic London injunction to 'op it. Bichan recalled how these shopwalkers operated:

> There were no 'walk-in' or open shops. Every big shop had shopwalkers, whose job it was to stand or stroll about the entrances which, by the way, were very seldom found open even in summer. These gentlemen somehow seemed to hold positions considered superior to the man behind the counter. He would be tall, usually with a waxed moustache, immaculate in frock coat, striped trousers and patent shoes. The customer on entering would be met by this dandy who would bow low and ask 'What can we have the pleasure of showing you, Madam?' On being told, the shopwalker would lead her to the appropriate counter and, sometimes snapping his fingers as if to command immediate attention, would call out 'Blankets one' or 'Sheets one', 'Dress materials one'... Then when the customer had completed her purchases, very often a dozen or so items, the bill was made out and the assistant would call out 'Sign'... The shopwalker would approach and the assistant would then proceed to call out the items starting from the top of his pile. When all was checked and found in order the shopwalker would bow to the customer, thank her for her patronage, and then resume his position inside the doorway.

This archaic system, in which customers were not free to wander a store at will, was, Bichan confirmed, in Britain 'shattered and revolutionised by one man, Mr Gordon Selfridge'. His shop had a different layout and look. The spare, uncluttered aspect of his windows, in stark contrast to the crammed displays of his competitors, was reflected inside the shop, where lower counters and absence of floor-to-ceiling displays gave a sense of elegant spaciousness. There was a crucial change, too, to the way customers were invited to shop. In Selfridges there was an information desk and no shopwalkers. In other ways British department stores were vulnerable to Gordon Selfridge's innovations. In common with American and French stores, Selfridge had no living-in hostels for employees and no unjust system of fines, which here allowed the Dickensian industrial relations that still existed a generation after HG Wells' time. His departments were altogether more consistent in their approach and the customers they were aimed at. He had a standardised system of staff training for everyone, followed by specialised merchandise training in the department. In Britain the department manager was often an independent local warlord, one who bought and laid out the merchandise, often to his own taste, trained the staff himself, and might be running a department with a different feel and even for a different clientele than the one across the aisle.

That's how life went in the typical London department store when Selfridges opened. Meanwhile the Lewis family fractured. Eliza returned home but the boys didn't, Oswald left the business but Spedan remained. But if Old John thought Spedan would stay in the harness he had put on him he was seriously mistaken. Spedan had seen the inefficiencies in his father's business, but he was uneasy about something else, something no one else gave a moment's thought to. It took the first sight of his father's books to make him really think. And it was a fall from a horse that gave Spedan the time to do so.

CHAPTER 4

# Spedan's Big Idea – and a Family at War

A vivid photograph of John Lewis in court, behind his solicitor, the Hon Charles Russell, on 18 March 1911.

Spedan Lewis at about the time he entered his father's business.

My father, my brother and I had been drawing from the business £10,000 a year upon its capital and a further £16,000 or more in profit. This latter amount was about as much as the whole of the staff except certain factory workers were getting between them. Hardly any of the staff had ever had more than a meagre living.

SPEDAN LEWIS IN *PARTNERSHIP FOR ALL*, 1948

It was on the edge of complete collapse. It was not merely a derelict. It was a desperate derelict, in the last stages of decay.

SPEDAN LEWIS, WRITING ABOUT PETER JONES
WHEN HE ARRIVED THERE IN JANUARY 1914

In the May of 1909, some weeks after his brother Oswald had left the business and Selfridges had opened, Spedan was thrown from his horse, which apparently shied as he took his normal morning ride down from his home through Regents Park to Oxford Street. He'd seriously damaged a lung, and though he ignored the pain for a couple of days his condition rapidly deteriorated, and was diagnosed as pleurisy and empyema. That's as nasty as it sounds: the main symptom is extreme chest pain, especially when breathing in. His condition needed a novel and dangerous operation, followed by another in the late summer of 1910. The prolonged recovery period meant that he spent much of the next three years shuttling between spells in the business and recuperation on the coast and the continent. That gave him the time to think.

## The Three and the Three Hundred

His first sight of his father's accounts had given him plenty to think about. The year before his fall he'd discovered that the 300 employees of the business were receiving close to £16,000 a year in total. Only four were being paid (as opposed to earning…) more than £250 a year for the long hours they toiled. But Spedan, his brother and his father were taking almost exactly that £16,000, to which could be added £10,000 a year in interest on their capital. Each was making therefore the equivalent today of about £800,000 a year, but paying very little tax, while their employees made an average equivalent to £4,500. No other major employer thought twice about that disparity – as still too few do today. As Spedan was to write later:

> In fact, as a whole the staff were getting just a bare living, with very little margin beyond absolute necessities and correspondingly little chance to get much fun out of life, and at the same time feel they were saving adequately for their retirements … Moreover the pay rates were not supplemented in any way. Absence for illness almost always meant stoppage of pay. Only in very special cases was there any help for that or in any other trouble. The business was forty years old but there was not a single pensioner or any prospect for anybody, and not a penny was spent on playing-fields or any other amenity for the staff. In all such ways the management could hardly have been more ruthlessly close-fisted. Obviously such a state of affairs could not have existed unless the general conditions at the time had been more or less similar. To me … all this seemed shocking.

It led him to conclude that someone who controlled a business shouldn't take out of it more than he would pay anyone else to do the same job. His father profoundly disagreed, and contended that many of his workers were lazy, and only did the minimum they could get away with. Spedan's retort was that since they had no stake whatever in the success of the business, they gained nothing by extra effort. As you might expect, when Spedan suggested that this was both unjust and counter-productive, the response was highly critical, encapsulated in a resounding expression that Spedan would recall with relish: 'Who do you suppose would bear the carking cares of business for such a miserable pittance as this would provide?' You don't have to know what 'carking' means to get the gist. Spedan dropped the matter and never returned to it with his father, who was often tetchy about money. For all his wealth, John Lewis was still nonplussed by the immense fortunes highlighted in the wills of his great competitors like William Whiteley and Frederick Gorringe. He'd made plenty, but not *that* much, and he couldn't fathom why not. Spedan said: 'He was bitterly mortified, and seriously assured us that the figures must be grossly exaggerated and published by their families out of mere vanity.'

His father lived extremely comfortably, but Spedan asked himself why he had not achieved more:

> Most [of his profits] had financed the growth of the business but I saw that quite a lot of them had gone into rather wrong-headed litigation, and a large remainder had gone into investments of which the making and the management were really nothing but a nuisance to their possessor. As I turned these things over in my mind, it occurred to me that, if a very much larger proportion of the income from the business had gone to the other people who were likewise giving their own working-lives to it, the business itself would have been vastly more efficient and my father's life would have been really far happier ... As all this became clearer and clearer to me, I came to see that an enterprise, a business, is a living thing with rights of its own. Its earnings ought to be used with real care for its own efficiency, exactly as a good farmer feels a duty to maintain and develop the fertility of the land that he farms and to leave it in better, rather than worse, 'heart' than when it came into his hands.

During 1910, the year after his accident, Spedan considered whether a more humane and inclusive way of doing business could mitigate the destructive effects of capitalism on society, effects that were particularly acute in pre-revolutionary Russia. They were becoming rife in Britain too, where strikes were being violently suppressed, as they were most notoriously in the summer of 1911. In the mid-nineteenth century the co-operative movements had emerged and thrived from their small tentative beginning with the twenty-eight Rochdale 'Pioneers' of 1844. They were societies of consumers: they worked well and became very substantial. Co-operative societies of *producers* were more difficult to establish and sustain, as the great social reformer Robert Owen had discovered in Scotland and America nearly a hundred years earlier. There were many entrepreneurs with a social conscience – Cadbury, Salt, Lever – but their measures to improve the lives of their employees didn't give them an explicit share in the profits of the business, didn't extend to allowing them to participate in decision-making, didn't undermine the deep-embedded pillars of capitalism. More recently experiments had begun in France, which Spedan may have heard of while recuperating there. He strove to devise a method of including employees in a business's success while ensuring that its health could be safeguarded. He concluded that 'capital should have a moderate fixed interest with a reasonable *but never unlimited* reward for taking a risk. All further earnings should go to all workers alike, from top to bottom.' But how exactly to do it?

By his own reckoning it was in the first few days of October of 1910 that he finally worked out the final details. He said it came upon him in the bath, although without, we presume, the subsequent Archimedean gallop through the streets. He knew he wanted to treat any business of his as a partnership of all its workers, but he couldn't work out how to make it self-financing. As he said, the solution 'suddenly flashed' upon him when he was in a nursing home recuperating from a second major operation. The idea was to distribute shares instead of cash. The shares needed to be freely saleable, but they must not have votes, otherwise outsiders could build up a share of the business. This hadn't occurred to him earlier because his father's business was still in private hands, had no shareholders, and he had no first-hand experience of the stock exchange at all.

> It may sound odd but it is a fact that, after I had got as far as conceiving the idea of treating a business as a partnership of all its workers, it was quite a while, a good many months, before I saw how such a business could be self-financing. The notion was so obvious that I am puzzled that it did not occur to me sooner.

Spedan was now a man with a plan, but with no business of his own to try it out on. At this point he was twenty-five. He found working for his father extremely trying: 'the perversity of some of his notions and the arbitrariness of his temper made the strain of working with him considerable.' He told his mother that if the worry and vexation didn't kill him by then he'd stick it out until he was thirty. 'He may live to see me forty and, though I think I can stand it until I am thirty, another ten years of it would be too much for anybody. By the end of it there would be nothing left of them.' In practice once a year there would be a violent argument, Spedan would disappear for a couple of days to cool off, Eliza would be sent to mediate, and he'd return without comment. Spedan said that in those Oxford Street years up to 1914 he rarely had a Saturday morning off, and took no holiday apart from three weeks in the summer. And when he came back from that, he said, he was forced to tackle so much that had gone wrong in his absence that he seriously considered taking no holiday at all. Had he not been given his own business to run in 1914 there seems little doubt that he'd have sought a career elsewhere, perhaps in politics where the Liberal whips had tried to interest him in a seat in parliament. But he stuck it out, did what he could to improve the business, and watched his father expend even more money in litigation, most notoriously in 1911, when the sleeping dog woke up.

## Landlords and Litigation – Part Two

In the high summer of 1909 the leader of the Liberal opposition David Lloyd George had delivered a sensational speech in one of the poorest parts of the East End of London. A wonderful Welsh orator, he lashed out at landlords, the aristocracy, and indeed everyone who didn't earn a living by the sweat of their own brows. He was merciless on landlords:

> Who is the landlord? The landlord is a gentleman ... who does not earn his wealth. He does not even take the trouble to receive his wealth. He has a host of agents and clerks to receive it for him. He does not even take the trouble to spend his wealth. He has a host of people around him to do the actual spending for him. He never sees it until he comes to enjoy it. His sole function, his chief pride, is stately consumption of wealth produced by others. What about the doctor's income? How does the doctor earn his income? The doctor is a man who visits our homes when they are darkened with the shadow of death: who, by his skill, his trained courage, his genius, wrings hope out of the grip of despair, wins life out of the fangs of the Great Destroyer. All blessings upon him and his divine art of healing that mends bruised bodies and anxious hearts. To compare the reward which he gets for that labour with the wealth which pours into the pockets of the landlord, purely owing to the possession of his monopoly, is a piece if, they will forgive me for saying so, of insolence which no intelligent man would tolerate.

Imagine a modern election enlivened by such rhetoric. He ended with a ringing: 'This system is not business, it is blackmail.' The aggrieved tenant John Lewis was paying a staggering £20,000 a year – nearly £2m today. Roused by Lloyd George's passion, John Lewis poked the sleeping Cavendish Square dog with a sharpened stick, erecting impassioned notices in his prime window space at the corner of Holles Street and Oxford Street:

> It is a great hardship upon those who by the cultivation of their business have created a value in the property which it did not possess before, that they should be liable in a limited time to be turned out of that property. They are very much in the condition of geese in Norfolk who at certain times of year are stripped of their feathers and then turned out to grow another crop.

This old (well-feathered) goose couldn't resist provoking his landlord. He mocked the young Baron, who was 'discovered behind the curtains pulling the wires for the imprisonment of his old tenant'. Under the headline

**THE WICKED LANDLORD**

he went on to lambast him with the righteous republican fervour of the penniless orphan made good:

> Under the feudal laws which unhappily still obtain in this country you, Lord Howard de Walden and Seaford, on the 21st year of your age, owing to the accident of birth, inherited political power as a life-long legislator. Coupled with this, as a landowner you stepped into enormous unearnt wealth, created entirely by the community in general and the occupier in particular. The Duke of Portland said ownership had both duties and pleasures; of the pleasures indeed with the energy of your youth have tasted freely, as witness your lovely villa in Monte Carlo, your steam yacht, your Motors, your racehorses, your palaces in London and the country.

Take that, and not surprisingly this riled the landlord so much that he sued John Lewis for libel, a case that eventually came to court in March 1911. Lewis spared no expense, lining up formidable advocates FE Smith, later Lord Birkenhead, and Edward Carson – Oswald's adviser in the spat with his father two years before – and one of their juniors was the son of Asquith, the Liberal prime minister. They did their best with the poor material at their disposal, but as the jury retired Smith turned to Spedan and told him that his father would lose, and the damages would be £3,000, over £250,000 today. But Old John's passionate advocacy in the witness box on behalf of the put-upon tenants of Britain clearly struck a chord with the jury. They took just twenty minutes to bring a verdict of guilty against John and to decide on the level of damages – one farthing, a quarter of one old penny, the by now traditional snub to the plaintiff: 'You win, but what on earth were you fighting for?' *The Times* next morning loftily announced a plague on both their houses, and the embarrassed de Walden capitulated. He no longer prevented John Lewis from doing what he liked in the shop, and allowed him to buy the properties' freeholds. In a curious sequel, many years later when Oswald joined the Territorial Army in the Westminster Dragoons, he found his commander to be the very same Lord Howard de Walden. His fellow officers were much amused. Lord Howard's widow later reported that Oswald had wryly enjoined her husband never to give in to his father: 'I fear the old man might die because he so enjoys being angry with you.' The landlord exhibited no personal animosity, it seems, and in December 1911 hatchets were ceremonially buried when John Lewis took his landlord round the shop. Of his vexatious litigant of a father, Spedan later wryly said:

> He said to me once that those two houses had cost him £50,000 more than they could possibly be worth. But he always loved a fight. He fought a great many law cases and he was always inclined to risk finding himself involved in a battle if the results were likely to be of public advantage ... Sir Edward Carson once told my brother: 'I have appeared for your father and I have appeared against him, and I would be puzzled to say which position was the more difficult of the two ...' When appearing against him, Carson had once addressed to his opposing barrister in urgent tones an appeal: 'Mr Duke, can't you control your client?', only to receive the discouraging reply 'No, I can't. You try.' (Much laughter in court).

He was by no means finished with litigation. He had what appears now an irrational loathing for inoculation, and, as Spedan said later:

> In 1913 on the wall of Chadwickham House, the boarding-house in Bolsover Street he was building, he put up an anti-inoculation notice. My father came upon an enraged doctor tearing it down. He chased him and, losing his puff, reached out and bashed him on his silk top hat with his umbrella. To judge from the hat, which was produced in Court, the blow was well aimed and had considerable merit. The doctor sued him for smashing his hat. The judge found for my father. He was seventy-seven at the time.

The judge in fact bound over both combatants to keep the peace. The lad sacked in Liverpool for fighting hadn't lost his pugnacity. Or his fearlessness. When he was over sixty he turned out of his stables in Weymouth Mews a drunken coachman, a man, Spedan said, 'who was threatening to brain with a shovel anyone who came up the narrow stairs to his room and whom two policemen were afraid to tackle'.

## Spedan at Oxford Street

Spedan later said that, the occasional violent argument excepted, during the initial period he was in very high favour with his father, who 'had never in his life worked with anyone who had spent his first nineteen years in learning to learn ... He told me once that he was amazed at the way in which my brother and I had learned ... in a day, to do things that he would not have expected us to grasp in less than six months.' That emphasises the danger of surrounding oneself with inferior minds, a mistake Spedan was determined never to make. He began by taking responsibility for the staff hostel at 42 Weymouth Street. Unhappy with its condition, Spedan tackled the abysmal quality and efficiency of its catering operation and 'cheerfully embezzled the savings for unauthorised mitigations of the prescribed austerity'. In other words, he found money surreptitiously to make a grim and cheerless place more attractive. He began to tackle the mountain of old stock, often confronted by idiocies in the way a range was re-ordered. He once had the whole stock of sewing silk laid out on a long counter. 'The result was farcical. The colours that were in frequent demand were present to the extent of one or two boxes, but certain colours that were in very slow demand were in piles of many boxes, and I remember that in one case there were twenty.' A wide-assortment policy demands meticulous attention to detail or you're sunk. Old John had once showed his detailed system of stock-lists to a relation of his wife, one of the Bristol Bakers, who retorted that it was all very perfect but how would he ever get anybody else to do the same thing? Well, John couldn't, but Spedan would.

From the outset at Oxford Street Spedan set about understanding the technical details of the business. He wanted to know about everything. He went out on the horse-and-cart delivery rounds, and was soon buying all the horses himself, and berated any driver found to be using a whip on them. He had no office, just a desk in the counting house, but he devised a means of note-taking that allowed him to carry masses of information in a tiny script on cards he kept in his pocket. He tried his hand at buying, and after a couple of early failures became a success, learning lessons that he would draw on later when he had his own shop. He flew dangerously upmarket on one occasion (Yearsley – he's never given a Christian name – was his father's expert buyer of silks):

> My father and Mr Yearsley were absolutely certain that my purchase of Oriental carved ivories and similar things would be disastrous, yet the stuff sold like butter before the sun. The Liberty's buyer stood in front of our window and said we were 'cutting the stuff to pieces'. The actual profit was 30–40%, and at that value the goods were staggeringly cheap. I never bought heavily, only lightly, and only stuff which I liked. They were no more aware than if they had been a couple of Red Indians of the existence of potential customers who would buy such stuff simply for visual pleasure. I bought nothing that I should not feel was a tolerably acceptable present if given to me.

They were selling it at about half Liberty's prices, and still taking an acceptable profit. Spedan was an aesthete who learnt to overcome his own taste – and distaste – and later said bluntly:

> I bought a lot of stuff that I wouldn't have had in my own house but seemed in its way genuinely attractive. Some very successful purchases made by Mrs McDermott and Mr Benton have revolted me. If you want to make millions you must cater for the very uncultivated. If you want to make hundreds of thousands, you must cater for a lowish grade of mezzo-brow.

Lowish grade of mezzo-brow? Is that what he thought the typical John Lewis customer was? He also began to disagree about merchandise with his father, who thought everything should be bought to last:

> In a very great many articles of our trade durability is of very little importance, and in comparatively few it is nearly all that matters. The policy of the John Lewis business has been settled by the habit of years upon lines that are disastrously incorrect in the extent to which they exaggerate the importance of durability and underestimate the importance of beauty and up-to-dateness.

Though he was careful not to introduce innovations his father might notice and angrily rescind, he did try out at the Oxford Street shop what he called a 'committee for communication', which would become a key plank in the structure of his Partnership in due course. He saw clearly that a better understanding between managers and managed was essential. One innovation he introduced wasn't actually at the shop. His father disapproved of games as a waste of time, but Spedan and Oswald didn't, even though they weren't particularly accomplished at competitive sport. They took a cycling holiday through southern England and Normandy. They persuaded their father to lay down a grass tennis court at Spedan Tower. Then at the height of his illness Spedan decided to take out a bank loan of £7,100 of his own money, a little over half a million today, to buy a house with a sports ground in its sixty-three acres. Grove Farm began Spedan's love affair with the idea of creating country retreats for his staff to enjoy, 'as if they'd had the same good fortune of birth'. He later wrote of its acquisition (and subsequent loss) in terms worthy of a romantic novelist:

> The contract came when I was too nearly dead to be able to close my fingers on the pen. My mother thought that, if the purchase came to light, there would be a tremendous family row and she urged me to break it off, but I answered that if I lived I should want it and, if I died, it would not matter. I knew they dared not excite me and, as I was too weak to grip the pen, somebody held my hand and guided it.

## Peter Jones

In 1864, the same year the young John Lewis had opened his shop, Peter Jones, the son of a Welsh hat-maker, had come to London with fourteen gold sovereigns in his pocket. He promptly entrusted them for safekeeping to a surprised young tailor's journeyman he had met on the train, saying he'd be back for them when he'd got a job. (That journeyman reappeared out of the blue forty years later and told his story at Peter Jones' funeral.) After working in drapers' shops in Newington and Leicester Square, Jones set up on his own out east in the Hackney Road. In 1871 he arrived in the working-class end of Chelsea, leased two small shops at 163 and 165 Marlborough Road, and set about knocking them into one to set up as a 'co-operative drapery shop'. Whatever that meant, it wasn't what Spedan would launch nearly fifty years later. Rebuilding was sluggish and for a spell Jones traded on the pavement outside. That's where he was when the building under construction behind him collapsed, trapping his wife under a heavy beam in the basement, and killing a young apprentice. From that awkward beginning in 1872, and reputedly helped by compensation from the landlord, his sales surged spectacularly. In 1874 he made £8,000, then in 1877 he decided on the key move to two small shops at the upmarket end of Chelsea, where the King's Road opens into Sloane Square (the road so named when it was widened from a footpath by Charles II so he could be driven to Hampton Court). In 1882 Jones was making close to £40,000, around £3.5m today. He expanded wherever he could buy property on the block facing Sloane Square, and by 1890 he had a continuous run from 2 to 14 King's Road, where he was now employing 300, the same as John Lewis.

In truth Jones was a far more considerate employer than Lewis, and he retained many of his staff for most of their working lives. Indeed in 1888 a drapery trade journal reported that there was much competition to join the company. At a time when employers weren't obliged to provide shop assistants with seats – it wasn't compulsory until Churchill's 1912 Shops Act – he was the first to do so. By 1890 he had converted twenty-eight shops and completed a massive rebuild, extending the store to five floors with ornate marble pillars and handsome plate glass windows. It was one of the first to be lit by electric light, and had its own fire brigade – by no means a luxury item. The profits topped £10,000 for the last five years of the century, and he successfully floated Peter Jones Ltd as a public company. He was chairman, and his two sons were on the board. That was just like John Lewis a few years later, but the fathers and sons were decidedly different in character. In 1903, after a record year with sales of £157,000 and profits of £12,000 (around £14m and £1m now), Jones withdrew from the business. He could then enjoy the benefits of his wealth, such as his substantial art collection. Not for long however, because within two years he was dead. Without him, the company then blundered by buying up cheap bankrupt stock and trying to offload it through frequent sales. His sons, their hearts not in it, were soon looking for a buyer. John Lewis sniffed a bargain.

In March 1906 the seventy-year-old John Lewis walked to Sloane Square, handed over twenty £1,000 banknotes and £2,500 in odd change, and bought Peter Jones. He installed himself as chairman and put his sons on the board. But he was reluctant to spend much time on the new shop, apart from immediately cutting the annual advertising budget from £2,000 to nil. In the following year sales plummeted by £20,000. By 1909 they had fallen below £95,000. Ordinary shareholders received no dividend and soon neither did preference shareholders, the ones who receive a fixed dividend before ordinary shareholders get any. John Lewis didn't have the temperament or energy to run both shops – he kept injecting cash into what he called 'that great bucket of a shop', but resented sending good money after bad. He suspected that the figures which had induced him to buy the shop had somehow been falsified. His trading methods were different from those by which Peter Jones was run; both were successful, but the awkward hybrid didn't flourish. Those who know the area now, and its customers, would be amazed both at what the shop sold, and to whom. Not the wealthy burghers of Belgravia, but their butlers and footmen and maidservants, and local small traders. It was perversely downmarket.

## At Last – a Shop of His Own

In April 1913 John Lewis, tired of Peter Jones and arguments over it with Spedan, handed him its chairmanship. In the following January the business posted a loss of £8,000 on sales of £100,000. Only two departments had shown a sales increase on the year, and – following a blazing row two months earlier – in exasperation late in 1914 John ceded day-to-day control to Spedan. (Crucially, though, he stayed on the board, and when Spedan missed a meeting through illness he summarily closed the greengrocery department.) Spedan asked if that meant he could do what he liked at Peter Jones. Yes, but: 'You must not neglect the Oxford Street shop. You must not go down there before five o'clock.' Spedan rolled his sleeves up, but was even more aghast at Peter Jones than when he'd lifted the covers at Oxford Street. As there, ancient stock had to be jettisoned immediately. So did several buyers. Spedan waited four weeks and then sacked five of them in one day. He said: 'In the next week the total turnover started to rise and in the first six months the whole House rose by 12%.' He went behind the scenes, lifted the lid off the can, and found a wriggling mass of worms.

> Nobody had dared to press to my notice the state of the stock. I found hats marked two and a half guineas for which I ... felt that the top price was a shilling. Just after I took over the chimneys were condemned by the district surveyor as dangerous. The drains were so worn out that the iron fire-doors used to be closed in the basement because the customers complained about the smell...
>
> The daily figures used to be telephoned to my house in Harrow. I can remember very well coming in one day and finding by the telephone a penciled note saying that the sales for the day were ahead by twenty pounds. I felt then that the back of the job was broken.

Spedan was too optimistic. Sales did go up by 12% in the first half year, but expenditure on repairs reduced profits sharply. Then came the war, and businesses everywhere began to struggle, but Spedan went on spending.

Peter Jones made a loss again in 1915, and Spedan asked his father to lend him cash – he still had that quarter share in Oxford Street that Oswald had given up for £50,000. The senior partner in the firm who audited the Peter Jones accounts had become seriously alarmed. Spedan said, 'He supposed himself to be a good judge of such matters and felt it his duty to write to my father that the course that I was taking would merely increase gravely the heavy losses that would be suffered by all concerned in the winding up of the business.' The auditor seemed to think winding up was inevitable.

His father promptly insisted that Spedan return the controlling Peter Jones shares that had been put into his name. Spedan declined. He thought the business was progressing powerfully, although the expenditure necessary to keep the ship afloat had certainly put Peter Jones through a tough period of retrenchment at the worst possible time for trade. Moreover, Spedan was convinced that the great growth of the Oxford Street business in the last ten years had been largely his own doing. He would go it alone. His father told Spedan that if he didn't return the Peter Jones shares he would terminate his involvement at Oxford Street. Spedan said that in that case he'd exchange his interest in Oxford Street for his father's remaining interest in Peter Jones – the debentures, some preference shares and some cash.

> That was an exchange of a quarter-partnership in one of the soundest businesses in England and the prospect of being my father's sole heir, for a controlling interest in about as forlorn a derelict as could easily have been found in the whole of the drapery trade ... The auditors, who had watched the accounts of Peter Jones for twenty years or more ... urged me not to make what they felt was the ruinous mistake of giving up my position and prospects in my father's business ... The Midland Bank, who had a branch adjoining Peter Jones, could have been the Partnership's bankers but declined the account ... I was still quite uncertain what would be the long-run effects of the tremendous operations that had followed upon my accident. My life might be comparatively short or I might find myself an invalid. I reckoned that, if the worst came to the worst, I should get out of the liquidation the amount of the debentures, £35,000. I was prepared to risk the rest.

Once John Lewis was persuaded that Spedan was immovable, he gave him his £50,000, and Spedan had nothing to do with the Oxford Street business for another eight years. While this had been going on, Oswald, out of the business since 1909, had got a Law degree at Oxford and qualified as a barrister. He was selected as prospective Liberal candidate for the comfortable rural constituency of North Dorset, but when war broke out he became an officer in the mounted Westminster Dragoons. (There, to his surprise, he recognised some of the old John Lewis delivery horses that had been dragooned into service.) The injuries sustained by his fall from the horse had given Spedan a C3 health rating and inevitably exempted him from call-up.

With a wry symmetry it was a fall from a horse in Egypt that propelled Oswald out of the army with a damaged hip – indeed you could say that horses decided the trajectory of both their lives. Instead perhaps of perishing in France, as so many did, Oswald was discharged in the summer of 1916. Thus, at the point when Spedan gave up his quarter share in John Lewis, Oswald was free of the war and able to start a political career.

He didn't. Somehow Eliza persuaded her hitherto intransigent husband, who hadn't exchanged a word with Oswald since 1909, to ask if he would care to return to the partnership he'd walked out on in such a litigious breach. He would, and he did, and he told his mother that they had restarted work together as though nothing had happened. So, in a bizarre twist, the position of 1909 was completely reversed. Back came Oswald through Oxford Street's revolving door, and out went Spedan. Back to Peter Jones, a shop in a mess, in trading conditions as stagnant as those the war, the country and its infantry were mired in. How would he cope? And what would happen when he brought his madcap ideas in? If he ever could.

CHAPTER 5

# Peter Jones – Thriving as Publicans

Peter Jones a little before John Lewis bought it. The King's Road frontage starts behind the three straw-hatted girls. The Star and Garter pub is on the right, bought by John Lewis in 1911 and one of the few 'departments' to make a profit.

He would arrive about four o'clock in the afternoon by taxi, for he had no car of his own at that time, usually at the Symons Street doorway, dash into our one and only antiquated rope-propelled lift and at once get down to work sending for the people he wished to see.

ROBERT BICHAN, WRITING IN THE GAZETTE IN 1967
ABOUT SPEDAN LEWIS IN 1915

Sad experience of a wicked world may make it extremely difficult … to believe that a programme so unusual and financially so disinterested can really be honest and have no catch in it.

SPEDAN LEWIS, RECALLING THE PETER JONES SHAREHOLDERS' MEETING OF 1920

Let's go back a couple of years to Peter Jones in the early days of the war, to see what Spedan was up against, and how he tackled his own shop and employees. We have an observant eye-witness, one who watched him from the shop floor and recorded his memories fifty years later. On 1 January 1915 the young sales assistant Robert Bichan took the train up from Streatham Common to Oxford Street to be interviewed by Spedan Lewis. Spedan remained standing at a desk in one of several cubicles acting as offices as he conducted a brief interview. He was satisfied: Bichan began at Peter Jones a fortnight later in the furnishing drapery department at £80 a year plus 1¼% commission on sales – about £100 a year in all. That was for hours that ran from 8.30 a.m. to 8 p.m., though the shop stayed open half an hour later in June, July and August, so for Bichan it meant leaving home at 7.15 and arriving back at about 9.45 at night. Bichan had been at the Bon Marché in Brixton, later to become a Partnership store a few months into the next World War. But, though Spedan was straining at the leash to start his profit-sharing scheme at Peter Jones, the business was far too rickety for him to contemplate that yet – if he ever would. Just how rickety Bichan was soon to find out, just as he discovered that it wasn't the stately upmarket emporium he'd anticipated. Take the stock for instance:

> I was naturally very thrilled at getting work in what I thought would be a better class of trade than the suburbs, but I was really astounded to find such cheap, almost tawdry, goods displayed in the fixtures. I recall quite clearly that on one end of the counter was a pile of 31" gaudy patterned cretonnes priced at 3¾d a yard and, a week or so later, in came rolls and rolls of the same. Further investigation through the various departments found cotton sheets at 7s 9d a pair... men's suits at 29s 6d up to 3 guineas or so; all goods more suited to the Fulham Road or Walham Green than Sloane Square. All this puzzled me very much for within a stone's throw of our very doorstep every house in, say, Cadogan Square, Eaton Square, Eaton Place and all the surrounding squares and streets were occupied by families with a butler, often a footman, and a staff of servants.
>
> It really was the most fantastic business for, although the nobility, the aristocracy, the stockbroker grade and all the people who occupied those huge costly houses in our district came to us almost daily, they did not buy their dresses, millinery and other fashion goods from us – not then anyway. Our trade with the upper classes was chiefly confined to the service departments, repairs, renovations, replacements of household equipment ... For instance they would not dream of coming to us for the curtains of their best rooms.

Now the staff. The war, said Bichan, had drained drapery firms of manpower, but that was helpful in Peter Jones' case for 'the quality of male assistants they had been struggling with left very much to be desired; by and large they were very illiterate and had a couldn't-care-less attitude.' On his very first day he was shown a book kept on the counter for recording customers' orders for household repairs. One entry ran: 'Somethink wrong with blind in bartheroom.' The customers were a mixed bag – you could get the lady of the house one minute and her cook the next: 'I remember my first customer was a lady of title and I nearly fainted. I felt nine feet tall. I was serving the nobility.' But not for long if Spedan didn't sort out the staff. Bichan again:

> In a day or so I found one of them apparently in the act of writing down the customer's name and address. The lady had said, and I recall the name quite clearly: 'Mrs Clayton-East'. The salesman muffed the first part and then said 'How do you spell it?' The lady replied, obviously annoyed and rightly so, rapping her fingers on the counter, 'C L A Y T O N' – a pause and then she said 'hyphen'. The assistant looked up and asked 'How do you spell hyphen, madam? H A...?' I could stand it no longer – I stepped in and saved the day and I shall never forget the whimsical look she gave me as her eyes met mine.

## Spedan Gets to Grips

Spedan had been given sole responsibility for the shop a year earlier. 'I put into Peter Jones almost all my leisure. Night after night I got home to Harrow about nine o'clock so tired that my voice was nearly gone.' He was working his way through the shop, wreaking long-needed change as he went. This was still the period he had to work in Oxford Street for most of the day. When he arrived at Peter Jones, as Bichan described, Spedan once again gave priority to tackling his employees' accommodation, which was in the top floor of the building, still subdivided as its component shops had been. He described it as wretchedly uncomfortable and a severe fire risk. The liberal-minded Peter Jones had equipped it handsomely with 'a well-stocked library, a piano for the musical, and two billiard tables.' By Bichan's time, only the piano remained, and it was no attraction to the musical:

> One was locked out after a certain time at night; the bedrooms were poorly furnished, often with only one washstand to three occupants, and there was no running water, not even cold; bath water was heated only on certain nights. There was an almost complete lack of social amenities, with no facilities for entertaining visitors, the only contribution to a form of cultural pursuit being an old vintage piano, many of its yellow keys refusing to respond to the touch. The decorations of these so-called sitting rooms consisted usually of the inevitable aspidistra and one or two drab reproductions of 'And when did you last see your father?' and Landseer prints of forlorn Highland cattle standing knee-deep in water. A zinc pail acting as a coal-bucket was already empty when the evening was young.

> The first action was to close the men's quarters and expand the women's. One of the very first things he insisted on was that each room should have running water, both hot and cold. Of course, this meant drastic alterations to the antiquated plumbing and hot water system. Still, it had to be done, and done it was, and really well. He allowed the girls to sort themselves out just as they pleased ... He ran it along the lines of a hotel, with a charge for each room – a single room warranting a higher charge than one with two occupants. Then, in order to further this 'freedom' feeling, the occupants of the rooms were each allowed to visit the curtain department and choose the material for their curtains and bedspreads.

At the same time Spedan removed all restrictions on personal freedom in the hostel. Anyone over twenty-one could come and go as they liked at any time. 'Their position in this respect', wrote Spedan, 'is exactly the same as a resident in a hotel.' The company had a duty of care for young women *in loco parentis*, so between eighteen and twenty-one they had to get a late pass from the Matron to be out after 10 p.m., and it was 9 p.m. if they were under eighteen. Night porters were engaged so that the hostels were open all night. The resulting accommodation was scrupulously hygienic, which a doctor later identified as the reason the hostel was completely free from the terrifying 1919 epidemic of flu. Another contribution to the health of the employees was the food, whose standard he set out to improve. Spedan was later to say that 'for most people eating is one of the chief pleasures of life, immensely important to good temper and liveliness of mind. Our dining room ought to be so managed that, when people leave the Partnership, they regret it regularly every meal-time.' As Bichan attests:

> Then came the staff dining-room, which up to that time must have surely have been the nearest copy of a Borstal [young offenders'] institution with its long trestle tables, its wooden chairs (many with portions of the back rails missing), the window blinds drab and faded and always at different levels of adjustment and drawn only at night and in the winter to hide us from view of the occupants of the flats opposite. The two male members of the maintenance staff, discarding their overalls and donning not very white coats, topped with ill-fitting chef's hats, took their place behind the serving tables to act as carvers...
>
> All this was swept away, and in a matter of weeks we were all enjoying our meals in an entirely new atmosphere with a number of interesting pictures on the walls, colourful curtains, black and red Tudor tile pattern linoleum, tables to seat two, four and six people, and an elbow chair to ensure comfort and space. The food came through from a modernised kitchen, piping hot and nicely served by waitresses immaculate in neatly laundered uniforms, with suitable headgear.

Spedan subsidised the staff dining room, and there always one very cheap main course on the menu. Later he would provide free milk for those under eighteen. The Peter Jones workroom, down in the bowels of the building, took longer to sort out. Bichan described its heroic occupants battling with adversity:

> There were two women sewing carpets, sometimes three, three upholstresses making curtains and loose covers, who were housed down in the basement under the pavement lights in Symons Street, part of it actually under the entrance. It had a flagstone floor, was badly lit and, in order to get a better view of their work, the machinists would move their machines under the pavement lights; but many's the time they had to be hurriedly removed when a sudden downpour of rain would bring a cascade of water belching down on to their work, causing utter confusion. Two upholsterers worked a few yards away, and, as their work was chiefly repairs, one can imagine the dust which filled the air almost constantly. To expect any human being to work under such conditions today would be quite unthinkable.

Spedan had avoided irritating his father by making no major *visible* changes to Peter Jones – although a dominating personality who didn't shirk an argument, he had always been careful to avoid lighting his father's blue touch paper. In particular he hadn't yet had the Peter Jones brass shop front cleaned, which his father thought a waste of money. Once Spedan was independent he had it done: 'a front that looked dirty, neglected, bankrupt, was in my view hopelessly bad policy for a business that ... was on Belgravia's back-door step and should be its village shop.' In keeping with this general sprucing-up he spent much time and effort trying to improve the attitude of his staff towards their customers, however unreasonable they were. In early 1917 he wrote:

> At the present time one or two of our Heads of Department tend to be rather unwisely cold in manner to casual customers ... One or two others get dangerously near to making their customers feel small, which is still worse, and one or two others are rather over-anxious to expect the feminine public to be reasonable, and to show decided resentment when this expectation meets its natural frequent disappointment.

## Thriving... by being Publicans

One of the few 'departments' making a profit at that time was, bizarrely, the Star and Garter, a pub owned by the shop at 26 Sloane Square on the King's Road corner. Years earlier the landlord had refused to sell it to Peter Jones even when offered £60,000 – nearly three times the sum John Lewis later bought the whole of the shop for. But its trade faded, and in 1911 John Lewis had bought it with the cigar shop next door for £15,875 at auction. He explained to the shareholders why he'd bought it: 'However well conducted the Star and Garter may be, no lady customer of Peter Jones cares to be seen stepping into or out of a public house, especially [one which has been] dirty and dilapidated for many years. I generally find lazy loafers hanging around the corner ... frequently an organ grinder or some objectionable tramp.' John Lewis, of course, had wanted the pub closed and its premises incorporated into the shop, but he'd have had to buy a piece of property behind it first, which proved difficult, so he had the pub tidied up and run 'in a quiet and respectable manner'. A surprise find in the cellar of forty gallons of 1875 Martell brandy brought a windfall which helped to boost the profits. In 1915 when Spedan chaired his first AGM a shareholder wanted to know whether the pub was to be kept on. Spedan was embarrassed but honest: 'Pro tem. I regret to say we are thriving exceedingly by being publicans.' And when pressed further – 'Is it the public house bringing in the money?' – he had to admit: 'It is the public house: on drapery last year there was nothing.'

Despite Drapery losing out to Intoxicating Liquor, Spedan was soon confident enough that the 'core business' was picking up that he decided to close the Star and Garter and bring the space into the shop. Obtusely, his father, who had tried to do that very thing when he bought it, now disagreed and tried to veto the move. But he failed, and in 1916 the huge star on the façade was removed, and the words Peter Jones faced Sloane Square for the first time. In explanation for the closure, Spedan told the shareholders that he was prepared to forgo the pub's £800 annual profit (about £70,000 today). Unfortunately the rebuilding cost, estimated at £350, was doubled when they found they had to reinforce the structure. John Lewis's obdurate reluctance to sell the Star and Garter was in spite of his forthright view, voiced when he acquired the pub in 1911:

> There are two businesses I will not follow for any profit going – publicking and pawnbroking. In one case they would ruin the man and in the other take advantage of him.

As for pawnbroking, the shop on the Peter Jones block at the *other* corner of Sloane Square when Robert Bichan arrived in 1915 was just that, a pawnbroker. And, as Bichan pointed out, strategically sited too:

> On the corner of Sloane Square and Symons Street was Millar and Fitch, without doubt one of the most widely known pawn shops in the whole of London; its dirty grimy windows, festooned in cobwebs, concealed from the passers-by deals in the pawning of pieces of family plate by the impecunious sons of the

> nobility who had bribed the butler to be allowed a few pieces 'just on loan for a few months'. When, many years later, the business was closed down and we took over the premises, I ... joined the demolition party for the thrill of ripping up the very first floorboard to reveal only a few of the golden sovereigns which, rumour had it, had over the years slipped through the cracking floor. So far as I remember only one sovereign was found, but coins of lesser value were numerous and were used, with no time wasted, to aid in washing down the dust in our throats with draughts of ale at The Antelope, known to all the Bohemians of Chelsea who crossed its threshold as The Pregnant Fawn.

The picture we have of Sloane Square's elegant wealth today is very different from this glitter-and-squalor of 100 years ago. Spedan recognised that 'in an out of the way site you must aim at having a few good customers rather than many who individually spend little'. His determination to drag Peter Jones upmarket and better the lives of his staff – he increased their salaries and lowered their working hours as well as improving their hostels – brought a rapid increase in sales but an even steeper rise in costs. He was most anxious to get the business into a profitable state so he could float his profit-sharing scheme. But he was opposed by virtually everyone else with any influence: this included his father, even though he had sold up his financial interest in the business. They already felt that improvement of the lot of his employees was both reckless and pointless. Spedan himself described their argument: 'They felt it ... merely utopian, an unpractical lavishness that must come in due course to grief, so that in the end it would be of no real benefit to anybody.' Among those who regarded Spedan as a spendthrift was his brother Oswald, as he later confided to his son Peter, who will enter the story many years on.

This 'unpractical lavishness' did indeed seem to be bleeding the business dry. Despite a reduction of trading hours to 9 a.m. to 6 p.m., the paysheet had doubled in the three years 1913–16 from £7,200 to £14,500. So had the cost of housekeeping in the hostel above the shop, up to nearly £6,000. Spedan's determination that pay-rates should keep pace with the fast-rising wartime inflation was responsible for only a third of that. At the end of 1916 the company secretary, Mr Pike, gave his bleak assessment of the position. Although the turnover of £167,000 was undeniably a great recovery, there were accumulated debts of £45,000 (about £3m today) and:

> Even on a £250,000 turnover the Company could only painfully slowly liquidate its liabilities, and it certainly could not possibly start a Profit Sharing scheme. I have looked the facts solidly in the face and I again tell you fearlessly unless you give somebody full authority to ruthlessly cut down the present extravagant method of running the Company, I consider the future is absolutely hopeless and nothing can convince me otherwise.

A sense of desperation and frustration runs through that extract, from a man exasperated by Spedan's stubbornness in pursuing his hopelessly impractical notions of 'fairness', which were ruining the business. But although he had no option but to postpone the introduction of his profit-sharing scheme, Spedan was not deterred. In 1918 he began to plough ahead with other unprecedented reforms that we'll discuss in the next chapter. Then the end of the war in November 1918 brought a sudden surge in well-being – and returning soldiers – and trade rocketed. Turnover leapt to £253,000, and although in truth most of that was inflation, Spedan now felt he could go to the shareholders and propose his new employee profit-sharing scheme. He couldn't just do it, as he would have been able to at the privately owned John Lewis in Oxford Street. Peter Jones was a public company, and he had to convince the shareholders at an annual meeting. How would they react? He proposed to reorganise the capital structure of the company. He would write down the Ordinary share capital to a quarter of its nominal value, and cancel the substantial arrears of Preference dividend with the promise of a higher dividend in future as compensation. He told them he was drawing no salary for himself whatever, nor would he pay himself any dividend on his holding of over 80% of the Ordinary shares. His scheme was clever, and he so dazzled the shareholders that his disarming honesty persuaded them. He pointed out that he could sell his shares for a vastly larger sum than he could get for it after the scheme was through. The extract at the head of the chapter comes from Spedan's recollection of the meeting, which included 'a prolonged debate of various points'. He then sums up blithely: 'The scheme was then adopted on a show of hands without any need for a vote.'

Some of the shareholders clearly felt they were being taken for turkeys and asked to vote for Christmas. But his sheer openness and self-confidence persuaded them that, at the very least, if they were turkeys he was turkey-in-chief. There was indeed no 'catch', neither for the old shareholders nor the nervous new, for each employee of Peter Jones received a proportion of a total of 7,000 new Preference shares, or rather share 'promises', representing 15% of their pay. It was the first Partnership Bonus, or 'Benefit' as it was then called. And soon after he told them they were no longer employees, but Partners, joining him in a new kind of enterprise. Did they feel like Partners in a genuine Partnership? No, not really. Did they believe these shares were as good as money? They were highly dubious: he was not *exactly* giving them shares, but share 'promises'. What did that mean? It all seemed too good to be true. Could they trust him? He set out to convince them.

CHAPTER 6

# Forging a Partnership

THE GAZETTE

OF PETER JONES, LIMITED,
SLOANE SQUARE, LONDON, S.W.3.

FOR THE PUBLICATION OF FACTS, OPINIONS AND IDEAS OF INTEREST TO ANY ONE WHOSE FORTUNES ARE FOR THE TIME CONNECTED IN SOME DEGREE WITH THOSE OF THE COMPANY.

SATURDAY, MARCH 16TH, 1918.

*Our Policy, Rules of Correspondence, etc., are on the last page of this issue.*

NOTICE FROM THE MANAGEMENT TO THE COMPANY'S STAFF.
Official Communications to this Paper are equivalent to House Notices, and must be known by every one whom they concern.

TO MY FELLOW-EMPLOYEES OF PETER JONES, LTD.

LADIES AND GENTLEMEN,

The front page of the first Gazette. The sub-heading is classic Spedan, and note the decorous 'fellow-employees', and the Ladies and Gentlemen...

'Oh, Matron, Florrie's got her share money!' 'What about it?' 'But are these things really money?' 'Of course they are really money, as I keep on telling you silly girls, and now perhaps you'll believe it.' Whereupon the questioner said: 'But I have got thirty of them! Fancy me worth thirty pounds!' – and she burst into tears.

SPEDAN LEWIS, RECALLING THE EARLY DAYS OF PROFIT SHARING,
IN *PARTNERSHIP FOR ALL*, 1948

## Spedan's Innovations – Sharing Knowledge

So what were the reforms that Spedan gradually brought into Peter Jones that would make it so different from all other department stores, and ultimately from almost any other business? How would he convince his employees that he meant what he said? From the outset he defined the key components of a genuine Partnership as the sharing of Knowledge, Gain and Power. He introduced a regular staff 'council' meeting; he improved pay and started his profit-sharing scheme; and he started a two-way journal he called the Gazette. He readily understood that a sense of the power of joint ownership would only emerge through shared knowledge. He had started early on by the simple expedient of posting the week's results by department, on cards along the stairs, annotated with his comments. That was well before he began the Gazette. He recalled, using the old-fashioned term 'House' for the shop:

> Another innovation that made the House gasp ... was the admission of the whole of the staff to knowledge of figures normally reckoned to be highly confidential. It had an extremely tonic effect upon the minds of the recipients. My father had carried secrecy even to the length of not merely not giving to his buyers figures of their own buyerships, but strenuously discouraging their attempting to keep any figures for themselves...
>
> The publication of these and other figures has always been a marked feature of the Gazette ... and I was told that one critic declared that in doing so we 'loaded the dice against ourselves'... but a Partnership must be very reluctant that any particular thing must be kept secret.

Early on after his arrival at Peter Jones, Spedan introduced a method of sharing information between managers and managed. He called this a committee for communication, something he'd tried with some success at Oxford Street in his early days there. The idea was that the shop assistants – not the managers – from different parts of the shop would elect representatives to regular meetings with him, so he could keep them abreast of events and they could make him aware of any grievance. He recalled how bitterly it was opposed by the Peter Jones buyers, who were in practice the middle tier of management of the shop, and used to ruling without question:

> How sensational an innovation that was in those days is shown in the fact that the buyers, who at that time were still managers of the selling departments for which they bought ... promptly took the very unusual step of sending me a 'round robin' to ask that I would hold a buyers' meeting, and at that meeting expressed extreme dislike of the idea. I listened to their objections and persisted

immediately. An important buyer tendered her resignation next morning. I ignored it and no-one left.

The buyers were opposed because they saw regular meetings of Spedan with their staff – who came to be called in the Partnership by the bluntly unflattering term 'rank and file' – as a threat to their power and autonomy. Spedan was determined to apply the same approach and standards across the business and wasn't going to allow local fiefdoms to remain. And although in the early committee for communication meetings he spoke much more than he listened, and was met by a degree of timidity, in due course people were emboldened to speak up, and it encouraged a crossover of ideas (and complaints) at the grassroots.

## The First Gazettes

Write a letter if you want to:

> Bring to light a grievance of your own or someone else's,
> Or to be told the reason of some rule or custom of the House,
> Or if you think that you can make a useful criticism, or suggestion, or put a stop to any mismanagement, or wrong-doing,
> Or if you feel that you ought to point out in this or that matter the Chairman, or anyone else, is wrong,
> Or if you want to let the management know that you take a keen interest in the company's welfare, or that you have special qualifications for some particular post better than, or different from, that which you occupy now.

That was Spedan's injunction printed on the back of the first Gazette, 16 March 1918. Very much as an experiment, he introduced an occasional newsletter. He wanted to start a genuine two-way debate between his staff and himself. He felt it wrong to give it away, so at first he charged a penny, around 15p today. It was by no means an immediate success, and for a long time he was virtually the only contributor. In order to encourage letters, which he allowed to be published anonymously to make people feel safe from retribution if – as they perhaps had reason to fear – they aroused his ire, he wrote many himself. His disguise would have been better had he changed his writing style, and particularly his eccentric placement of commas, which gave the game away. He was by now a prodigiously prolific writer. In fact he had difficulty knowing when to stop, and his effusions at first generated dislike of his new-fangled Gazette. But Spedan could find a silver lining in any glowering cloud: 'We understand that the Gazette is more unpopular than it has ever been. I am more glad to hear that it is unpopular than there is no feeling at all.' He deliberately kicked off an early controversy by proposing that everyone's pay rates should be published. This at least got some letters going, especially from the courageous Betty Wilson, who signed her own name and wasn't put off by Spedan's typical: 'We are very much obliged to Miss Wilson ... but we are bound to say that she seems to have an odd idea of what constitutes a fact.' However, as the spring of 1918 progressed, trading prospects became so uncertain that some board members wanted the Gazette to stop, lest doom and gloom should spread. Spedan demurred because:

> The prospect of times of especial difficulty was a particularly strong argument against delay in providing the management with a much more efficient and continuous method of communicating with the staff and vice-versa.

It was a pivotal moment. Spedan showed the courage of his convictions by asking the entire staff to vote on whether they should keep the Gazette. The result was very nearly even, 187 to continue, 191 to stop – and six hedging their bets by putting an X against both options... To Spedan that was a glass half-full, so the Gazette continued, the charge now two pence, with twelve pages instead of sixteen, and coming out three-weekly instead of fortnightly. It soon reverted to fortnightly, but there was another crisis in 1921, when the splendidly truculent works manager Mr Cuthbertson proposed in an early 'staff council' meeting that the Gazette should be abandoned: 'There's very little in it, and only 20% buy it.' Put to the vote, the figures came out at 9–9. The chairman sweated in Spedan's absence about whether he had a legitimate casting vote, but eventually decided discretion was the better part of valour and referred the tied vote to Spedan, who saw another glass half full, and wrote ringingly in response:

> Government is an evil, a necessary evil, but still an evil, and the more light you can keep shining on it the better.

Spedan's long articles had filled the first few issues, but at first they hardly encouraged others to write. Some managers did start to contribute, though he hardly helped his cause by occasionally in reply letting off with both barrels. In early 1919 a forthright buyer named Gertrude Jardine had written to complain about a sacking, a letter to which he took exception. Rather than rebut it point by point, he chose to draw a natural history parallel by introducing his readers to the Weasel tribe, of which one of the most interesting was the Skunk, which released a noxious cloud of poison gas when alarmed, but failed to use its little brain, so fired it off indiscriminately at harmless innocent passers-by. *Five pages* of this as he warmed to his theme left Miss Jardine in little doubt as to the intended parallel. It turned out later that she had been right about the unfairness of the sacking, and he apologised publicly. Another letter to the Gazette, complaining that the company should no longer employ 'Aliens, even though they have perhaps been Allies during the War', received (extremely long) short shrift.

A little later an anonymous correspondent took him to task. How can you possibly encourage letter writers, anonymous or not, when you employ 'Billingsgate Language' to put down a writer, yet accuse us of being 'dull or lazy' in not writing? Spedan responded with an engaging lack of repentance: 'I *should* have said that the reason why you don't write to the Gazette is that some of you are dull, and either lazy *or chicken-hearted or both*. See how ready I am to accept correction!' Spedan enjoyed these blunt exchanges, and gradually correspondents recognised that he harboured no grudge: he just wanted a vigorous open debate. And that gradually filtered down to the more timorous on the selling floor. When he surprised everyone by introducing an extra week's *paid* spring holiday in 1919, someone plucked up courage to ask:

> They say we are not being paid for the spring holiday before we go. It is all right for the girls in the House who have no food to buy, but what of the poor work-girls that have widowed mothers and daughters to help, to keep the home together, and many of whom have no parents at all, and landladies waiting patiently for the week's rent before they go? Hope you will kindly consider it.

Spedan replied by pointing out that, since they weren't paid in advance for a week in which they did work, they shouldn't expect to get paid in advance for a week in which they didn't. But he took the point and said anyone who wished to apply for it in advance would get it. He was trying to encourage requests like this, to avoid resentment simmering under the surface, particularly from the ordinary employee.

Gradually they plucked up courage. In the spring of 1920 there was a flurry of witty letters written in verse form or as literary spoofs. One was a parody of Kipling's *If*, another a clever retailing version of the *Rubaiyat* of Omar Khayyam, to which the editor gallantly riposted with a neatly turned pair of verses in the same style. The third was a set of brief articles about a new sports club. In 1920 Spedan received a tempting offer to buy Grove Farm, one he accepted because he had suddenly become drastically short of cash. Although he promptly bought a smaller replacement as a sports club, the seven-acre Broom Hall near Teddington with a river frontage on the Thames, he was subsequently angry with himself over the sale. It was still grieving him fifty years later:

> It had been meant for a fairyland and had become one. For years after I lost it I used to dream now and again that I had got it back ... nothing will make up for the loss of those sixty acres, adjoining, as they did, two railway stations (South

Harrow and Sudbury Hill) by which the ground could be reached in twenty minutes from Marylebone or forty-five minutes from Sloane Square.

At the time he was anxious to encourage Partners to use Broom Hall, and in this he was helped by a delicious pastiche of Daisy Ashford's bizarre runaway best-seller of 1919, *The Young Visiters*, spelt just like that. This feverish romance had been published through the intervention of JM Barrie, the author of *Peter Pan*, many years after the 1890s when Daisy had written it in a notebook at the age of nine. In three successive Gazettes the anonymous author 'HS' introduced readers to the dashing Mr Speeden and his new club, Ashfordesque mis-spellings and all. Below is its start and end:

**CHAP. I.**

Mr Speeden was a youngish man of 33 with a loud voice and curly hair. He was fond of inviting people to report to him about his bizness, which was a sumpshious affair at Sloan Square. He had a tipist with fair hair and a terri-cotta coat and one day he said Madam do you think the staff would like a club by the river. Oh yes she said getting very nervous and fijetty and wear would it be? Oh not on my vast estate at Harro said Mr Speeden with an airy wave of his lofty hand I think we will try Teddington now take down.

**CHAP. V.** *Ellapse of some months.*

After Pammela and her people got back to Slone Square they told many peaple grate and small about Old Brume Hall and when the fine wether came the thorghtful Mr Speeden said I think I will comandear a comodius viacle to take the Staff to and from the Club it will lesson the expense of the jerney. So a massive lorry filled with seats and a driver took the staff to the Club every night they wanted to go. And to of the bigwigs conspired and borght a hughe gramafone and the Wardon got three good boats a skif a punt and a dingy and now every day the Club has some young visiters so I will end my little tail and the Club lived happily ever after.

Sadly, Broom Hall didn't survive long, but a few years later its successor did.

## Sharing Gain

Spedan was clear that he had to do two things to make people genuinely feel they were co-owners of the business. He needed to make pay rates fairer, and he had to find the right way to share the profits of the business – as soon as it had enough worth sharing. As we've seen, he couldn't tackle the latter until the first distribution of early 1920, but he could deal with pay and, moreover, its make-up. When Robert Bichan started in early 1915 he earned a fixed salary, plus a bonus in commission calculated as a proportion of his department's takings each week. That in itself was a change from the old system whereby you got commission on your *own* sales only. This had meant that the department's senior sales staff would jealously guard 'their' customers, the biggest payers, and it generated unhealthily divisive competition and a rigid pecking order unrelated to ability. Spedan soon changed this, as some other shops, including Bainbridges of Newcastle, had done, with a commission based on what the department as a whole had achieved. But he didn't want any sense of unfairness to linger further: this method meant some were richer because of the department they were in, and there were considerable fluctuations week by week. So if you were in a department unaffected by the general trade lift at Christmas, you were unable to find extra for Christmas presents and luxuries.

Spedan concluded that the only just solution was to abolish commission and increase everyone's pay rates proportionately. Then he could begin to pay more fairly according to responsibility, ability and experience. But he incurred such serious opposition that he later reflected in the Gazette: 'The selling staff were very much against my scheme for fixed salaries rather than commission, and by their opposition deprived themselves for eighteen months of a reform that seems to be universally popular.' He was sensible enough to lift pay rates by more than enough at the same time, recognising that if you give people a little less than they expect they'll resent it, but give them a little more and they'll applaud you warmly – and work with more enthusiasm. The difference in cost is often very small, the effect on enthusiasm for work substantial. One further reform he made was to introduce a minimum wage, way ahead of its time. Everyone was to receive whatever the market 'value' was for his job, but subject to a minimum linked to the Minister of Labour's cost-of-living index, and designed to stay always a little ahead of the minimum wage of competitors. One 'Worried Wife' – he didn't limit letters to employees only – had written in to explain how difficult it was to make ends meet on £2 10s a week, around £100 today:

| | | |
|---|---|---|
| Rent | 11s 6d | £23 now |
| Coals | 2s 1½d | £4.25 |
| Meat | 10s | £20 |
| Vegetables | 2s | £4 |
| Groceries | 10s | £20 |
| Provisions | 5s | £10 |
| Bread | 5s | £10 |
| Milk/eggs (for child) | 1s 6d | £3 |
| Oddments | 1s 6d | £3 |
| Husband's pocket money | 1s 4½d | £2.75 |

The husband, with his pocket money of little more than two pence a day – hence perhaps the reluctance to spend it on a Gazette – will have been glad of the anonymity rule. Of course Spedan might have written the letter himself, for you couldn't always tell, but it seems unlikely.

When he was at last able to start his profit-sharing scheme he wanted to distribute in shares the equivalent of 15% of everyone's salary. But his father still exerted an influence, and he had to tread carefully:

> By the spring of 1920 the plan, that had been in all essentials completed by October 1910, was in full operation with the exception of the form in which the Partnership Benefit was to be distributed. However as long as my father lived it seemed undesirable to issue the Partnership Benefit in the form of a security that could be sold on the stock exchange. It was thought that this would bring the whole experiment to his notice and be a ceaseless puzzle and vexation to him. To get over this difficulty the Partnership Benefit was issued not in actual shares and stock but in printed documents with a handsome orange stamp called Share Promises. In due course it could be exchanged for the number of shares it mentioned together with a cumulative yearly dividend of 7½%, which was paid punctually on 1 June and 1 December.

He chose those dates so that people got a little extra in time for Christmas and the summer holiday. This dividend was indeed paid regularly in cash until World War II, but Spedan was unable to turn these share 'promises' into real shares until 1929, after his father's death. As you might expect, the idea of a share promise was a bit sophisticated for the selling floor, however impressive the orange stamp was, and many people didn't believe a word of it – until, that is, they realised that the shares could be cashed in, if only initially at a time of need. One important ally was Adeline Bakewell, the indefatigable hostel Matron. Spedan described her with relish as 'a woman of very broad, imaginative mind, a ferocious Bolshevist who gladly acquiesced in an experimental arrangement that the tenure of her post should depend on a) her keeping within her budget, b) conforming to the rules of the Partnership, and c) yearly re-election by her customers.' She worked hard to convince her doubtful charges that the share promises were real. One case caught Spedan's fancy:

> Among my letters one morning there was a report that an unmarried girl in one of the staff kitchens was expecting a child and was leaving and wanted to encash her holding of sixteen pounds' worth of Share Promises she had received as Partnership Benefit. I marked the paper 'Sanctioned' and passed it out.

A few days later the Matron reported that Florrie's share money had caused a flurry of excitement among a group of girls. In Spedan's words the conversation went as described at the head of the chapter. Florrie's £30 would be worth over £1,000 today. These were the days before companies' occupational pensions, and indeed Lloyd George's national pension scheme, which had been introduced in the face of much opposition in his 'People's Budget' of 1909, still only catered for those over seventy. It was means-tested, and provided 'subsistence' of a maximum of 5s a week, less than £25 today, a start but hardly enough to subsist on. Spedan was trying to persuade people to save, and felt that the advantage of an annual share distribution was that it encouraged people to try to do so, especially those who wouldn't if they were simply given a little bit extra each week. He felt that 'probably a good many people managed to refrain from deciding to sell stocks who might not succeed in resisting the temptation to nibble away a bit of ready money.'

Gradually people got the idea, though most still wanted to sell them back to the business for cash straight away, and Spedan, as in Florrie's case, had to institute a rule that people who wanted to sell must make out a good case to him first. He tried in the Gazette to discourage people from selling them, suggesting instead that if necessary they borrow against them as security. He realised early on that his terminology was misleading, so to make it absolutely clear:

> I think we had better drop the term 'Profit Sharing' in favour of Partnership Benefit. Profit Sharing has come to bear a special meaning, namely a system of business in which profit is shared between workers and owners of capital. In our case the workers get the whole profit and the sharing is entirely among themselves.

The word Benefit was later changed to Bonus. Within days of the announcement of the first profit distribution a Gazette notice of 10 April 1920 used the words Partnership and Partner for the first time. Spedan was delighted when the terms became common currency 'within days'. At times he still railed at those he thought wilfully dense: 'If anyone should hear of a good drug for common or garden fatheadedness he would do a real service to the Profit Sharing.' But most finally seemed to be getting it.

## The Responsibilities of Co-Ownership

Unfortunately they didn't entirely share his vision of what being a 'Partner' meant in terms of responsibilities as well as gain. He was adamant that if you were to share the profits of a business among its workers, you must ensure that none of them took advantage of their fellow-owners, by error or design. So he resolved to re-introduce a system of fines, so that identifiable errors that led to a loss of income for the shop (such as mischarging, or till losses) were deducted from pay. In fact from the outset he wouldn't let anyone be part of the profit-sharing scheme unless they first signed up to his fines proposal. At first he was almost universally opposed, by selling floor and management alike. This certainly gave a fillip to the Letters column:

> Fines!! Ugh! They take one back to the days of *very* long hours, small salaries, hard-earned commission, and penalties by fining.

> The House is unanimous in its opinion that the proposal of the staff paying departmental losses is atrocious ... We know the Chairman has a hard heart, as admitted by himself in this week's Gazette ... I can only hope that this letter can soften that portion of his anatomy.

This second letter smacks of Spedan writing to himself. He replied blithely, 'This is just the sort of letter we want and it is a very great pity that we get so few of them', and then used it, naturally, as an opportunity to expand again on his reason for insisting on a fining system. People eventually, and reluctantly, came round, helped by evidence that management were in the same boat. John Wenden, one of the Peter Jones shop superintendents, cheerfully confessed in a Gazette letter that he would be paying a substantial fine for failing to sign something he should have done, and pointing out that it would make him much more careful in future. Wenden, a wonderfully engaging and popular character, was the only Peter Jones employee in 1919 to have been there since 1900 – he had in fact joined in 1878. When he retired in 1926 as 'chief superintendent' Spedan granted him a pension for life *equal to his full pay*. Wenden was regarded as a genius at dealing with the impossibly demanding customer, a species still sometimes observable at Peter Jones in the present day. The extent to which Spedan had weeded out the poor staff he and Bichan had found at the start of the war was evident from an elaborately detailed chart printed in the Gazette in early 1919. Only 3% remained from when Spedan arrived in 1914, and only half had been at Peter Jones for more than two years.

Spedan made sure everyone knew he was subject to the same rules himself. He made clear that in a Partnership of workers he was firmly against perquisites, now shortened to 'perks', such as the acceptance of gifts from suppliers. In a notice about this in 1919 he pointed out that he would pay for the use of a typewriter at home in Grove Farm, and for the time of the staff secretary, who had done a special private job for him. He was then caught out himself when someone from the selling floor asked in the Gazette whether management, like them, had to pay for pencils. That was useful, for he could respond: 'Good gracious! Now I come to think of it, I don't believe I pay for my own. The finance director will see that the rule is strictly enforced in future. How very useful the Gazette is!'

## Sharing Power

Once Spedan was able to foresee a profit distribution he started the first 'staff council', in the Peter Jones restaurant on 31 October 1919. He'd taken a long holiday in the summer of 1919, and the Gazette didn't appear at all between 14 June and 6 September. In that first issue, after this unprecedented (and unrepeated) gap of twelve weeks, he announced a 39% increase in sales in the first half-year, and proposed an experimental staff council that he would chair himself at first. It would contain eighteen members, with directors present and able to speak *but not to vote*. This non-voting feature didn't last long, but it indicates how bold he intended to be in devolving power. At one of the first meetings the tone was set when the selling assistant Robert Bichan, an able democrat, proposed that the staff in the hostel should be paid weekly instead of four-weekly, a privilege enjoyed only by those who 'lived out'. In a long debate Spedan opposed the motion, Bichan defended it stoutly, and it was passed by 14 to 1. Spedan accepted the decision with a good grace (though one wonders whether he was just being artful, and opposing it when he didn't really care one way or the other). He thus sent a signal to the staff, which he underlined soon afterwards in the Christmas 1919 issue of the Gazette:

> I hear that the first two meetings of the staff council were a great surprise to a large proportion of the House. They did not expect that the actual powers of the council would be so great.

Spedan's experiment was starting to work, and it was people like Bichan from the shop floor, and two indefatigable older men, Messrs Wenden and Glass, from the management side, who were supporting him. Spedan frequently disagreed with Bichan in the council, but made it absolutely clear that he regarded him as a model Partnership 'citizen'. Some years later Bichan managed to outsmart Spedan and reverse a decision to sack an assistant who had attacked another in an argument over commission, and knocked out several teeth. Despite the victim pleading on his behalf, Spedan sacked the assailant on the spot. But the following day Spedan had to go abroad, and in his absence Bichan persuaded the council to reinstate the man. On his return Spedan was so tickled by Bichan's gall that he allowed him to stay, despite being told he shouldn't let himself be outwitted.

Soon others were encouraged by Spedan's patent lack of animosity, despite the trenchant expression of his views. At times he was exasperated, like the occasion he compared those opposing new ideas and change with the mediaeval priesthood, who 'responded to new scientific ideas by burning and torturing the innovators', but he chiselled away. By early 1920 he was confident enough in his experiment to announce boldly that the council would in future decide the level of profit-sharing, and that he would no longer come to council meetings. He stuck with neither commitment for very long, although he didn't attend council meetings often, and stopped entirely from 1926, but this was a measure of his confidence after eighteen months of the Gazette and only three council meetings. The participants, not least its first chairman, his cousin Murray Lewis, probably wished Spedan was in the proverbial council tent rather than outside it. Spedan started to write long screeds of observations after each meeting. But, as he said in February 1920 after the first meeting he'd not attended:

> My review I fear is nearly all in the nature of ultra-candid criticism. This is because I'm extraordinarily anxious that the council should become capable of taking substantial powers.

His new baby had only just started to walk, but he was already encouraging it to run. Unfortunately the whole business was soon tottering.

CHAPTER 7

# A Tale of Two Shops

The *Daily Mail* of 29 April 1920, showing John Lewis workers leaving a meeting at Mortimer Hall after voting to continue their strike. Their employer, the Mail reported, was 'continuing his attitude of determined resistance'.

As a shop Peter Jones was an unqualified success. But Profit is one thing, Finance another. In this I had a terrible time. As I look back, I still marvel that we got through.

SPEDAN LEWIS, IN *PARTNERSHIP FOR ALL*, 1948

Difficult man, John Lewis. Very difficult. Not like that stone there, which is Portland stone and wears away in our London fog. He's like that over there, Aberdeen granite. Horses' hooves won't wear that away.

JOHN BURNS, THE FORMER LIBERAL CABINET MINISTER AND ANTI-WAR CAMPAIGNER, SPEAKING DURING THE STRIKE AT JOHN LEWIS IN 1920, QUOTED IN PHILIP HOFFMAN'S *THEY ALSO SERVE*, 1948

No sooner had Spedan begun his profit sharing scheme at Peter Jones in early 1920 than trading turned sour. The post-war boom went into reverse. Retailers found themselves with a level of stock suited to a fast turnover, but it wasn't turning. The sharper of Peter Jones's competitors introduced deep price cuts across the board and cancelled outstanding orders. Spedan, normally so far-sighted, did nothing and paid the penalty. He'd suffered a relapse and was very ill. Then at just the wrong moment the cabinet (of a Liberal-Conservative coalition government) twisted his arm to let them take away his new finance director. He'd recruited Percival Waterfield from the upper echelons of the civil service, but he was wanted for the tortuous Irish independence negotiations, work for which he was later knighted.

Spedan's remaining subordinates were perhaps slow off the mark, but he cannot escape blame. His general manager was his cousin Murray Lewis, grandson of John Lewis's uncle William. Robert Bichan called Murray a 'very pleasant and likeable gentleman', but 'a complete square peg in a round hole – he lacked authority and was slow in making decisions.' Perhaps he dithered and failed to keep Spedan posted, a salutary failure of communication *within* management when Spedan was desperately trying to improve it *between* management and the shop floor. Another lesson for Spedan was that, doubtless out of family loyalty, he kept his cousin on far too long. That's a mistake he would make occasionally again. Spedan summed up his naivety in 1920 years later, with his usual frankness. He'd thought everything was going swimmingly:

> The workers in Peter Jones constantly heard the choiceness of their stock, the moderation of the prices and the extreme absence of any sort of trickery, praised warmly by customers ... and at the same time there was exhilaration at the rapid growth of the business ... There was the separate interest and pleasant excitement of the successive innovations that were steadily bringing the real Partnership into being.

But:

> All my notions of management had been formed in a business in which there was constantly a great superfluity of ready money. Half the transactions at John Lewis were for cash, half on credit, and most of the customers paid within a month. At Peter Jones 80% of trade was on credit, and they were most recalcitrant in settling accounts. Things went terribly wrong but that particular experience did us an immensely good turn. It gave me the idea of setting up a system of budgetary control. An eminent banker ridiculed the idea as being quite inapplicable to a business of our kind but it turned out well.

Peter Jones made a loss in 1921 and 1922 (in which year Spedan was again ill), paid no Partnership Benefit, and was often acutely short of cash. Bichan recorded the view from the shop floor:

> The lasting peace and the land 'fit for heroes to live in', which our politicians had told us was to follow the war, proved to be a bit of wishful thinking, for the country was faced with over two million unemployed. The labour exchange just down the King's Road in Chelsea was seldom without its long queue waiting for the 'Dole'. Outside our very doors we had a daily parade of ex-servicemen's brass bands complete with drums and, of course, the collecting box, exhorting us to 'Pack up your troubles' and 'Keep the home fires burning'.
>
> It was about this time that the business of Peter Jones found itself extremely short of ready cash. Although the quality of our trade was improving fast and we could all feel proud of our achievements our expenses were very high indeed. The whole central heating system was being modernised at great expense and antiquated fixturing was being replaced to meet our fast expanding trade in higher-class goods. There were occasions when this extreme shortage of cash became most embarrassing ... On a Friday a charming young lady from 'Bought Ledgers' could be seen making a hurried tour of the cash desks to scrape enough money together to placate a small queue of suppliers (chiefly furniture makers in a small way of business) with something on account.

Things were indeed getting dire. Some pay had to be cut, and many of the staff immediately sold their shares back to Spedan, despite his plea in the Gazette to invest extra capital in 'their' business – they didn't want it to be *theirs* if it was likely to go bust. Spedan even tried advertising, God forbid, with the slogan 'The best value in London and the most obliging staff.' It didn't help, and he was forced to liquidate most of his assets. The sale of Grove Farm yielded him £20,000, a bit less than £1m today and double what he'd paid for it in real terms, and it made a real difference. But that hurt, as we've seen, and an uncharacteristic cloud hung over him for many months. In a letter to a friend he even considered selling Peter Jones and buying another shop – John Barnes in the Finchley Road, for example (now, ironically, a Waitrose) – or giving it all up for the life of a wandering naturalist. A love of wildlife, nurtured in the grounds of Spedan Tower and Hampstead Heath, had become his life's consuming hobby along with the new science of ecology.

Early in 1920 Oswald had urged Spedan to accept an offer from Whiteley's of £200,000 (£8m now) to buy his shares in Peter Jones, but Spedan declined. The contrast between them at this point is striking – Oswald was safely ensconced in an Oxford Street shop comfortably weathering the depression with a £60,000 profit for the year. But the depression wasn't all it had to weather. Although the Peter Jones workers weren't convinced yet by their 'Partnership', in comparison with those at John Lewis's shop they were content and cosseted, largely insulated from the worries that beset Spedan. But their John Lewis equivalents were far from happy. At the outbreak of war, when – persuaded by Spedan – his father announced he would make good any difference between the peacetime pay and military service pay of anyone called up, John had been something of a hero to his shop workers. He later spoilt it, however, for with Spedan out of the way at Peter Jones he tried to renege on the arrangement (he failed, defeated in a court case for once). But now, never well paid at the best of times, the John Lewis workers were suffering increasing hardship because the escalation of prices since the war hadn't been offset by a matching rise in pay. After fifty years of virtually zero inflation since he'd opened the shop, the value of the pound dropped to less than half its pre-war value. There were cases of severe hardship, because some shop workers had received no increase at all since the start of the war: Peter Jones of course was a major exception.

## Strife and Strike at Oxford Street

The shop workers at the Army & Navy Stores were particularly badly paid. They set out a list of demands, based on a proposal set out by the shop assistants' union, and all 4,000 employees went on strike in December 1919 after the management had brushed aside their demands. The case quickly excited national interest – shop workers weren't notably radical, and the strikers were supported by the press, particularly by Lord Northcliffe who owned *The Times*. The Army & Navy management capitulated and agreed to abide by an Arbitration Court ruling, which eventually accepted most of the union's recommendations; these, covering wages and living-in deductions, make entirely reasonable reading today. Most department stores followed this lead immediately, including Bourne & Hollingsworth. Uncharacteristically, John Lewis, now eighty-four, and someone who rarely met any of his competitors, went to see Hollingsworth, who advised him to follow suit. He then actually signed an agreement, which the union leader Philip Hoffman took to a meeting of John Lewis staff at the Wigmore Hall. They didn't believe he'd abide by it, and they were right. Old John started sacking staff and engaged new employees who had to agree not to be members of the union while in his employment. At an Arbitration Court called to discuss staff grievances Oswald represented his father, and was told flatly by its chairman: 'You know, Mr Lewis, these things are not done these days.'

They were by Old John, to whom a union leader was a red rag to a bull, ageing certainly but still powerful if goaded into a charge. Via Oswald the Court made five recommendations to him – essentially to accept the agreement and allow free right of association. John simply ignored them and remained bullish, despite a private visit from the Court's unhappy chairman. The staff threatened to strike, and John responded by putting up notices which contained this:

> To our Young Men and Maidens...What is it that gives rise to this unwholesome atmosphere? It is the vapourings of the accursed trade Unionists. However great the sacrifice, I will not at the bidding of any unscrupulous league forgo my rights ... While this scoundrel [the strike leader] lies in bed at six o'clock in the morning he bullies my young women, more or less delicate, to tread the pavements as pickets ... What can be the feelings of the fathers of these respectable young women when they learn that their daughters are ... marching in procession through the streets?

Language like that was hardly calculated to placate his young men and women, maidens or not. On Saturday 24 April 1920 John reluctantly agreed to receive a deputation of four, who included a shop girl, Hilda Canham, and the buyer Turner Thomas, a courageous man who stood to lose a substantial sum because of the terms of his engagement. They put each of the five recommendations to John Lewis and he rejected them all, whereupon they voted five to one for strike action. Hoffman warned them that in his opinion anyone going out on strike would never be allowed back, but they pressed on regardless, and came out the next Monday morning. That was the day of a planned sale at John Lewis of a huge job lot of government silk. On that day 400 of the 500 employees downed collars, but John Lewis corralled the loyal remainder – or blacklegs, depending on your viewpoint – into the silk department, closed the rest of the shop, and sold all his sale merchandise, priced down at 1s 11d a yard, by four o'clock. John Lewis was triumphant. Next day he was back, starting to replace his strikers with new non-union recruits.

This strike, because they were rare in the retail trade, caught the public's imagination, and the strikers stayed out for five weeks, bolstered by financial support and a sympathetic press. While the papers admired the indomitable old man's shop and his principles, they thought he was misguided and mean-minded. He didn't care, he had enough money to see the strike out and the strikers didn't. He cheerfully ignored Northcliffe's *Times*, which expressed the majority view by saying:

> It is probable that Mr John Lewis and his fellow directors will presently find cause to change their minds. The shopping public has no sympathy nowadays with obsolete ideas about trade unionism and the right of workpeople to fair treatment.

Much of the shopping public showed their sympathy by cheering the staff as they marched arm in arm down Oxford Street and round Cavendish and

Hanover Squares each morning with placards. Hilda Canham became the 'girl in brown', the public face of the strike. The strikers received donations totalling £2,500, of which £300 each came from shop assistants at Harrods and Army & Navy. West End actors gave them a special benefit performance led by Sybil Thorndike (later Dame Sybil) – who had worked part-time at Peter Jones – and even Queen Mary let it be known that she'd sent a donation. Railway workers for a time declined to deliver stock, and electrical engineers refused to maintain the lifts. Oswald and the credit manager John Moss tried to negotiate with the strikers staying in the hostel – John wanted them out, but even he recognised that it was hardly good policy to summarily evict them. Eventually they were given twenty-four hours' notice and were all found accommodation by well-wishers.

Hoffman, trying to figure out a way to soften John Lewis's resistance, had talked to their mutual friend John Burns, a Liberal politician who had failed to persuade Lewis to purge his contempt at Brixton prison. Burns promised to go to Hampstead see Mrs Lewis and then the obdurate old man. He failed. Some strikers began to trickle back, but soon the old man told a journalist that he wouldn't take any more back, even if they came to him 'crawling on hands and knees', and he was true to his word. He got others in, and by 2 June the strike was over. The strikers all found other jobs at better rates, many at Pontings, whose general manager said he hadn't had such excellent girls come into the trade for years. Spedan, observing from Chelsea but powerless to act, clearly sympathised entirely with the strikers, but thought the tactics of the union leaders were wrong. This is how he summed it up:

> The strike ... seemed to have two main causes. Many of the staff were acutely dissatisfied with the proportion that had come their way of the profits it was obvious to them that the firm was making ... Secondly they were exasperated with the frequency of what seemed to them to be merely arbitrary dismissals. To my own mind some of those dismissals were quite indefensible and were evidence that my father had passed the latest age at which he ought to have retained such responsibility and power – as was his persistent mismanagement of Peter Jones from 1906 to 1914 in the teeth of the grave loss that it was causing.

Spedan too was exasperated. In the Peter Jones Gazette he had gone through the strikers' demands for improvements in pay and conditions point by point to show that his Partners had most of them in place already, and more beside. Where they didn't, he backdated the increases. At Oxford Street Old John's profits suffered, true, but not by much. He could see his elder son, with his dangerously generous new-fangled methods, foundering at Peter Jones. Spedan claimed to be on high ground morally, but in practice he was on soft sand. John was pleased to be out of that Sloane Square 'bucket of a shop'. Seeing Spedan's losses mount there, Oswald offered to buy him out of his share of the eventual inheritance of their father's wealth. That would give Spedan a much-needed cash injection while at the same time, of course, eventually ensuring the whole of the Oxford Street shop for Oswald. But Spedan wouldn't yield, simply gritted his teeth and funded the Peter Jones losses from his own shrinking savings. Then in 1922 he again fell ill, and Oswald wrote:

> Isn't it best to admit you've tried, tried all you know, and failed? Other men have failed before, and not even had the consolation that what they tried to do was well worth doing (if it could be done).

No. Spedan could be as stubborn as his father, but in a different cause.

## A Reconciliation – and New Recruits

Spedan hung on, and was unexpectedly rewarded in 1922 when his mother persuaded her husband to take a look at Peter Jones. Old John, now eighty-six but barely slowing down, was surprised and impressed by what he saw, even to the extent of writing Oswald a note suggesting they should apply some of the ideas at Oxford Street. 'The place is a credit to the boy, a very great credit.' So what were the trading ideas Spedan, the 'boy' of thirty-seven, was exploring, and which would eventually pull the shop through? His principal aim was to drag a downmarket business in an upmarket area up to the level of its residents – and to drag his buying and selling staff up there too. His conviction that a good buyer was worth his weight in silver, if not gold, led him to experiment, and to pay really well. He misfired a few times, but one success was worth several failures:

> A buyer, who was drawing £350 a year and whose sales for several past years barely reached five figures, was suddenly replaced by a newcomer, who was to draw £1,000 and who was, moreover, to bring with him a lieutenant at £600 ... It did in fact increase the sales of the department by 400% within a very short time and it simultaneously gave really important help to other departments to whose customers the availability of a much better stock of goods of that particular kind was a real boon.

He had a growing conviction, moreover, that you needed first-class brains to make a real difference to any challenging venture. So he set out to hire them. It was Spedan's second big idea, but it was to have almost as profound an effect as his first – and it would change his life. He went to the university authorities at Oxford and asked them for the details of their top woman graduates, and invited them to work for him. In retailing, a profession hitherto beyond the pale? Robert Bichan, from his shop-floor vantage point, was among those who at first not surprisingly resented the arrival of Bright Young Things, playing at shops and blocking future progress for himself and his colleagues. But he came to see the benefit of Spedan's approach:

> He took the view that if you want to sell nice things that are a joy to possess and which enhance life, who better to sell them than young people who have been brought up with them? Thus it was that we on the shop floor found ourselves with a sprinkling of young ladies dispersed all over the departments. He had labelled them 'learners' in preference to 'trainees'. I recall that we, as rank and file, were inclined to take a dim view of this new experiment and one heard criticisms from all sides, even from buyers who were naturally slow to welcome the added expense to their departmental costings. The Chairman at once dispelled this particular complaint by making it known that he himself would pay the major portion of their weekly pay. This was to be £6, double the wage of the average assistant.

Spedan himself tackled the resentment head-on. By now, the Gazette was more widely read and correspondents were becoming bolder, just as Spedan intended. To one Gazette complaint about his recruitment methods he responded with a knowing and disarming bluntness:

> You are wrong. You have always needed somebody clever enough to stand up to me. Like many people of a strong creative faculty I produce a host of ideas, good, bad and indifferent. You need somebody ... to act as a filter.

By 1928 Peter Jones alone had over seventy learners in a permanent staff total of under 400, most on the selling floor. Spedan was well aware of the dangers of this recruitment policy, but he was certain that finding a first-class buyer was the simplest way to make a huge difference to the bottom line. Moreover, these girls from the well-off middle class brought their friends and parents into the shop, and for a while he paid a substantial commission to anyone who introduced a new customer, until he realised the system was being abused, and was too costly anyway. The well-heeled wife of the buyer General Hogg earned herself an extra £30 in 1928, over £1,000 today. The whole recruitment scheme was risky, but he was prepared to carry some failures, and he eventually weeded those out. Like the glamorous debutante, perhaps, remembered by Albert Sherring, who, on being handed a piece of silk to be matched, exclaimed, 'Oh Madam, what a putrid colour!' Some stayed for just four weeks, pocketed their first month's pay, and were off. One such was Amy Johnson, a graduate from Hull, who found a more rewarding career, and fame, as a pioneering long-distance pilot. But a brilliant new young buyer could freshen up a department, turn a good profit, and bring the shop up with it. It was a virtuous circle. One nervous graduate arrived in the linens department, as Bichan recalled:

> The department had been doing its normal amount of business year after year with nothing outstandingly brilliant in the range of goods it stocked. A learner, who had come in with several university degrees and who had been tried out in various jobs, was suddenly invited to take on the buyership of this department. Very reluctantly and with doubts as to her success she had a go. In no time at all the department became alive, exciting, displaying really eye-catching things like exotic table mats and embroidered bed-linen, and I shall never forget the thrill we all had when one customer bought three pairs of sheets at thirty-four guineas a pair.

No wonder – the assistant was taking in a single transaction the equivalent of nearly £5,000 today, about thirty-five times his own weekly pay. At first Spedan paid the women buyers as well as he did the men, without the pay discrimination then rife. Gertrude Parrett arrived as a learner in 1925 at £200 and was earning £500 as umbrella buyer in 1928. There was no bar to married women, as there was elsewhere, and Mrs Elspeth Fox Pitt, a 'première vendeuse', sold designer gowns from her own separate showroom in the shop. She brought in a huge number of customers. Nor was youth a handicap: Laura Bowen joined after graduating from London University in 1927 and by 1930 had been catapulted to general manager of Peter Jones by the age of twenty-four. In that year there were more women buyers than men. Another was the intrepid Florence Lorimer, who had accompanied Gertrude Stein on expeditions abroad, and brought a wide knowledge of antiquities when she joined in 1925. Spedan gave her £5,500 to fund a buying tour of Punjab, Kashmir and Afghanistan, and paid her a salary of £750 when her purchases sold well. The multiplier for these figures to get today's values is a bit less than fifty, so a salary of £500 equates to £30,000, but in fact this was a substantial salary for a buyer back then, let alone a woman. Above all, at a time when nobody did it, Spedan tried to make it easy for women to return to work after having children. He accorded them 'intermittent' status, gave them extended leave after childbirth and even a marriage gratuity.

Robert Bichan enjoyed jousting with these clever young ladies when they were on the selling floor. At one point in 1922 he was working in the second-hand furniture department, which lay between the receiving dock and the shoe department.

> In the shoe department at that time was another young lady learner who seemed to spend a lot of time marking off stock, for she would pass the spot where I was usually to be found many times a day carrying about six boxes of shoes from the receiving dock. She had to walk almost the whole length of my department before reaching her own. I got so used to her passing that I would chant Kipling's 'Boots, boots, boots, boots', and she would reply, 'Junk, junk, junk, junk', referring to the conglomeration of second-hand furniture that surrounded me. Little did I realise who I was teasing.

## Beatrice Hunter

The new boot buyer was Beatrice Hunter, already thirty-two in 1922, five years younger than Spedan. She had been a contemporary of Florence Lorimer at Oxford, and had taught English before joining the civil service during the war. She had become a factory inspector, but in common with many other unmarried middle-class women was now out of work. The government had needed them during the war, but with high unemployment, and the traditional breadwinners returning from the front, they were discarded. Beatrice was, Spedan later said, a very strong feminist. Spedan offered her a buyership at £350 a year. The stock of those boots she found when she started did not impress her. Her old college magazine included a typo that said she was 'burying boots at Peter Jones'. She commented that in view of the dilapidation of the stock she had taken over she wished she had thought of that expedient. Some of her letters to a friend at that time have survived, and they give us a lively picture of the young Spedan in action. First, a month before she began:

> I am going into trade. I've been offered a buyership at Peter Jones, Sloane Square. It's a cheapish drapers and ladies' outfitters ... The Chairman is the son of John Lewis of Oxford Street ... He has a mad stunt of employing University women ... but the commercial world is very suspicious of outsiders – the idea of taking in completely inexperienced people in responsible positions is quite a new one.

Note that to be in 'trade' was certainly not the done thing in circles like hers. She started on 9 October 1922, and, in a notebook she'd used to jot down some notes on the poet Keats, she wrote:

> Begin at PJ today. Feel as one does at first when trying to speak a foreign language in its own country ... I learn that L's temper is dreaded – expected as much but it is not cheering. The showroom is untidy and the stock looks pretty dud – that however is in my favour – more to make a show on. Not an encouraging day but I found this in Boswell last night – a good omen – Johnson wanted to practise as an advocate without a degree in civil law. Said he: 'I am a total stranger to these studies, but whatever is a profession and maintains numbers must be within reach of common abilities and some degree of industry.'

She had both ability and industry in abundance. A month after she'd begun:

> I've been having a hectic time. It's terrifying to be plunged into full responsibility without any experience at all. I have four shop girls under me from whom I have to conceal my ignorance ... After years of working on paper it's alarming to

> be so concrete – real money and real shoes and, worst of, real individual customers to cope with … I've made no awful gaffe but it may come any moment. I've been stock-taking and doing twelve hours a day but hope to take life more easily soon. Another snag is that one practically stands all day.

That passage, especially the final sentence, will strike a chord with every subsequent 'senior learner' parachuted straight onto the sales floor. Spedan already seems to have taken an early shine to her:

> I thought the Chairman himself was going to be a difficulty but he has been awfully nice so far – he is a great joke – a real idealist, a wild enthusiast but also a rather sharp business man. He is in some ways engagingly transparent. He plays to the gallery and never dreams that the gallery may contain a critic. He loves to have two of us in the office at once and switch from one topic to the other with complete mastery of both, he loves to demonstrate that no detail escapes him and he loves to do the 'human touch' in the middle of it all. But you can't call it affectation because he's so obviously in the audience and beguiled himself. And he's treated me with every kindness and consideration and been awfully patient with every kind of silly question … and he's no end of a sportsman, of course, to be making the experiment at all. I don't think anyone else would do it.

Spedan's great experiment, and a mind teeming with ideas, is what unlikely recruits into retailing like Beatrice found so compelling. In two letters in January 1923 she confesses the down side, that he's a man of mercurial temperament who may switch tack at any minute. You have to hang on tight and accept the danger:

> Life continues hectic and uncertain … It is nerve racking because one feels one's whole position hangs on the Chairman's caprice – and he may change his mind at any moment, in fact he frequently does … It is a perpetual gamble but anyhow it isn't dull – the whole thing, of course is more like a Musical Comedy than real life, priceless from morning to night … He himself provides a large part of the entertainment of the job. Enough amusement to keep one giggling for a month. I am convinced Himself is always sincere. He hasn't the slightest intention of letting anyone down, but he changes like the maddest weathercock … He bubbles over with new ideas, he pours forth ten-page memoranda from morning to night – no one can get on with the job because he's always butting in with a new and better idea – I've never met so much restless energy in all my life.

She then launches into a recalled conversation in which, while he's ostensibly explaining how to subdivide an assortment (Oxford shoes) they spiral off trying to cap each other in spouting quotations. There's no doubt Spedan gets an enormous kick out of finding a trained mind not afraid to joust with him, as she stresses a few months later, after he whisks her off during the working day – something a work-hard play-hard man has no scruples about – to play tennis at Roehampton with Oswald and a friend.

> I have grown pretty friendly with him lately – I don't think it'll last, I don't think he's the lasting kind, but he has recently discovered I have a tongue and as he has one too he enjoys sparring with me. I am going to ask him one day whether he engaged me as a boot buyer or a court fool ... He told me the other day that I had a disconcerting way of listening to him with the utmost deference while suggesting all the time in the most delicate way in the world that he was merely blithering. As he frequently does blither it was very good for him.

Without a doubt Spedan had met his match, and he recognised it. He had found someone strong and clever enough to stand up to him. And he *was* the lasting kind, for they were married on 8 October 1923, just a year after her arrival at Peter Jones. It's soon clear that he became reliant on her as a sounding-board for ideas, one who wouldn't be cowed and who gave as good as she got. Beatrice was relieved to find she was popular at Spedan Tower, though the regular weekly dinner took some getting used to for one of her tastes: no wine or cigarettes allowed. The Lewises liked her. 'As I'm not too conspicuously modern in any way I go down well.' On religion: 'I think Mrs Lewis consoles herself with the idea that I am at heart an ardent church woman, and he that I don't swallow Genesis whole.' It undoubtedly helped that she became pregnant straight away: 'I was popular with them before, but my stock has gone up enormously – from their point of view this is the real justification for my existence.'

## Settlements

1924 brought a grandson for John Lewis, and a real reconciliation with his son. The following year Spedan was able to announce the first Partnership Bonus for five years. It's salutary to speculate on what would have happened had there been no reconciliation. Would Peter Jones have recovered without the cash John Lewis now gave Spedan to pump into it? Or would it have gone under and the Partnership idea with it, a footnote to history as a bizarre experiment dreamt up by a maverick mind, doomed to failure? Probably it would have made it through, but it's an arguable point. Anyway, John Lewis brought Spedan back into Oxford Street with a formal one-third of the business, and the brothers concluded between themselves that when their father died Spedan, the one with retailing in his blood, would have the business and Oswald, keen to embark on a political career, the cash.

So all was at last roses in the Lewis garden? Had the intransigent father now mellowed towards his two very different sons so they could all work together? Not yet. After a long life battling to keep her warring family from bursting apart, Eliza died in November 1925, removing a restraining influence on John, who went over to Peter Jones three months later and had a stand-up row with Spedan. The old man was now eighty-nine, and still took the old 1911 Rolls into the Oxford Street shop most days. The shop bush telegraph still worked. What he wore, apparently, was a signal of his mood – 'If he wears his green muffler, you could relax, but if he was in his top hat, watch it, someone was for the chop.'

Spedan and Oswald had a problem. Spedan was impatient for control of the business and Oswald wanted money and freedom to pursue a political career. They needed to settle things between them: neither could afford to wait till their father died. Knowing him, he'd live to 100. After a long debate they eventually settled, without telling their father, that Oswald would give up his share of the business for a lump sum, which Spedan took out a bank loan to provide. In October 1926 Oswald took off round the world also without telling his father, who, as they'd predicted, expelled him from the Partnership a second time. While away, Oswald mused in a letter on the oddity of life and of his and Spedan's respective talents and prospects:

> Consider the case of Spedan and myself. Spedan, imaginative, eloquent, enthusiastic, with a lively perception and excellent memory, could have had a brilliant political career. And he has elected to take over our family business and will in time (unless I am greatly mistaken) come to a most colossal crash in consequence. I, on the other hand, shrewd and level-headed (dear me, I'm afraid I shan't be able to add 'modest'), anyhow methodical, and adequately endowed with commonsense ... could have had quite a successful business career, whereas I shall make but an indifferent politician.

Fortunately Oswald was wrong. Although he never reached high office he became the Conservative MP for Colchester in 1929 and held the seat until the Labour landslide of 1945. He had started a Liberal but changed party, as Winston Churchill famously did, when the Liberal vote collapsed at the 1924 election. (Perhaps Oswald would have been at home in the Tory-Liberal coalition of 2010.) And although he came close on occasions, Spedan never did suffer that 'colossal crash'. He now ran the John Lewis shop in all but name as well as Peter Jones. Old John went in to Oxford Street less and less, and was properly reconciled with Spedan, who toured the shop with him on his ninety-second birthday. The old man at least agreed to see Oswald after his return and parted with him on amiable terms. On 8 June 1928 John Lewis died peacefully at Spedan Tower. Spedan came into the whole of the business at the age of forty-two, when he might have expected it twenty years earlier. Once he could tie it all up legally, he'd be free at last of all encumbrances, and he was armed with a pent-up energy ready to burst out in all directions. Which it did.

132, OXFORD STREET, and
27 & 28, HOLLES STREET, LONDON, W.

JOHN LEWIS,
SILK MERCER,
DRAPER AND FANCY WAREHOUSEMAN.

Book 70 22 Ent. 7 Date 6 187

16 ... 3/6½ 2 16 8

ABOVE LEFT: A John Lewis letterhead of 1877.
ABOVE RIGHT: A delivery horse and van outside the Weymouth Mews stables.
RIGHT: John Lewis's house Spedan Tower in Hampstead.
BELOW: Oxford Street in the 1890s, John Lewis on the left.

## Four early shop cartoons

ABOVE: Closing time.
RIGHT: 'Take my seat dear'.
BELOW LEFT: Hostel life.
BELOW RIGHT: Aristocratic assistants.

WASHING DAY!

ABOVE LEFT: Robert Bichan, one of the first Peter Jones councillors.
ABOVE RIGHT: Philip Hoffman, later the shop assistants' union leader.
LEFT: A Harrods window photographed the day before Selfridges opened in 1909.
BELOW: A Selfridges window the day before opening.

ABOVE LEFT: Oswald Lewis in 1906.
ABOVE RIGHT: Spedan on holiday in France in 1907.
RIGHT: Spedan and a now moustached Oswald in a John Lewis cricket team in 1907.
BELOW: Grove Farm, the home during World War I that Spedan loved and lost.

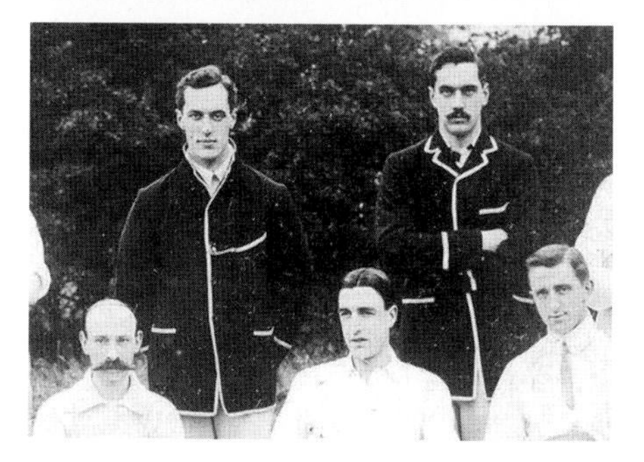

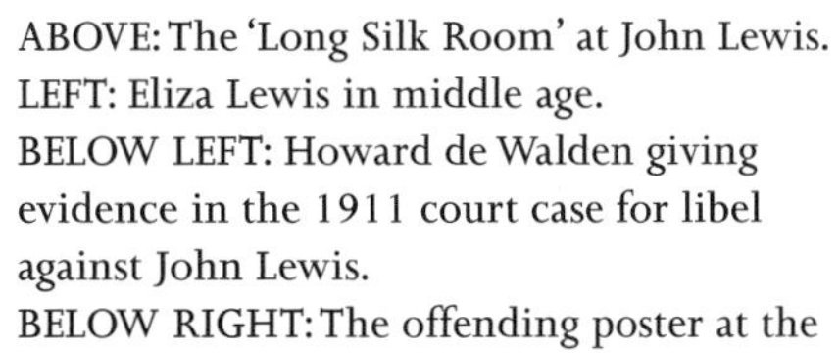

ABOVE: The 'Long Silk Room' at John Lewis.
LEFT: Eliza Lewis in middle age.
BELOW LEFT: Howard de Walden giving evidence in the 1911 court case for libel against John Lewis.
BELOW RIGHT: The offending poster at the Holles St corner.

Four newspaper photos from the strike of 1920

WEST END SHOP GIRLS' STRIKE.

**SHOPGIRL AS STRIKE LEADER.**—A meeting at Whitefield's Tabernacle yesterday of the Strike Committee of the employees of Messrs. John Lewis & Co., the Oxford-street drapers. The girl member of the committee is Miss Hilda Canham. [*Daily Mail Photograph.*]

ABOVE: Shows the strike committee, with Hilda Canham standing,
BELOW: John Lewis flanked by two cheery strikers, Hilda Canham and Bobbie Stirling.

MISS HILDA CANHAN. MR. JOHN LEWIS. MISS "BOBBIE" STIRLING.
Leading figures in the strike of shop assistants at Messrs. John Lewis & Co.'s drapery store in Oxford-street, W.

ABOVE LEFT: Beatrice with her three young children.
ABOVE RIGHT: Spedan and Beatrice (hidden) with the children. The eldest, John Hunter Lewis, died tragically, soon after.
LEFT: John Lewis was reconciled with Spedan in the mid-1920s.
BELOW: Peter Jones at about the same time.

ABOVE LEFT: Harvesting on the Leckford estate in the 1930s.
ABOVE RIGHT: The spacious interior of Waitrose Gerrards Cross in the 1930s.
LEFT: Kitchen equipment unfamiliar to us today...
BELOW: A Christmas 1913 advert for Waitrose. For quality at competitive prices has no equal.

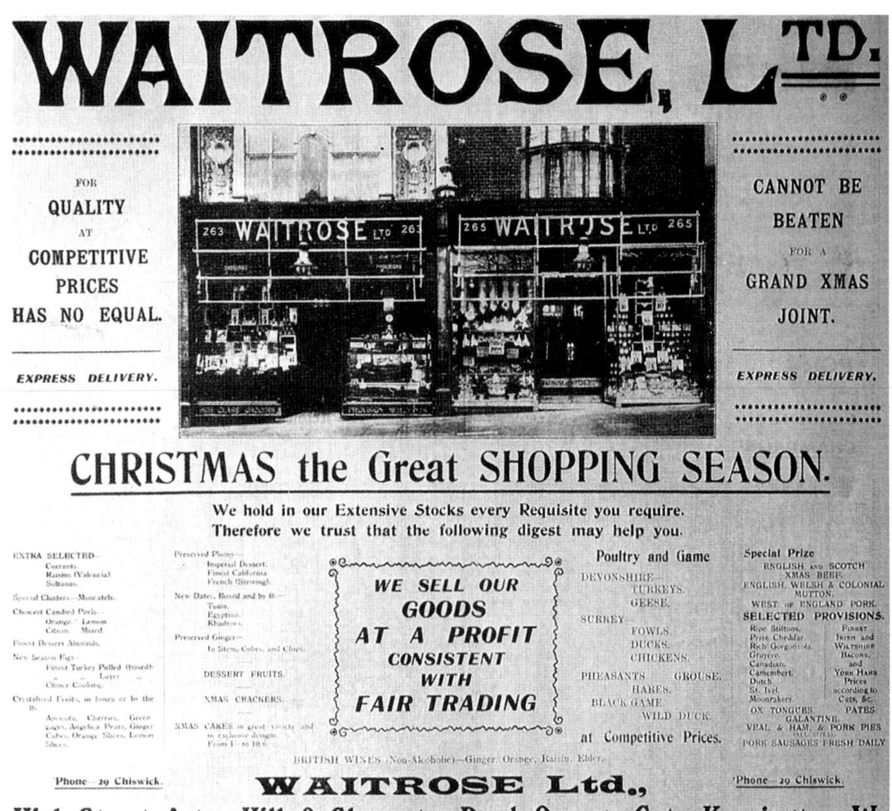

CHAPTER 8

# Full Steam Ahead

An illustration from a 1920s booklet advertising Peter Jones's autumn fashions, with the old shop behind. And the new Peter Jones in the 1960s, with its architect William Crabtree.

If my wife and I had chosen to sell out, we should have had a seven-figure fortune that invested in sound securities would have produced an income of upwards of £40,000 a year [around £2m today]. A life of leisure with resources so large was attractive. On the other hand, the course that we took had for us, our temperaments being what they were, attractions still stronger.

SPEDAN LEWIS, IN *PARTNERSHIP FOR ALL*, 1948

From 1927 to 1939 was for me a time of youthful zest and energy spilling over in all directions; nothing was too zany to look into and everything was possible.

SIR BERNARD MILLER IN THE 1970s,
REFLECTING ON HIS PARTNERSHIP CAREER

When his father died in June 1928, Spedan immediately kick-started his plan to incorporate the John Lewis business into 'his' Partnership. Despite all that had gone before, he did his father the posthumous honour of calling the new combined business after him, and not himself. It wasn't to be named, as it might well have been, the Spedan Lewis Partnership. He described his father's achievement like this, and these precepts had become his own:

> From first to last throughout the whole of his long career my father held steadily to a simple policy of genuine solid service. He took immense pains to have constantly in stock the greatest possible choice of goods of certain kinds. He took equal pains to give really good value and to win in all other ways a first-rate reputation for general trustworthiness. It was his success in those aims that made me feel it would be good for the Partnership to bear his name.

## The 'Settlement' of 1929

Spedan now needed to bring John Lewis employees into the Partnership, and make the handover of his ownership legally watertight. After the problems that followed his illness and absence in 1922 and the subsequent injection of money from his father, so successful was trade at Peter Jones that he had been able to distribute at a rate of 15% of pay in 1924, 20% in each of the years 1925–27, and even at the odd figure of 23⅓% in 1928. Now he had to do two things. He must redeem his Partners' 'Share Promises' – they amounted to £76,632, a little under £4m today – and turn them into proper shares that could be traded on the stock exchange. Moreover, he had to combine John Lewis with Peter Jones in a new Partnership, into what he termed a co-operative society of producers. The idea was to sell the two businesses to its new owners, the Partners, who would pay him back gradually out of future profits. He felt strongly that no one person should own more than they needed for their personal use and as insurance against bad times, and to pass on to their descendants. As he put it:

> My wife and I had decided that for the rest of our lives we would limit our private expenditure to a certain rate. If we held to that programme then the money that we had already would cover the whole of that expenditure no matter how long we should live, and would indeed leave a large remainder (that should, we intended, go to the Partnership) beyond provision for children, ill-health or accident.

Essentially he chose to sell his fortune to the Partners, current and prospective, receiving his payment out of future profits. He did not, as some came to think, give his fortune away. How exactly to do it was something he'd been discussing with advisors for some time, and they came up with a device called an irrevocable settlement in trust. This would be not quite irrevocable (see the Glossary on p. 311 to understand precisely why) but it would long outlast Spedan. The effect was to make an interest-free loan of the two businesses to the members of the new Partnership, a loan to be paid back out of the profits over an extended period. The business was valued at a figure an expert advisor reckoned he could get readily for cash on the money market. Because it was interest-free over such a long period, at the end of which the value of the pound had almost exactly halved, it was a sale to the Partnership at substantially less than its value (and in fact he didn't in the end take the full amount). Spedan took the money in the form of bonds that were created in 1929 which would provide no interest or dividend, but would be paid back steadily each year out of future profits. That is what he would live off. He would, moreover, take no salary or fees, and hence not share in any future bonuses, so in effect he was giving his services free to the Partnership for the rest of his working life.

It's important to recognise that, while Spedan was being exceedingly generous by in effect yielding up the bulk of his wealth to give to Partners current and future, and working for nothing, he was not giving up power. He would stay as Chairman, though subject to the constraints he had imposed on himself by creating a democratic council structure. He could, in fact, overrule any decision the council made, though he seldom did so. In extremis he was more likely to expound the reasons for his disagreement – at great length – and ask them to consider it again. He also created a system whereby three trustees were elected by the council annually. They would hold sixty of the only hundred voting shares, so could effectively vote him out of office – only if they were all of one mind, though, for he held the other forty. In effect he could only be displaced if he was manifestly deranged. Spedan spent the next twenty years juggling a desire to keep control of his infant Partnership with the need to set it on its own feet. Though World War II did put major obstacles in the way, in practice he managed the balance pretty well – until, that is, after he retired in 1955. A dozen years after that, an academic study of the Partnership concluded that Spedan had given himself and his successor unusually strong powers:

> The Chairman's view of what is good for the business takes precedence over all other considerations. Indeed it would appear that the Chairman has greater power than either his counterparts in the more usual kind of public enterprise or the heads of the nationalised industries.

## Reforming John Lewis

Before looking at how Spedan set out to get his new Partnership motoring into the 1930s, let's examine how, while his father was still alive, he tackled the covert job of bringing the operation of his father's shop to something like Peter Jones. Since he had come back into the management of the Oxford Street business in 1926, Spedan had been stealthily making reforms. But he had to be careful: John was ninety, and came into the shop less often, but when he did so Spedan wanted to be sure he got no whiff of the changes being instituted, lest there be another conflagration. For instance, horrified at some of the low salaries paid there, Spedan had them increased up to a par with Peter Jones. But since his father would occasionally ask to look at the books, he couldn't risk a confrontation, and so had two sets of wages books kept, making sure the fictitious set was brought out whenever his father appeared. Late in 1926 he held his first joint council meeting of Peter Jones and John Lewis, though he enjoined secrecy:

> I hope that no talk of this sort will get into any newspapers other than the Gazette itself. It might make a good deal of mischief between my father and myself and it could be of no help to us at this stage.

Note the inference that his father had no interest in reading the Gazette. Spedan restarted his old committee for communication at John Lewis, and followed it by giving staff there for the first time a paid spring holiday. He began to include the John Lewis trading figures in the Gazette, of which he had 200 on sale at Oxford Street, but, to his resigned disappointment if not his surprise, most of his staff there neither read it nor embraced the changes as readily as he felt they should:

> Many of them do not understand the principles I follow, but meet every proposal with a timidity and suspicion that would be appropriate if they were dealing with someone who was quite unscrupulous and cruelly greedy.

Of course, most of those who might have warmly welcomed change had probably moved elsewhere, and left at John Lewis were those too old, conservative or cautious to try somewhere new. Albert Sherring remembered that time:

> The first reaction of the old stagers was profound scepticism. It has always been the same whenever new ways and changes are proposed ... So it was when the Partnership came to Oxford Street. 'It won't work', was a very mild statement. 'Share promises? What's the good of them?' It was like this: Mr John Lewis was still a force to be reckoned with, and Mr Spedan Lewis was not yet able to go ahead with his plans.
>
> Then we had the first committee for communications meetings. It used to be the custom to pay the staff on Saturdays. This did not give wives a chance to do

> the shopping if hubby got home about two or three in the afternoon, so could Partners be paid on Fridays? Certainly they can. Then there was the medical room, run by Sister and trained Nurses. Sick pay comes when it is most needed and one does not forget those baskets of fruit that used to be delivered at one's door.

Another shop assistant remembered that first meeting:

> We all sat round a large table and the Founder asked us in turn if we had any complaints and suggestions. My word, was I nervous when my turn came. I had, and that was the early morning duty. Partners felt that they were underpaid for the extra hours they worked. I think it was five shillings a week and their breakfast and those who lived in Chadwickham missed their breakfast there. After that, I thought to myself I've had it now ... but he thoroughly looked into it and it resulted in nearly 100% increase, plus extra for loss of breakfast for those that lived in.

One of the most visibly striking and psychologically important changes was dress. Peter Jones assistants had long since been liberated from the rigid straitjackets of their uniform, but Albert Sherring pointed out that at John Lewis it hadn't changed for fifty years:

> The old draper's store was a very sombre place ... [Before 1928] male assistants dressed in a black frock coat with striped trousers. It was not a very comfortable outfit to serve in, especially in the summer ... [Later] the men wore much more comfortable clothes, and gone is the 'Black Clothing Feeling', for ever. No wonder Partners look more pleasant. Imagine smiling faces in an old-fashioned draper's! What did they have to smile about?

Spedan loosened other restrictions. Little had happened to maintain the improvements at the John Lewis hostel in Weymouth Street since he had tackled it with such gusto twenty years earlier. Sherring said, 'Even the stag's head looked fed up.' Spedan immediately brought the hostel in Weymouth Street, and the newer one in Bolsover Street called Chadwickham House – named by his father after the Victorian sanitation reformer Edwin Chadwick – up to Peter Jones standards. He encouraged dances by having installed at Chadwickham a dance floor of sprung maple reckoned to be the best in London after the Savoy Hotel. In the shop he instituted a morning and afternoon coffee and tea break, unheard of before according to Sherring, and relaxed the rules on leaving the store during working hours. Smoking was still – and would always be – rigorously banned in the workplace, but 'smoking restrooms' were introduced. Albert Sherring remembered the easing of the previous grimness with pleasure, but best of all was the first profit distribution to include the new Partners in John Lewis. That first Bonus distribution was well over 20%, in shares, and the dividend they produced was still 7½% every six months:

> Then in 1929 everyone had a real windfall; even porters got as much as £100 in shares. Furthermore Partners were invited up to the counting house to sell up to a half of their shares if they wanted to. And it is true to say that nearly all the Partners did go, to receive 22s 6d for each share they sold. Interest at the rate of 1s 6d in the £1 was paid each first of June and December. You could rely on that.

## Expansion in Oxford Street

In the middle of 1928 Spedan was tipped off by a senior manager in the competing department store to the east of the John Lewis shop, the Oxford Circus side, that it was about to be put up for sale. He needed to move quickly, and he did, acquiring on 18 September TJ Harries, a business which took up most of the block between Holles Street and John Princes Street. It had about as much floor area as did John Lewis, so the sales area was doubled at a stroke, but it had the particular advantage that its window frontage on Oxford Street was much longer than John Lewis's. It was separated from the parent shop by a bank on the corner and two small shops, but that didn't matter, and it allowed Spedan to move some of the departments that languished for lack of window space, like fashions, to a much better location. That rebalanced the business, because the immensely strong 'piece goods' trade, in which John Lewis had come to dominate to the extent that rivals no longer tried hard to compete, was soon to diminish. Spedan didn't know this yet, though his sharp long-serving silk buyer Yearsley had foreseen it. Spedan said of him: 'For years Yearsley had deliberately and systematically disregarded the regulations he was supposed to be following.' This he admired, unless of course the regulations were his own. In the case of the trade in piece goods, which are fabrics sold in standard lengths:

> Mr Yearsley once astonished me by saying that if ever he set up for himself he would confine himself to new departments, such was the dwindling demand for piece goods. For my own part I did not foresee it, but in fact the trade was now near to a sudden and very great contraction. Had we foreseen that, we must have jumped at the chance to get the Harries business with its incomparably better frontage. Our decision however was based upon a much broader and simpler notion. We simply looked at the fact that the Partnership already had competitors whose scale of operations was far larger. We would transfer to the new shop with its abundance of window display all those departments of my father's business that had been comparatively underdeveloped. This decision seems now an admirable stroke of policy. In fact it was in that respect a lucky fluke.

Spedan was everywhere in the early 1930s. A young school-leaver who arrived at sixteen in 1929, Stanley Carter, later described the Oxford Street shop and Spedan's influence at the time he joined:

> There was a great change between 1929 and 1939. In 1929 it was all Edwardian in behaviour and dress. Spedan interviewed each buyer once a year and they dressed in silk hat and morning dress for the interview. Most didn't wear such clothes every day, but some did.
>
> Spedan dominated and had an all-pervasive influence over that critically important decade. His ideas about Partnership and shopkeeping were drummed into us hour by hour, day by day, so that we lived and breathed by his standards. When I look back all else pales into insignificance. I can't find words to express his great importance. All we did we measured by what Spedan would think of it. His energy never flagged. He was meticulously accurate in all he did. If you were working with him you were swept off your feet. The whole place was drenched with his personality.
>
> There was a very strong feeling that the Partnership was different. It was largely a loyalty to Spedan himself. When I met people from other stores, what struck me was a lack of loyalty or belonging. Among crucial differences was the sharing of information between managers and managed, which was unheard of elsewhere. Similar was his determination to find people with exceptional degrees, or who had done well in other jobs. They introduced a heightened standard of efficiency, and an enlightened mode of thought that stimulated everyone round them. Spedan said he wanted people who were like catfish, with two very large barbs to tickle other fish up and make them dash around the tank.

Spedan compared the Harries purchase to a chess move that you decide on without having a clear-cut plan in mind, but one which you make on sound general principles, like getting pieces on 'good' squares, or freeing them for later action. (Spedan was an enthusiastic and not inconsiderable chess player, and indeed was so impressed by the brainpower of players that could beat him that he often recruited them.) The decision to buy Harries would seem even more vital in retrospect. It wasn't the end of the expansion in Oxford Street either, because by another coincidental stroke of fortune the DH Evans business came up for sale in 1936, eight years after Evans himself had died penniless. DH Evans at that time shared with John Lewis the block between Holles Street and Old Cavendish Street, and it was too good an opportunity to miss, even at a price of nearly £850,000 (over £40m today). Another upheaval, but when it ended John Lewis covered the best part of two blocks – in fact twice as much space as it occupies in 2010. It was now the largest store in London with the biggest expanse of windows. So it could compete with anyone in every facet of the department store trade.

## Expansion Outside London

The late 1920s and early 1930s saw a severe depression in Britain. Unemployment peaked at 25% and it was never lower than 15% throughout the 1930s. That was accompanied by deflation, a rare phenomenon, which cut prices by a third on average in the 1920s, and everywhere pay was getting cut. Profits dropped in 1931, a year when, unknown to all but a few, the Partnership came perilously close to insolvency, an event which led Spedan to introduce an even tighter system of budgetary control. With sharply falling sales, Spedan decided to impose a pay cut across the board, except for those on the lowest incomes. The cost of living had, after all, gone down, so Partners were better off. This led to the curious outcome of a 10% pay cut at the same time as a 15% Bonus was announced for the previous year. Partners were effectively having their salaries part-paid in shares that they couldn't immediately cash, and they were uneasy, finding it hard to understand Spedan's long-winded explanations in the Gazette. In a period when businesses were laying off employees in great numbers, however, the question boiled down to 'Take your pick – pay cut or redundancies?' The answer would probably have been, 'I'll have my pay and make someone else redundant.' Nevertheless, with evidence of unemployment and hardship only too visible (if much less so in London than in the north) the Partners buckled down without much public complaint in the Gazette. Moreover, the depression, as with the banking crisis of 2008, but on a far greater scale, put some old retail businesses under severe pressure and gave those on a sound footing expansion opportunities.

So it was that once trade improved and pay levels were restored at the beginning of 1933 Spedan decided to seize the opportunity to start what he called 'branch trading'. In that year he bought Jessops of Nottingham and Lance & Lance in Weston-super-Mare, the Somerset holiday resort where his Speed great-aunts had worked and lived. In 1934 he bought stores in two more coastal towns: Tyrrell and Green of Southampton and the much smaller Knight and Lee in Southsea. These all came on the market because they were failing during the depression. In Spedan's words they were 'businesses under-performing through lack of investment in staff and systems, or long-established family enterprises that had lost their way.' So the Partnership was saddling itself with businesses that were housed in tired, neglected buildings, with ancient fixtures, and poor staff facilities. Moreover, it brought a large influx of new employees Spedan was determined should be made Partners immediately, be paid properly, and get the same facilities makeover he'd instituted everywhere he went. He wasn't going to have a second-class citizenry, and he was adamant that they should have an equal share of the profits even if their own business was making a loss – as some were at takeover.

The new Partners in these four locations were at first fearful – they'd suffered the combination of a worldwide recession, high unemployment and a failing business – but once they saw the injection of money into their shops the majority were relieved at how well placed they were. Jessops of Nottingham had been family-run, first by the magnificently named Zebedee Jessop, and then by his son William, who in 1912 had refused to shut for a midweek half day, as the new Shops Act stipulated. Then he refused to pay the £1 fine – 'I am a freeborn Briton' – until it had mounted by degrees to £128, when he was persuaded to part with a guinea in settlement. The view of his freeborn British employees is not recorded. The Jessops were determinedly old-fashioned. Orders were delivered by porters with wooden cases strapped to their shoulders like coolies. All their account statements were written by hand until an ancient typewriter – still the only one of two in Jessops when the Partnership acquired it in 1933 – was bought in 1920. In that year the annual turnover was £145,000, but by 1933 it had slithered down below £60,000. By 1950 it had gone up by a factor of twelve. When the Partnership took over, out went much of the stock in a fire sale; John Lewis buyers travelled up to look it over and re-plan the assortment, and Spedan introduced a slick system that enabled anything out of stock to be replenished from Oxford Street by van the next day. Most buyers enjoyed their day out, but one of them needed two. A Joseph Morris, the lace buyer – who was still wearing a wing collar when he retired after the war – blithely found himself in nearby Griffin and Spalding by mistake. He toured the department, handing out advice and criticism to a nonplussed local staff. He didn't discover his mistake till he got back to London and was asked why he hadn't arrived at Jessops. Conditions there can be imagined – when Spedan took it over part of the ground floor was still occupied by a foundry over 100 years old. When they 'cast', twice a day, the back of the ground floor was covered with steam and dust.

Ruth Dexter, working at one of those two old typewriters, recalled that they used to have no more than the normal retail two weeks' holiday, but said, 'When the Partnership came and we had the spring holiday week we were in clover.' The store now closed on weekdays half an hour earlier, and the new Partners received 1933's Bonus of 10% of pay despite their shop running at a loss. Pay went up, the hostel was closed, the smoke-filled dining room replaced. Out went the primitive loos, which had no hot water, and towels that were changed just once a week. In came Partnership methods and disciplines, brought in by brisk women who struck fear into those not up to the mark, but not Ruth Dexter. Muriel Elliott, later one of the flotilla of personal secretaries that Spedan kept occupied round the clock, came up to Nottingham to sort out the staff paperwork. Ruth supplied her with tea and typing – on a new typewriter – and was amazed and gratified to be sent strawberries and cream when she was later off sick.

Spedan's reason for expansion was to increase his buying power and to forestall the threat from the 'multiple' stores like Marks & Spencer that were now expanding much more rapidly than department stores. He also had a distinct sense of foreboding, earlier than most, about the threat of another European war, only too uncomfortably aware that his two London shops would be vulnerable to air attack. Although both the port of Southampton and the industrial city of Nottingham would also be likely targets, he was at least parcelling his all-too-breakable eggs into several baskets. It's worth remarking that when he made his first purchase out of London his fear of bombing was regarded as rather daft – even distasteful – by most of his managers, a fact recalled by one with chagrin in the Gazette late in 1940. He remembered the Chairman's announcement in John Lewis, ending with a telling reminder of how Britons shied away from any suggestion that there might be another war:

> He was explaining the new policy of spreading our trade to different branches, and then went on to say that in his mind had been the thought of *war* – (I remember a slight shudder went through the audience) – war, that might well mean that trade would forsake London for the provinces. I believe he even mentioned the destruction of our London shops. After the meeting, many remarks were heard to the effect that the Chairman was warmongering.

## A Team of All the Talents – for Life?

As well as bringing in bright young women from university, Spedan persuaded several high-flying men to come into his Partnership, often after they had spent years in completely different careers. His aim was to create a group of brilliant minds – with whom he enjoyed a vigorous debate – who shared his vision and could help him with the Partnership's rapid expansion. In the late 1920s and 1930s he recruited a collection of educated people attracted by his ideas, from varying backgrounds. They became his key lieutenants in the 1930s and through the war that followed. Although Spedan had been ahead of his time in recruiting women to important buying and selling jobs, all these new arrivals were men. His main men were Michael (later Sir Metford) Watkins, Bernard Miller, Sebastian Earl, Tom Robinson and Max Baker. Of these, Spedan came to lean most heavily on Watkins and Miller.

Michael Watkins, the son of a railway worker, was commissioned in the Great War in 1917 when not yet eighteen. He won a scholarship to and got a double First at Cambridge after the war, and had been happily teaching maths at Spedan's old school when he was lured away in 1926. His sympathy for the Jarrow marchers had led him to voice his opposition when the boys volunteered to drive trains and buses during that year's General Strike. His card was marked at Westminster as a result, and his old housemaster there put him on to Spedan, who he'd been at school with. Watkins' enthusiastic acceptance letter affirms that it was excitement at Spedan's ideas that had landed him, and he plunged avidly into this new world. Within a year he was the Partnership's financial adviser, and by the mid-1930s was director of trading (the equivalent now of the MD of John Lewis) with an overall responsibility for the selling branches. Spedan admired his mind:

> The steel of his mind is very beautifully tempered. It gets very near to the quality of those legendary sword blades of which the cutting and piercing powers were extreme but could yet bend without damage to a complete circle.

A friend of Spedan's, the architect Charles Reilly, was impressed by Spedan's approach, and by people like Watkins:

> His great invention, the John Lewis Partnership, is to me something like a great university ... I have not met, outside the permanent members of a university, men like Michael Watkins who, with clearly a very subtle and acute brain seems to care, not only for most of the things my young artist and socialist friends care for, but who takes extreme pains not to tread on other people's feelings. To find such men holding positions of great responsibility in a highly successful business is a great surprise.

Bernard Miller came straight from Oxford, where as a History First he had beaten his famous contemporary AJP Taylor to the annual essay prize with a piece on Robert Harley, first Earl of Oxford. (Harley Street was named after him, and he'd been an earlier owner of the de Walden estate on which John Lewis stood.) Miller had no intention of becoming a retailer, but Spedan bowled him over, and he joined in 1927 in the John Lewis silk room, although when they found out he was colour-blind he was soon sequestered to be Spedan's PA. After taking on a succession of other jobs, often holding down several at once, he settled finally as director of estimates, then an important planning function. He recalled:

> I was expecting to teach or enter the civil service. An interview with Spedan Lewis changed all that. I was so swept away by him that I forgot all the things I had in mind; he seemed to be on the point of explosion all the time. The counter of the long silk room in Oxford Street brought me down to earth with a bump. For some weeks, I was literally worn out at the end of the day, but that passed and I soon found myself involved in all kinds of activity that reflected the many-sided nature of the Partnership and its Founder. When I began it was still in many ways Victorian, with buyers in tail-coats and department-supervisors in frock-coats. I moved from selling silks to working on the new constitution as personal assistant to the Chairman ...

> There was little office space in John Lewis so I worked in 1928 in a fitting-room in the costume department on the first floor of the John Lewis building. It was not easy to concentrate; the sales patter of a very successful buyer in the adjoining fitting-room was an irresistible diversion. Another was the occasional foray of old John Lewis. His arrival was signalled well in advance, and I and others had to put on our [top] hats and go out into the shop, so that he should not be upset by seeing idle young men sitting at desks in fitting-rooms! John Lewis was short, but a most impressive figure with his flowing white beard; seeing him together with his son Spedan, tall with a strong, handsome face, I was vividly conscious of the personal dynamism that had gone into the business and that was going into the creation of the Partnership.

The so-called 'long silk room' was an institution, and the spiritual centre of the Oxford Street shop. Every senior learner at Oxford Street began there, as did legions of many more junior recruits. The post-war silk buyer HH Jones began there in 1931 (at 13s a week with 6s 10d deducted for food, and a black jacket and striped trousers to buy at £2 10s). Summoned at midday down to the basement, he found a cricket pitch edged with skis set up by the sports buyer, Bernard Miller, who was juggling several jobs at that point. Recalling the old 1930s shop, Albert Sherring described his favourite places:

> The Silk department was always the busiest, and it was a common sight in the old Long Silk Room to see customers three or four deep in front of each assistant. The range of shades was astonishing, with over 600 for crêpe-de-Chine alone.

The other three of Spedan's five were Earl, Tom Robinson, and Baker. The strikingly handsome Sebastian Earl had been Head of School at Eton, won a scholarship to Oxford with an essay on Capital and Labour – a perfect grounding for Spedan's ideas – rowed four times in the Boat Race, and won a rowing silver medal at the 1920 Antwerp Olympics. He joined the Partnership in 1932 after starting his career in the Black Country iron industry. Earl began as Gazette editor for a year before joining Spedan's growing close-knit entourage, frequently switching jobs until the war. Tom Robinson was an accountant who quickly became the Partnership's finance expert; before joining, he later told Spedan, he never knew what it was like to look forward to work on a Monday morning. One high-flying recruit who had actually *worked* in retailing was Max Baker, who had been a silk buyer and merchandise manager for ten years after getting a First in Natural Sciences at Cambridge. He was a rarity at the time, a man with a top degree who had gone into retailing elsewhere.

Spedan possessed great attention to detail, impeccable logic that he took further than most, and a formidable energy despite often being laid low by debilitating illness. But he usually recognised his limitations; he had a growing family, and by 1930 lived on an estate in the Hampshire village of Leckford that was turning into a major agricultural project of his own. In 1935 he decided to prepare for a withdrawal from constant active control of the business, and set about firming up his 'investment' in the brilliant team he'd recruited by trying to bind them to the Partnership with lifetime contracts. Some agreed willingly, some vacillated before accepting, some baulked. Michael Watkins' contract took him to sixty-five, starting at £3,000 a year (c £160,000 today) with eight weeks' holiday and a minimum of thirty hours a week in the office. That seems outstandingly generous until you realise that he never took anything like that holiday, and he probably worked well over sixty hours a week. With Spedan, you were rarely off duty unless you were on holiday – he never bothered you then, though one can imagine that he couldn't have resisted the invasive temptations of modern communications. Anyway, as Bernard Miller said, it was always more than just a nine-to-five job:

> I couldn't claim I was originally an apostle of the Partnership and that was what I had come for, but it was something that clicked into place. He made me feel it wasn't just a question of money but that he had ideas which were really a twentieth century manifestation of the sort of thing that had been stirring in the early part of the nineteenth ... Before long I was clerk to the newly amalgamated council of John Lewis and Peter Jones, and secretary of the two committees of claims. I planted bulbs at Odney, started the chess club, failed to start a debating society, arranged tennis fixtures and was much involved with the Odney Club.

Miller also acted in the revues, which were encouraged by Spedan and became a feature of the Partnership in the 1930s, often directed by Beatrice Lewis at the Fortune Theatre. He played hockey, tennis and cricket at the Partnership's new 'Odney' Club in Cookham, which we'll look at in a moment. It was perhaps there that Miller saw most of one of the young women 'learners', the athletic Jessica ffoulkes, whose performances at the many Odney sporting events seemed to have the same effect as did Miss Joan Hunter Dunn on John Betjeman. He married her. It's hard not to see the period as a marriage mart, for Spedan was keen to introduce suitable young women into his entourage, and would invite them down to Hampshire at weekends. That's how Michael Watkins met and married his wife, who had been selling furs in John Lewis Oxford Street. Sebastian Earl married someone from a similar circle, the portrait painter Honor Maugham, daughter of the baronet brother of the novelist Somerset Maugham.

There was a strong social glue binding the men around Spedan, all caught up with his drive and vision. Nowadays one would instinctively look for evidence of tension and rivalries, and jockeying for position. But even reading between the lines of the copious reporting of the period any tendency towards this seems to be subsumed into a shared enthusiasm for Spedan's great project. This of course was tempered by their making, at times, common cause in resisting some of Spedan's more exotic, and often quixotic, ideas. But Spedan's love of a fierce debate spread to his team, and never seemed to leave the participants bearing grudges. They argued things out. Spedan likened his team to Gladstone's cabinet. In a letter to Michael Watkins he wrote in almost romantic terms (we happy few, we band of brothers...) and ends with a comparison which readers in the twenty-first century may find odd:

> We are a band of people consciously engaged in pioneer work of such a nature that preconceptions are most undesirable, and we ought to cultivate ... Gladstone's 'Cabinet Mind' ... and develop a habit of expressing our ideas clearly and candidly to each other and thereafter examining them dispassionately to create one whole, of which the parts work with a minimum of friction. In such an association there must be a casting vote, which falls to me, but ... I desire to give as great scope as possible to the majority view as against my own. Our entity is a state within a state and the relationships of its leaders should resemble as closely as possible those of the members of a good specimen of the British Cabinet.

Spedan rarely did important things by diktat, although one can sense wearily lifted eyebrows when he announced yet another learner to be accommodated, one Spedan had been impressed by at dinner, or over the chess board. But he was often right, especially about chess. Playing for Hampshire he came across Hugh Alexander, one of the few British chess players to be able to compete with the great Russians. Alexander was lured away from a comfortable job as maths master at Winchester with an offer to double his salary to £1,200. 'I'd have come for 700', said the delighted Alexander. Spedan mollified his sometimes exasperated colleagues by paying a proportion of the most expensive learners' salaries out of his own pocket. Another recruit was acquired virtually sight unseen. At a chess congress in Margate in 1938 Spedan was beaten by a fourteen-year-old, one of several schoolboys from an ordinary Liverpool secondary school who all produced some precociously brilliant chess. Once his conqueror told him who had taught him – just a middle-aged teacher, one not even very good at chess himself – Spedan resolved to recruit the man. Thus arrived Edgar Pennell, a disorganised genius who after the war became the Partnership's inspirational head of training.

## Expansion – Everywhere He Could

In 1935, with the Partnership now consisting of six separate department stores and employing over 10,000, and his new team in place, Spedan went into what he called 'experimental retirement'. In reality that meant leaving the day-to-day running to his lieutenants to give himself time to explore any opportunities for expansion, and pursue ideas that appealed to him. He went on happily experimenting with organisational structure, especially moving key people about in the top jobs, something they seemed to bear stoically. Max Baker, a great admirer who became in later years the man who imparted Spedan's wisdom to generations of learners, nevertheless felt he couldn't resist tinkering. 'You didn't plant a seed, then dig it up six months later to inspect the roots,' he'd say of Spedan's constant need to re-invent parts of his enterprise. The more businesses he acquired, the heavier the responsibility that devolved on that team, particularly in integrating the four new department stores totally into the Partnership. Their buying had to be centralised, shop floor practices overhauled, stock assortments and fixturing upgraded, the new Partners' facilities improved, their recruitment and discipline practices brought into line. Moreover, it wasn't just geographical expansion into more shops. Spedan was keen to secure sources of supply of products that he felt would give the Partnership distinction at a price his customers could afford. So he sought and seized opportunities to acquire a hat factory, a leather factory, a chocolate factory, and one that made the decorated furniture then in vogue. In Clearings, a new building in Chelsea where the extra stock for Peter Jones was now housed, there was a factory that made beds. And for Peter Jones itself he wanted nothing less than a total rebuild.

## Rebuilding Peter Jones

This project was one close to Spedan's heart. The original Peter Jones, an amalgamation of many single shops, had different floor levels and poor lighting, and moving stock about was extremely awkward. He had planned its replacement originally in 1926, and at the end of 1929 he sent for a young man who had only just qualified. Spedan had been sent the drawings from his thesis design by his friend Charles Reilly, the head of Liverpool School of Architecture. The young man explained:

> I had a letter from Spedan Lewis asking me to see him ... He was a distinguished man in appearance, handsome in a Byronic fashion and obviously someone very much out of the ordinary ... He offered me the job of doing research work in connection with a rebuilding of the Peter Jones site in Sloane Square. On 1 January 1930 I reported for duty. Very much on my own and with no guidance or briefing I worked out a series of possible developments for the site. There was a scheme for a cinema surrounded by a shop and another for a hotel... One afternoon, unexpectedly, Lewis and Michael Watkins came to my office and I proudly displayed my work. I remember the Chairman perched on the edge of my rickety table and spilled the ink on his pinstripe trousers.

William Crabtree, straight out of university, impressed Spedan enough to land the plum job of rebuilding Peter Jones and, moreover, to a revolutionary design. With Michael Watkins, Crabtree visited Germany and was attracted and influenced by Erich Mendelsohn's design for the Schecken (now Kaufhof) department store in Chemnitz. Then there was a bad-news-good-news setback. While Crabtree was wrestling with the complex fill-in job of creating a hydraulic lift for the basement of John Lewis Oxford Street at the Holles Street end, Spedan bluntly told him his job was over. The depression had really kicked in and Spedan decided he had to postpone the Peter Jones rebuild. 'What about the Oxford Street lift?' asked Crabtree. Spedan frowned, said he'd think about it, and then uncharacteristically failed to follow it up. So Crabtree got his head down and laboured on. Spedan forgot he'd 'released' him, and with Beatrice took him to Paris to get ideas for a rebuild of part of the John Lewis East House, the converted Harries acquisition, after dry rot had been found there.

Crabtree was still there when some time later work restarted on the new design for Peter Jones. The good news about the depression for Crabtree's design and his later reputation was that there wasn't the money available for the heavy masonry buildings then prevalent, and so he chose to construct a cheaper, yet revolutionary, structure with a steel and glass façade. It was cantilevered, built with beams supported at only one end. Despite the usual difficulties, including Crabtree and Professor Reilly having to convince fellow architects that they weren't total crackpots, the building, with its distinctive sweeping curve at the King's Road corner, finally opened in 1937. Reilly was heavily involved in steering the project through, and the completed building immediately created great interest and enthusiasm. The famous curve came about because the council demanded that a bit should be chopped off each corner facing Sloane Square, and so, as Crabtree said: 'We sliced a bit more off the King's Road corner to give it a sort of natural movement.' So necessity mothered the invention, described by an architectural historian in these glowing terms:

> The curtain wall, with its thin mullions and centrally pivoted windows, seems an astonishing anticipation of today's techniques. It has the most successful splay corner in London ... achieved simply by making a double curve so that the splay itself is given an exaggerated bulge which prevents the volume slipping away like jelly... a simple trick worthy of Nash. The overall plan is like a corner piece of Yorkshire pudding ... You can see it a thousand times, and it will never fail to give a little kick of exhilaration.

In 1939 it was voted the best building 'of our time' by a panel of sixty-three eminent people in the *Architects' Journal*. The new Peter Jones received fourteen votes and Battersea Power Station was second with ten. Spedan was particularly pleased with the eventual building, which he described as quite different from any other shop in London at the time. In a 1935

Gazette article he wrote commending its design especially for its substantial window area, and condemning the waste of such crucial visual space caused by the typical 'sham masonry' design of department stores. He had given Crabtree these instructions which, inverted, are a catalogue of the problems with traditional big shops:

> You must get into the building the very utmost amount of daylight. It must be very airy. It must be cool in summer and warm in winter. It must be very easy to get from one floor to another. You must not lose a single inch of window space against the street. The inside of the building must allow to the utmost extent of re-arrangement if it should come at some future time to be used for selling things quite different from those that had been sold in it previously.

## A Country Club – and a 'Grubby Grocer'?

Between the wars Spedan made two further key purchases that would have a profound effect on the Partnership in the long run, one from a trading perspective, the other – less tangibly but nevertheless culturally important – from a social one. This was a recreation centre he called the Odney Club, close to the Thames at Cookham, thirty miles west of London. Despite a mixed reception from the council when he announced the idea in May 1926, Spedan pressed ahead and within two years had bought five houses, eventually extended to seven. Into Odney he poured all the pent-up enthusiasm to provide relaxation facilities for Partners that he'd had to suppress since forced to sell Grove Farm and Broom Hall. Odney's houses fringed an estate near the confluence of the Thames and a tiny tributary called the Lullebrook, and Spedan had them converted into hotel accommodation.

Odney was close to where twenty years earlier Kenneth Grahame had written the children's classic *Wind in the Willows*. His model for Mr Toad had been Colonel Ricardo, who had owned one of the four purchased houses, Lullebrook Manor, and driven around in a flamboyant yellow Rolls Royce, gaily tooting his horn at all and sundry. The Odney estate had a winsome rural English three-men-in-a-boat charm, and Partners were soon staying there at 1s 6d a night plus 3s 6d for four meals a day, playing tennis and cricket, netball and hockey, and messing about on the river. (And going in subsidised parties to see AA Milne's new musical adaptation of Grahame's book, *Toad of Toad Hall*, at the Lyric Theatre for Christmas in 1929.) Odney was run by the amiable retired Major General Llewellyn Price-Davies, known incongruously as 'Mary', who had won the Victoria Cross for gallantry at a Boer War skirmish in 1901. He wasn't the 'very image of a modern major-general', but he ran the place like a country club that *everyone* could stay at. His regular reports of Odney goings-on at the Gazette brought a note of engaging whimsy that managed to stay – mostly – on the safe side of condescension.

In the late 1930s, when Spedan was clear war was imminent, his fear of possible bombing made him increasingly anxious that his senior management should live outside the dangers of London. Miller and Watkins had shared an office at Odney in 1929 when Miller was Watkins' assistant for a spell, and they both settled and brought up families in Cookham. They were enthusiastic participants in the annual 'Rag Regatta', where staff turned up to see Partnership bigwigs take a dunking, and were rarely disappointed. There the Miller sons and Watkins daughters lived carefree lives in wartime. Peter and Michael Miller, both later to be Partnership directors, were allowed to take a boat out on the river by themselves when they were still very young, and were summoned in for meals by their mother blowing a blast on her whistle from the steps of The Orchards, one of the Partnership-owned houses on the edge of the estate. Margaret Watkins reckons that she could row almost before she could walk. For them it was a magical place, if not entirely so for their fathers in the anxious wartime days.

The second purchase was in 1937, and nobody then imagined how important it would be. Spedan bought a little food business, largely located in the outskirts of London. It had just ten shops, typically occupying a couple of frontages in a suburban shopping parade. Its turnover was only about 4% of the Partnership's, and most Partners who gave it more than a moment's thought wondered why Spedan was bothering. It would be nearly sold off several times in the next thirty years. It was called Waitrose.

CHAPTER 9

# The Waitrose of Wallace Waite

An early Waitrose at 190 Acton Lane. Note that 'we save you money', not a typical boast of today's Waitrose.

> The Founder wanted to get into the food business, and he may well have been right, but all he bought were ten little grocery shops ... Small, inefficient, unimpressive, and it carried no weight. People thought it was a loser. Everyone was glad that we decided to keep its name. We didn't want the name and reputation of John Lewis dragged down.
>
> STANLEY CARTER, WHO WENT ON TO RUN WAITROSE FROM 1967 TO 1973, REFLECTING IN 1990

Michael Watkins bought on the Partnership's behalf those 'ten little grocery shops' in October 1937. At that time they were making a £21,000 profit on a turnover of £167,000, the equivalent of around £100,000 on £8m today. That was only 4% of the Partnership's trade at the time. By then Waitrose as a trade name had existed nearly thirty years – it was incorporated in 1908. Its origins went back four years before that, when three men in their early twenties opened a small shop at 263 Acton Hill in West London. Wallace Waite, Arthur Rose and David Taylor had split away from a grocery chain called Coopers, though, as the chosen name suggests, Taylor left early. And while Rose concentrated on the accounts, the real grocer was Waite.

## Apprenticed at Twelve

Wallace Wyndham Waite was born in 1881, one of the eleven children of William Waite, an itinerant railway foreman who crisscrossed the country working on major railway projects. At one stage his team was building the railway bridge between Bath and Shepton Mallet, so at ten Wallace was at Shepton Grammar School, as the orphaned John Lewis had been nearly fifty years earlier – a nice coincidence. It was in early 1893, on the day before his twelfth birthday, that he was apprenticed for three years to a substantial grocer named Pegler in Pontypool, one of the places his father had lived. According to his daughter Monica, Wallace had wanted to become a farmer, and indeed had worked for the two previous years on his uncle's farm, but his father decided what each of his eight sons would do, and brooked no opposition. William Waite later went to work in China on the Kowloon tunnel project – and according to Monica stayed there, abandoning his family.

Wallace Waite told Monica how miserable he had been as a living-in apprentice of just twelve years old, working long hours and going to bed exhausted with nothing but a wedge of bread and a cup of cocoa. His wages were meagre – he received nothing in that first year, £5 a year in the second, and £10 in the third. Determined from an early stage to own his own shop, he saved half his wages and went to night school as soon as he could. That was in London, where he arrived in 1897 with the apocryphal pound in his pocket, going on to work for a series of grocers within cycling range of Paddington Station. Every Saturday he'd leave the shop when it closed at nine in the evening, cycle to the station, and take the last train back to Shepton Mallet to spend Sunday with Kathleen Hall, the daughter of a Shepton clothier. Early on Monday he'd be back on the milk train in time to open the shop. Eventually they married in Shepton in 1908 when he was twenty-seven. And by then he did have his own business.

In 1904 he was working for the Coopers branch in Woking, when the three young men found a shop to rent in a new shopping parade in West

London, and the name *Waite, Rose and Taylor* was emblazoned in gold lettering over the facia of 263 Acton High Street. Acton was a rapidly growing residential area, and Waite's determination for honest dealing – 'I wanted to lift the food trade to a higher plane' – made them a success at a time when grocers had a justified reputation for food adulteration. Operating with tight margins, often against intense local competition, grocers had for years been saving costs and 'prettifying' products however they could. Bread was whitened with alum and often contained sand and ashes. Tea was glazed with black lead, and 'red' Gloucester cheese was brightened with red lead. Gravel, leaves and twigs were ground up and added to pepper, still an expensive import. Confectionery was sometimes found with a lab-full of dangerous metals added – copper carbonate, lead sulphate, mercury bisulphate and Venetian lead. Everyone was doing it, but Waite wouldn't. The engagingly outspoken GK Chesterton, author of the Father Brown stories and much else, loathed grocers, not least because of their questionable dealings. This extract is from his *Song of the Grocer*:

> He sells us sands of Araby
> As sugar for cash down;
> He sweeps his shop and sells the dust
> 'The purest salt in town',
> He crams with cans of poisoned meat
> Poor subjects of the King,
> And when they die by thousands
> Why, he laughs like anything.

From early on Waite aimed high – he told his daughter that he'd always wanted a royal warrant and a shop in Oxford Street – so Waitrose was among the few which refused to adulterate its food in this way. The young business thrived (despite fierce local price-cutting which saw an intransigent competitor go bankrupt) and survived the departure of Taylor back to Coopers two years later. In 1908 Waite and Rose were confident enough to buy the next door shops at 265 and 267 and embark on a major refit. That year they joined their names to create Waitrose as a private limited company, and further cemented the partnership when Rose married Waite's sister Bertha in 1910. According to an early employee, 'Rose was a small dark man, always immaculate – when we saw him coming through the door we used to smarten up a bit – while Mr Waite, he was the big one.'

## Waitrose Begins

That first Waitrose shop cut a dash. When it reopened in September 1908 it had mahogany counters inlaid with satinwood, and walls lined with marble, mirrors, tiles and glazed bricks, decorated in the art nouveau style. Numbers 263 and 265 had grocery, provisions, meat, fish and greengrocery departments, and 267 was a flower shop. Fridges were not yet available: to keep food cold they converted the basement to a cold store with nine-inch thick walls, and an eighteen-inch concrete floor with a rack capable of carrying two tons of ice. Upstairs there was a 'ripening room' with large windows to catch all the sun Acton could offer. The manager and his family lived above the shop, and above them slept half a dozen apprentices and older assistants in an attic dormitory.

Wallace Waite was no longer in the shop day to day, but out developing the business. Three more small shops were opened in Acton, trading downmarket for cash only, and Waite won contracts to supply hotels and hospitals. Two small London warehouses provided the extra storage space they needed. In 1912 they sold off some of the smaller shops so they could open a new larger one on Gloucester Road, in wealthier Kensington. That's the trade Waite wanted. He was an energetic opportunist, and in 1914 he spotted an opening that led him to prosper in World War I, and that in large part insulated the business from the problems of the 1920s.

The opportunity had been spotted by one of his many brothers who had joined up, and it was a long way from London. The army was building its new headquarters at the massive camp at Catterick Bridge in Yorkshire. There wasn't a large town nearer than Darlington, and the building contractors needed someone to feed and supply the workmen, so Waite set up a company called Catterick Supply Stores, using the racecourse grandstand as a depot. The first hut to be finished was turned into a canteen, and Waite employed his wife's cousin George England to run it. Waite was running the business alone at this juncture, because his partner had volunteered for war service. Although Rose survived, he returned from the war in poor shape. According to Monica he became lackadaisical, 'sat cloistered in his office reading novels', and left Waite to tidy up the accounts at home in the evenings. By 1924 he'd had a nervous breakdown and departed.

By the mid-1920s Waite essentially had two different chains. Waitrose had several small shops in more prosperous suburbs, plus a few downmarket businesses – what we would later call a cash-and-carry – which traded as Wyndhams, derived from his middle name. Monica Waite had been born above the Gloucester Road shop in 1914, but by the end of the war the family had moved to a Surrey suburb. Monica remembered going out from their home in the family's chauffeur-driven car each Saturday night, 'branching' – checking that every shop had been properly closed for the weekend. Sometimes during school holidays they would sit in the car on a daytime round, watching 'with a slightly pious glee' as their father ran his gloved finger along a shop's windows to test for dirt, and tick off the apprentice responsible if it wasn't clean.

Monica described how for a special display of Danish produce the Gloucester Road window was strewn with straw to accommodate live piglets. Although large numbers of people gathered to gawp, the mess meant a withdrawal of the piglets after a couple of days. This bizarre display ran somewhat counter to Waite's usual concerns at a time when elsewhere hygiene was generally slapdash, regulation lax, and enforcement poor. While the local preparation and presentation of food was something of an art form in the best shops, food hygiene standards back in the 1920s were pretty appalling compared with today's. One wonders at the response of those affronted Kensington customers of Gloucester Road to whose lapdogs he would refuse entry. After several altercations he eventually compromised by providing chains for the dogs outside the shop.

## A Grocer's Shop in the 1920s

Harold Tobias began as an apprentice at another provisions store in 1923. Fifty years after he first started, he recalled what the grocery trade had been like. His first job was scrubbing down the counter with Monkey Brand polish and a pumice stone, cleaning the windows, and skinning cheeses and frozen rabbits. There was a clear job gradation at a grocer's: the first step up meant you were beating up butter and carving meats by hand (not so simple, as weekend juniors starting in Waitrose today can attest). Next came wrapping goods and taking cash for the 'scalesman', who was the shop manager's right-hand man. Grocery apprentices saw themselves and were indeed regarded as the lowest form of shop life. Tobias – a success who disproved his own statement – said: 'People who went into retailing at that time were either dim-witted or couldn't get into the army.' Conditions where he began were little improved from the days of Wallace Waite's own apprenticeship thirty years earlier: 'We didn't have rest rooms like branches do now. Our rest room was an egg box we sat on to drink our tea, from jars.' Most had ordinary glass jam jars – a halfpenny back when you returned them to the shop. (The most senior staff had what were called gallipots, *stone* marmalade jars. Luxury...)

At that time competition was fierce, profit margins were extremely tight, and shady practices commonplace in the trade, if not in the Waitrose of Wallace Waite, who was determined to rise above it. When Tobias first became a scalesman he was told in forthright terms that his scales must earn the wages for the whole shop. 'It was easy to make the scales bounce while weighing out. As the tray with the goods on went down, you could sweep them off before the tray could rise again. That made a penny or two extra. Multiply that up...' Like members of many communities who didn't want their conversation overheard, they used back slang. So 'Toh no elacs' could warn of a customer who was known to watch the scales closely. 'Dlo woc' was a less specific warning. Unwary customers could also be diddled by a form of bastard decimalisation. 'When calculating how much a sale came to we would add the pence aloud quickly – twelve, seventeen, thirty-two: three and two all right madam?' In fact thirty-two old pence was two shillings and eight pence, so the customer had been swindled out of six-pence, paying an extra 20%. Page 313 explains the exacting intricacies of pre-decimal currency.

Like most provisions, butter arrived in bulk and had to be packaged in the shop. The assistant had to prepare the butter by softening it with wooden beaters, constantly dipped in water, ostensibly to wet it – but as a spin-off to dilute it. One young grocer said his father boasted he could 'knock four pounds of water into a hundredweight of butter when it was patted up into quarter and half pounds', an increase of nearly 4%, useful when margins were low. Moreover, Tobias said you ended by stamping a different motif on each finished block, and charged a different price for the same product. You chiselled out extra income where you could. Frozen Australian rabbits for example arrived in sixty-pound cases and were sold at 4½d a pound, with useless pieces such as half a head hidden under a hind leg when it was sold. Bottles of wine were kept without the labels giving the year. Whatever year the customer asked for, the appropriate label was stuck on ...

That's something for critics of today's supermarkets to ponder. 'Sharp practices were not regarded as dishonest then. It was the accepted behaviour of the food trade, but not in Waitrose.' Like Waite, Tobias had been keen to run his own shops. In 1937, by coincidence on the very day Wallace Waite sold Waitrose to the Partnership, he opened his own store in Kingsbury in North London, and owned seven by the time he was called up in 1943. (The call-up regulations exempted him until that point, but had recently been tightened.) Tobias sold four shops to Waitrose, which he went on to join when demobbed in 1946. He found a salutary contrast when he sold his shops to the Partnership – they were extremely honest traders, to an extent that first he felt was naive. 'It was very foreign to us. They wouldn't let us do things like putting pieces of fat between rashers of bacon, but insisted that whatever was on top must be the same all the way through.' Soon the poacher had turned gamekeeper: 'Don't talk about the good old days ... They were bad old days in trading practices, hygiene and working conditions. I soon realised that the Partnership's way of trading was the right way.' He became a passionate advocate in the industry for honesty in product packaging and dating – as late as the 1960s bacon, for example, used to be labelled with an obscure date code, rather than a clear date the customer could understand. In 1963 he became production manager, a new post, responsible for all prepackaging in Waitrose. For many years after his formal retirement he worked part-time, unable to get grocery out of his blood, at the smallest Waitrose shop, Temple Fortune.

## Madam Was Your Bread and Butter

Waitrose, like some of the better grocery chains, was keen to educate its staff. When he began at Waitrose in January 1928 the young apprentice Harold Tickner had a heavy training load. He had been interviewed for his apprenticeship by Wallace Waite in his sparsely furnished office in the Gloucester Road shop. An hour's grilling, punctuated by the dripping of a leaky pipe into a bucket in the corner, led to his first job which he 'gladly accepted, starting at the princely sum of twenty-two shillings a week', a bit over £50 now. It was a week of more than seventy hours still: Tickner was confronted with trading hours of eight to eight, Monday to Saturday, extending to nine at night on the Saturday, though often there was a midweek half-closing day, and work to do before and after the shop traded. For a fourteen-year-old Waitrose apprentice this included three mornings a week at the local college, plus two mornings starting at six at Smithfield meat market. One of his first reports read: '... he has made a very good show with trussing a fowl for roasting and another for boiling. He also trussed a rabbit for boiling ... With more experience he will get the necessary speed which is very essential.' You can imagine that young boy (grocery apprentices were never girls) laboriously grappling with the meat on a freezing winter morning, without any heating at the back of the shop. And swatting away the flies in the summer. To Harold Tickner, those three years as an apprentice were of lasting value. He duly got his Institute of Grocers certificate at seventeen, together with his copy of Lord Leverhulme's *Self Help*, which was given to everyone who passed.

> Above all, though, the priority asset of customer relationship and service was the most important. Whether you liked it or not, Madam was your bread and butter, though quite often I was relieved to see her go as I bowed her out of the shop.

For Waitrose, as for many shopkeepers across the country, the 1920s were a tough period. By maintaining stringent standards and keeping the customer happy Wallace Waite came out of the decade better than most. In 1928 he was able to open a substantial shop in leafy and prosperous Gerrards Cross, at that stage the Waitrose furthest west, out at the borders of John Betjeman's Metroland. Its fanfared opening heralded it as a marble palace, with five spacious departments under one roof, decorated with potted palms, and with ample seating provided for customers. Orders could be phoned in and were delivered daily in a fleet of smart black vans, with credit more freely available than hitherto. The assistants were still overwhelmingly male, though now you might see a woman employed in the flower department or as a cashier. There is a photo of its interior on Plate 8.

Such a 'waste' of space would be anathema to modern supermarket designers, but back then the range of foods and brands available was microscopically small by today's standards, and making the customer comfortable while the grocer took her order was more important. In those days there were very few 'own label' products about, although Waite was keen to start his own branding. Monica recalled that whenever he was considering a new trademark he'd bring the problem home and encourage his children to come up with names – thus 'Sunnybrook' butter entered the lists. By 1937 he had some twenty own-brand lines, tea was specially blended at each branch to suit the local water supply, and coffee was roasted on the premises and freshly ground for each customer. At the Ealing branch they caused a local sensation by selling milk in cardboard cartons, not bottles, from the local dairy. Gerrards Cross did a lot of contract work for big events like weddings and shows, where Waite himself would be the overall coordinator. Imaginative and energetic, he was keen to support the development of 'Empire' produce, often winning prizes for promotional window displays. That brought him an MBE for his work on the Empire Marketing Board. He managed to secure a royal warrant for his branch at Windsor to supply the household of George V. Queen Mary would even occasionally sweep in for her favourite honey soap – an alarming arrival once causing a relief manager to keel over behind the counter in a faint.

In the early 1930s, when deflation was leading to wage cuts for shop workers, Waite was industrious in working for national improvements in hours and wages for shop assistants. He was admired by shop trade union organisers such as Philip Hoffman, because unlike other grocers he recognised that shop assistants couldn't be expected to keep up standards when they worked such long hours. He hadn't forgotten his own grinding apprenticeship. He set out to improve pay rates and working hours, especially for juniors, making common cause with the shop assistants' union: grocery wages had been cut on average by 25% in the previous ten years, double the rate of deflation. At a meeting in July 1935 of the Metropolitan Grocers' Association, who resisted all improvements, in Hoffman's words:

> Mr WW Waite ... a doughty Daniel, marched into the lions' den and advocated Trade Boards for Grocery. The Press were excluded ... so Mr Waite sent his speech to them afterwards. In it he read out a very long list of low wages being paid all over the country ... The step taken by Mr Waite crystallised support and counsel for wage-fixing machinery in the Grocery Trade.

In May 1937, Waite on behalf of Waitrose signed a landmark agreement with the shop assistants' union, and it received much publicity. Hoffman:

> The speech of Mr Waite was robust, full of understanding and sympathy, and appreciative of the work the Union had been doing over the years ... Mr Waite was a courageous, likeable man.

## Into the Partnership – Why?

In 1937 Wallace Waite was fifty-six. With none of his sons interested in taking over the business, he was looking for someone he trusted to sell it to. A chance meeting with Michael Watkins led to discussions with the Partnership, who took it over on 1 October. The 164 employees were made Partners immediately, with full entitlements. For Harold Tickner they were conditions unknown to them at that time: 'three weeks' holiday a year, an annual issue of shares in Partnership Bonus, the right to vote ... and the position of "Partner" in one's own firm.' Waite demanded nothing for the business's goodwill, but out of loyalty to his team extracted the unusual (and potentially damaging) promise that managers and heads of department would be retained for five years. This was before the current 'TUPE' arrangements (standing for Transfer of Undertakings, Protection of Employment) that protect employees after a takeover today, if hardly to that extent. Of course, the outbreak of war two years later made that promise void. Wallace Waite initially stayed on as MD, though Joe Webster, who had been running the London region of Co-op stores, was brought in to become a counterweight to his somewhat dictatorial approach. Waite, who had exercised virtually sole command of his business for over twenty years, not unexpectedly found it hard to submit himself to the rigours of Partnership rules. In 1940, with rationing making the grocery business a paper nightmare as well as a logistical one, Waite retired to indulge his old love for farming, something Spedan could well understand. Monica described the family as self-sufficient for food in World War II, even able to make their own butter when it was tightly rationed. That and the lack of financial cares consoled him for giving up his own business.

In the Gazette of 16 October 1937 Spedan, announcing the arrival of Waitrose – under the eccentric single-word heading of 'Victual' – was keen to stress its quality:

> Each of the ten branches delivers over a radius of five miles, so between them they cover fairly completely the residential portions of the western half of London and the western Home Counties ... The business has a very high reputation, not only for the quality of its goods, but also for the way in which it has been built up and carried on. It is no secret that many provision shops ... have owed a good deal of their success to the bribing of servants of their customers. Messrs Waitrose Ltd has never used any such methods. The policy has tended, of course, to delay the success of a new branch, but it has won them in the provision trade a goodwill of the same kind as the Partnership's own.

There's an interesting sidelight in that passage on how some grocers engaged in business with upmarket households. Spedan seems bent on deflecting possible criticism by stressing the similarity of the Waitrose trading principles to the Partnership's own, and to distance those 'ten little shops' from the rest of the grocery trade, which Stanley Carter and some of his somewhat superior John Lewis colleagues so looked down on. The 'western Home Counties' was something of an exaggeration too. Doubtless Waite's reputation for honest dealing and his determination to raise pay levels in the grocery trade would have attracted Spedan and settled any doubts. He didn't take part personally in the takeover negotiations, and hadn't even met Waite when he talked to the Partnership council at the end of October. In a typically forthright and open speech he exposes the risks, and clarifies his reasons for buying a food business:

> There is only one thing that worries me. I hear continuously reports that Mr Waite is a man of exceptional ability. I have not yet met him. So I am bound to worry for when he is no longer available ... However I think the betting is ten to one that the thing will turn out well. I have my eye on the hotel business. I have always wanted to go into hotels ... If we can make a real success of the provisioning side and then start financing hotels, look at the lovely tied business you will get in furnishings and linens and china besides all the food. Oh, it is a beautiful thought.

A beautiful thought for Spedan perhaps. But it was clear from the reaction from those in the department store business, as the chapter heading quote from Stanley Carter shows, that many doubted his wisdom – and those ten to one odds. One Gazette letter writer complained that it was a kind of business 'alien to the company'. Moreover, some were still doubting it fifty years later. Carter would end his career running that 'small, inefficient and unimpressive business'. He arrived there in 1967 nearly forty years after joining John Lewis as a shop assistant. By that time he was a shopkeeping legend, someone we'll hear about in Chapter 13.

Meanwhile let's return to the Partnership in pre-war Britain. The eight years that followed, 1938 to 1945, were for Spedan and the Partnership the most unnerving and dangerous in its history, before or since. This period throws up a series of issues that illustrate the benefits and disadvantages of a co-owned business, and which define the Partnership for future generations.

CHAPTER 10

# Waiting for War

The rag regatta at Odney in June 1939. A combative rowing event has thrown into the water the high-powered pairing of Bernard Miller, above, and Michael Watkins, below. The tall man looking innocent in the boat in the foreground is the shop assistant Paul Roake, later to be the inadvertent focus of a heated wartime council debate.

The Partnership … will hold, of course, to its main principle of trying to behave to all its members as a decent family behaves to its own … For each Partner absent on public service the Partnership will go as far as ever it can in making up the whole of any difference between his service pay and his remuneration from the Partnership.

SPEDAN LEWIS, GAZETTE OF 9 SEPTEMBER 1939

If a comet hit the earth, some … would spend their last minutes in writing anonymous letters blaming the management for it.

SPEDAN LEWIS, GAZETTE OF 23 SEPTEMBER 1939

As the 1930s progressed Spedan came up to London less and less. That didn't stop him sending off missives of advice, instruction and observations from his retreat in the little village of Leckford in Hampshire, which in 1929 he'd bought – yes, the entire village – with its charming house of amber sandstone with mock Tudor chimneys. There he was attended by a set of secretaries who worked in rotation, typing the bulk of the nearly 40,000 numbered memoranda he produced between 1917 and 1955, a colossal output. To a friend he confessed, 'You will not be surprised that my five stenographers are considered bad risks by insurance societies, and martyrs, though quite mistakenly, by themselves.' His habits included the Churchillian eccentricity of having a secretary parked outside the bathroom with the door ajar so that she could catch and record his *bons mots* as he loofahed his back.

Spedan enjoyed the life of a country landowner, improving his tenants' living and working conditions, which he was disgusted to discover were among the worst in England. Warned that increasing their pay would incur the wrath of his farming neighbours, he adopted the simple expedient of reducing to zero the rent on their tied cottages, which he promptly set about overhauling. He built a golf course and a cricket ground, and experimented with livestock and different crops. He liked to tinker with nature. He planted a 'wild' patch of crocus bulbs one September by having his groundsmen collect conkers, paint half of them white, then walk round the designated area dropping them randomly from a bucket. They were to plant a yellow crocus bulb where a white conker had fallen, a purple in place of a natural brown one... but only after they had inspected the outcome and swapped conkers over if they thought the result not random enough. He had an impulse to order his world – or in this case to re-order it in a disorderly fashion. He was an early espouser of the new science of ecology, to which he later said he'd have liked to devote his life. His view was neatly expressed by his nephew Peter in 1989, when 'green' issues started to emerge:

> The green issue seems to mean anything that people instinctively like the sound of but, equally instinctively, are not prepared to take up or pay for if they have a choice. Man is Nature's Sole Mistake. The free market will not fix it. Indeed, mankind being what it is, the free market is the cause of the trouble, because the harm is indirect, long term, and not necessarily suffered by the perpetrator.

Spedan's family life was briefly idyllic but ultimately desperately sad. Beatrice and he had three children in five years – John, Jill and Edward – but tragedy had struck in 1931 when the much-loved oldest, John, caught meningitis at the age of eight and died three days later. As a consequence of the shock Beatrice lost the fourth child she was carrying, and with it any chance of another. Quite apart from their personal tragedy, it's clear that Spedan already had it in his mind to steer this elder son towards the succession. In 1955, when his father reached his self-appointed retirement age of seventy, John would have been thirty-two, at which age Spedan had been running Peter Jones solo for three years. So, with his father's benevolent guidance, he could take over ... But it wasn't to be. The other two children, Jill and Edward, had a privileged but bizarre upbringing. Their father was so habituated to having a secretary on hand to record his thoughts that his observations to his children at mealtimes were noted, recorded, and later card-indexed with everything else. You'd have to be a pretty exceptional young person to overcome the fear of being upbraided because you failed to recall something your father could prove he had told you at a specific date and time.

## Overstretched

After the pay cut of 1931 had been restored early in 1933, on the face of it things continued impressively, with sales nearly doubling in real terms between 1932 and 1937, and trading profit holding up reasonably well. But the company's structure made it difficult to raise capital when it was needed. From 1933 the cost of absorbing four new department stores, and then the massive work necessary to overhaul the newly acquired DH Evans business in the west house – the original site – while the new ex-Harries was called the east house, led to a Bonus level that stayed below 10%. For 1934 it dropped to 9%, paid only to those earning below £400 p.a. (now about £21,000), albeit the vast majority. For 1935 it was 7%, for 1936 it was 8%.

Then in January 1938 came an unexpected sting. Spedan warned that there would probably be no annual Bonus, but also that there would be a general wage cut some time that year. He again explained the reasoning at great length, but Partners were puzzled and hurt: with the economy and unemployment improving, they were less understanding than they had been in 1931. Every company's employees had suffered pay cuts earlier in the decade, but not now. Why us? All right – and several articulate Gazette letters were clearly from those at management level – we understand that sales have been poor since the second half of 1937, but if the business was strong enough to make all these acquisitions, culminating in the Waitrose distraction, why on earth are prospects so poor now? To put it bluntly, have you tried to tackle too much? In an open business like the Partnership's, there was no shortage of dissatisfaction: all the better for being out in the open, perhaps, but nonetheless an unwelcome embarrassment.

## Criticism From Within

The following three pivotal years, from 1938 to 1940, were the toughest for the Partnership since 1922. The Board held fire for six months until the results were clear up to the end of June 1938. At that point Bernard Miller announced that the actual half-year profit available for distribution had dropped in a year from £53,000 to just £13,000. (Multiply all these figures by fifty to get the 2010 equivalent.) The shortfall was due to a drop in sales, half at Peter Jones, half at John Lewis Oxford Street. Trade was seriously depressed in the West End, and the government was levying a heavy new charge for National Defence that cost the business £17,500 a year. Spedan told Partners that they would be laid off only as a last resort, so the only way out was to introduce the pay cut he had warned them about. It would be 5% for all but the lowest paid, and would yield £24,000 in a year. It would probably have to continue throughout 1939 but should end in early 1940. Why don't we graduate it, asked Spedan rhetorically, so the highest burden falls on the highest earners? This had in fact been suggested by the Communist Party of St Marylebone, who had got hold of the Gazette, as anyone could who tried hard enough. Well, those on the Partnership's minimum pay rate (not a *national* minimum wage – there wasn't a formal one – but a level higher than the lowest paid elsewhere) wouldn't be cut. The group on the minimum pay rate amounted to £352,000 of the £887,000 annual paysheet, a very substantial percentage. Of the rest, so comparatively light was the Partnership's top management that if those earning above, say, £1,500 p.a. (circa £75,000 now) took a 10% cut, only £4,000 would be available for redistribution. The Chairman, Partners were reminded, draws no pay at all. He didn't need to, of course, because each year he was taking from the Partnership's profit the annual repayment of his loan to it: more to the point was that he would not take that annual repayment either this year or next. Nor did he, in the event, throughout the war.

Dissatisfaction rumbled on through late 1938. The Gazette (now regularly over thirty pages long) published, of course, its anonymous letters column, but also the minutes of every major meeting. Board meetings, estimates meetings, council meetings, communication meetings in each branch. It also published the detailed results of each department in each branch and for each buyership. Not in terms of money, but as percentages of shift between this week, the previous week, and the equivalent week last year. So Partners – and the rest of the world – could see their washing constantly displayed, whether clean or soiled. This was unprecedented in a large business and created a mixture of pride and dismay inside the Partnership, astonished admiration from commentators, and often malicious glee from competitors glad they could avoid the same rigmarole for their own staff – and glad they could make use of the information provided.

In early 1939 Spedan ran into trouble for his neglect of letters. First, there was a complaint in March that a letter written in January by 'Unpunished' had received neither acknowledgement nor reply. It was an important rule that letters were publicly acknowledged on receipt and answered as quickly as possible, ideally within three weeks. The original letter had, in a swingeing attack, taken Spedan to task for banging on in his 1938 Christmas message for 6,500 words of self-justification, without proper explanation of several recent serious setbacks. Why, having acquired the Harries and DH Evans buildings and rebuilt Peter Jones, have you continued so imprudently with the expensive refurbishment of the DH Evans space when money was so tight? Why acquire Waitrose, a company whose business is alien to the Partnership's? Why have you in the last three years distributed in shares money that should have been placed in reserve? And on top of all this we've had the shock of learning that pay was to be cut by 5%. We're all pleased with generous holidays, kindness and attention when ill, good cheap lunches, but it's not enough to produce a happy and contented staff. Odney? The majority can only afford to go there occasionally. Why has Mr Lewis continued to trumpet the benefits of the Partnership without explaining his mistakes?

That's what you get in an open business. The letters were answered carefully, point by point, not this time by Spedan but by his directors, including Bernard Miller and Michael Watkins, with their normal courtesy – though Watkins, in one flash of exasperation, began a reply with: 'I sympathise with you in this matter. I object to having to come to work at all: I would sooner draw my pay for staying at home.' (Not true, of course – he was a total workaholic.) The accusations were answerable, but the questioner had hit home. Had they grown too far too fast? In retrospect the most dangerous action was to go ahead with the major rebuilding of the DH Evans space in the west block. They could have waited, but they took the risk of short-term difficulty in order to gain long-term benefit. They'd have got away with it had there been no war. Spedan's image was dented further when in May 1939 he had to admit to a major bungle over another letter. In dealing in France with a backlog of work, he had only now, a year later, found one dated June 1938. The writer, over the pseudonym 'Puzzled', asked why John Lewis, held up as an example for others to follow, cut wages when competitors had not done so. Spedan was fed up with his inability to get across what he could see as simple truths and others couldn't. His reply was long and tetchy, including:

> What other word than stupid can one properly use of such a paragraph as this?... Muddle-headed ... 'Puzzled', and the other people for whom he is speaking ... are out of their depth but they do not know it and it seems impossible to get the idea into their heads.

## A War Footing

Spedan was very much on edge. Another war was looming, and almost everyone who could bear to think about it was starting to regard it as inevitable. Could it be staved off for a while or restricted in scope, and could trade hold up at least until the Partnership had finished its rebuilding, restored pay to its level before the cut, and restarted the annual Bonus? The Partnership had been preparing for war for a long time. It had been back in October 1936, following the use of poison gas by Italian troops in Ethiopia, and the first destructive bombing in the vicious Spanish Civil War, when an ordinary shop assistant, ET Kingsman, wrote to the Gazette. In a carefully considered proposal he suggested that store basements should be prepared for use as refuges, that the Partnership should hold open the jobs of those called up on war service, and – more controversially – that their service pay should be made up to its Partnership level out of profits that would have otherwise been distributed as Bonus. Spedan promptly asked the Partnership council to consider it. Next month Bernard Miller produced an exhaustive survey, showing the potential cost of subsidising war service if half the men aged eighteen to forty were called up, and the council voted to set aside up to half a year's profit to do it. (That there was little prospect of much profit in wartime went unsaid.) The Partnership would doubtless have got itself organised pretty soon, but it's striking – and a measure of the growing maturity of Partners and of the Gazette letter column – that the move should be triggered by an ordinary Partner's query.

The Partnership quietly prepared for war, converting basement spaces for use as shelters when and where it could. In April 1938, the month after Hitler marched into Austria, every Partnership branch was instructed to have ARP (air raid precaution) procedures in place and to have had a dummy run by mid-May. September brought the Munich crisis, when Britain and France tacitly allowed Germany to invade Czechoslovakia without reprisal. At that point plans were put into place to use Odney and Leckford as evacuation centres for the families of London Partners in the event of war. In January 1939 Spedan wrote a long Gazette article assessing probable United States action. The Americans would come in, he was convinced, despite their apparent isolationist stance, the moment the fascist powers looked like winning. But it might not be until there had been in Europe 'a terrible amount of destruction'. In May the Gazette could claim that Partnership shops were the best prepared for war in the country, with their roofs coated with special fire-resisting materials, reinforced air raid shelters in each basement, and regular ARP drills. Steps were in place to ensure copies of all crucial documents were made and stored away from Oxford Street and Sloane Square.

Spedan, increasingly restless, starting to fret at being away from the centre, decided in early 1939 to alleviate the burden mounting on his subordinates, notably Michael Watkins, and returned from his self-imposed retreat as director of selling. He prowled round the windows of Oxford Street and Peter Jones, and wrote long pieces in the Gazette pointing out their deficiencies. Watkins, while studiously careful not to offend, clearly regarded the intrusion onto his patch as profoundly irritating. He'd obviously rather have had someone who was reporting to *him* doing that legwork. After a few similar forays Spedan backed off.

Through the spring and summer of 1939 the threat of war was hardly mentioned in the Gazette. Optimism returned and trade started to pick up. There was a prickle of industrial unrest, quickly quashed: the Gazette reported on a meeting with the national secretary of the TGWU (Transport and General Workers Union), who had been approached by some drivers interested in joining the union. That's fine, said the Gazette report, for our aims are the same as theirs, but striking will affect fellow-Partners. Strikers wouldn't be sacked but they might have Partnership privileges withdrawn. Enshrined in regulation 26 was that any Partner had the right to join a union, but that in any conflict the Partner shall obey the Partnership and not the union. A driver immediately wrote to the Gazette saying that 95% of his colleagues didn't want to join the union, because it offered no advantage. Moreover, the union minimum pay was 52s 6d a week against the Partnership's 57 shillings, and one week's holiday against the Partnership's four and a half. Later in the year the shop assistants' union attempted to recruit Partners with a misleading circular. Spedan rounded on this specific action at length, but nevertheless concluded: 'I agree entirely with those who consider that on the whole the trades unions have done tremendous good.'

Over the years unions would intermittently approach Partners looking for a foothold, largely because they wanted inside their ranks groups with better pay and conditions, which they could use as a lever against less generous employers. Incidentally, if they'd wanted to find a weakness in 1939 they could have pointed to the fact that the Partnership's minimum wage scale, net of meals, for sales and office staff aged 24 was 53s 10d for men but 33s 10d for women, in other words nearly 40% less. That seems pretty shocking to us, but the comparable union rates were 50s and 29s, so they weren't likely to make an issue of it.

In that spring of 1939 the Gazette imaginatively sent out a questionnaire inviting Partners to say how they would have spent the profit available for distribution for the last Bonus-paying year, 1937. Partners were told how the £76,300 was actually spent, and here's the response:

| Spending on | Board decision | Partners' view |
|---|---|---|
| Additional holiday | nil | 2,179 |
| Close on some Saturdays | nil | 548 |
| The Odney Club | 11,100 | 4,613 |
| Minimum wage subsidy | 1,900* | 4,745 |
| Meal subsidy | 2,000 | 2,031 |
| Staff Discount (then 8.3%) | 2,500 | 3,443 |
| Annual Bonus Shares | 51,500 (6%) | 48,690 |
| Clubs and Societies | 1,000 | 769 |
| Partners in need | 2,800 | 3,026 |
| Pensions | 2,600 | 4,994 |
| Charities | 900 | 861 |

*It's this low because the scheme began late in the year. Next year it was £6,500.

This showed a broad convergence of views with the board's except in two major respects. First, they would have given less than half of the subsidy to the Odney club, echoing the complaint in the letter from Unpunished. In reality, Odney's cost to Partners was held extremely low, and there was help with rail fares as well, so overall the subsidy was the equivalent of 1.3 percentage points of Partnership profit. The reason people didn't use it was less due to the cost than to the middle-class atmosphere and its range of activities. And second, they felt that double the amount should be spent on pensions, and Spedan duly took note. As in almost every business at this time there was no occupational scheme. In the Partnership pensions were doled out to the deserving long-servers, like John Wenden, in a generous but ad hoc way.

## Play Must Go On …

From its inception down to the present day most Partners would prefer to spend less on amenities like Odney. The world's joiners were enthusiastic, whereas the non-participators just wanted the money. Spedan's Partnership resolutely continued in its determination to give staff possibilities for enjoyment and education that they wouldn't get elsewhere. The Gazette reported every jot and tittle of that activity. Cricket, tennis and chess were particularly strong, and every Partnership match was reported. On successive Gazette pages in June 1939, for example, we read that the young England batsman, Denis Compton, playing cricket at Odney one Sunday in the middle of a match for Middlesex against the touring West Indians, was run out by a direct hit on the stumps. On the following page we're told that one of the Partnership's top management, Hugh Alexander, has just beaten the former world chess champion Dr Euwe in playing top board for England against Holland. The game was dutifully analysed in the following week's issue.

Alexander's arrival had prompted Spedan to plan a national chess centre to be housed in Oxford Street. To run it he engaged the world female chess champion, Vera Menchik, who had a Czech father and British mother. But before it could be opened both Alexander and Menchik went off to Argentina at the beginning of August 1939 to play in the world chess Olympiad in Buenos Aires. Alexander captained England, who got through the qualifying stages, but the moment war was declared the team members decided they should come back immediately. Menchik stayed and won the women's tournament with the same ease she'd won every world championship since 1927. Incidentally, the England team was the only one to withdraw. Ignoring calls to return, the whole German team stayed, winning the tournament narrowly from, of all countries, the Poland Germany had just invaded. All five German players stayed and sought asylum in South America, and most were not Jewish. The wide extent of pre-war anti-Nazi feeling in Germany has been largely forgotten.

## War – and an Exodus

In the summer of 1939 Spedan had started keeping Partners abreast of the worsening situation in Europe. His articles were based on his gleanings from the wide range of newspapers and journals he consumed. While he dutifully summarises all shades of opinion, in retrospect it's clear that he errs on the side of optimism. Partly perhaps it's his own wishful thinking (and that of most commentators, to be fair) but there is clearly a desire to keep up the spirits of his own foot soldiers. Late in July he seizes on a report from the *Sunday Times* City Editor, just back from the continent, under the heading 'Why Peace is Likely', to return to his own earlier conclusion that German rearmament doesn't necessarily mean that 'the rulers of Germany are blindly bent upon gambling on another war'. Oh dear. Spedan isn't the only one seizing on any glimpse of a silver lining in the clouds, but the lining disappears once the heavens open at the end of August. War was declared on 3 September after the stunning news of the Russo-German pact and the carve-up of Poland.

At once the Partnership had an acute problem. When Spedan withdrew from active leadership in the mid-1930s, his entourage, all men, consciously or unconsciously dispensed with his policy of hunting for high-powered women. Instead they recruited a number of retired military men – excellent, many of them – but it made the company vulnerable if war broke out. This led to a great forced shift round at the top. When Hugh Alexander arrived back after a fraught journey from Argentina he found himself the new personnel director, because they'd lost not just the incumbent, Rear Admiral Varyl Robinson, but his assistant, another naval man. The engaging news editor of the Gazette, Geoffrey Snagge, was also called up from the naval reserve. Captain Trouton, the director of building, and Major Fausset, the manager of plant and stores, were drafted back to the army. Michael Watkins' assistant George Watson and the buyer George Walton disappeared. Off went Commander Fitzroy Newdigate, Major Lewis Smith, and Captain Peace, the general managers respectively of John Lewis, Tyrrell and Green in Southampton, and Knight and Lee in Southsea. Half the six department store heads lost in a single month. A little careless?

Sales halved in the first two weeks of the war, being badly hit at Peter Jones, where many well-heeled customers had abandoned London for their country retreats. Spedan took personal charge, and on behalf of the board immediately announced three things. He confirmed the promise that Partners called up would have their service pay brought up to their Partnership rate. He laid off 300 of its 6,000 Partners (5%) and promised to re-employ them whenever possible, although a good few of them wanted to get out of London anyway. And in order to hold the line at that redundancy level he asked all remaining Partners to consider a 'deferment' of a proportion of their pay. The level would be of their own choice, and it would be paid back 'when circumstances permitted' plus interest at 5% p.a. In practice less than 3% of the pay of weekly paid Partners was deferred in this way – if they weren't on a minimum pay level already they were still enduring the previous year's 5% cut – but around 20% of *monthly* pay was. That was gratifying, as was the chorus of thanks from Partners who had been called up and were having their fourteen-shilling weekly service pay made up. In fact some were even deferring an unexpectedly high proportion of their pay supplement. Bernard Miller soon realised why, for in the Partnership's uncharacteristic but laudable haste it had failed to spot the scale of the free board and lodging, clothing and travel that servicemen were provided with. This unwonted generosity was unfair to other Partners, so at the end of November they had to write to all the servicemen telling them the subsidy would be reduced, and asking them to pay back the overpayment as soon as they could. Their uncomplaining response brought Spedan 'more pleasure and encouragement than almost anything in the last twenty-five years'.

Pleasure and encouragement was what he was in great need of. He was putting a brave face on it, starting to pour out his views in the Gazette at a rate which suggested that he knew paper rationing was imminent. He upbraided past Gazette editors for failing to make simple things clear (see pot v. kettle):

> This is strong evidence that past editors of the Gazette should have been nailed up on the door of the editorial office as gamekeepers nail up rats, stoats, hedgehogs and similar criminals.

He was letting his normal restraint off the leash. The 'If a comet hit the earth' reply, quoted at the head of the chapter, was typical. But he'd started the anonymous letters system... The next week he responded with an eight-page diatribe to a letter by a professed outsider, criticising the Partnership for amateurish shopkeeping and system-clogging paperwork. In the next issue he gave Partners four pages on the war (peace is still possible), five pages on Maynard Keynes' proposal for compulsory National Savings (a Good Thing), and three more on the rise in the cost of living (awkward). Rising inflation was clearly prompting a rethink, when on 8 January in its first debate of 1940 the Partnership council tackled the still unresolved 5% cut that had applied since late in 1938. Because of the rise of the cost of living since the war began, Mr Dewing, a driver from the John Lewis garage, proposed that the 5% cut should be removed forthwith. Other firms had given increases, why can't we? Dewing found the door at least ajar: Bernard Miller accepted the argument in principle, but said that it would load £20,000 onto the annual pay sheet at a bad time. In the council debate Miller suggested that the 5% cut should be added to each person's voluntarily deferred pay – so they'd get it eventually – except in cases of hardship when the Partner could apply to the committee for claims. Michael Watkins, however, who'd sympathised so much with the Jarrow marchers, wanted to help the Partners most seriously affected, and hence suggested raising the minimum wage level. Sebastian Earl was the hard man, 'reluctantly' declining to support either proposal, preferring that the claims committee should (as usual) deal with any hardship cases. In the end it was the Miller 'add to deferred pay' proposal that was tabled, and it got through by 36 votes to 19.

It's particularly noticeable how there has clearly been no attempt to thrash out an agreed management line before the debate. There was (gentlemanly) public disagreement among Spedan's main lieutenants. That was the way then. A letter writer in 1958 bemoaned the loss of 'the sight of Messrs Watkins, Miller and Earl, all very senior Partners, having a set-to in the council'. Spedan himself agreed with Dewing's recommendation – clearly delighted that the motion had been brought by an ordinary Partner, even though he'd had to accept an amendment – and the board duly passed it. A further intriguing sidelight on the way the Partnership's decision-making worked was provided by the next proposal on the 8 January council agenda. The question was whether conscientious objectors, when called up and given work outside the armed forces, should receive the same subsidy as those in the line of fire. Hugh Alexander as personnel director had raised it at a board meeting in December. The board said firmly: 'If it were up to us, we wouldn't give it.' Spedan felt nevertheless that the council should debate it; he clearly had some reservations but studiously didn't state them. That observation was published at the end of December. Next week there was an anonymous letter from someone, convinced he was backing a loser, but nevertheless elegantly articulating the case for a subsidy, and ending:

> I believe that if the Partnership gives subsidy to conscientious objectors its action will be in keeping with those countless other unreasonable, quixotic actions that have helped to make the history of the British people a book in which today we can have some pride.

That letter was published on Friday 5 January, doubtless designed to influence the council debate on the following Monday. At that meeting Hugh Alexander proposed that the subsidy *should* be paid to conscientious objectors. He read out a letter from a Partner who was a Quaker, a member of the Society of Friends, a key component of whose creed is that in no circumstances will they harm another person. This Partner was now a corporal in a Friends' Ambulance Unit about to leave for Finland. Alexander's case was that if the Government is convinced that such a man is genuine in his objection to fighting, and carries out the vital war work to which the Government assigns him, why should we rule otherwise? The country is at war today largely because of the high value it set upon the liberty of thought of the individual. His speech was clearly powerful, but every other speaker opposed him, managers and rank-and-file alike, including Michael Watkins, Sebastian Earl, and the buyer Stanley Carter, who had decidedly forthright views. The motion was defeated by 38 to 18 in an open vote (i.e. a secret ballot wasn't called): a stronger showing for the proposal than might have been expected given the strength of feeling against it evidenced by the debate.

The Quaker letter writer was unnamed, but it turns out to have been Paul Roake, who'd joined in 1938 as a salesman in John Lewis. At weekends he had hurled his 6' 7" frame about the rugby pitch at Odney, and in the summer evenings of 1939 had been stage manager of the Partnership Revue directed by Beatrice Lewis in the Peter Jones theatre. Still fit and well seventy years later, Roake explained that one day in late 1939 he was filling sandbags outside Peter Jones, the next he was reporting for duty at the Friends' ambulance HQ, and a few months later he was in Finland. His unit was on the Finnish side of the lines in the desperate defence of their country against a Russian invasion. When this 'Winter War' ended in March the twenty ambulances with their crews were donated to Norway, which was invaded by Germany the following month, and Roake arrived there overland via neutral Sweden. His eventual narrow escape after Norway's rapid defeat was on the deck of a cargo ship jammed with fleeing troops.

It's clear that Spedan empathised with people like Roake, and in July 1940 the issue was raised again in the Partnership council, in a slightly different guise. A shop assistant in John Lewis, Miss Miles, proposed that conscientious objectors should neither be dismissed from the Partnership nor prevented from joining it. She was supported by Bernard Miller on commercial rather than ethical grounds, and Messrs Earl and Watkins too had softened their stance. Everyone else who spoke was against it, Stanley Carter considering that feeling was running so high (his was, certainly) that it 'would interfere with the Partnership's efficiency'. This time there was a secret ballot on a revised proposal that existing Partner objectors should be allowed to stay, but no more would be recruited, and it sneaked through by 25 votes to 21. Spedan now made his feelings clear. He was cross that the issue was debated when there were fewer than fifty councillors present out of a possible 120. He told the council that it would have been better advised to form a committee to consider it and report back – 'four votes seems a small tail to wag a very large dog' of over 5,000 constituents. He was sure such a committee would have ensured that moral standards were maintained:

> The council would have kept the Partnership at the level of decency that is one of the chief glories of our own country and would not have lowered it to the level of the enemy for whose blind ruthlessness we profess to feel such scorn. Some conscientious objectors are loathsome humbugs. Some are silly fools. Some are the very cream of mankind, people who combine utter unselfishness, extreme kindliness and magnificent courage.

In other words, don't throw the cream out with the humbugs. The episode helped the Partnership get its attitude to conscientious objectors straight. The following year a counting house manager, Roland Clarke, was called up and declined to fight, and the tribunal assigned him a job as an evening and night porter at Brompton Hospital, doing fifty-two hours a week. Not only that, he worked as taxation accountant in the mornings, taking him close to seventy-five hours. He was one of the cream, as Spedan pointed out: 'He might well have been directed to a Government service such as the costing department of the Ministry of Supply, like other accountants of his age, some from the Partnership, but to his credit he chose to face the Tribunal and to accept its ruling.' Spedan didn't forget Roake, moreover. When he was later captaining an ambulance unit in the Middle East he got a letter from Spedan asking him to call when he was released, and he duly rejoined the Partnership in 1947, retiring in 1977. In 2010 he was ninety-two, still helping Vision Aid, the charity he helped to found after he retired, from his home in Wells,

## A Wartime Windfall

On 3 February 1940 Spedan was able to reveal a windfall that Michael Watkins and Bernard Miller had been quietly waiting for since late October. Waiting, and giving an occasional encouraging shake to the tree of the American Gordon Selfridge. Selfridge had progressively bought up between the wars a number of – literally – Suburban and Provincial Stores, SPS. Short of money – he lived a notoriously extravagant lifestyle – and extremely concerned about the coming war, he started to discuss their possible sale to the Partnership. In helpful contrast, he was trying to divest and rationalise at a time when the Partnership was keen to do the opposite and take any opportunity to trade outside a London so vulnerable to air raids, even though its financial position remained tense. The cost was only £30,000 (£1.5m today), which seems in retrospect the tiniest of snips, but many of the shops were making a loss, in tired old buildings with tatty fixturing: the windfall had some rotting fruit as well as ripe. Even at the price, most people wouldn't have risked it, but Spedan was the opposite of risk-averse. After much debate with Watkins and Miller he seized the opportunity, and arguably it's because he did so that the Partnership was able to survive the war. (Incidentally Selfridge, founder of the great store, stayed in England during the war but died in sad obscurity and penury in Putney in 1947 at the age of eighty-nine.)

So for a knock-down price the Partnership acquired four shops in South London, two in North London, and shops outside London in Liverpool, Harrogate, Sheffield, Peterborough, Cambridge, Reading, Windsor, Gloucester and Watford. Their sizes were very different, but the total annual turnover came to £3.3m (£250m today) and pushed the total 'branch' sales figure above that of Peter Jones and John Lewis combined. Spedan told Partners of the benefit the extra volume would bring to buying power, at the expense of extra strain on buyers and top management, now having to deal with twenty-one branches rather than six. He emphasised that the Partnership would now be far better insulated against social change and the probable decline of the West End as a trading centre. The new group would be run for now as a completely separate business outside the Partnership structure. He headed off the expected criticism by pointing out that, while the acquisitions of the 1930s had brought the prospect of great long-term gain (it'll come, it will...) at the cost of much short-term expense, this would be different. There could be no question yet of any physical refurbishment, and Spedan was careful to stress that on this occasion the SPS employees would not become Partners immediately, but would have to wait until their branch was 'pulling its own weight'. That opaque comment meant in effect that you'd be welcomed into the fold if you were profitable, but probably sold if not. In fact none was sold until the end of the war. He addressed those existing Partners who he feared would say 'But if you can find the money to buy these shops, why couldn't you find the same amount to restore our pay?' by pointing out the difference between income and capital. (If they didn't get it before they won't now, but I'll keep on trying to explain it ...)

A week after his announcement of the SPS acquisition Spedan told their understandably nervous employees that they would have a week's paid holiday in the spring – rescinding an initial decision not to change their employment terms. Any pay cuts they'd received since the start of the war would, as for existing Partners, be treated as deferred pay, so they'd get it back as a lump sum some time later. That generosity and the signal it gave dispelled their anxiety instantly. He addressed the new SPS employees with a description of the Partnership, long, but as simply expressed and effective as anything he wrote. This is from its last paragraph – number 129:

> I hope you will like the Partnership. Developments along these lines are, so it seems to me, the natural next step beyond the family in the evolution of human society. The Family has had its day. We are entering the Age of Corporations. In business of all kinds saving and investing is becoming a function of the Many Small instead of the Few Great. Management is ceasing to be combined with ownership.

But for the moment the jury was still out on Spedan's experiment. One of the John Lewis preference shareholders remaining from the pre-Spedan days, writing in the same issue on the previous week's announcement that the half-yearly 7½% dividend would not be paid, was in no doubt:

> Of course you cannot pay the preference dividend. Your methods, and your so-called Ideals, are all well and good in theory, but if put into practice in running a public company, heaven protect the shareholders, for failure is foredoomed.

Spedan's last paragraph to the SPS newcomers ended:

> In this field there is still to be done a great deal of invention and experiment. It is important work and urgent, a principal need of this present time. We are doing a bit of it.

The Partnership is still doing its bit of it today. The rest? Investing is becoming a function of the Many Small instead of the Few Great? Hardly. In 1979, when Mrs Thatcher became prime minister, half the investment in UK public companies was made by individuals. In 2009 the figure was 8%.

## False Hopes in the Phoney War

Soon after this Spedan lost another top man, Hugh Alexander, who in Spedan's cryptic phrase was obliged to leave because 'the Government needed a mathematician.' Indeed it did – he went to Bletchley Park, where in 1942 he took over the famous Hut 8 from the future computing pioneer Alan Turing, working on the German Navy's Enigma code. He returned to the Partnership after the war but was persuaded away to become head of cryptoanalysis at GCHQ, the government's secret communications headquarters. (There is a recurrent link with Bletchley Park. Spedan was a friend of Stuart Menzies, later head of the Secret Service, who set it up. There's also an unsubstantiated story that Menzies planned SOE – the wartime Special Operations Executive – while staying at Odney.) Meanwhile, all remained quiet on the Western Front: Germany still hadn't moved as March ticked into the April of 1940. Spedan kept up a stream of optimism, despite a serious bout of pneumonia that he subsequently said had nearly killed him. Lord Horder is his distinguished doctor:

> My last holiday was in May 1940. I earned it by surviving by a very small margin a touch of pneumonia with heart complications. It was a fortnight before I could walk more than a few steps very gently in the flat, and when I proposed to shave myself Lord Horder reacted as if I intended to go mountaineering.

In the month after the war began Spedan had told readers that in *Mein Kampf* (he was one of the few Britons to actually read it – he read everything) Hitler said that if his country ever had to ally with Russia it would lead to war and inevitably to Germany's ruin. In the Gazette of 20 April 1940 he reported a distinguished economist's view that Germany was getting into the same financial trouble as in 1917 and couldn't fight a long war. Unfortunately that was the week in which Germany exploded into Denmark and Holland. On 3 May Spedan reported Germany as 'badly short of petrol and steel', but it didn't stop them carving through Belgium and France to the coast by the end of May, two weeks after the Partnership had stopped regular overnight ARP patrols, hastily restored. In the last week of May Dunkirk was being evacuated, in what Churchill called 'a colossal military disaster, but ... a miracle of deliverance', due to the Germans' unaccountable paralysis at the key moment. But Spedan still felt able to tell Partners of his wife's young cousin who had just been evacuated from Dunkirk. On the way home he had called in at Leckford to report that although we had taken terrible material losses, Germany had too, so that 'they couldn't last beyond November'. Hmmm.

Spedan used that Gazette issue to hope that the end of the war would 'quicken the movement towards less privilege and more equality of opportunity, the movement from which has arisen free education, old age pensions, and so on'. But we still had to win it. The threats of bombing and invasion were palpable, but as the summer progressed still no bombs fell on mainland Britain. It wasn't until 12 August that German bombers attacked British airfields with huge bombing raids. Then on 24 August Spedan felt confident enough to pass on an *Economist* report that while the country was 'not yet out of the wood ... our resounding aerial victories had visibly shaken Nazi power.' The next week he reminded readers that the previous

October he had reckoned the war would be over by October 1941 – now he felt it would be even earlier. It's as though he was determined to swim against every tide he saw, knowing it must turn in the end, to keep his Partners' spirits up – and his own.

In the last week of August little Knight and Lee in Southsea was hit and seriously damaged. A week later Hitler ordered air attacks to be switched from strategic targets to the cities for the first time. Ten days later, on 16 September, Hitler cancelled preparations for an invasion of Britain. But the bombing went on unabated, and the very next evening the roof fell in on John Lewis. Literally.

CHAPTER 11

# Bombed Shops and Spedan's Welfare State

On the 18th September, that is to say in the early hours of yesterday morning, the more important of our two great shops in Oxford Street was struck by a large 'oil-bomb' and by at least one high-explosive bomb ... The strong wind was doubly unfortunate. In whatever direction it had been blowing it would have increased immensely the effect of the oil-bomb ... The wind was westerly and it drove the fire across Holles Street onto our East House. That was not burnt so completely as the West but the damage is very great.

FROM A LETTER WRITTEN BY SPEDAN LEWIS TO PARTNERS AND OTHER SHAREHOLDERS, 19 SEPTEMBER 1940

I had about twelve people sleeping, and just as I got there the second bomb fell somewhere in front of me. I had one moment of sheer panic. I could have sworn that the walls in front were going to collapse and that the ceiling would then come down upon us all. It was a curious feeling: it was not so much seen as felt – as though someone had put far too much into a cardboard hat-box and you know it must give way. However the awful moment passed and I went on.

EXTRACT FROM A LETTER TO BEATRICE LEWIS PRINTED ANONYMOUSLY IN THE GAZETTE OF 19 OCTOBER 1940

In the Gazette of 19 October 1940 a letter written to Beatrice Lewis was printed in its entirety. Nothing else can quite convey the events of the night of 18 September with such vivid immediacy. The writer is unnamed, but the context suggests she is a Miss Katherine Austin, then the secretary of the John Lewis staff manager. She had been looking after the evacuees in the basement of John Lewis for the previous ten nights.

> No one seems to be turning up to be interviewed, so, although I disapprove of writing personal letters in business hours I will write this one. (There go the sirens again – the third time this morning – just my luck! I may have to break off and go to the basement if the guns start) …
>
> I wasn't actually on the Watch that Tuesday night as I was 'mothering' the evacuees, and had been for the previous ten days. I never knew how many I was going to have to find beds for, as some would try to get home and get stuck on the way, or actually get home to find a time-bomb and that they were roped off – so back they came to the haven of J.L. I just loved doing that job. I think I had about thirty there that night, including Mr and Mrs Moss and Mrs Pennell and Miss Rosser. Some of the others were terribly nervy after what they had already been through in their homes …
>
> We had had a pretty worrying night on the Monday when The Langham Hotel was hit and I do not think any of us except the evacuees got to bed before two o'clock. The ARP post had to leave the Langham and go to the RIBA and the manager rang us at about 1 a.m. and asked us if we could give breakfasts to about 200 as he had had to evacuate them to shelters. Capt Burnett gaily said yes although none of us had the slightest idea of whether we had enough eggs or bacon or even if any bread or milk would be delivered after such a bad night!
>
> However we need not have worried, as Mrs Tatem turned up trumps as usual with enough eggs and bacon for three months. Butterfield, Lynn and I got up at 6.45 a.m. and went up to the Restaurant and laid tables and messed about in the kitchen to our heart's content until the regular staff arrived. We had just got all the 'guests' assembled at 8.30 when the sirens went and we had to get them all down to the shelters again. It was at once decided that at all costs the poor things must have coffee so (while CP harangued us to get us down from the 5th floor) we filled dozens of coffee pots and carried down tray-loads of cups and saucers and everyone had at least two cups! After the All Clear had gone they all went upstairs and had eggs and bacon and more coffee and then made a collection among themselves of £6 2s for our Spitfire Fund … Then at 11 we had our own breakfast.
>
> We were all, bar the Watch, in bed by 6.45 p.m. or so until wakened about 12 by the first direct hit. I put my trousers on back to front – I was very annoyed

> because it must have wasted a quarter of a minute. I told those sleeping near me to dress and wait, and I ran along to the Control Room. The water was pouring down behind our little switchboard and they were already trying to get an ambulance for the wounded firemen. Mr Pennell was evacuating no 3 shelter (which was also letting in water) into no 13. I followed them to the Returns room, where I had about twelve people sleeping, and just as I got there the second bomb fell somewhere in front of me. I had one moment of sheer panic. I could have sworn that the walls in front were going to collapse and that the ceiling would then come down upon us all. It was a curious feeling: it was not so much seen as felt – as though someone had put far too much into a cardboard hat-box and you know it must give way. However the awful moment passed and I went on.

Look-outs on the roof had telephoned to the control room to report exactly what they'd seen. Partners there, while water seeped through and poured down the switch-board, stayed at their posts to take down precise details on pre-printed forms and these were passed on to the Watch, who told the waiting fire squads where to go. The second bomb hit at just after midnight, as the writer was leading her charges away from the shelter in danger of flooding. That night there were about 200 people in the several John Lewis basement shelters. Half were Partners and half a collection of local residents only recently bombed out of their homes and awaiting somewhere permanent. The four young women on duty in the Partnership first aid post, trained but untested, had to deal with three dead firemen killed by the second bomb, and many injured. They were helped by a passing Harley Street skin specialist and an off-duty Australian soldier. Katherine Austin shepherded her charges to the staff dining room by the watchman's box. The Mr Moss she mentions was the long-serving credit manager, the man who interviewed the 1920 strikers with Oswald Lewis; CP is Edward Coad Prior, the MD of the shop's west house; Enid Rosser (later Locket) was the Partnership's legal adviser. The duty managers that night were Michael Watkins' deputy Captain Burnett, Mr Stenson the goods manager, and Edgar Pennell (the former chess teacher), then assistant personnel director. Pennell gradually evacuated the 200, spreading them wherever there were spaces from basement shelter to basement shelter down to Selfridges, while Captain Burnett with a team of others was trying to get all the fire-doors shut to stop the fire spreading to the new part of the building (the old DH Evans). But it was hopeless. Subsequently they stayed in the watchman's box for about an hour until the police insisted they evacuate. As they left she saw fire pouring out of the windows of the new building – she hadn't realised it was aflame. She continues:

> Mrs Moon of house catering was firmly clutching a large biscuit-tin containing the day's takings. Someone else had wrenched the Spitfire Fund box off the wall

as he passed, and I was not to be parted from the £4 14s 6d that I had collected from the evacuees for suppers and breakfasts. We were a rich but dismal party ... We trudged through shattered glass down to Lilley and Skinner's, who very kindly opened their shelter specially for us.

Capt. Burnett then started making plans for the morning, and spent the greater part of the remainder of the night trudging about with Mr Stenson and Mr Pennell between the various shelters right as far as Selfridge's and in getting in touch with the matron at Chadwickham. When the All Clear went about six, we walked to Chadwickham, where we found tea and biscuits ready for us and a lounge, already converted into an office, with small tables, pens and paper all set out. At seven o'clock we started 'receiving' the staff who had been caught by the men of the Watch acting as scouts round the cordon at JL ... I cannot tell you how helpful all those men were, and our grand little first aiders stood up to their first big job marvellously.

I am sorry this is so lengthy, but I did want to tell you as much as I could. I am afraid it is now Saturday morning (because I had to do *some* work yesterday) and the third warning has just sounded plus guns. Please give my love to Mr Lewis and tell him we will fight like _ _ _ _ to pull things together again. That word expresses our feelings best, but if you think he would disapprove, please substitute another.

*There is a map showing the places the writer mentions on page 317.*

The day after the bomb struck, the fires still burning, Spedan sent a description of the events to all the John Lewis credit customers and shareholders, assuring them that duplicate records of their accounts had been sent for safe-keeping each night. Partners read it the same day. Spedan makes it clear that everything humanly possible had been done to prepare for such an event:

Before the war began, the more vulnerable parts of the roof had been covered with steel plates, and volunteers from all ranks of the Partnership had been trained as a fire watch. On two previous occasions the general efficiency of the plates and the watch had proved an adequate defence against ordinary incendiary bombs. Of these there had been eight. But the oil-bomb combined, as it was, with high-explosive and helped by a strong wind, overwhelmed all these precautions and the efforts of the regular firemen. They arrived with extreme promptitude and worked with the greatest bravery but the bomb had spread burning oil throughout the building. Within a very few minutes it was running in the street gutters.

Another high-explosive bomb fell just after the firemen had arrived. It killed three of them and injured several others. The Partnership will supplement to

> whatever extent seems necessary any other provision for the dependents of those who were killed and any help to those who were injured. These deaths and injuries meant a dreadful call, met admirably, upon the courage and competence of those members of the Partnership who were on duty in the First Aid Post.

## Fighting Back

Spedan was never better than when responding to a crisis. Every Partner in Oxford Street – whose place of work had been destroyed – was sent a postcard the following day which told them that their pay would be available for collection as normal on Friday. At that point the shop was still burning, and no one could tell how severe the damage was. In the following week's Gazette Spedan's war-report headline on the front page was:

GERMANY HAS BEGUN TO CRACK

Classic Spedan bravado. He told the Oxford Street Partners that the majority of them would be dispersed around the Partnership – an incidental advantage of having acquired the SPS branches a few months before – and that any who were laid off would be brought back at the earliest opportunity. There were though some 2,000 Partners in Oxford Street, so there was inevitably some difficulty in placing them, and some had to be temporarily released. A crack in the Partners-all-pulling-together façade appeared when John Lewis refugees in Peter Jones complained in the Gazette about the snobbishness of their new hosts, who in turn criticised the John Lewis immigrants for 'incessant rudeness'. The dawn handbags were soon put away, but it's a sign of how nervy the bombing campaign had made everyone working in Central London, with constant air raid warnings interrupting the day, forcing the rush to the basement. Will it be us this time? It was, for Partners in Southampton, target for some of the most intense bombing, which was switched to port cities in November. After a six-hour raid at the end of that month, in which most of the windows were blown out, they took a direct hit a few days later.

Peter Jones survived – indeed lost not a single pane of glass – despite several bombs landing in and around Sloane Square. Now only that branch and those in Nottingham and Weston-super-Mare remained unscathed of the six branches with which the Partnership had started the war (although the Nottingham carpet and soft-furnishing factories had already been burnt down). Then in 1942 the Weston shop was destroyed as well, the Gazette describing it next day as a desert of twisted girders, blackened smouldering remains and crazily tottering walls. (For its MD Robert Hurst bad luck came in threes, for he had been general manager at both Oxford Street *and* Southampton when they were burnt down.) Spedan's 1930s strategic expansion had foundered because three of the four branches he bought were on the coast. It really was the SPS acquisition that was keeping the Partnership in the black.

At Oxford Street the major question was how soon they could get part of the less damaged east house up and running, not least because by now the supply position was getting really difficult. The value of the stock destroyed was £848,000 (£38m today) and the departments they were planning to re-open had to be restocked in less than a month. That's because at the end of October new government supply restrictions would come into force, effectively rationing the amount of replacement stock they could get. Only the value of the stock was insured by the government, incidentally, not the buildings or fixtures and fittings. Perhaps the only piece of luck was that the bomb hadn't dropped a month later, otherwise they'd have found it impossible to restock anything like a full assortment. Within a month, after heroic work from the Partnership's own building team and the buyers, part of the fire-blackened east house was able to reopen, housing all the clothing departments. There was universal amazement from Partners and customers, one wryly commenting that she was 'glad it was now so much smaller – so many fewer departments to get redirected to'. By the end of November more departments had opened in the east house, and by the end of January the Southampton shop was trading in several little outlets clustered round the cathedral in Winchester, fifteen miles away, and in smaller new premises within Southampton itself. Gallingly, much of the still-usable west house was promptly requisitioned for government offices.

The Partnership was now an archipelago, dotted around the country with its central island still metaphorically smouldering. Three men bore the brunt of a colossal workload. Sebastian Earl toured the country bringing the SPS branches up to standard – in terms of methods, if not of facilities in war-strapped and rationed Britain. Michael Watkins wrote later of Earl when he was forced to retire from the Partnership:

> His job involved ceaseless travelling in conditions of great discomfort. All hours of the day and night found him running to catch or miss trains. Any moment that he might have snatched for leisure or sleep he filled with the reading and writing of reports, information and advice ... Yet with all this he pulled more than his weight ... and enjoyed nothing better than a dash to a good fire, where his own enthusiasm was only exceeded by the anxiety of his friends for him.

When Earl died in 1983 Bernard Miller added this to his obituary in *The Times*:

> As director of selling through the war his development of branch trading added very greatly to the strength of the business. He brought support and encouragement wherever he went and inspired affection and admiration in equal measure

> ... His courage, loyalty, honesty and complete candour made him an ideal colleague, with whom it was a privilege to share both bad times and good.

The same could be said of Michael Watkins, and there wasn't much that was good in 1940 and 1941. He was in overall control as director of trading, and took personal charge of the post-bomb work, supervising the gradual resettlement of Oxford Street, helping the buyers fight the constant difficulties of getting enough stock when there were increasing shortages coupled with rationing. Britain in wartime – and for some time afterwards – operated as a centrally directed economy. Ration coupons were introduced, and the planners attempted to flex the coupon allocation to match the availability of products. But it was often hit-and-miss – the fluctuation in the supply of stockings led for example in 1942 to female office staff petitioning successfully to be allowed to wear slacks, as long as they went nowhere near the selling floor. (Permission was soon rescinded, and it took another fifty years for trousers to be allowed again.) Not only was Watkins worrying about all this, he had been 'invited' by the government to organise the provision of the nation's clothing. He it was who invented the idea of the 'Utility' range, which began with clothing and extended to furniture, and for which he would be knighted in the 1946 New Year's Honours List. (He called himself Sir Metford Watkins because there was another Sir Michael.) On taking up the task he was adamant that he wouldn't leave his Partnership job, so essentially he was then doing two full-time jobs in parallel. He took no holiday till 1944, when Spedan insisted he went away, out of contact. In 1942 Spedan wrote of him in the Gazette:

> For some time past I have been hearing from various quarters again and again what extremely important work Mr Watkins as Director General of Civilian Clothing has done for our country ... [It] is one of the sadly few jobs that by reason of their efficiency have shone out in our public affairs against the general welter of incompetence and sloth ... He has slaved month after month for no material recompense.

By the end of the war Watkins was completely exhausted and his health starting to deteriorate, though his sense of humour was holding up. In November 1945 Spedan announced that Watkins would go on three months' holiday in the summer of 1946, reporting in the Gazette that:

> On the 9th of November the director of trading said that he 'wished he felt a bit less like a squeezed lemon in the rubbish-bin behind a second-rate temperance hotel in Wigan ... There was no indication that the sensations of the lemon included even the first beginnings of mouldiness, yet ... even these symptoms require radical measures for recuperation.

## Pensions

The Third Man of the trio was Bernard Miller, and he held the purse-strings. To him fell the task of calculating the cost of Spedan's next trick – pensions. The idea of a pension scheme had been discussed quietly for some time with a view to introducing it as soon as practicable, but Spedan saw that to announce it now would give an important morale boost after the damage caused by the bombing. He later set out the reasons for not implementing a scheme earlier:

> We thought that earnings ought to be distributed completely each year and every worker ought to be left free to make his own arrangements for his retirement. Partners had asked occasionally that a Pension Fund should be started and in 1940 we woke up to the fact that, if the whole of the earnings were distributed every year, too many participants would spend their Benefit as fast as they got it and would then expect a pension when they retired.

Although the 5% pay cut had been added to the 'Deferred Pay' pot at the beginning of 1941, it still wasn't in Partners' pay packets yet, and there was no possibility of a Bonus again until at least the war's end, which even Spedan now admitted couldn't be 1941. (Oh well, 1942 perhaps ...) In a long article at the end of July 1941 Spedan spelt out plans for a *non-contributory* pension scheme, one of the first anywhere outside the civil service and the armed forces. He reckoned that in peace time the Partnership should be able to keep up an average annual Bonus of 12%, and they planned on that basis. His priorities were in this order – pay, then amenities, then pensions, then any Bonus last of all. Miller calculated that the initial scheme would add 5% to the paysheet. Was it workable? Yes. Would the Partners like it, if it meant a consequent reduction in Bonus? Spedan sent the plan to the Partnership council, adding:

> I am very anxious indeed that whatever scheme we adopt shall be extremely clear, extremely definite and as liberal as ever we can make it. Let us have either no pension scheme at all or else a very good one. That is how the Partnership ought to do everything. Either leave the thing alone or else do it very well.

They put it to the Partnership council. The Partnership could afford to start it now because it would not have to pay out very much at all at first – the problems of bloated pension fund liabilities were still fifty years away. The first scheme was at first available only to Partners of fifteen years' service, but women would qualify at fifty and men at sixty, five years *before* the State retirement age. (The actuarial oddity of giving it sooner to women, who would live on several years longer than men, excited no comment.)

The pension would be calculated by dividing the number of years' service by sixty, and multiplying it by the average pay over that period. The council, largely made up of people who had served or were close to completing the qualifying fifteen years, voted for it with alacrity and unanimity the following month, September 1941. It was clearly more generous than any of the other schemes about, despite the length of the qualifying period. Not only were pensions to be provided for women, but so were dowries for women about to marry. That sounds remarkably old-fashioned to us now – almost mediaeval – but we must remember that women at that time in the civil service and most of the teaching profession (and many private companies) had to leave as soon as they got married. The dowry value was set at 5% of the pay accumulated to date, up to a maximum of half a year's pay, for any woman with more than five years of service. So for example a woman earning £250 a year, with ten years' service, would get a lump sum of £125, (about £5,000 today). Sadly, the idea was eventually dropped because it didn't attract the tax relief that pension contributions did.

## Women

The position of women started to be the subject of debate. Later, at the council meeting that agreed to start the pension scheme, a discussion of the Partnership's minimum wage emphasised – to those who didn't already know – the size of the discrepancy between pay rates for men and women. The forthright Elaine Burton, a radical thinker recruited a year earlier who did a series of Partnership planning jobs during the war, expressed amazement at the pay rate disparity between men and women. Burton promptly proposed that women's rates should be raised by 50%, up to the men's level. She was fully aware that the proposal would be defeated but she wanted the issue aired. And aired it was too at one of an occasional series of Brains Trusts held at Peter Jones in the following August, 1942. To the question: 'Does the Brains Trust consider that women should be paid less than men for the same work, and, if so, why?' the report of the panel's answer included:

> The Brains Trust was rather surprisingly unanimous in the view that men should be paid more than women ... The Question-Master said that he ought, perhaps, to apologise for not having a lady on the Brains Trust, but the committee took the view, he thought, that men make a better Brains Trust than women.

Sounds of explosions off, if not in the room. The panelists included Max Baker, whose service call-up was announced in the next issue, when his successor as overall buying director, ironically, was to be one Violet Young. Baker's view on the question had been: 'Women's brains might be equal in capacity, but men's were usually the better trained.' Perhaps he'd trained her more assiduously than most. Probably not – she was yet another Oxford First.

A few months later, in early 1943, a Gazette letter writer proposed that married women should no longer be employed after the war because they would block the places of returning men or single women. Spedan took the opportunity to reiterate his unshakeable view that the Partnership should recruit the right person for the job – male, female married or single, Jew, gentile, British or 'alien'... Elaine Burton weighed in, pointing out the many ways married women were disadvantaged. After teaching, she had gone to live with an unemployed miner's family in the Rhondda to find out for herself the real effects of the Depression. Later she had become a member of a new organisation, the Common Wealth party, started by the popular writer JB Priestley among others, which envisaged a form of common ownership unlike the Labour Party's monolithic state model. During the wartime three-party coalition (Conservative, Labour, Liberal – now there's an idea) the main parties tacitly agreed not to contest by-elections, 'in the national interest'. But the Common Wealth party decided to put up a candidate and force proper by-elections, and one such was at Hartlepool that June, in which Burton stood and was defeated. She eventually became a Labour MP in 1950 and was subsequently knighted as Baroness Burton. The Common Wealth party's principles were close to Spedan's, but he made it a firm rule never to align himself with any party in public.

A year later, in the middle of 1944, there was another Brains Trust. Again there was a panel of five, but this time there's a woman, Enid Locket the legal adviser (who had been on duty on the night of the fire). Again there was a question on equal pay for women, to which the panel unanimously responded by saying there should be equal pay for equal performance, man or woman. The tide of argument was turning perhaps, but not enough to effect change – the Partnership paid the market rate at the very least, with more for the best performers, but the rate for women in all the lower-paid jobs still lagged by a third. Spedan was unmoved too. Usually ahead of the pack with reform, he had been badly stung by a number of women buyers in the 1930s who had gone through long training periods and then left. He would only go so far as saying women should have 'no less than 80% of the pay of a man doing the equivalent job'. One innovation he did pioneer, however: 'There shall be no avoidable discrimination against married women. Expectant mothers shall have leave of absence for *not less than* thirteen weeks, of which five shall be after the birth.' It wasn't paid maternity leave, but it was a start, long before it became law. Spedan had first-hand experience of course, for Beatrice had worked as Gazette editor during and after a pregnancy.

In fact during the war women were undoubtedly holding down more important middle management jobs in the Partnership than elsewhere.

Throughout the war about a third of John Lewis department store heads were women, and though the figure diminished afterwards, it did so only gradually. One job almost always held by a woman was the chief registrar: the ombudsman figure in central management charged with looking after Partners' interests, through a network of individual registrars in each branch. They were independent of the local management, and looked after each individual's personal records. Before the war the chief registrar was Sylvia Barrington Ward (who married the Peter Jones architect William Crabtree in 1940), and she was followed by Marion McEwan, an Oxford First with long experience of industry. It was an indication of the world of work outside the Partnership that McEwan was the only woman in a committee of seventeen, set up by the Minister of Labour in early 1945, to construct a scheme for training ex-servicemen and women in business administration and salesmanship.

## Anticipating the Welfare State

Spedan spent much of 1942 and 1943 overhauling the Partnership's constitution and rules. He was pleased to see similar ideas incorporated in the famous Beveridge Report, which recommended major improvements to the nation's welfare provisions. The wartime monitors from 'Mass Observation' reported that these were enthusiastically welcomed by almost the entire population. Most of them would be enacted by the Labour government that took power after the war, but it's not usually recognised that most Conservative MPs were in favour of its general thrust too. Knowing that much of what he proposed might become the province of the State, Spedan nevertheless published his revised set of Partnership rules in the summer of 1943, and the council picked over them in August, with very little change. So Spedan's own Partnership 'welfare state' was more or less completely in place by 1943.

He had always been keen on providing 'life tenure' in the Partnership for anyone who deserved it, something that he felt could be discerned in a Partner after seven years' experience. So he put in place an arrangement of formal annual reviews for the first seven years of a Partner's working life; this was duly passed into the rules, if not without some disquiet. Was there a risk that, with a comfortable pension beckoning, some would freewheel, and could there could be a danger, in Spedan's words, of the Partnership (as he felt often happened in the civil service) becoming 'silted up with inefficient workers who combine incompetence with a lack of social conscience'? In the end he decided that the risk of people becoming 'disastrously slack' was worth taking in a co-operative business, where fellow-Partners wouldn't tolerate idleness. Finally in 1945 the question of working hours came up as a Brains Trust question. What did the panel think of a five-day week? Since retailing was a six (or five and a half) day occupation, this would inevitably mean some extra staff, but the panel, again with four men and a woman, voted unanimously for it. Spedan concurred in the following week's Gazette and, with the TUC starting to campaign for a forty-hour week, he agreed that five eight-hour working days was something the Partnership should aim at. (This was a revival of a short-lived campaign the TUC had championed a generation earlier, under the slogan 'eight hours' work, eight hours' play, eight hours' sleep', which of course is roughly what we have now, a hundred years on.)

## Coming to an End

Spedan continued to write long pieces about the war. It seems somewhat self-indulgent in retrospect, but there's no doubt from the letters written by Partners in the armed forces that their Gazettes were welcomed as much for Spedan's summing up and speculation as for anything else. Indeed, they were often eagerly anticipated by service colleagues, and there's clear evidence from post-war recruiting that Spedan's ideas had a marked impact, and led several returning soldiers, who had known Partners in the conflict, to join the business after their demob. The war took its inevitable toll, and each report of a man decorated, missing, captured or dead was itemised in the Gazette. The sudden and alarming V1 rocket campaign in the summer of 1944 abruptly blotted out the recent euphoria after June's D-Day invasion of France. Londoners were unnerved by the eerie drone, cut-out, silence … and explosion (if you heard the last one, you had been spared) which took the lives of several London Partners. One of the Partnership's great characters, Lieutenant Colonel Maurice Trouton – of whom Spedan said discretion was never the better part of valour – had arrived back from the war to become overall planning director. Only a couple of weeks after taking part in the Brains Trust on equal pay he was killed when his home was demolished in one of the first V1 raids. The chess champion Vera Menchik and her sister Olga, who had each joined the Partnership during the war in research jobs, were killed by a direct V1 hit on their home in 1944. Hugh Alexander led the Gazette tributes from Bletchley Park.

As 1945 began some anxiety surfaced in the Partnership about the effect of home-coming servicemen on the existing workforce, particularly among women who were now in middle management positions. Spedan pointed out that inevitably the returnees' arrivals would be staggered, so he felt all could be accommodated. But he had several high-level reorganisation headaches. Few of the senior Partnership management had actually been killed, but the health of many had deteriorated due to the strain of the war years. In many ways those left behind to run the Partnership suffered more than those from top management positions who had joined the war effort. They were still young. Only Varyl Robinson, now knighted, was over sixty, and he came back as personnel director for a short time before retiring when he lost his hearing. In late 1945 Michael Watkins, still only forty-five, suffered a major breakdown in health and could only work part-time. Sebastian Earl was also in his forties at the end of the war, but was worn out, took extended leave, and eventually left in 1947. The chief accountant and council president Tom Robinson (there were two Robinsons) died in harness in 1946 at the age of fifty-two. The chief registrar Marion McEwan died the day after speaking at a Partnership council meeting in 1947. By 1948 the only one of Spedan's pre-war close entourage still with him full-time was Bernard Miller, who was in effect the last man standing.

In the immediate post-war years Spedan urgently set about replacing this 'lost generation', energetically but indiscriminately. He recruited a number of major figures who had held important jobs inside government and the forces during the war, but for several reasons most lasted only a short time. Some were lured back to government, some fell out with Spedan, some found commerce or the Partnership uncongenial, some had health breakdowns. Max Baker later said that Spedan recruited several apparent high-flyers from the Indian civil service, but hardly any could stand the insistent daily pressure of retailing. Gordon Welchman, a Bletchley Park colleague of Hugh Alexander, stayed two years before disappearing to academe in the United States. He had been research director. A new financial adviser, Major General Sir Charles King, lasted no longer, nor did a personnel director, a building director, and as many as four chief accountants in five years. Spedan was sixty in 1945 and over-anxious to get a new team in place, but his approach led to confusion and lack of continuity, and his tendency to pick and choose where he intervened was wearying for those who had to steer the business day to day. Though his Partnership constitution allowed a Chairman to continue till seventy-five, Spedan made it clear that seventy was his limit, which would take him to 1955. Even that seems old to us, but many leaders carried on well past everyone else's retirement age. Winston Churchill was already seventy at the end of the war, when so unceremoniously sent to the opposition backbenches by an electorate keen for the kind of reform that Beveridge had recommended. Moreover, he was Prime Minister at eighty and still an MP at ninety. His replacement as Prime Minister in 1945, his wartime deputy Clem Attlee, was himself two years older than Spedan. The balance of attraction between wisdom and charisma in our top politicians was very different in those days compared with our era of television exposure, aggressive interviewing and snappy sound bites.

## A Constitution, and Elected Board Members

At the end of the war Spedan completed his reworking of the Partnership's constitution, and assembled *Partnership For All*, a book to explain the

Partnership and its origins that was eventually published in 1948. He had decided to finalise the handover of his share of the business to the Partners, the process he'd begun in 1929. In 1942 he had recruited one of his wife's English tutors at Oxford, John Crofts, who for the previous twenty years had been an English professor at Bristol University. He wanted Crofts to do two things. The first was to start a new department, under someone he called the Partners' counsellor, which would hold a watching brief on behalf of the business over both the Partnership and the individual Partner. The second intention was to use Crofts to help in redrafting the constitution. It had evolved over the years as an aggregation of several articles, rules, regulations and job definitions, and he now wanted to present it in a more coherent form. Inside the front cover of Spedan's first book *Partnership For All* an elaborate diagram of the Partnership opens out, which the book goes on to explain. In contrast to much of Spedan's writings in the Gazette, *Partnership For All* was immensely readable. Often in the Gazette and in letters you have to reread his longer sentences (sometimes only once) to crack their meaning, so thick are they with multiple clauses and double or triple-negatives. He was an inspiring raconteur and speaker, who spoke what he thought and wrote what he spoke.

Trevor Fry, later an upholstery buyer, was one of the 'Bevin Boys', who worked down the coal mines as an alternative to war service. Spedan took him on in the mid-1940s after being impressed by a wartime article he'd written for the *Spectator* about primitive pit conditions in Kent. The eighteen-year-old Fry was summoned to Hampshire:

> I was picked up at the station in an old horse and carriage. We had lunch, where he and Beatrice had a quarrel over some obscure ornithological point. She gave as good as she got. He was an absolutely riveting man. You had to listen to every word and be totally direct and honest. Otherwise he'd play with you like a cat with a mouse, and every now and then he'd jump on you and ask a question out of the blue. His writings do sound terribly dull. But he had great delivery and pace – he could have been an old actor of the Shakespearean school.

Spedan's dutiful secretaries took it all down in shorthand and typed it as it was, and he seldom changed anything when it was typed up. *Partnership For All*, however, bears the unmistakable mark of another editorial hand, with sentences chopped up and ideas simply expressed. The book tells the story of how the Partnership came about from 1909 onwards, with engaging honesty that doesn't shirk from describing the family's tribulations at its beginning.

There was one key change from the pre-war Partnership. In June 1946 Spedan for the first time asked the Partnership council to elect five members to the Central Board. The election would be open to everyone, anywhere in the business, but in reality no one outside the Council was well enough known, and of the five eventually elected three were operational directors, one a general manager and one a buyer. Partners outside the management structure would eventually get elected, as Spedan wished, but not yet. What the Partnership had in 1946, then, was a board of twelve – Spedan, Beatrice (as deputy chairman), plus five members he appointed and five elected by the council. The five appointed members were in fact the holders of specific posts, from what he called the 'critical side', to distinguish them from the holders of operational posts. These 'critical' directors were a financial adviser, an internal auditor, a chief registrar, a Partners' counsellor, and a general inspector. They formed an elaborate safety net, watching over in turn finance, accounting probity, Partners' records everywhere, and the rights of the individual Partner, while the general inspector had a freewheeling role investigating anything that seemed to be misfiring. It's notable that these were the five Spedan appointed to the board. He *didn't* appoint operational directors, those running selling, buying, personnel, maintenance and expansion, financial operations and accountancy. This led to the Partnership council balancing things up by electing operational leaders, without any of the ordinary Partners that Spedan hoped might be there.

This 'critical side' looks over-elaborate to modern eyes (and to others at the time), but it was an early attempt at what is now today called 'corporate governance'. In that it was well ahead of its time. Many observers thought it a recipe for laborious decision-making, although one, writing in *Management Today* in the 1960s, compared it to President Kennedy's espousal of 'binocular vision' – two pairs of eyes give you a better focus. There was certainly potential for overlap and aggravation, especially in finance and personnel, but Spedan was determined, after his losses of key people, to 'double-bank' for safety. It meant that those who stayed past 1950 were those who could get on with each other and make the structure work, in particular Bernard Miller, Max Baker, Paul May and Elizabeth Barling. Baker succeeded Watkins as trading director. May and Barling were two more Oxford Firsts. May was an old Westminster School boy who Spedan had personally helped to pay his way through Oxford when his father's business collapsed. In the 1930s he'd been a contented silk buyer, then spent the war supervising the factories that turned silk into parachutes, and was surprised after it ended to find himself landing in the chair of the financial adviser. Elizabeth Barling, like her predecessor, brought to the chief registrar job considerable wartime industrial experience.

## An Under-Powered Business

Britain had been impoverished and almost bankrupted by the war. Rationing had to remain in place. One American observer, after spending a few days in London in 1946 on his way back home from Moscow, said that with their long queues and grey drabness there was very little difference between the two capital cities. The new Labour government's Welfare State, welcomed by Spedan, had to be paid for, as had the reconstruction of heavily bombed cities and of industries running on antiquated machinery. (As Germany was to discover, in the long run industries benefited by being forced to start afresh, helped by Marshall Aid money from the United States.) In Britain taxes rose, both on businesses and individuals, and there were shortages everywhere, not least of fuel in the frightful winter of 1946–7. But, worst of all for the Partnership, steel for rebuilding the bombed John Lewis was strictly rationed, and despite its lobbying the Partnership couldn't lift itself up the priority list. Their repeated requests for permission to acquire steel were turned down throughout Labour's postwar period in office.

One wonders if they tried to lobby a short-lived government minister, George Brown, later deputy prime minister. Brown was Minister of Works for six months before the Conservatives won the October 1951 election. Perhaps they didn't register that he'd been a Partner. Sacked from a previous job for trying to persuade fellow employees to join a union, he became a fur salesman and an energetic councillor in John Lewis Oxford Street from 1932 to 1937. He seems not to have tried union recruitment there; in a 1962 Gazette correspondence in which he sparred with Spedan he said:

> My time there left me with a conviction that the Partnership was mixing up ideals which I really liked with an unnecessary paternalism ... It's odd, but I still think of myself as a Partner. I'm rather proud to think that I was a member of it for so long.

With its crippled flagship barely paying its way in Oxford Street, how in the 1940s was Spedan's reconstructed team to drive the business forward, and deliver enough profit to start paying out a Bonus again? Although the purchase of the SPS chain had given the Partnership a substantial increase in dispersed selling space, it was the original John Lewis shop that had been the great motor of the business. Its sales had been more than double that of any other branch and its pre-bomb profit made up about a third of the whole Partnership's. But the steel to rebuild John Lewis was not released until 1955, and the reconstruction not complete until 1960, when the shop had shrunk back to the original west house. After much discussion they decided it was better to have a smaller shop, funded partly from the sale of the east house. So for twenty years the business was missing its great profit engine. The crucial measure of any business's success is profit, not sales – 'sales are vanity, profit is sanity' runs the old catch phrase. The average trading profit percentage in the Partnership's department stores in the 1940s and 1950s was around 8% of sales; in John Lewis itself it was less than half that. It was like an expensive car unable to exceed 30 mph.

From 1940 until the late 1950s John Lewis Oxford Street traded from a partially reconstructed east house, and in the west in an agglomeration of temporary buildings and space open to the elements. Robert Owen was a salesman in the garden furniture department. (As a foundling who never knew his parents, Owen had been named after the pioneering co-operative industrialist.) In 1940 he was a fifteen-year-old factory teaboy, living in a hostel in Albany Street. Woken on the night of the West End bombing, the curiosity of youth outweighing the danger, he walked down Great Portland Street and stood on the Oxford Street pavement opposite John Lewis as it blazed, 'chunks of shrapnel raining down on the street'. Owen remembers one early morning in the late 1940s, when he and his manager had manhandled the garden furniture out onto a levelled area of bomb site – as usual when the weather was fine – for customers passing down Oxford Street to amble round, when 'that vile black and green' Rolls Royce rolled to a halt, the window opened, and Spedan on a rare visit, said, 'Very nice stock – are you selling it for nothing?' Owen's manager had to explain that its price tickets were yet to be attached for the day. This was the state John Lewis was in right up to the second half of the 1950s, a struggling collection of separate buildings on a bomb site.

Immediately after the war, the Partnership had been able to resume an annual Bonus distribution after a gap of eight years. For 1946 and 1947 it was 6%, but then trade fell back – everywhere, not just in the Partnership – and there was another lean period of five years without a Bonus. Between 1947 and 1952 total sales only increased by 11% in real terms, and what free profit there was went into the new pension fund. This was especially galling to Spedan. As one competitor put it: 'They talk endlessly about sharing their profit, but there's none to share.' At this time, and right into the 1970s, the business couldn't raise money on the financial markets, so everything had to be funded out of the retained profit. There was no spare money for refreshing tired shops.

## Totalitarians in the Partnership?

There was a constant low-key background murmuring of grumbles in the Gazette after the war. Spedan, now in his sixties, responded with increasing irritation and occasional splenetic outbursts. The Partnership got itself into a fearful tangle in 1949 over communists. It was a reasonable question, for a co-owned business with a strong democratic element, to ask whether those holding anti-democratic, 'totalitarian', views merited membership. Communism in its original meaning of 'citizens holding everything in common' would not necessarily have been anathema to a partnership of producers. Spedan in fact before the war had been attracted by the theory of Russia's commonly owned businesses, which did at first have a measure of democracy. But he was soon repelled by the dictatorial reality; in the immediate postwar period a series of Soviet-sponsored coups resulted in a swathe of Eastern Europe taken over by communists who had not been democratically elected. Moreover, in Britain at the time there were several attempts by communists to infiltrate the leadership of trade unions, some successful, and the Soviet Union made no secret of its desire to bring down the governments of Western Europe from within.

In early 1949, following alarm caused by an impassioned and intemperate speech by a communist Partner in a secret council session, Spedan asked the council to consider whether the Partnership should exclude totalitarians – communists and fascists – from membership. He didn't think the issue through properly himself before passing it to them, and he paid the price – he said later he'd set a stone in motion and caused an avalanche. After an uncharacteristic series of drafting blunders and sloppy thinking the Council voted to exclude communists, but in a separate motion decided *not* to do so for fascists. Further, they blithely proposed to ask existing and new members to sign an undertaking that they were not communists and did not have communist sympathies. With a Conservative MP as its president at the time, Colin Thornton-Kemsley, the council had walked into a horrible trap.

Spedan immediately asked them to reconsider the fascist question, and at their next meeting they added fascists to the embargo, but the damage was done. With the story blazoned all over the Gazette in its usual detail, customers, journalists and MPs (of every shade) wrote forthright letters of disgust, 400 in all in the following weeks. Are you fascist sympathisers? Don't you remember why we just fought a war? Chief registrar Elizabeth Barling wrote Spedan a withering critique of the council decision: 'It was painful to see how easily fear and hatred could be fanned into acceptance of a proposal as devoid of commonsense as of charity'. She doubtless regretted her own failure to speak in the debate – she had left it to Professor Crofts. How can we possibly know if any such undertaking signed by a Partner is genuine, she asked? As Prime Minister Attlee had wryly put it: 'Someone who is contemplating high treason is unlikely to boggle about an oath.' Spedan tried to tread a dignified path through the mess, but the mud clung to his ankles. Eventually the furore died down, and six months later he revealed that just one single person had been dismissed from the Partnership as a consequence (and it wasn't the man whose speech had started it all).

It had all been terrible publicity, smacking for some of the McCarthy witch-hunt for communists in the United States, which had begun in 1947. Spedan, far from having his Partnership system admired as he wished, was finding it criticised from both sides of the political divide. The Labour Party in government, heavily subsidised by the trade unions, saw it as anti-union, and were not disposed to help when the Partnership petitioned for the steel to rebuild John Lewis. The Conservatives were suspicious of a business that they saw as clearly anti-capitalist. The Liberals, who might have been sympathetic, were struggling on with just a dozen MPs. However much Spedan said that he was in favour of trade unions as long as they were democratically elected, he wasn't believed. At the start of 1948 he'd reiterated that trade unionism has done 'enormous good' and was 'still very much needed', before going on to deplore its excesses, which included unions competing against each other in the same industry, and union officials seeking power for themselves. In fact later that year some drivers at Clearings, the Peter Jones warehouse and transport depot in Chelsea, had asked once more if they could join the TGWU (the Transport and General Workers Union). Yes, of course, as long as you hold a secret ballot among the drivers. They did, they voted for it, and Spedan accepted the decision with a good grace. Ironically, at the end of 1949 the TGWU *itself* decided to require all its 560 officials to sign a similar undertaking that they were not communists, and sacked the nine who refused.

Spedan was glad to see the end of the 1940s. In 1950, the year he reached sixty-five, he would finalise one outstanding issue, his settlement with the Partnership, and would tackle another: the identity of his successor, over which he had been brooding for some time.

CHAPTER 12

# The Fractious Fifties

**Spedan at the council meeting on the day of his retirement, 22 September 1955, his seventieth birthday. Bernard Miller is standing on the right, behind the flowers.**

What is the Chairman to do? As little as possible. That is the essence of the plan. In theory the Partnership should get along perfectly well without any Chairman.

SPEDAN LEWIS'S FIRST WORDS IN HIS CHAPTER ON THE CHAIRMANSHIP, IN *PARTNERSHIP FOR ALL*, 1948

I think when history is written it will be said paradoxically that Spedan Lewis was the only man who could not have run his own constitution.

LAWRENCE NEAL, FROM A SPEECH AT THE PARTNERSHIP COUNCIL DINNER FOLLOWING SPEDAN'S DEATH, SEPTEMBER 1963

The Gazette of 29 April 1950 contained a nine-page supplement explaining the details of the 'Final Settlement' and its 1929 forerunner, the articles of the constitution, together with some explanatory notes. Spedan explained that he'd originally intended to wait only about ten years from 1929 before finalising the settlement, but the war's disruption inevitably delayed it. It's expressed as an exchange of promises between Spedan and the Partners. He undertakes to hand over to them his controlling share, in exchange for a promise that the Partnership will continue to be conducted as he had laid down. Bernard Miller later summed up the two legal stages in simple terms:

> The first settlement established that the *profit* belonged to the workers. The second settlement established that the *property* of the business belonged to the workers. A very important step forward.

## The Succession

Spedan may have handed the business over in trust for the Partners, but he still saw himself as its monarch: 'It is a constitutional monarchy, with as much as seemed safe of democracy and correspondingly little of monarchy.' But he was still a king, one with far more powers than any since James II. He was one who expected to retire in five years time to become a wise old adviser, but a monarch nonetheless. And monarchs don't usually abdicate willingly. Who should succeed him? Of those outside his family, Michael Watkins had clearly been the preferred choice, but his illness had gradually worsened. Spedan was assiduous in finding ways to reduce the strain and keep him going part-time from the wartime home he'd found for him in Leckford, but in late November of 1950 he died. The news came in a telegram from Spedan as a Partnership council meeting was about to start. The meeting was abandoned, with members in shock and tears, one saying, 'This is the worst news the Partnership has ever had.' Any lingering hope Spedan had that Watkins might ever become well enough to take over the Chairmanship had vanished long before, and now he decided to announce his successor as Chairman.

The safe pair of hands of Bernard Miller was the obvious default option. Calm and unemotional, with a quick mind and a prodigious appetite for work, he had been a key player as director of estimates for ten years. He was now a committed Partnership man living down at Odney with his family, and would be fifty-one in 1955. Was he the man? Spedan still had one surviving son, Edward, and he'd become increasingly keen on the idea of starting him in the Partnership and encouraging him to take over in five years' time. After studying Law at Oxford, Edward went to work in the hardware department of the partial bomb site that was John Lewis. He was known to be uneasy about a job in his father's Partnership. Robert Owen, the man who as a lad had watched the shop burn down, became a friend of Edward's when they were both selling assistants. Owen asked him once if he wanted to become Chairman one day. Edward made a face and intimated that his life had been dominated by the Partnership since the day he was born, and he had serious doubts about whether that was what he wanted for the rest of it. His twenty-first birthday had been celebrated in July 1950 with big parties at Odney and Leckford, almost as if he was the crown prince of Spedan's 'constitutional monarchy'. Six months later, a few days before Christmas 1950, Spedan wrote in the Gazette that he had conducted a long conversation with his son in which he offered him the Chairmanship after his own retirement in 1955. He said that Edward asked for the night to think it over, and the following morning had declined it (this conversation in fact took place the previous August).

Spedan ends the piece by hoping that since Edward would be forty when Bernard Miller retired he might yet take over. Yet for Spedan, as he wrote much later: 'It was a bitter renunciation of a lifelong hope.' Whether Edward ever seriously entertained the prospect of becoming Chairman is extremely doubtful. Since the age of ten he'd seen the business fight its way through first the bad luck of the war and the bombing, and later the really tough post-war period of rationing and shortages. Did he want that heavy responsibility? In the end he decided to become a lawyer, and was eventually called to the Bar. By an odd coincidence so was his cousin Peter, Oswald's son, on the very same day, 8 February 1956. By then it seemed more than likely that Spedan would be the last Lewis to be associated with the John Lewis Partnership.

From 1951 onward Bernard Miller, formally deputy chairman, was virtually acting as Chairman, while Spedan stayed largely in Longstock House. Longstock was the larger house across the Test valley that Spedan had moved to from Leckford – so he now had two villages. (For his health Spedan had taken to wintering in South Africa. While there he had decided that the Partnership should as an experiment open a chain of small drapery shops in Capetown and Johannesburg. However good the prospect looked at the time, the long supply chains to England, and the abrupt change in South Africa's policy to one of apartheid, the pernicious 'separate development' of the races, rapidly turned it into a failure.) In 1951, after the Conservatives regained power, Bernard Miller had another attempt via his friend Sir Wavell Wakefield, Conservative MP and a renowned former England rugby captain, to extract some steel from the government's tight clutches to start the rebuilding of John Lewis Oxford Street. Miller thought the Partnership was being unfairly treated, and told Wakefield:

> From 1945 to 1951 we recognised that factories and housing reconstruction would take priority. But the rebuilding of shops is now under way outside London, notably in Liverpool, Southampton and Plymouth, and it seemed reasonable to hope that we should be given a licence. We applied in July 1951 but

were refused. Now nearly two years later £10m has been appropriated for the rebuilding of the City, with greatly improved prospects for steel supply. So we made another approach last week and were met with a blank refusal.

Wakefield tried the Ministry of Works but still had no joy. What was worse was that, with the cost of building rising by 9% each year, the replacement cost was now three times as high as the original estimate. By the time they did eventually get started, in 1955, the cost was four times as much. Other price inflation had only doubled. In the end it came in at £7m, the equivalent of £130m in 2010. It might have been higher still had Bernard Miller not responded in alarm to Spedan's suggestion to ask the famous French modernist architect Le Corbusier to design it: 'At his age? Has he done anything like that before?'

One of the Parnership's lobbyists in this period, with experience in the City of London and with a long record on parliamentary committees, was the new part-time financial operations director, appointed in the same month, December 1950, that Edward declined the Chairmanship. He was sixty-three, and while no stranger to the business he had not been part of it for nearly forty years. It was Oswald Lewis. He came to join his brother's 'strange crew' at a time when the Partnership's finances were seriously stretched. He had been a casualty of the Labour election landslide of 1945, and as he was hardly working flat out he agreed to Spedan's request to return part-time. But he couldn't yet extract any steel from the government, and for Spedan this inability to rebuild was especially galling, because his London competitors had emerged from the war unscathed. He had, incidentally, concluded that the Oxford Street shop had been the victim of its proximity to the BBC headquarters in Langham Place, a key German target – the Langham Hotel and the Queen's Hall had been hit in the same week as John Lewis in Oxford Street. In one tetchy article he railed at the decision to plant the BBC there, instead of half a mile away in the middle of Regents Park, where the bombs could have dropped harmlessly. He didn't sound as if he was joking.

## The Korean War Crisis – and Another Pay Cut

Although there was no repetition of the mass unemployment at the end of World War I, trade in Britain continued to be difficult at the start of the 1950s. Despite the return of members of the forces to work, and a consequent baby boom, there was no boost to trade. Rationing was still there, money and supplies were short, and Spedan's temper shorter still. The test came in early 1952, when it gradually became clear that the Partnership was suddenly doing worse than its competitors. After limping along for five years a couple of percent above inflation, Partnership sales plummeted by 8% in the second half of 1951. Spedan came back from an extended five-month winter holiday in South Africa to find the situation grave. How had it happened? There were two things. In sticking rigorously to its policy of wide assortment and solid value, the Partnership had lost sales. Its trade had been taken by competitors who recognised that a new generation with homes to furnish, young mouths to feed, and pay packets reduced by higher taxes, were obliged to buy cheap and cared less than their parents had about how long products would last.

As the war in Korea, begun in 1950, reached stalemate, a flood of hitherto embargoed products began to arrive from the Far East. Wholesale prices dropped sharply, and the Partnership was caught napping in early 1952 with substantial stocks of fabrics that they had to sell at a loss with massive mark-downs. They wouldn't have been caught, had the usual warning systems worked. 'Merchandise advisers' had been planted in each buying group to ensure that buyers didn't overspend their 'purchase ration'. Eric Pearce (later a buying director himself) saw what was happening and warned the overall buying director Max Baker of the danger, but said, 'He didn't do anything till it was too late – I think he was worried that the Chairman wouldn't be keen.' Everyone was under pressure – Baker himself was in the middle of a two-year period in which he took no holiday at all. Baker later asserted that he had tried to persuade Spedan of the need to abandon its assortment and pricing policies temporarily, but couldn't budge him.

When he arrived back from South Africa at the end of March 1952 Spedan found a long paper on the trading prospects from the financial adviser, Paul May, and summoned his team to Longstock. It was a grim discussion: the 1951 profit was only £250,000 against an estimate of £600,000, and almost all of that had to go to the pension fund and to reserves. As a mitigating circumstance Spedan explained in the Gazette that the Partnership's tax bill for 1952 was estimated to be £262,000, whereas it had been just £10,000 in 1938, a measure of how much company tax bills had rocketed because of legislation during the war and afterwards. At the beginning of 1952 a pay freeze had been imposed, and he warned Partners that another mandatory pay cut might prove necessary for those earning more than £1,000 a year, but we'd wait and see how the figures panned out after the spring. They worsened: sales for the first half-year of 1952 were 18% lower than those for a year earlier. At the end of June Spedan announced that they would have to cut £165,000 from the paysheet, a drop of nearly 5%, by means of a 'general decrease'. This would take the form of a temporary pay cut from August 1952, skewed so that it would be:

20% for those with an annual salary of over £2,000 (around £54,000 today)
15% for those earning above £1,000 (£27,000)
10% for those earning above £600 (£16,000)
5% for those earning £600 or less, unless on the Partnership minimum wage or a negotiated union pay scale.

In the event, national wage council rises, sanctioned by the government soon afterwards, fortunately meant that the 5% cut for those on low wages was never implemented. The effect therefore was that the cut hit the higher earners disproportionately. For those with over seven years' service zero-interest hardship loans would be available. Whether these cuts would count as 'deferred pay', paid back later as the voluntary wartime cuts had been, was left open by Spedan for later debate. He stressed that it was out of the question to cut the dividends of shareholders (most of them Partners, of course, though some original ones still remained) or to raid the Pension Fund. He anticipated a call to save on Partnership amenities – things like subsidised dining rooms and the Odney Club – by pointing out that if they were cut completely it would save just 1.5% of the paysheet, about £55,000, of which the taxman would take nearly half. The argument in favour of cutting amenities rather than touching pay had been expressed wittily in the Gazette in a letter written as a calypso by someone calling himself 'Rum Jamaican' in February 1953. It expressed what a lot of people felt about the Partnership's amenities, which while available to everyone, were seen to be aimed at a few, middle management working in London and the Home Counties, and essentially elitist. This was its final verse:

Bad times will cut out bonuses, but glad and calm we feel,
For we're subsidising Glyndebourne, and that clever boy, Boyd Neel,
And I'll work like twenty Partners while Leckford Abbas stays
For the fishermen of England to have peaceful holidays.

In 1949 Spedan had been instrumental in saving John Christie's open-air operas at Glyndebourne in Sussex, by means of a seven-year covenant to cover losses up to a maximum of £12,500, and by guaranteeing that the Partnership would take a large number of seats each year. These were then balloted for by Partners at half price, the same discount they could get for tickets to the theatre, another pastime seen as elitist. Boyd Neel was the leader of a professional orchestra which had been engaged at the beginning of 1951 to give a concert for London Partners each month. Leckford Abbas, Spedan's Hampshire home until he moved across the River Test to the grander Longstock House on the other side, was now available for any Partner to stay at rates comparable to Odney's. While there they could fish in the Test, a famous trout river where fishing permits were eagerly sought. Leckford and its fishing were open to anyone at very reasonable rates, but not 'anyone' went, only experienced fishermen. That was the problem. One Partnership councillor irritated Spedan by pointing out that 'an amenity associated with a privileged class' had a bad effect on morale. Although Spedan was adamant that these activities were subsidised and priced to be within the reach of the ordinary Partner, he can hardly have been surprised by that statement, or by

Rum Jamaican's sly verse and other exhortations to 'cut amenities first, pay second'. He replied intemperately to the calypso, as did the part-time Gazette editor, his daughter Jill, who at twenty-five was beginning a trial period in the Partnership. Her trenchant dismissal of Rum Calypso's doggerel incited a further rash of letters – a lesson that all Gazette editors learnt the hard way. Make sure it's not petrol in the hose that you use to douse the flames.

After a month, which allowed time for more antipathy to the pay cut in letters to the Gazette and to Spedan himself, notably from two members of the previous Labour government, Jennie Lee and Mannie Shinwell, the Partnership council met at the end of July 1952. This time they were better prepared. The financial adviser Paul May proposed a series of options for amenity cuts. In the event it was a sensible debate, steered briskly by Oswald Lewis, its new president, who had stepped down as financial operations director and would hold the council presidency for a further ten years. He enjoyed it – it was like having his own parliament. The council voted in turn by decent margins to halve the expenditure on Odney (closing some of the holiday houses); not however to touch the camp at Leckford, used almost entirely by the lower-paid; to end the Boyd Neel arrangement entirely; *not* to reduce any social subsidies such as for Glyndebourne, theatres, concerts and branch societies, but to abandon the annual in-house opera; to halve the education budget; and to reduce its own council expenditure. It ended, against Paul May's mild opposition, with a vote to recommend to the Chairman that the pay cut should be a deferment, and hence repaid.

In the end Spedan and his team managed the pay cut well, and after the following Christmas it was repealed, and everyone moreover was repaid the amount they'd lost *plus* 5% interest. But he was tired and ill, so was Beatrice, and he began to lose patience with his detractors. To writers questioning the leadership of a business that had performed so badly that it was forced to cut pay when its competitors were (comparatively) thriving, he reiterated the fearful effect of the 1940 bomb, among other things. But the more forthright he was, the more emboldened were his detractors, who fired off further letters, including this derisive observation:

> Reading Spedan Lewis is like watching a three-ring circus, or perhaps a melodrama where the identity of the villain is in doubt till the end. Unfortunately at this stage the villain is still a bit of a mystery. The character with the highest number of black marks, however, is the bomb that would not have hit John Lewis had the BBC been in Regents Park, but Joe Stalin and Clem Atlee run it a close second ... The impression is growing ... that our much-vaunted Partnership is just a rich man's toy and the council just a crumbling façade.

Unpleasant, but with that little grain of truth that gets under the skin. But soon Spedan was devastated by something far worse, the death of his wife Beatrice. Spedan, in the pre-war days when he was uncertain how long his health would hold out, often spoke of her as a possible successor as Chairman. Quite apart from being the person with whom Spedan discussed his ideas, she had always been active in Partnership affairs. In the 1930s, as well as formally being the Partnership's deputy chairman, she had been a pioneering member of several women's organisations. Particularly keen on the theatre, she had directed, reviewed, and generally encouraged the pre-war Partnership plays and revues, and had helped to resuscitate the Partnership's dramatic society after the war. She produced its first postwar revue in 1947, and in 1951 directed their production of Granville-Barker's powerful play *The Voysey Inheritance*. The cast included their daughter Jill and the name part was played by Peter Yaghmourian, later a buyer, who recalled how delightful Beatrice was to work with. In December 1952 she had been well (and game) enough to play the substantial part of Mrs Conway in JB Priestley's time-slip play *Time and the Conways*. It was a profound shock to everyone and a dreadful blow to Spedan when she died of cancer in June 1953.

Since they'd married he had rarely been without her; now she was gone and Jill and Edward were mostly away in London, so he was very often alone. As Chairman he could summon people down to Longstock to discuss issues with him. He expected that to continue after his retirement. That in the event it didn't was a cause of sadness and puzzlement, and ultimately a growing bitterness. He later said in a letter:

> I was stunned by the loss, so utterly unexpected and in so terrible a way, of the wife to whom in our last years together I said more than once I could be well content to spend any years that might remain to me on a desert island with no company but hers.

For now, though, Spedan was able to preside over a recovery that began that same year, 1953. That was the year that signalled the end of postwar austerity. The coronation of the young Queen Elizabeth seemed to give a lift to the nation's spirits, helped by the first ascent of Mount Everest, by a British-led team, and (even more difficult) the recapture of the cricket Ashes from Australia. At the start of 1954, after seven dismal years, Spedan was able to announce a Bonus of 4%, modest enough but psychologically important, not least for him. With 8% in the following two years he was at least able to go out on a comparative high. In the following fifty-five years it only dropped below 8% once, when it was 7% in 1958. After the terrible war years, the grim post-war struggle, the dangerous days of 1952, and the abject misery of 1953, he could at least hand the Chairmanship over in 1955 to Bernard Miller with the Partnership back in reasonable order. And Oxford Street had just got its steel at last.

## Bernard Miller and a Short-lived Honeymoon

Bernard Miller took over on Spedan's seventieth birthday on 22 September 1955, marked by an event at the Central Hall, Westminster full of gracious speeches and much warmth. A month later the staged demolition of the John Lewis west house began, kicking off the Miller chairmanship with a long-delayed feeling of renewal. Little changed apart from that – Miller's hallmark was careful long-term planning and steady evolutionary change. The annual Bonus remained at 8%, Spedan kept writing to the Gazette: if not so frequently and extensively as before, he still had plenty to say, and he was accorded space whenever he wanted it. It had been ever thus and his successor wasn't going to deny him that privilege. Spedan appeared each year at September's annual Partnership council dinner and would give the first speech each time, and propose a toast to the Chairman. In 1957 he ended by telling his audience that they seemed to be doing very well indeed, and interposed merrily when Bernard Miller told the story of a journalist misnaming him as Mr Spender Lewis: 'My father when he heard it roared with approbation.' Spedan's speech was followed that night by one from Lord Shackleton, son of the famous Antarctic explorer and a retired Labour MP, installed in Spedan's last months as the Partnership's first male chief registrar. Shackleton had worked for the BBC, and said Spedan bore a striking resemblance to its founder Lord Reith: two highly original creative minds with a distinctively pungent writing style. He might have added their commanding physical presence and their inability to suffer fools gladly. In 1958 Spedan was again charmingly entertaining and polite, apologising at the outset to those who would have heard his stories before, advising them to stave off boredom: 'Take to drink so far as you have not already done so sufficiently.'

But in 1959 the trouble started. Wide-ranging letters began appearing from 'Allesina', anonymous, but the content, style and punctuation were manifestly Spedan's. Similar letters arrived from a (far from) 'Benevolent Onlooker'. It's unclear what triggered it, but his contention was that the Partnership was not expanding fast enough. The underlying problem was that he felt neglected: he was used to being asked for sage advice which was listened to and acted on, and it wasn't happening any more. He had offered it, but the Partnership – his creation, his child – listened politely but no longer sought it. He began to feel he shouldn't have retired until he was seventy-five, in 1960. What began as a bee in his bonnet became before long a fizzing of angry hornets. He blamed himself for letting go too soon, and increasingly he found reasons to criticise Bernard Miller. Miller's son Michael remembers: 'Those endless phone conversations my father had with Spedan; my father was so patient – but firm with him.' Without telling Miller, several of his team went down to Longstock individually in turn to attempt to persuade Spedan to desist. They made little headway.

At the 1959 council dinner, with his brother in the chair as its President as usual, Spedan gave an obscure and melancholy speech without exhibiting outright hostility. But he brooded on, and in June 1960 the affair turned into a very public shambles, which shocked alike those who revered Spedan and those who supported his successor – and most did both. Spedan now trained his guns on management rates of pay, which he felt were decidedly too low to attract the best people. He had always been prepared to pay really well for talented people. Perhaps they were too low, but Miller had turned his attention first to the lower-paid. Spedan then demanded that the Partnership council debate two motions, put on his behalf on 18 July: a woolly proposal that the Chairman should consult his predecessor more, and a concrete one proposing that Spedan should have up to a *quarter* of the Gazette set aside for him. But Spedan hadn't exactly endeared himself to all but his ardent supporters by being interviewed for the *Daily Express* the week before. In a piece headed ON THE SHELF he spoke with sadness about being 'shut out of his own firm'. Not surprisingly his proposals were sorrowfully but decisively defeated by 89 votes to 10 and 81 to 6. What other company would do anything similar in such an appallingly public manner? Bernard Miller wrote a dignified endorsement of the decision the following week, emphasising that he would continue to reply to Spedan's letters and publish what his predecessor wished. His more-in-sorrow-than-anger conduct seems almost saintly, and cemented the respect in which he was now held within the business. Spedan was allowed to follow with six pages of self-justification, shot through with words like 'bitterly', but he had shot his bolt, at least in public.

He didn't appear at the Partnership council dinner in September 1960 and Oswald began proceedings at an event which he called 'Hamlet without the Prince', and finished with diplomatic remarks about both Spedan and Bernard Miller. All seemed to have blown over, but Spedan did appear again in 1961, still spoiling for a fight, ending accurately enough with 'I intended to get into mischief tonight and I think I have,' and once more at the 1962 dinner. At both meetings a deeply uncomfortable Oswald, unable to restrain his elder brother, continued to preside, and Bernard Miller remained outwardly imperturbable. What each year's distinguished guest speaker thought of it all can be readily imagined. 1962 was the last such meeting at which the retiring Oswald and the unrepentant Spedan appeared. 'You are playing the fool with my life-work and breaking my heart', he said. He died the following February at the age of seventy-seven, in the house he'd retreated to in Longstock village – he'd given his old home to the Partnership's Chairman in perpetuity – and his ashes were scattered at sea.

It was a distressing way to end. Spedan's life-work had been a long battle to bring a brilliant idea to fruition against all the slings and arrows that fortune bombarded him with. As his nephew Peter Lewis later said, 'He acted decisively in real life where so many men only talk and dream.' The Gazette in the week after his death repeated his comment, 'The Partnership is not only something to live by, it is something to live for.' A man who had been his PA in the 1930s said: 'I was staggered at his clarity, vigour, humour and humanity, and at the interest, enthusiasm and affection he excited.' Beatrice, who was a clear-sighted critic, had said of him that she 'had known many people to be kind but knew of no one who took greater trouble over their kindnesses.' Spedan dispensed such kindnesses quietly – many turn up unexpectedly in his letters to Partners – and it led to a Partnership tradition of 'random acts of kindness' that often broke through the careful rules set up for dealing with hardship.

If only Spedan could have retired with dignity and watched his Partnership prosper again, as it was beginning to do. Three months after Spedan's two demands to the Council had been rejected in 1960 John Lewis Oxford Street had fully re-opened. The shop, labouring painfully since 1940, now began to move ahead with remarkable speed. From 1960 to 1965 its sales doubled, as they might well have done in any hands. But in that time its profit had increased by a factor of more than five. That astonishing result was down to one man, a hard-nosed disciple of Spedan's trading methods who had joined the Partnership from school in 1929 at the age of sixteen, doing day-to-day, minute-by-minute on the selling floor what no Oxford First or military hero could manage to the same degree. They could organise, plan, debate, and make farsighted decisions, but few of them had the combination of knowledge, instinct and sheer bloody-mindedness to get right down to the basics to make a big shop work to full capacity. To modernise John Lewis, Bernard Miller knew that you needed someone who, like Spedan, would 'act decisively, not just talk and dream'. Miller made his most important trading appointment – he called up Stanley Carter.

ABOVE: John Lewis still burning the day after the 1940 bombing.
RIGHT: Pedestrians in Oxford Street after a small part had reopened.
BELOW LEFT: The devastation in the basement.
BELOW RIGHT: Partners with potential customers outside the burnt-out shop.

ABOVE: A council meeting of 1948, Michael Watkins presiding.
LEFT: Spedan with his successor Bernard Miller and his wife.
BELOW LEFT: Spedan inspects a new sailing club yacht in 1955.
BELOW RIGHT: Spedan returning from abroad in April 1955.

# The rebuilding of the Oxford Street shop from 1955–60

ABOVE: The single storey shop at the Holles Street junction.
RIGHT: The new building under construction later in the year.
BELOW LEFT: Clearing rubble in front of a (long-lived) temporary hangar.
BELOW RIGHT: Part of the 'west house' was still a hole in the ground when Peter Lewis joined in 1959.

ABOVE: The Odney potter John Bew with his team, c 1950.
RIGHT: Spedan's optimistic early plan for Odney.
BELOW LEFT: Robert Sayle of Peterborough, destroyed by fire in 1956.
BELOW RIGHT: The Partnership Ball at the Royal Albert Hall in 1956.

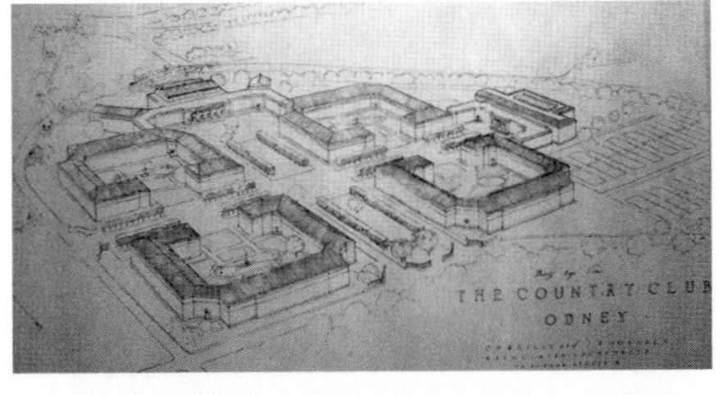

## Post-war Waitrose

ABOVE: The first custom-built supermarket at Streatham, before opening in 1955.
LEFT: A pre-conversion interior at Leigh-on-Sea in 1951.
BELOW LEFT: The interior of a 1950s Waitrose converted to self-service.
BELOW: Another Waitrose Slough promotion from the early 1960s, before Stanley Carter. It's hard to believe now that Waitrose used to be like that, so startlingly different from the understated John Lewis of the time.

ABOVE, RIGHT and BELOW LEFT are from sketches from the 1954 revue, which show the selling floor and office dress then current.
BOTTOM RIGHT: The year 2000 revival Never Knowingly Understood – 'What has Spedan ever done for us?'

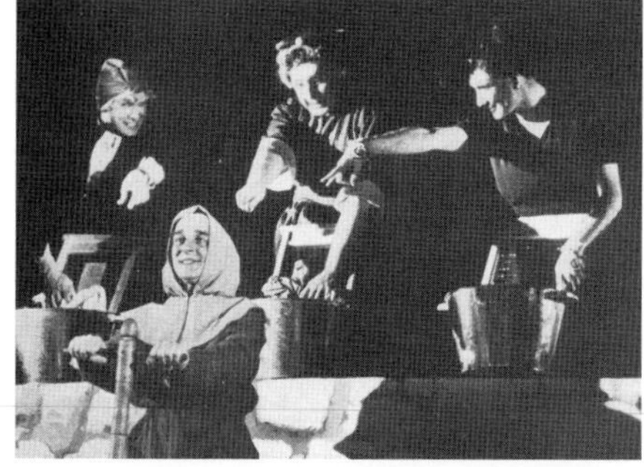

ABOVE LEFT: Barbara Hepworth beneath her sculpture for the Holles Street corner in 1963 before – ABOVE RIGHT – it is hoisted into place.
BELOW LEFT: The sculpture in position.
BELOW CENTRE: The old JLP symbol.
BELOW RIGHT: An early advert for John Lewis TV and radio.

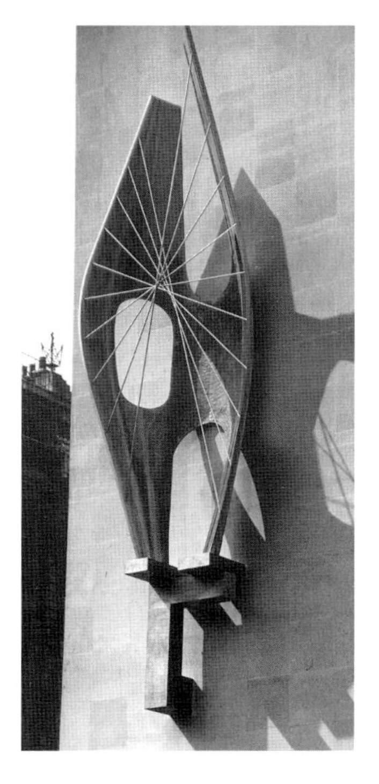

## Some key figures from the late 1930s

ABOVE: Michael Watkins.
RIGHT: Hugh Alexander, the British chess champion.
BELOW LEFT: Sebastian Earl.
BELOW RIGHT: Old grocers meet up in 1963. Wallace Waite front centre, with among others Harold Tobias and Harold Tickner.

ABOVE LEFT: George, last of the retailing Bainbridges, beneath the portrait of its founder Emerson Muschamp Bainbridge.
ABOVE RIGHT: The 'Bevin Boy' Trevor Fry with the future playwright Peter Shaffer.
RIGHT: Roy Jenkins, working at the Partnership before becoming a cabinet minister.
BELOW: Muriel Ward Jackson and Max Baker.

## Long-serving leading figures of the 1970s and 80s

TOP LEFT: Ian Anderson, management services director, then John Lewis MD.
TOP RIGHT: John Foster, Waitrose MD.
BOTTOM LEFT: Harry Legg, research and expansion director.
BOTTOM RIGHT: John Sadler, finance director.

## Caricatures from the Gazette reports of Partnership council meetings in the early 1980s

Ian Bassett

Harry Tossell

David Ramsey

David Stevens

John Stott

John James

## Personnel Directors and Chief Registrars from the 1980s and 90s

TOP: Two generations – Stephen May, long-serving personnel director, with his father Paul May, a major post-war figure.
ABOVE LEFT: Dudley Cloake, management services director, Partners' counsellor and personnel director.
ABOVE CENTRE: Ken Temple, chief-registrar and Partners' counsellor.
ABOVE RIGHT: Ian Alexander, personnel director, who was finance director and deputy chairman when he died in 2005.

Three long-serving councillors. TOP: Terry Stredder, who followed his father on to the Council. LEFT: David Jones, former board member, who became council president in 2010. BELOW LEFT: Anne Buckley, board member in 2010. BELOW RIGHT: Noel Saunders, the MD at Oxford Street who oversaw its recent massive refurbishment.

## Four of the Partnership's appointed board members in 2010

TOP LEFT: Marisa Cassoni, finance director.
TOP RIGHT: David Barclay, a non-executive director made deputy chairman in 2007.
BOTTOM LEFT: Andy Street, John Lewis MD.
BOTTOM RIGHT: Patrick Lewis, great-grandson of John, Partners' counsellor.

CHAPTER 13

# Reaping the Whirlwind – Stanley Carter

One Christmas Eve there was a crisis in one of the other departments. We were slack in furniture so I went over to cover. Stanley Carter saw me there and exploded. 'You're sacked. Leave the building immediately.' I stayed, but made myself scarce if I saw him coming. He seemed to be everywhere that day, but then he always was. Anyway, as we were closing down he came past and I couldn't avoid him. 'Night, Withers. Happy Christmas. See you on Tuesday.' So I had a Christmas after all.

STAN WITHERS, CHRISTMAS EVE AT HEELAS OF READING, 1950s

He was a legend in his lifetime. He was more akin to Spedan than any of us.

MAX BAKER, CARTER'S DIRECTOR OF TRADING WHEN HE WAS AT OXFORD STREET, 1973

A cynical retailing historian in 1955 might have summarised the Partnership like this. A successful established department store in Oxford Street, set up in 1864 by a self-made man on simple but robust trading principles, is taken over by his son over sixty years later. The son is a curious cove, with the lofty – but dangerously socialist – ideal of creating out of this successful shop a business empire for its employees and an ideas playground for himself. He spends money liberally on his staff and on expansion, extends rapidly in the 1930s but over-stretches. In that period he acquires four failing businesses in the provinces, three of which are on the coast, rebuilds his own Peter Jones store at great expense, and more than doubles the size of the original Oxford Street shop. By the end of 1940 this shop lies in ruins, as do two of the three coastal shops (and the other is hit in 1942). When he retires in 1955 his much-vaunted Partnership has only five times in the past eighteen years paid an annual Bonus for its long-suffering employees, who he insists on calling Partners as though they were his equals. An equality only of misery perhaps, for they enjoyed an average annual Bonus of under 2% in that period. And all this by insisting on running the business with a coterie of Oxbridge graduates good at passing exams in exotic but impractical subjects but with no prior retailing experience, and a handful of distinguished military men (ditto). Hardly a proper retailer among them. All right, he was unlucky with the Oxford Street bomb, but a good general makes his own luck, doesn't he? And here we are in 1955 and the expensive Oxford Street rebuild hasn't even begun yet. How long will that take?

That's by no means an unreasonable conclusion in 1955. But by the time of Miller's retirement in 1972 there had been a transformation. It was done with more contraction than expansion, and by taking John and Spedan Lewis's principles and applying them with imagination, intelligence, and a painstaking (and pains-giving) attention to detail. On Bernard Miller's unobtrusive but steely watch in that period were three key men. One was Max Baker, an experienced retailer when he arrived in 1932; the second, Paul May, had become one since arriving from university in 1932. The third made himself one under Spedan's eye in Oxford Street from the moment he joined as a sixteen-year-old school leaver in 1929, Stanley Carter. It was in 1955 that Carter returned from an unwise two-year spell at Selfridges, bringing back a recharged respect for the Partnership. We'll look at the wider picture, and the May and Baker contributions, in Chapter 15, but this chapter is about Carter and his revitalisation of Oxford Street. It will contain only about a quarter of the stories that are told about him. We'll go back to the beginning of his career, because it gives us a chance to track one individual through four difficult Partnership decades and into the safe haven of the 1970s.

## Carter Before Oxford Street

Stanley Carter was a paradox, a man who was a success in the Partnership despite, and some would say because of, the fact that he was a bully who broke all the unwritten rules of Partnership behaviour in his dealings with people. He would either inspire you or destroy you: there seemed to be no middle ground. 'Respect' in its modern usage he granted if he thought you were good at your job, and only then. He was born in 1912, the son of an upholsterer father and a mother who had worked at Court as a dressmaker, practical and exacting parents with a feeling for fabrics. He had started at Peter Jones at sixteen in the summer of 1929 with a school certificate from one of the then 'technical' schools, which were designed to teach practical subjects instead of Latin and Greek. He began as an assistant in household linens. Spotted and encouraged by the linens buyer Elizabeth Hope Glen (one of Spedan's Oxford graduate recruits), he enrolled in the City and Guilds classes to learn about textiles on weekday evenings. Miss Glen insisted that he stop half an hour early and have a cup of tea before leaving for his evening's study, an uncharacteristic generosity for the time which impressed him deeply. He said there was little attention spent on 'selling' when he joined. Buyers ran the department, and Spedan himself was much more interested in buying and merchandising the goods – but in the 1930s specialist selling department managers were brought in, and the overwhelming control of the god-like buyer was gradually curtailed.

In the 1920s Spedan found, against his better judgement, that he'd had to reintroduce commission for selling staff. In Peter Jones when Stanley arrived it was paid out of a department pool to avoid damaging competition between staff for the best customers. Stanley started at 8s 4d basic a week plus 4s 10d average commission, just over 13 shillings, about £36 a week today. He was so impressive that within six months his basic pay had doubled. He set himself to learn everything he could about the merchandise, and eighteen months later was transferred to furnishing fabrics in John Lewis. He became such an expert on linings that while still a teenager he became known as the Lining King. Spedan had an office nearby and constantly popped out onto the selling floor where Stanley was working. He found Spedan totally inspiring, and set himself to emulate him.

In 1932 he was sent to Bradford to spend three months in a wool mill, before returning for a stint in the novel merchandise-testing laboratory set up in Oxford Street by Walter Halstead. Halstead instantly recognised his worth – and his marketability – reporting that Carter was 'dangerously underpaid'. As a result he became salaried, starting at £208 (£11,000 now) with annual increments of £52 for the next five years built into his contract – that was the way contracts were expressed in the business in the 1930s. In response he wrote a polite but unsuccessful letter requesting a starting rate of £234 with annual increments of £78 – prompting the dry comment that 'he has a keen sense of his own value.'

By 1936 he knew everything there was to know about fabrics and moved to become a deputy buyer, and at the end of 1937, at only twenty-five, a full buyer. A month later, Max Baker, who had by then become overall buying director, regarded him as someone 'exceptionally well suited' to the buying side: 'He displays considerable initiative and vision, but needs to acquire balance.' Ah, balance, that enemy of invention. He would be criticised for that lack of balance throughout his Partnership career, but would rely on others to provide it for him. In this he was not unlike Spedan himself, and he, too, could leave victims in his wake. Several months before his appointment he'd openly criticised a buyer who he felt was incompetent. Incompetence he couldn't stand, and if the Partnership in later years had one major fault in handling people it was that it was *too* kindly, too slow to identify and deal with poor performers. Stanley Carter had no such qualms, and made it clear when he regarded someone as not up to the job, be he employee or colleague. The power and influence he could exert as a buyer excited him, and at first he was inclined to overreach himself. 'When he first had a big buyership it went just a little to his head,' said Max Baker. In the restrained language of the Partnership in those days 'just a little' could be translated as 'rather a lot'.

In 1942 he was called up and went into the RAF as a navigator, at which he excelled and became a trainer. His pioneering work on polar navigation earned him honorary membership of the Royal Meteorological Society. He kept up a lively correspondence with Spedan, including a five-page letter from the United States describing in precise detail the novel self-service cafeteria arrangements that fascinated him, a typical effusion of enthusiasm about a piece of organisation he admired. Within a year of returning he was director of buying for the now quaintly titled 'ironmongery and turnery', when he worked from Chadwickham House for a spell. Trevor Fry, who worked for him then, said:

> He would go down the stairs at Chadwickham like a machine gun. Swam every lunch hour, but still came back bursting with energy. I remember him writing CHRIST!!! in red ink across a pile of papers. I had tremendous respect for him, but I was fortunate because he liked me.

## Resignation and Return

In 1949 Carter had a spat with Spedan over a pay rise which he deemed insufficient, which irritated Spedan, who nonetheless was surprised to get a resignation letter out of the blue that June. Stanley attributed his departure, rather unconvincingly, to his disquiet over the recent decision to exclude totalitarians from the Partnership. He complained that the Partnership council vote 'was not free', that he was fed up with 'management by committee', and felt that the total separation of buying and selling was a mistake. He'd also fallen foul of one of Spedan's legion of external appointees who was kept on despite being 'utterly useless and unsuited to retail'. He wrote a seventeen-page letter from his holiday in Brittany, and got a classic from Spedan in reply of ninety-six numbered paragraphs. It's clear, however, from subsequent events that Sebastian Earl, who had now recovered from the health breakdown and was running Selfridges, had offered him a substantial rise to move there. (Spedan's response to hearing that Earl had gone to a competitor could be imagined; Earl's wife Honor said later that he'd left because overwork was destroying him – he could never turn Spedan down.) Despite Carter's affection for the Partnership, the Selfridges prospect was too good to resist. He left the Partnership after working out his final six months, typically 'handing over his buying directorship in very good shape .... He clearly put in a lot of hard work right up to the moment of his leaving.' That was Bernard Miller's valediction on the formal Partnership 'leaving note', and Stanley was wise not to slacken off. He'd need Miller's support two years later, when he was back: he found the grass outside a good deal less attractive than reliable old Partnership green. In reply to Miller's offer to return he wrote:

> Frankly, I have had it driven home to me over the past two years that although other organisations may be able to offer lucrative careers, none can offer the special qualities of friendliness, benevolence and family spirit which are characteristic of the Partnership ... What struck me when I met people from other stores was a lack of loyalty or belonging. Among the crucial differences was the sharing of knowledge between managers and the managed, which is unheard of elsewhere.

At the age of forty he now embarked on a period of fifteen years in which he became the 'enforcer', sent to trouble spots round the Partnership. First he was tested at Pratts of Streatham, where a young section manager recalls being startled at and affronted by his complete overhaul of her 'notions' section. Department store MDs didn't stoop to that sort of thing, but Carter did. Woe betide you, pointed out his assistant Richard March later, if you were ever out of stock of *any* of the hundreds of coloured Sylko cotton reels which were haberdashery's stock-in-trade. Carter wanted people to come to his shop without thinking twice, because they *knew* they'd find what they needed. A favourite word in his vocabulary was 'cornucopia'. A shop and a display in its windows or on its fixtures had to leave you with the impression that it was overflowing with plenty.

## The Enforcer

From Pratts he went to Heelas of Reading, a long-established store which the Partnership had just taken over, integrating the Partners from the smaller Reading shop of AH Bull which the Partnership had acquired as part of SPS in 1940. 'We didn't know what had hit us,' said Stan Withers, a young section manager originally from AH Bull, describing the days after Carter arrived at Heelas. 'He was everywhere. You couldn't relax for a second ... He took the place by the scruff of the neck ... There were casualties, people who had been stuck in their ways for years, those who couldn't adapt. But most could. He transformed the place.' Withers once saw him bounding past startled customers up the down escalator, so eager was he to get back to his office to make a call.

> He had eyes in the back of his head. He'd bustle in each morning through furniture, my department, head down, apparently engrossed in his own thoughts. Then he'd suddenly stop, turn, and point to a distant corner. 'Why hasn't that wardrobe got a price ticket on it?' 'Ah, sir, I ordered new tickets on Tuesday.' 'Why aren't they here yet? Give me that phone.' And he'd put the fear of God into some poor individual making tickets, then crash the phone down on its cradle. Drastic, and frightening, but it worked. Marvellous man.

Within a year Carter had lifted the profits by a third through 'a combined attack on weak spots, applied with conviction and drive', as the then selling director Max Baker's review said in August 1957. Those comments were tempered, typically, by the addition of: 'He has tended to exceed the speed limit. There is no doubt that the morale of the branch is high, but the pace that Mr Carter is setting is a bit of a strain.' Again, Partnership-speak for 'He's putting pressure on morale, let's hope he doesn't break it.' Max Baker, who as we'll see in Chapter 15 was instrumental in developing a coherent approach to selling in department stores, was a great supporter of Carter, and was constantly passing on his successful practical ideas to other managing directors.

The new Chairman Bernard Miller was aware of the danger to Stanley's health as well as to that of his Partners. He wrote at the end of that year: 'Do let me urge you to run no risk whatever of overworking yourself and trying to do too much too quickly. There is a limit to the extent to which you can deal with the detail.' There wasn't. There was no chance of restraining the bulldog in Carter, and provided he didn't savage too many people, Miller was content to let him off the leash. A revitalised Heelas was followed in early 1958 by the ultimate prize, John Lewis Oxford Street. The shop had been labouring under rebuilding work since 1955, and was still in a constant state of turmoil, with department moves taking place all the time.

## Oxford Street

Carter was made joint managing director, an arrangement intended to enable him to focus on improving the selling operation – though no limitation of his scope was ever successful – allowing his harassed joint MD to deal with the admin of running the shop, and picking up any pieces Carter left lying in his wake. Often they couldn't stand his pace. Bernard Miller at the end of 1960: 'The Partnership is grateful to you for bearing, in addition to the strain of getting the shop ready for operation, two joint managing directors who have fallen far short of the requirements of their post and failed lamentably to give you the help they should have provided.' By the time the Oxford Street shop re-opened fully in 1960 the previous year's results had been 'outstandingly good' and Carter received a substantial pay rise as reward, but he wasn't satisfied. He'd got the percentage of profits to sales, the best measure of performance, up from just under 4% to over 5, but it was still way short of the Partnership's department store average of 10%. Where were the economies of scale they should be finding in that great big shop? It was something of a sprawling mess, and Carter set out to revamp it. At first he couldn't manage both the overhaul and the task of getting both sales and profit up, and it obsessed him, especially as the Chairman dangled a carrot in March 1961: 'It is a fine effort to achieve a turnover of £6m, though the drop in profit percentage is no surprise ... A salary of £10,000 is possible if you can achieve the average Partnership trading profit.' At that point he was earning £6,500 a year, so he needed no incentive, but he was frank in his reply, aghast at presiding over a temporary drop in profit percentage, albeit a small one on a big sales increase:

> I am profoundly disappointed, and indeed ashamed, that John Lewis made such a poor profit showing and I was concerned that the Partnership may be valuing my work too highly ... I think the [pay] award should be withdrawn.

To an outsider this response to a pay increase doubtless seems bizarre. But it had its roots in the Partnership's quaint custom, continued for many years after, to require the recipient of an annual pay increase, if he was senior enough, to reply indicating whether he thought it was 'fair and reasonable'. To Carter, ready enough to press for a larger rise whenever he'd exceeded his target, it was logical to refuse it if he failed. It was, of course, something of a ritual dance. He knew by now that his Chairman was most unlikely to concur, and indeed he didn't, in a neatly phrased letter that essentially said: 'I decide these things, and I firmly expect you to get the profit up again next year.' And so he did. Between 1960, when the rebuilding was complete, and 1965, he'd not quite doubled the annual sales from £6.1m to £11.9m. But in that time the Oxford Street trading profit rose from £229,000 to

£1.175m, a factor of more than five – astonishing. The importance of that can be gauged by the fact that by this time the branch provided nearly 30% of the Partnership's total profit. When he'd begun it was just 8%. Indeed between 1960 and 1965 more than half the Partnership's increased profit came from this one shop. More strikingly still, in 1960 the Oxford Street profit was the equivalent of a quarter of the 14% Bonus payout. In 1966, Carter's last full year there, it represented *all* of the 12% Bonus. If Oxford Street hadn't improved by such a margin the Bonus would have been smaller (though not zero) and far less would have been available for future expansion. Carter's Oxford Street was now the great reconditioned engine powering the Partnership's recovery. No wonder Miller gave him a strong incentive. So how did Carter do it?

## Respect but not Affection

He did it by a ferocious energy, an attention to detail that was fanatical, and an ability to inspire by inculcating a combination of fear and adulation. It wasn't plain sailing for anyone. Cecil Gotts, the experienced but nerve-racked manager of the crucial china and glass department, was a constant target of Carter's critical attention. So were other managers, and his feverish search for perfection left some so exasperated that letters began to appear in the local weekly John Lewis Chronicle. These local versions of the Gazette carried the same anonymous letter column that the Partnership's Gazette did. Their specific complaint was that Carter would humiliate them on the selling floor in front of customers, which led to a debate in a local branch council meeting criticising his behaviour, for which Stanley was required to leave the room. His defenders outnumbered his critics by a substantial margin, but the discussion had the desired effect, faithfully recorded in the minutes, which the Chairman always read.

Bernard Miller, a very good listener adept at giving no clue to the nervous recipient of what he expected you to say, came down to Oxford Street and interviewed each department manager, and subsequently wrote letters to Carter and his long-suffering general manager, the cultured and witty Edgar Price. He used the incident, which had reached the press and was splattered over the *Daily Express*, as a reason for writing a long Gazette article. The Partnership's system does work, Miller concluded, because this kind of problem is revealed and dealt with before it completely explodes – though in truth it got close here. He summarised his conclusion privately to Carter, careful to couch his criticism in urbane language – he was talking to the chief dairyman of his cash cow, after all:

> I have concluded that the allegations of discontent and unsettlement have been greatly exaggerated, but there is some fire beneath the smoke, and it evidences

> some shortcomings in the performance of the management team of the branch as a whole. The general impression that I have ... is that the whole atmosphere of the John Lewis management is too stern, too austere, and too lacking in warmth and, for want of a better word, friendliness. Your own overwhelming energy ... leads to unfortunate personal incidents and to some failure to keep detail in proper perspective ... You have respect but not affection.

'Respect but not affection' was a telling phrase, because it illustrated Miller's view about how working life ought to be, and his temperament. While sympathising with Carter over 'the lax standards of the current generation', he felt that the management had allowed a 'yawning gap between top and bottom in the branch' to develop: 'I had an impression of remoteness and aloofness.' Although Spedan himself was an authoritarian, he was almost always courteous and respectful in public. Carter, known to be decidedly in awe of Miller, acknowledged he'd crossed the borderline of that courtesy, wrote a chastened letter of apology to his Chairman, and moderated his behaviour. Well, a bit.

Down in the basement the young Philip Morgan had no such qualms. In 1960, after coming on a careers course for the Partnership during his A-level year at his Somerset public school, he had alarmed his parents by deciding there and then it was the career he wanted. Doing the rounds as an A-level trainee – not so grand a procession as a *graduate* trainee might expect – he was picked out by Carter early on as a bright prospect. Before long he was a section manager in china and glass, where Carter pounced on a consignment of new items he'd spotted before they'd even been displayed. These were the so-called 'Pagoda' jars, glass containers that stacked inside each other. 'How are you going to display them?' 'Well, Mr Carter, I thought...' 'No, this is what we'll do.' And he was away, scouring the branch for as many items of different colour he could find to fill them with: bath salts, cotton wool, anything. One of his favourite expressions was that the merchandise had to *speak*, and in this case the pagoda jars trumpeted their presence. He saturated the promotional display window, the one in pole position on the corner of Holles Street, put the stock in the basement by the down escalator, and sold thirteen *thousand* in a fortnight, hounding the buyer to get him to corner the supplier's stock.

## An Inspiration to a New Generation

Philip Morgan took over hardware in 1965, at twenty-four the youngest department manager by ten years. His department (and in truth himself) was 'intensively cultivated' by Carter, who had decided hardware had huge growth potential. One night they went back to Carter's flat in the Marylebone Road to carry on poring over the plans, armed with the usual gin-and-tonics of disturbing strength. Carter, in the customary striped trousers and bowler hat, got in the back of Philip's mini, breathing down his neck and barking out directions. When Philip pointed out he still had his little JLP-symbol badge on, Carter said, 'Oh, never take it off. I've got one on my pyjamas.' He still can't figure out whether Carter was joking. A few days later Carter came down to hardware and decided to merchandise all the plastic containers together. They had to move the cash-and-wrap point, one of the innovations they'd introduced, but that meant repositioning an electric socket. 'I'll get Mr Pond to find an electrician.' 'No, no, no, we haven't got time for that. Here.' And Carter had whipped a screwdriver from his pocket and was down on his hands and knees when Philip said: 'Er, Mr Carter, Tom Pond's just come into the department.' In a flash Carter had given Philip the screwdriver and disappeared. Pond was the maintenance manager, and one of the few prepared to stand up to the boss: 'Where is he? I'll catch the bugger one day. What the hell does he need a maintenance manager for if he insists on doing everything himself?'

Everyone has a pack of Stanley Carter stories, and they seem apocryphal until three people tell you the same one. As when in a weekly meeting with his management team somebody inadvertently wound him up and he slammed his pencil on the table. Like a three-dimensional pinball, somehow it bounced up and off wall and ceiling straight back into his hand. Everyone was so helpless with barely suppressed laughter – and not suppressed at all when recalling it – that he had to join in, and the miscreant escaped censure. However much his rages were feared, he generated such sheer adrenalin-fuelled excitement round him that there was a sense of real wartime camaraderie, even if it was his managers looking out for each other when Stanley was about. A quick phone call: 'He's coming your way with a head of steam up…' His life outside the Partnership – and he did have one, was equally full of enthusiasms. One was for fungi, about which he was (naturally) a national expert, in particular a group known as slime moulds, which are just as unattractive as they sound. Once he was amazed, on his way to the shop, to find a species of fungus unknown to Britain growing between paving stones in Oxford Street, an event recorded by an opportunist press cameraman who was passing. On one later occasion on a tour of Waitrose branches he made his driver stop because he'd seen a rare toadstool on a roundabout. Not so remarkable, you'd think, but he insisted he stop *on* the roundabout. The English language doesn't often fail, but 'incorrigible' just isn't strong enough.

He was in his element at John Lewis. The early 1960s was a time when there was much product innovation. Derek Rawlings, who arrived there as a merchandise manager from Southampton on the day Carter had signed a contract for new walnut fixturing with glass tops, remembers the day they put the first automatic washing machine in Britain in the shop window, the

Hoover Keymatic. One day 'Colour in the Bathroom' was the slogan, when plain coloured towels arrived for the first time, a John Lewis staple and best-seller to this day. It's hard to visualise, at that time when cars were only black, that towels were only white, as were sheets and pillowcases. Soon it was 'Colour in the Bedroom'. Buyers had to get used to Carter's peremptory demands, of course. If something went well, he wanted all the stock he could get, because in John Lewis he could sell a lot fast. Tough on the other branches. Peter Yaghmourian – who had fallen foul of Carter on the selling floor – moved to the buying side to sell stockings and the new tights.

> Then I had a marvellous relationship with him. You had to learn how to play him though. I had a new line of support stockings. I told him casually that Bainbridges in Newcastle were selling more than Oxford Street. He took the bait, and soon we had a window stuffed full of them, blazoned with 'Knee-High Know-How'.

Another Carter advocate was Trevor Fry, by then the buyer of upholstery and the man who took the photo of him at the head of the chapter, and of every Partnership worthy for thirty years:

> He was so outspoken, but very stimulating to deal with. Did a tremendous lot of good for the Partnership. Turned round the department stores by his example, no doubt at all. Breath of fresh air.

By 1965 the Oxford Street profit was way above its previous maximum level, and few thought it could go on rising, not least because trading conditions in 1966 were so tough. It was expected to fall – it went up by 10%. And he was determined it would go on rising – there was so much he felt he had left to do. One of the key underlying reasons for his success was a determination to go for better quality shop assistants and pay them more. The higher paysheet was more than offset by his drive for sales and cost savings wherever he went. He was fifty-four, and aiming to see out his time in that great bustling shop, when in the summer of 1967 Bernard Miller called him in and asked him to take over Waitrose. It was a bombshell to Stanley and a gamble for the Partnership. Could he make his drive, energy and trading principles work as the MD of a chain of twenty-five undistinguished food shops? He hadn't worked in food, and he'd never run a widely spread business – could he do it without exploding? Waitrose was at a crossroads, and there were still those who wanted to sell it. Carter was perhaps its last chance, a point Miller made perfectly clear to him.

CHAPTER 14

# What Shall We Do With Waitrose?

The kind of promotional display common in Waitrose when Stanley Carter arrived as MD in 1967. Note the pattern clashes – and be grateful the photos aren't in colour. The Waitrose assortment's a little wider these days, too.

> After a while I remarked one day to the director of trading that, if the drapery departments did not take care, they would find that Mr Webster's enterprising temperament had turned the Partnership into a food business with minor wings in the way of clothes and furniture.

SPEDAN LEWIS, JOKING ABOUT JOE WEBSTER,
RECRUITED IN 1937 TO BUY A FOOD BUSINESS

> Upon the food business, Walton and May are inclined to think it is satisfactorily profitable. I am myself in favour of getting rid of it … Let's do it quickly while the going is good.

REPORT FROM BERNARD MILLER
TO SPEDAN LEWIS, FEBRUARY 1952

How had Waitrose fared in the thirty years between its arrival in 1937 and Stanley Carter's appearance there in 1967? The first quote at the head of the chapter was intended as a joke at the time, and doubtless Spedan would probably have been nonplussed by the position today. The second illustrates the dilemma in which Waitrose in its early days constantly placed the Partnership's management. With the arrival of the war, Spedan's dream of using this new small food chain as a springboard to a hotel business abruptly vanished. It then became a question of whether it was pulling its weight sufficiently to justify its demands on the Partnership's scarce capital resources, and – of course – its share of any Partnership Bonus once that could be restarted. During the war and the immediate post-war period the management's attitude to Waitrose was simply opportunistic. Individual shops were sold if they weren't making money. Small new chains in the London area were bought: Bees and Tees, and Schofield and Martin, and later a chain with a substantial wholesale business, Kinghams. None really added much – the Partnership's leaders had the best intentions, but they were tinkering. They didn't know what to do with it.

## Waitrose – Low Margin, and Marginalised

Essentially Waitrose was at the Partnership's margin, a distant province rarely visited. The people who ran John Lewis, from Spedan onwards, were department store men to the hilt – none had ever worked in food. Almost all the Partnership's top officials had started life in the long John Lewis silk room. John Lewis in Oxford Street, despite the decline of the pre-war fabric trade, still had vast areas devoted to dress fabrics and furnishing materials, and its range and variety were staggering. Every week the Gazette listed the results of each department store and of each buyership. In 1966, the year before Stanley Carter moved from Oxford Street to Waitrose, each of seventy-seven department store buyerships was listed – Waitrose had five – and twenty-five trading branches, of which the whole of Waitrose was merely one. Until 1968, the year after Stanley Carter took it over, its turnover was below that of John Lewis Oxford Street alone. It was out of Partner sight, and out of the corporate mind. In Spedan's last full year the annual Gazette index has just ten entries for Waitrose. It has thirty each for Odney and the Sailing Club, 300 for the department stores – and over 200 for Spedan himself. Waitrose simply didn't matter.

For most of its early life in the Partnership Waitrose was run by Joe Webster. Known as 'Uncle Joe' – but with considerably more personal warmth than Stalin – he had been recruited in early 1937 when Spedan was considering the move into food. A grocer since the age of fourteen, he had been running the London region of the Co-op grocery chain, then a huge business, at the time Michael Watkins met him and lured him away. One key factor in his recruitment was dissatisfaction with how the Co-op had treated his subordinates, and a conviction that the Partnership would be fairer. It was, although in his first three years he had an awkward coexistence with Wallace Waite. Spedan had confirmed Waite as MD of Waitrose, with Webster as its Chairman and Waite's successor, hoping that the Partnership's collegiate style of management would rub off on them. It was never likely to unless they got along personally, for both were used to a single command. They didn't, and it was no help that they were obliged to share a tiny office in Gloucester Road. As Waite wrote to Watkins in one letter of weary complaint:

> I am working with Webster in a room little larger than a rabbit hutch and have had to share the telephone. I have a placid disposition ... otherwise I could not have endured the irritation and inconvenience ... Two experienced officers of the Partnership predicted at joining that I would be mad within six months but then I would begin to enjoy myself. I am not mad, but at times nearly demoralised.

Waite resented Webster's interference and inflated salary, while Webster chafed at the terms of the Waitrose purchase, which gave Waite an annual commission of 20% of the profits, a sweetener designed to keep him from a tendency to freewheel. What united them was their belief that the Partnership was damaging Waitrose's profits by setting unreasonably high standards. They complained for instance that the standard of safety demanded for electrical fittings was unreasonably high. The understandable attitude of two hard-bitten grocers who had left school at eleven and fourteen is revealed in Watkins' dry reply to that letter of Waite's:

> Perhaps you would elaborate on what you mean by 'the Partnership will never make a satisfactory profit unless a brake is put on expenditure'... Taken in conjunction with your next paragraph it would suggest the company has been carrying the salaries of various inexperienced people whose only qualification is a university education. In fact the reduction of gross profit is the government's fault, coupled with the decision of the Partnership to subsidise the incomes of those Partners on military service.

In the end it was the difficulties brought by the war to the grocery trade that persuaded Waite to retire at the end of September 1940, and to enjoy himself by dabbling in farming down in Cookham – he might have derided the cost of the amenities but he loved Odney. He never did achieve one aim he told Spedan he had nursed since he opened his first shop, that through Waitrose he would 'have the best food store in London, serve the monarch, and have a store in Oxford Street.' Seventy years later, it has arguably got there, but those first years after 1940 were pretty thankless ones for Joe Webster, who took sole charge for the following ten years. Money was tight, rationing was still in force well into the 1950s, and grocery shops were tiny by modern standards. Chains could gain some economies of scale, but it's important to remember, looking back from a period of almost total dominance by the modern supermarket groups with their slick distribution networks and tight grip on suppliers, that the food business back then was essentially controlled by the suppliers of the main brands and by the big wholesalers.

## The Post-War Waitrose

What was a Waitrose shop like then? Until 1950 they were very similar to how they'd been when acquired in 1937. Then there had been ten small shops, each of just one to three frontages. There was no self-service, so everyone was catered to by an assistant, and paid a cashier at a cash desk in the recesses of the shop. Every shop had a different assortment. Each sold groceries, which were largely in tins, and provisions, the name given to products like sugar and butter and flour, which still largely arrived in bulk and were packed on the premises. Nine of the ten shops sold confectionery, nine poultry, four of them had butchers and two had fishmongers. The configuration all came down to how much space there was and what the local competition was like. Although most of the shops were profitable, and their buying was largely centralised, it could hardly be called a chain in the modern sense. The only thing in which the shops were consistent was that they all delivered free via vans – or by boys on bicycles – within a radius of five miles. There was a central warehouse of sorts, attached to the shop at Gloucester Road which doubled as the head office, but it was terribly congested, and its basement, as the son of its meat buyer recalled from a visit with his father, was infested with feral cats – perhaps descendants of the cats that grocers always used to keep to control vermin.

After the war, although food sales regularly increased at above the rate achieved in the rest of the Partnership, it was largely because food price inflation was greater, and Waitrose struggled to make a worthwhile profit. Particularly bad were 1948 and 1949. Webster was getting to the end of his working life and his tether. Spedan tried to introduce new blood in 1948, and brought in an old school friend, the Cambridge Regius Professor of Greek, to work with Webster, who promptly resigned in an understandable huff. He didn't think a propensity to read Ancient Persian for fun in the lunch hour an ideal background for the food business. The prof soon went, and Spedan hastily persuaded Webster to return. But there were major problems with Waitrose that couldn't be easily solved.

Bernard Miller's reports when general inspector in 1948, as well as regretting a necessary series of price cuts to match the Co-op, revealed major problems with 'shocking' unexplained wastage. In those days before computers, it was extremely difficult to match up what you'd taken at the till with what you'd paid for goods plus the difference between cost price and selling price: the buyer's mark-up. The difference is known as wastage in the retail trade. 'Explained' wastage is what you accumulate by adding the value of everything you know you've thrown away because it's no longer saleable (and only because your eyes or nose told you it had gone off – there was nothing on the packet to warn you back then). The gap you're left with is the 'unexplained' wastage, made up of three main components. One is inaccurate pricing – most items had to be price-labelled when they arrived at the shop. The second comprises natural losses during the process of (say) turning a side of beef into a set of joints, which was then done in the shop. The third is pilferage. Anyone can steal – customers, shop assistants, or delivery men. And managers in warehouses, as when a wines manager was caught by the waiting police at the Gloucester Road warehouse in 1949.

Webster, a grocery boss of the old school, didn't want the expense of a suggested new central warehouse, nor did he like interference from busybodies like registrars, and he thought the Partnership's amenities – like the extra week's holiday in the spring, which his competitors didn't have to provide – an unnecessary drain on his profits. When Webster retired in 1950 Spedan asked for a detailed review of Waitrose from Thornton Kemsley, the Conservative MP who had presided over the ill-fated Partnership council debate on totalitarians the previous year. The review concluded that profits in the food business had been eroded by diminishing margins and rising overheads, and that money invested in non-food would have a better return. So, sell Waitrose? No, for crucially he decided that there were useful other reasons why it shouldn't be sold, notably that it improved buying power in providing supplies for department store restaurants and staff dining rooms, and – the argument that really persuaded Spedan – it spread the risk. Waitrose was another, different, basket in which to hold the Partnership's fragile eggs. But it was clearly a finely balanced argument, and hardly a ringing endorsement for owning a food business. Indeed it again came up for debate when the Partnership ran into such trouble in the latter stages of the Korean War and had to cut pay. The quote from the head of the chapter from Bernard Miller illustrates how close the business came to being sold in 1952, and it was looked at again at least twice more in the 1950s. The question once arose again in 1955, and the person asked to look at it was the Labour politician Roy Jenkins, as part of an overall review of the Partnership's performance. Spedan had admired his book *Pursuit of Progress*, and recruited him part-time in 1953, as Jenkins summarised later with a typical sharp brevity in *A Life at the Centre*:

> He was living in Stockbridge in semi-retirement and pouring out memoranda interspersed with not very readable books. He was an eccentric autocrat of strong personality ... He believed in recruiting a highly educated management, paying them only moderately, forbidding commissions and kick-backs for buyers from

> suppliers, giving them a share in the profits but only in the same proportion of their salaries as junior staff received ... The mathematicians and philosophers stood up very well against the street-wise traders more favoured by some chains.

Roy Jenkins, the brilliant son of a Welsh miners' union official who had become an MP, had got a First at Oxford, had been at Bletchley Park in the war, and was elected a Labour MP in 1948. Spedan recruited him to work a day and a half a week as financial adviser, the finance director's 'shadow' in Spedan's construct. Muriel Ward Jackson (née Jenkins, but no relation), was no mental slouch herself, yet she later described how Roy – an unforgiving name for someone who couldn't pronounce his 'R' – would sit in meetings looking bored and say nothing, while some knotty debate flowed to and fro. But when asked to sum up, he would produce in two or three crisp sentences a perfect résumé of the arguments. He left after ten years to join the new Labour government of Harold Wilson, and took his forensic mind to the Home Office and the Exchequer, where he was Chancellor from 1967 to 1970. It was earlier, though, as Home Secretary, that he made the most lasting impact. From 1965 to 1967 he presided over a series of reforms that led to what became known as the 'permissive' society (though he preferred the word 'civilised'). In that two-year period he suspended capital punishment in advance of its abolition, relaxed the tough divorce laws, ended theatre censorship, and supported the private members' bills that legalised abortion and decriminalised homosexuality – what you might call in retail a pretty impressive rate of return.

Jenkins' analysis of the Partnership's performance in 1955 concluded that the department store business was not achieving the economies of scale it should, and that competitors were performing better, particularly the fast-growing multiples like Marks & Spencer. Moreover, the wages bill was now increasing faster than turnover. 'Should we,' he asked, 'improve our footing in the food trade, or shed it?' On balance, he was for growing it: although margins in food had declined, expenses had reduced more rapidly, and food might provide a hedge against fluctuating inflation rates. He felt it would be wise to move rapidly into the new form of 'supermarket' operation. The fact that Bernard Miller's reply to Jenkins' paper doesn't mention Waitrose at all tends to confirm that throughout the 1950s and into the 1960s it was in the Partnership's peripheral vision, spotted only occasionally. But the arrival from abroad of these new supermarkets did at least focus attention on it in its own right.

## Self-Service and the Supermarket

Bill Anderson was the son of Scots parents living in Essex when he'd started as a grocer's lad at the age of fourteen in 1937 – working every day of the week *including* Sundays then. After spending the war in the navy, he was attracted by a poster in the window of a Schofield and Martin shop in Southend detailing the benefits of the Partnership, which had just taken it over. By 1951 he was deputy manager of the Alexander Street shop in Southend at the point when George Walton, then running Waitrose, decided that it should try self-service, which he'd seen in the United States and Sweden. Anderson, a self-made man with a practical bent, was asked to be its first manager, at £7 3s 10d a week, a good wage, he reckoned then, though in fact less than £10,000 p.a. today. He set about the conversion:

> The area supervisor was in charge – Sid Staples, a lovely man. I discovered quite by chance that he was a spiritual healer. Always interested in people, and you felt better after speaking to him. Anyway, he was responsible for the opening, and we closed the shop for a fortnight and ripped out all the old-fashioned fittings and started from scratch. A dozen other Waitrose branch managers came down from London to help – they were eager to see what we'd finish up with. When we opened all the local traders scoffed at us, said that the customers would pinch everything. In no time we halved the staff numbers and trade absolutely took off. George Walton wrote to us all before it opened, saying he was sure the experiment would be a success, and if it wasn't, well, we'd probably have to close Waitrose!

So it was in that hand-to-mouth manner that Waitrose became one of the first in England to try self-service, and it was clear from its success that the business would have to go that way to survive. And thieving? Anderson said that losses were more often down to staff than to customers, although, in the days when there was very little central warehousing, it was suppliers that were the worst.

> There were lots of delivery men on the take, even their managers. There was a local bread supplier I was suspicious of, so I came in early one day to check it in myself. The loaves came in racks: the top rack was full but there were gaps dotted about all the way down. I got the directors in and hauled them over the coals. They must have known.

Money was still in acutely short supply, so, although individual branches were gradually converted to self-service, the first custom-built 'supermarket' wasn't opened until 1955, a fortnight before Spedan retired. It was at Streatham in south London, and had 2,500 square feet of selling area, microscopic by today's standards. Fifty years later the ideal size in Waitrose was regarded as ten times that, and in many competitors twenty times. Even then it was a building conversion on the site of a men's outfitters. Three months later came Epsom, the first to be built on an empty site, at 3,300 square feet. Both openings received lavish illustrated coverage in the Gazette. Their jazzy neon signage, massive plate glass windows with a clear view of the shop inside, brilliant internal lighting and open shelves were clearly highly novel, and appeared jarringly American-influenced to a business that prided itself on understated displays and personal service.

At the end of that same year Waitrose had thirty-three shops and there were small food departments in three of the twenty-two department stores. But Waitrose sales were only 7% of the total, and profit even less. By the time Stanley Carter arrived in 1967 Waitrose had sold all its smaller shops, converted those remaining to self-service and built several new small supermarkets. Many of them, incidentally, were on the sites of closing cinemas, at a time when television was becoming the entertainment of choice. Seven were converted over the next few years, despite unhelpful features like steps to the front door, sloping floors, and thirty-five foot high ceilings. At Slough the cinema projectionist's room became the manager's office, his bridge, with a sea-captain's view of the decks below. The 1960s rationalisation reduced the number of shops to twenty-two, but increased sales nearly fourfold in real terms. That was getting close to 20% of the Partnership's total sales: more significant, certainly, but it still provided less than 10% of the profit. Thus any £1 spent in a John Lewis department store was worth twice as much in profit as if it were spent in a Waitrose. Admittedly, it was far easier to find sites for a small supermarket than for a full-blown department store, but there was plenty of refurbishment to be done in old department store buildings. Why spend it on Waitrose when the return was so small? It was clear that other food businesses were doing better. Could Waitrose increase its profit contribution – and, if not, was the chain worth keeping? Despite the all-for-one, one-for-all principle of equal Bonus percentage for everyone, some thought it was unfair that Waitrose Partners got more than its contribution deserved, and department store Partners correspondingly less. In May 1964, in one of a series of articles to mark fifty years of Partnership, Bernard Miller articulated this concern:

> The Partnership has now developed a considerable separate self-service business, in which the relation of profit to its paysheet may prove to be very different from that in department stores, and it may develop other activities such as manufacturing, in which much greater differences may be found. How far then should the Partnership continue the principle of the common pool, which means that members engaged in work with a higher ratio of labour cost to profit get much of their Bonus from the members in other kinds of work in which the ratio is much lower? Should such activities be split off into separate Partnerships, each with their own different rates of Bonus?

## Get Carter

Into this frontier town rode Stanley Carter, worker of miracles at Heelas and John Lewis Oxford Street. Could he bring the retailing principles and zeal he'd used to transform Oxford Street to a business about which, though a food-lover, he confessed he knew nothing? Perhaps, too, he wouldn't meet quite such dislike of his methods in the rough-and-tumble of the food trade as he had at times in the genteel world of the department store, with its on-site registrars reminding everyone of Partnership principles, and pursing their lips at his intemperate rages. He told his team at the outset that he was entirely ignorant about food, but that he would learn fast, that selling was selling whatever the product was, and their standards of shopkeeping were to be as exemplary as anywhere else. His intent was clear, and his reputation had preceded him on a fast horse. The operations manager Gerry Kelliher was warned about Carter by a colleague: 'I don't envy you – that man is evil. I'll never work for him again.' (He did). Kelliher described the free-and-easy Monday morning nine o'clock meeting with Carter's predecessor George Walton. 'George was an affable chap who would roll in by about nine-thirty, and the sherry would come out when the meeting was over. When Stanley arrived the first thing he told us was that the meeting would start at nine sharp and there would be no sherry.'

Waitrose was a very small player. Of its much larger competitors Tesco was growing fast but still well downmarket, the Co-op was vast but losing ground, and at that time it was Sainsbury's that Waitrose strived to emulate. They were much larger, with a strong own-brand portfolio that was rapidly increasing, a clean house style with a set of first-class local managers who enforced a consistent approach, and were starting to 'manage' their suppliers. Carter's first priorities were to increase the number of Waitrose branches, improve shopkeeping standards, develop a much clearer and consistent house style, and sort out the in-house warehousing. This was now largely based on premises at Greenford, opened in 1960, struggling to operate efficiently and clearly not big enough for the expansion he had in mind. A key ally in this 'dash for growth' was Harry Legg, the new Partnership services director who had been 'acquired' along with Kinghams. He kept his cards, said someone, not so much close to his chest as secreted under his skin. He had been for a spell the Waitrose buying director and knew its problems only too well. By December 1967 the Board was discussing a proposal to build a warehouse on farmland much further west of London at Bracknell 'New Town', close to the new M4. If they added an office building they could at last get all the Waitrose management under one roof, instead of dotted about in three locations. It would take a while to get operational, of course, and in the meantime Stanley Carter would get to grips with a rather chaotic product assortment.

In April 1968 a new buying director was captured from Sainsbury's. Peter Falconer had little problem coping with Stanley Carter – he had dealt with worse at Sainsbury's – and shared his vision. Over the next thirty years he would be responsible for transforming the buying operation. His predecessor, Ian Anderson – who had taken exception to being railroaded by Carter, not least because of a refusal to continue blanket reductions on whole ranges – went off to run management services. It turned into a good career move for Anderson, running a new Partnership directorate to oversee the massive increase in computing that had just begun with the arrival of the first generation of new IBM 'mainframe' computers. Meanwhile Falconer would not only preside over a rationalisation and huge expansion of the product assortment, but also an increase in own-brand ranges with distinctive packaging, which had begun so tentatively that there were embarrassingly few when he arrived. That own-brand push coincided with Bernard Miller's decision to bring more coherence to the Partnership's overall design philosophy by inviting the noted husband-and-wife team of Robin and Lucienne Day to act as overall design consultants. The timing was fortuitous. The Waitrose branches had been something of a visual ragbag, and Carter's planned expansion in branches and own-brand products benefited from a more disciplined approach. He wanted to remove clutter from the shops, and in particular to concentrate more on food, and reduce an ill-chosen selection of non-food.

## Shopkeeping Standards

Gordon Parris, who started as a lad of sixteen in Dorking with his mother and two brothers, remembers the jumble that Waitrose branches sold at that time.

> Those were the days of reduction posters in the windows, garish hanging decorations, suppliers' promotions. Anything went – needles and cotton, records, kids' toys, shirts, even metal chickens advertising the poultry fixture. There was no range discipline – if you could fit it on the shelves you could sell it. And there were reduction stickers plastered all over the windows. Mr Carter got rid of all that.

The brash young Bill Bishop, already at eighteen a section manager at the biggest Waitrose supermarket at Slough (actually the biggest in England for a spell, at a now laughable 14,000 square feet) remembers: 'It was huge. Typical of Waitrose then – didn't know what to do with it. We got a Mini in the shop once on a promotion – it came in sideways through the window. We sold Italian glassware. Masses of china.' At nineteen he was deputy manager at Henley.

> That's where I first met Mr Carter. We had stuff from the Slough non-food assortment. Mr Carter came round and I said to him: 'How can we sell that?' Just odd bits of the blue band crockery range. He didn't need telling. He said we must get back to doing proper ranges, define what we're here to sell, and sell it in a proper way. In weeks whole ranges of rubbish were moved out. We started selling more fresh, too – that's when it all began.

A shopkeeper of Carter's mentality, experience and exacting standards, used to storming through every floor of his department store, was not going to sit in his office at Greenford. One person who remembers him vividly was Brian O'Callaghan, who'd joined Waitrose from Bourne & Hollingsworth and would later be the MD of the whole of John Lewis. He was still in 2010 the only senior trader to have gone in that direction rather than the other way. O'Callaghan was a branch manager, soon promoted to operations manager, in charge of a cluster of branches. The second branch group he was in charge of included an old shop in Banstead, on the Surrey downs. 'It was highly profitable but so tiny it was hard to keep up decent shopkeeping standards. In fact it was something of a shambles. Stanley waited just a week after he'd appointed me, then raided it. I got a missile next day.' (O'Callaghan learnt missile technology from Carter, and much else besides.) Those Carter visits are legendary. Some branch managers, tipped off from the centre that Mr Carter was in the car in their area, would post a scout outside the shop so they'd get warning. He was small and hard to pick out. Gordon Parris, when at Hounslow, his first managership, said:

> I could spot most people coming, but not Mr Carter – he'd just suddenly be there and your legs would turn to putty. He never shouted at me, though. He was a gent, really. He was all right if you were straight with him. He could sniff a feeble excuse and you'd cop it. I've seen it. I liked it – you knew where you stood.

He would come into the shop, immaculately dressed and courteous – he'd learnt to control his temper, at least in front of customers – and demand to see *everything*. 'He'd stand on the baskets we had on the bottom shelf then,' said David Gumm, later Parris's manager at Guildford, 'and run his fingers along the spine at the top of the fixture looking for dirt.' He'd often start with the toilets, which he regarded as a marker of hygiene standards in the shop. Tony Paine recalls accompanying him into the gents' loo and watching him scrape his fingernail round the toilet bowl rim. 'See that? Uric acid, that's what that is. Show me what you use to clean it with. No, no, that's no good.' Philip Morgan had a similar story from Oxford Street, and remembered when Carter decided to test every floor cleaner they sold. He took Morgan, when he was running hardware, into the Partners' dining room and they each got down on their hands and knees on the squared lino. They went through the whole assortment of cleaning fluids on a series of test squares to see which worked best and – almost as important – used least of the cleaning fluid. He would not allow soft toilet paper in the Partners' loos in Oxford Street for years after it first appeared because of the expense and high usage rates. John Pass, a branch manager turned staff trainer, remembers him in the open-plan office in Bracknell examining rolls of own-brand loo paper when it first arrived. He not only counted the sheets, but made sure that the first sheet was usable because that's what gave customers their first impression (as it were...) of the product.

He was a cleanliness obsessive in the days when hygiene discipline was poorer throughout the food supply chain. His backstage tours forced improved standards from everyone he came across, managers and suppliers alike, or they'd reap his wrath. But his prime focus was on making sure that the customers got what they wanted. On his unannounced visits he would scan each run of fixtures for gaps on the shelves, and establish *exactly* how each one had arisen. Woe betide you if he found the stock in the branch's warehouse storage space and not out on the shelf. If he discovered it was a supply failure he'd take you to the back office to listen while he harangued a hapless buyer. Typical was the opening of the branch at Witney. John Pass met him for the first time there in 1970 on its opening day, which coincided with a national shortage of pepper. The shop had started fully stocked, but such was Witney's pent-up pepper demand that by eleven they were completely out. Carter to buyer: 'If the Americans can put a man on the moon we can find pepper. Get it here at once.' And down went the phone with the usual clatter, though this time it didn't smash. David Ramsey, an operations manager who spent many years as an elected board member, recalled him at Epsom when the strip lights had failed on a refrigeration unit. 'They were waiting for a replacement from Canada. Carter blew up, went down the High Street, found some that fitted, and installed them himself. Absolutely incredible attention to detail. He smashed any complacency.'

Several managers spoke of a twofold effect. It made you quake in your shoes, all right, and determined never to be on the receiving end if you could help it, but it told you that he was giving hell to the buyers – and through them their suppliers – to make sure you got what you needed. In every dispersed business there's a natural tension between 'us in the firing line', and 'those in the centre' who 'simply don't understand the pressures we're under.' Carter, the big chief, was telling them he did understand and thus helped to improve the buyer/seller relationship. He and Falconer got buyers out in the branches more to see the effect of their decisions, or failures, and created a virtuous circle. And Carter, with an aggressive opening programme planned, was always on the lookout for bright young potential managers, many of whom thrived on his methods and vision. He created a cadre of young managers who bought in to his methods, and they were the rock-solid core of the Waitrose operation for the next thirty years. Many left school at sixteen with a threadbare education, but Carter's inspiration convinced them of what they could do: Parris some years later became Mayor of Windsor, Bishop later managed major Waitrose transformation projects, and in 2010 Pass was president of the Waitrose council. Some of those he spotted on his rounds, like Bill Bishop, were fast-tracked to branch managerships at an age impossible for department store staff. Carter rarely praised you to your face – he often found it embarrassing – but he always wrote up a detailed report of his visits to the area manager, who would show it to you. If it said for example that you were 'shaping up towards becoming one of our top flight of managers', as it did for Tony Paine, it somehow had more effect than saying it to your face. And it galvanised you.

However, not all relished it. He was still, frankly, a natural bully who simply wouldn't survive in the Partnership of 2010, when standards of Partner behaviour are laid down. One branch manager, Brian Ryder, said that Carter was such a strong personality he could make anything work, even if it was wrong. 'He just terrorised people into submission.' Kelliher remembered him bringing the John Lewis 'intensive cultivation' idea to Waitrose and trying it with the little Epsom branch that had been its first custom-built supermarket. 'I told him it was the wrong branch with the wrong manager, but he ignored me. I was right and he eventually gave in. I had a thick skin and I stood up to him.' Other skins were thinner. If you'd been Cartered you remembered it and you either didn't make the same – or any similar – mistake again, or else you left hurriedly before you were pushed. Or you were invited to leave, or, in the familiar Gazette euphemism, 'moved to other work in the Partnership'. Or, it being the Partnership, you attacked him in the Gazette. Carter had arrived in October 1967. In the spring and summer of 1968 a spate of critical letters began, thinly disguised attacks on him and his regime, at least one of which was clearly from a disgruntled branch manager. This was seven years after the same thing had happened at John Lewis. In early August Bernard Miller stepped in and decided to convene what he called a branch managers' committee for communication, a construct devised for the occasion: these committees were normally solely for non-management Partners. He met twenty-three of the twenty-five branch managers in London for two hours, and four days later published the results in the Gazette, which included:

> There was general agreement among the branch managers that there was no substance in the claims ... that changes in management had lowered the morale and dissipated the spirit of Waitrose Partners generally ... I told the meeting that I welcomed the example of the Partnership's system working as it should, and that ... [these concerns] have led to a meeting out of which has come much that is useful.

Bernard Miller that day circulated a detailed summary of the points raised to the managers and their chief, made it quite clear that he expected them to be vigorously tackled by Carter and his team, and privately gave Carter total support for what he was trying to do and the way he was doing it. Miller was a master at defusing these conflicts and using them to advantage. He would sit there calmly and, managers said, encourage them to say what they thought without fear of retribution. Moreover, he would walk away with a detailed knowledge of the position which no MD's formal report or spruced-up branch visit could provide him with.

## Tackling the Supply Chain

One of the defects in the supply of fresh products in those days was the lack of clear date coding on products. We're so used now to easily visible and understandable 'sell-by' dates, now more likely to be 'display until/use by' or 'sell by/best before', that we forget that there was a time when there was none of it. Suppliers marked products with their own codes, obscure to anyone else. Waitrose found themselves in the vanguard of reform, an unfamiliar place for them back then, almost by accident. They'd got wind that Marks & Spencer were considering 'open' date coding. Carter asked Peter Falconer if it could be done, and found himself on television – something Partnership management *never* did, promising that Waitrose would be first. Moreover, to Falconer's consternation, he committed publicly to starting in two weeks. 'We had no control over our suppliers, of course, and they weren't keen,' said Falconer. 'But we did pack some of our own meat at Slough, so we worked flat out and got some prepacked meat products open-coded by his deadline.' Waitrose at that stage tended to be followers, not innovators, but several managers told me that the effect on morale of seeing their chief on television announcing a new approach was immense.

Control of supply was a perpetual problem in the food business then. Carter was determined to start to distribute centrally a far greater proportion of products, and the new Bracknell warehouse would be the key. Although he managed to double the number of branches to fifty in his six-year tenure, from 1967 to 1973, in the process tripling the selling area, he couldn't quite match the spectacular profit increase he'd achieved at Oxford Street. But he got close. The sales lift he achieved in real terms in that period was just over a threefold rise, taking into account inflation which was beginning its 1970s surge – £1 in 1970 was worth just 37p in 1980. The profit increase in real terms was greater, just over four times, but he knew it could be improved even further with more efficient and cost-effective distribution. Buyers could get distinctly better terms from suppliers if they had to deliver to one central warehouse instead of to fifty branches, and if the warehouse operation could be automated as far as possible for 'dry goods' – tins and packs delivered in cases on wooden pallets – the operation at the new warehouse at Bracknell would be faster and distinctly more reliable.

Eager to exploit new automated warehouse technology, late in 1968 Harry Legg with Carter's support chose a system from the German manufacturers AEG for £2.5m (around £35m today) that was automated to an unprecedented degree. The then deputy finance director John Sadler felt it was expensive and over-engineered, but Legg and Carter won the day. They were convinced the long-term benefits would be substantial, and with an aggressive branch opening programme it needed to be operational soon because Greenford was creaking. Bracknell, though, was dogged with problems from the start. The builders were late getting on site, a subcontractor went bust, there was a major steel shortage which lengthened the time it took to supply from a fortnight in early 1969 to four months by the end of the year and for most of 1970. Legg listed this catalogue of problems, but was bound to admit: 'No doubt incompetence has played some part.'

In late 1969 the performance of the Greenford warehouse was deteriorating under pressure, and Carter looked round for someone to investigate it, especially the huge stock losses. Someone alerted him to a young man far from enamoured of his next move, managing haberdashery at the run-down Bon Marché in Brixton. Dudley Cloake was fed up with the stuffy formality of 1960s department store life, and considering returning to New Zealand where he'd been a government economist. Carter sent him to Greenford to investigate its problems. Cloake arrived in a warehouse housed in four former factory units on a 1930s industrial estate and bursting at the seams. Congestion and poor planning meant constant delays in getting stock to the branches. Indeed fruit and vegetables would often not arrive at the furthest shops till mid-afternoon, and the drivers had instituted an overtime ban. His subsequent damning report on Greenford landed him with the job of taking it over (from a manager so in awe of Carter that he stood at attention whenever he answered the phone to him).

Cloake survived that frying-pan experience, which included moving fruit and vegetable distribution temporarily elsewhere so Greenford could cope with the 1970 Christmas peak, only to be lobbed into the fire that the commissioning of the Bracknell warehouse turned out to be. 1970 had been a vile year for food businesses, with power cuts, strikes, a foot-and-mouth outbreak, and volatile world commodity markets. 1971 was little better. The Bracknell office space at last was occupied in the summer of 1971, and fruit and vegetables moved in, but that was comparatively easy. It was too variable, and had to be distributed too quickly, for the process to be automated. When the fully-automated warehouse eventually started for dry goods in 1972 everything that could give trouble did, from the novel palletising machine that stacked cases on pallets in different configurations depending on their dimensions, to the computer-controlled cranes that fetched and carried the pallets into and out of storage spaces in one of six aisles each sixty feet high, to the tow chain system. On that trundled round the trucks into which the branch orders were picked (by twelve real people, who for this final stage could not be dispensed with).

Eventually, once it settled down, it was an object of wonder for visiting distribution experts from everywhere – especially Japan, at that time leading the world in this sort of automation. It was decades ahead of its time, and seems now an aberration totally out of character with the soundly risk-averse Partnership at the period. In fact it was nearly a disaster. Cloake supervised its long-drawn-out installation through 1972 and 1973. 'We'd got a house in the new town very close by, so near that I could hear the crane alarms going off at night whenever they failed, which they did constantly at the start. I could hear all the messages on my walkie-talkie too. It was hell for a long time. The ultimate aim was the flexibility of a seven-day operation, and we got there in the end.' They did, but not, sadly, in time for Stanley Carter to see the benefits before he retired.

Carter kept a restless eye on Bracknell's progress, especially the training manual. Training was crucial. As part of his determination to create coherent operating standards across Waitrose – and as a by-product to understand the business himself from top to bottom – he had decided at an early stage to write a comprehensive operating manual for branch managers. Before then there had been a collection of instructions on different subjects, written by several hands at different times. For one morning each week he painstakingly went through a section with the two operations managers, often working into the afternoon without a break for food or drink. He co-opted his new assistant, the charming and long-suffering Richard March, as amanuensis.

> We'd start on some section in the morning, and plough on with barely a halt – unless he was called away to bark at someone on the phone – till about seven. 'What time is it? Is it really? Good heavens!' He'd phone his wife, and we'd be back at his flat and on into the night. He had amazing stamina. I didn't mind the work, it was the gin and tonics he poured out. The tonic bottle would last as long as the gin bottle, and I had to take evasive action at times. Anyway, the gin probably helped keep his drains clear…

Carter's *Branch Manager's Handbook* formed the basis of the Waitrose operation for many years thereafter. He didn't leave it there, for he was determined to crank up staff training to make sure everyone got the same message and knew exactly what they were supposed to do. Cash register training, for example, was not just for checkout operators, but for everyone. Bill Bishop remembers the till training he was forced to go through: 'We did it as part of a course at Gloucester Road. At the end of the day they made us take a basket of sixteen items through the till in a set time with no mistakes before we could go home. I was last out of course.' John Pass had been brought in from the branches to strengthen staff training, and he wound up creating a set of operating manuals for the automated warehouse from an entirely inappropriate set of originals translated from AEG's German. 'Twice a week I had to show Mr Carter what I'd written, and he went through it to make sure a warehouseman could understand it.'

## The Non-Stop Soloist

Stanley Carter's compulsion to understand everything, however, increasingly got him into trouble with his immediate team. It took him a while to get the right people and organisation, but by 1969 he'd replaced two successive general managers underneath him with a two-man team of Derek Saward and Jeremy Grindle, an administration/operations split that worked well – when he allowed it to. But, even though he'd left some areas to himself, like design, he just couldn't stop himself trampling all over their pitches. They wouldn't stand for it and eventually their complaints reached Bernard Miller. Miller knew Carter's health was deteriorating. He would soon have to have heart surgery, not surprisingly. Derek Saward said that when he was getting angry you could watch the blood rise up from his neck till the top of his bald head was a bright red glow. 'Except, the tips of ears always stayed white, very strange.' Miller didn't want him to fall by the wayside as Michael Watkins and the others of Spedan's pre-war entourage had done, and was constantly upbraiding him for not taking enough holiday. (Typically he'd take ten days out of the thirty due, and he would work weekends.) On this occasion, having spoken to Carter's immediate team, Miller instructed him to take a break straight away, but, as was his style, finished by mollifying stern criticism with an uplifting compliment:

> You have been pushing yourself and others too hard, and are involved too closely in what they are doing. I must recognise that discord and tension do exist and we must concentrate on removing it. Take two blocks of not less than a fortnight holiday this year, as I think that a complete withdrawal from business worries twice a year is very good business for the Partnership in respect of someone with such responsibilities as yours. Take two weeks' holiday by the end of March without fail.
>
> The tremendous advance Waitrose has made in this period is very greatly due to the impulse and the drive you have communicated to all members of the team. When you hand it over it will be a monument to successful shopkeeping and trading flair. Under your stewardship Waitrose has developed a character and a reputation which will set it apart from other food chains and which will ultimately bring great success.

Quite a way to go out for someone who had wondered what Spedan had been thinking of when he bought that scruffy food chain. Clearly, too, Carter had completely changed Miller's sceptical view of Waitrose, which was struggling so badly when he took over as Chairman seventeen years before. Now let's look at what had happened in the John Lewis department store business in that period, building on the great resurgence of Oxford Street.

CHAPTER 15

# The Miller's Tale

OB (Sir Bernard) Miller around the time of his retirement, and John Lewis Oxford Street at Christmas 1964 showing the new Hepworth sculpture, in place and floodlit.

OB Miller was pleasant, precise, with a very decisive brain. He used a quarter of the words Spedan would, and was his complete opposite as a personality, though like him he could talk for an hour without a single note. He did a great job turning the Partnership into an up-to-date business.

TREVOR FRY, BUYER AND PARTNERSHIP PHOTOGRAPHER, SPEAKING IN 2002

Let's return to the Partnership when Bernard Miller took over in 1955, and look at how it performed under his guidance between then and his retirement in 1972. Between those years the Partnership went from being an intriguing but unfulfilled experiment to a rock-solid business that was outperforming its competitors. It did so despite carrying out virtually no expansion. At the end of the period it had two fewer department stores that it had when it began, the Waitrose expansion under Carter had barely got under way, and yet the Partnership ended with sales three times and profits six times higher in real terms than in 1955. The Bonus payout was 18% in Miller's last year, and had averaged 15% for the previous eight years from 1965 to 1972. By any measure that's a spectacular improvement, especially considering the parlous state of the Partnership in the early 1950s. And it was done by the very opposite of exploiting the workforce. During the period the working week of John Lewis shop assistants had been reduced across the board, their holidays increased and their average take-home pay including annual bonus was up by close to 50% in real terms. His successor as Chairman put it like this:

> When I arrived in 1959 the whole of the Oxford Street south west corner was just a hole in the ground. The minimum holiday was three weeks. The working week was five and a half days. We had a half-finished Trewins and Tyrrell & Green, half a Robert Sayle, half a George Henry Lee.

It looks like magic, but it was done by sheer persistence in following through Spedan's trading principles, and, it must be said, by resisting all his old distractions. Admittedly we were entering the era the Conservative government described as a time when 'we had never had it so good', and the 1960s was a decade that saw a UK population increase of three million, the largest in a single decade since the Edwardian period. Trading conditions were therefore on the whole much better, but how did Miller's team capitalise on it so successfully? We've seen how John Lewis in Oxford Street was rebuilt and energised by the turbocharged Stanley Carter, and Waitrose rescued from a muddled obscurity, but what other forces were at play? It could be simply described as deciding the right trading format and sticking to it; improving each shop bit by bit; improving the buying operation; taking no unnecessary financial risks – no adventures. All was underpinned by sticking to Spedan's trading principles.

These threads came together in two of the best Partnership thinkers to survive the war, two men known before long as May and Baker. May and Baker was a well-known pre-war pharmaceutical company, long ago split up and absorbed by Big Pharma. In the Partnership it meant Paul May and Max Baker. After the war the contented pre-war silk buyer Paul May found his ability and judgement catapulting him into a series of top positions including finance, and ending with research and expansion, when he was also deputy chairman. Max Baker's impact in Miller's era was on the way the selling branches operated, but before the war it had been in centralising buying, bolting Spedan's ideas into place. Let's look first at buying.

## The Art and Practice of Buying

The customer wants the right product in the right place at the right time, at the right price. It's no good having well-positioned shops displaying goods in a seductive setting, with eager, courteous and well-informed service, if the customer doesn't like the product or its price. Buyers selecting the right merchandise and pricing it shrewdly are absolutely crucial if a retailer is to satisfy customers and persuade them to return. The shops do the selling, but top-class buyers are essential to generate profit. Once you have the right range, pricing it accurately has always been an immensely powerful creator of profit. If you can put a little extra on the price without damaging sales, or if by cutting the price you can improve sales to more than recoup what you've lost, you have a very simple and powerful lever in your hands – provided you can do it without alienating the customer. It is of course just as true today. At the beginning of 2010, for example, analysts reported that two of the largest UK supermarket groups, which had trumpeted major – and genuine – price reductions in the run-up to Christmas, had also quietly slightly increased prices on a substantial number of products in the same period. They gave customers savings on the swings and took more back on the roundabouts, trusting that with so many lines nowadays (and no price on the item) no one would realise that prices had increased.

John Lewis buyers have never been able to do that, because of the Never Knowingly Undersold principle, rigorously enforced. It had been in place formally since the early 1920s. It's ironic that a writer as chronically verbose as Spedan could come up with a three-word slogan that seems almost wilfully dense. It means in essence 'We won't let any competitor sell a specific product for less than us once we know they're doing it.' Clearly, if another shop lowers a price it'll take some time for the intelligence to come in. 'Intelligence' was indeed the name of the department that monitored prices since its establishment under one Countess Golfarelli in the 1930s. John Lewis had and still has its own scouts out checking competitors' prices. This may be hard to believe – all half a million John Lewis products? In theory a willing platoon of scouts, because shop assistants were and still are paid a bonus for any undersale they report. Many would scour the competition in their lunch hours for pin money, and it's the existence of that bonus that stresses to the selling assistant that John Lewis is serious about reporting undersales and lowering prices as a result. Moreover, the system is helped by the commitment to refund the difference if an item is brought in identical to one sold in a John Lewis shop, if the customer has bought it elsewhere. Customers may not understand exactly what those three words mean, but they get the gist of it pretty quickly if the shop uncomplainingly gives them the difference.

A key question here is 'Who is a competitor?' Spedan recognised from the outset that it was unreasonable and impracticable to allow someone who'd bought something in Glasgow to claim an undersale in Peter Jones. So, after some experiment, he developed an exclusion zone around his shops. It didn't apply outside a specific radius, small in London but larger elsewhere once provincial shops like Jessops of Nottingham were acquired. In 1921, formulating the policy to a Peter Jones buyer, Spedan wrote:

> Profit or no profit, we must never be undersold ... The only occasion on which I should ever consent to a departure from this rule would be if a competitor had a class of business so different or were situated so far away that he ought not to be regarded as a competitor of ourselves at all. I should certainly never let myself be undersold by any shop of any standing trading within two miles of these premises.

Two miles was not unreasonable when most customers came on foot or in an omnibus, or by taxi. Spedan later amplified the distance criterion to be one where 'the cost of journeying to the competitor is negligible in time, trouble and money.' The 'different class of business' stipulation was soon dropped. The policy has come under strain many times, up to and including the present day. In 1946, when post-war supply was difficult and a quota system operated nationally, he and Bernard Miller considered abandoning the slogan, if not the principle. However, as he wrote to Michael Watkins, 'We think this slogan is valuable for its psychological effect on the minds of our own people as well as for its direct effect upon the public.' This short-term double-whammy – losing money on the selling price for an extended period *and* paying your staff to initiate the process – was clearly regarded as the necessary cost of establishing in customers' minds that they really couldn't find a product elsewhere cheaper than the price at which the Partnership sold it. What is more, the Partnership was scrupulously honest about the pricing and description of sales merchandise long before (in the late 1960s) legislation arrived to ban the widespread practice of advertising a product as, for example, 20% off, when it had in reality never been offered for sale at the higher price. The effect was that John Lewis buyers didn't have the freedom to manipulate price to anything like the same extent as other retailers, though they could use the local undersale system to warn them if they'd priced it too high.

## Caring for Your Suppliers

So it became even more imperative for the John Lewis buyer to get the range right (the 'assortment' in the Partnership's terminology), and to strike the best possible buying deals with suppliers. 'Best possible', moreover, didn't mean screwing as much out of them as you possibly could. There existed in the Partnership a genuine culture of cultivating your supplier, especially if he was operating in a small way and providing something that the competition didn't possess. With the River Arno flooded and many of Florence's basements under water on 4 November 1966 (a public holiday, so many businesses were closed) it wasn't just priceless works of art that were damaged. The Partnership despatched Rex Probert, its buyer of gifts and mirrors, to bale out financially – if not literally – many of his and other buyers' small Florentine suppliers with interest-free loans to keep them afloat. The long-serving assistant buyer of gloves, Mabel Hammett, underlined how vital it was in this period to make sure that your best suppliers survived. You played a long game, and you didn't drive them into the ground. Yes, you could probably extract more profit from a small supplier, but theirs was usually a distinctive product for which you could charge a higher price anyway, so why imperil your source of distinction? Trevor Fry, when a furniture buyer, said he learnt that you had to try to inspire suppliers to be imaginative:

> I'd get an idea, and lob it at a couple of suppliers. I'd say I know you won't be able to do it, but never mind. They'd be desperate to try after that. You had to cultivate good personal relations to get that response. I dealt with little firms in Denmark – no one here could polish teak like they could. You needed to really understand your customer too, and not listen to some of the Partnership's senior management. Try this, they'd say, but they didn't have a feel for the trade, especially if they shopped at Peter Jones.

Another buyer with a mission in 1966 was Peter Yaghmourian. He was the son of an Armenian immigrant who had been a tailor at Tyrrell & Green when it had been bombed. His father had taken three days to tramp home from Southampton to London in November 1940, because there was no transport. (That was nothing to him – he had walked across Armenia in his youth to escape the Turkish pogrom.) Yaghmourian junior was the stockings buyer when in 1966 the rise and rise of the mini-skirt led to increased demand for the new-fangled tights, hitherto virtually only sold to ballet dancers and ice skaters – and hence achieving remarkably high sales at Pratts of Streatham, where there was a nearby ice rink. His English suppliers, used to fashion trends being dictated by Paris and not by London, were convinced tights were a six-day wonder. So Yaghmourian found a small Austrian supplier, run by two brothers who were concentration camp survivors. Against much internal opposition (ladder one stocking, and you replace only that one; ladder tights and it costs you far more – they'll never sell) he risked an order for 10,000 pairs. Overriding internal disapproval, he had the crafty idea of selling them as 'seconds', and they were soon flying out of the door at 18s 11d. Young women *had* to have them, and staid old John Lewis was the only place you could get them.

The point of the story is that when Lady Sieff, wife of the chairman of Marks & Spencer, taxed her husband with the distasteful truth that she could only get the tights she wanted at John Lewis, of all places, Lord Sieff's buyers made contact with the Austrian company and proposed to buy a quantity that would dwarf the John Lewis orders. The Austrians shocked them by refusing it. They enjoyed the relationship with John Lewis, they were making 'enough' money – an old-fashioned concept in tune with the Partnership's – and they didn't want the character of their business to change. Their experiences had perhaps given them a deeper perspective on life. Before long such was the John Lewis volume that Yaghmourian could get the selling price down to 12s 11d, and later even to 9s 11d, below the ten shillings mark, then a psychologically vital barrier for customers. This strategy was not far off the equivalent of a shop selling something for £9.95 today when nobody else can afford to sell it for under £12.50. Yaghmourian had the sales volume that enabled him to get the supplier's cost price down.

## Centralising Buying – Control v Flair

Sales volume, vital for improving margins. When Spedan had taken over John Lewis in the late 1920s he immediately recognised the advantages of centralising buying. He might only have two shops, and Peter Jones was in many ways so distinctive that it had to retain many local buyers, but he could start to generate some economies of scale and the cost price reductions that volume would bring. The arrival of the four provincial shops in the 1930s, where his buyers tramped round overhauling stock, gave another push to centralised buying. Enter Max Baker. He arrived from a business that had special expertise in centralised buying: the department store chain confusingly called Lewis's, then led by Frederick Marquis (later, Lord Woolton, the wartime Minister of Food, who gave his name to 'Woolton Pie', essentially a pie full of any ingredient except for those you might expect). Marquis had set up centralised buying to cover his three largest stores, in Manchester, Liverpool and Birmingham. Few had centralised the buying process as comprehensively as Marquis had, and Baker built now on what he had learnt there. In the Partnership Baker implemented Spedan's approach, working with his boss Michael Watkins, then director of trading. Thirty years later Baker wrote at his retirement:

> Spedan had instituted half-yearly buyership reviews, and in those days he conducted every one himself ... It proved to be a most powerful tool in putting and keeping a keen edge on their work ... Within a year of my coming into the Partnership, he withdrew from day-to-day executive work. Watkins and I set ourselves to clarifying and defining the policy and organisation of the buying side as a central buying operation; new control, stock planning and purchase rationing systems were set up and the relationships between central buyers and the selling side were crystallised ... Then in 1940 came the sudden great extra load of taking over the whole of the Selfridge Provincial Stores group, lock, stock and barrel, largely reorganising it and turning it over to central buying ... It could hardly have been a sterner test of the soundness of the principles and of the basic systems that had been established. There never seemed to be even a remote danger of breakdown, though ... I marvel that we came through as well as we did.

Although the restrictions and shortages of the war were so disruptive to the buying process, the very constraints only served to emphasise the benefits of concentrating all the buying with a limited set of experts in London. You had to take note of local differences of course, which regional branches were quick to stress, but overall the advantages were huge. It also enabled a much more explicit form of cost control, vested in purse-holders called central merchandise advisors (CMAs), whose job in each buying directorate was to keep tight control of each buyer's 'purchase ration', which was set in advance. Mostly women, like the formidable Miss Fanny Razzell – rarely did a name fit the owner's personality less – these CMAs exerted a control that could be too strict if trading conditions changed or new product ranges suddenly emerged, but which meant that a buying disaster like that of the Korean War period (Chapter 12) was extremely rare. And buyers were protected against themselves, especially if their skills were a result of instinct and flair rather than sober calculation. A combination of flair and calculation was the ideal, though it was rare.

The buyers themselves were a formidable bunch, too. Spedan's search for the perfect buyer before the war had brought him several who developed immense reputations in their trades – men like the unexpectedly brilliant Indian Army veteran General Hogg. Spedan paid them far more than his father would have done: they got a commission on sales above a certain level, they stayed with the business for years and set an indelible stamp on their product range. Once he had found good buyers, Spedan didn't like to chop and change, and he often kept them in the same product area for most of their working lives. Curiously, after his initial successful experiment in the 1920s, he was put off appointing women buyers because – as he saw it – for all their particular sense of taste and style, they were just too likely to go and get married and disappear. This may have come about because in a few cases he was 'spurned', as he saw it, by a bright prospect leaving soon after being trained. (Actually in the overall scheme of things his original women buyer recruits stayed longer than his men. In 1955, when Miller took over, of eighteen buyers still there who had been recruited by Spedan before 1930, thirteen were women. Students of glass ceilings, however, will note that of the then nine buying *directors*, not one was a woman. By 2000, incidentally, the position was very different. Four of the now six buying directors were women, and as many as forty-six of sixty-four buyers were, a quite remarkable shift. Moreover, it would soon be five out of six: one glass ceiling less, at any rate.)

Miller maintained Spedan's continuity and longevity among his buyers and their directors. Of those in place when Miller retired in 1972, almost half had been in the business when he'd taken over in 1955, and they had often been buying the same merchandise for over ten years. Typical was Eric Pearce, who joined when he was demobbed in 1947, became a buyer in the early 1950s, and was a buying director from 1959 until he retired in 1981. His early mentor was the brilliant Patrick Mahon: Pearce regarded Mahon as the best buyer of his time and Carter as the best shopkeeper. Patrick Mahon had a double First in Modern Languages when he joined Bletchley Park in January 1942 at the age of twenty-one and was another Partner who had been sent to Hut 8, led first by Alan Turing the computing pioneer, and later by Hugh Alexander, who encouraged him to join the Partnership after the war. He did so after writing a history (then classified) of Hut 8, and later described himself as 'in charge of the German Navy at the age of twenty-two'. He started in buying, which according to his widow Liz Mahon, later a buyer herself, he loved with a passion. The passion led him to analyse the job intensely and extend the work done by Baker and Watkins before the war. Mahon was a buying director at twenty-seven, a year after first being made a buyer; his work rate and intellectual energy were such that he acquired a succession of extra jobs at intervals. One of these jobs was as research director, and Miller clearly wanted him to introduce more efficiency into the business. A drawback of giving buyers their head is that they were each inclined to invent a different way of doing the same thing. In 1959 Mahon wrote a piece in the Gazette on the topic that suggests he had been running into some resistance:

> Business efficiency covers all our activities: what people do and why they do it. Enquiries have revealed so many extraordinary and unproductive activities. We need to introduce a 'No Sacred Cows' initiative. The research director simply cannot surrender to the entrenched conservatism with which he is surrounded and he has got to battle endlessly to maintain the idea that we are a modern and go-ahead business, receptive to new ideas and intolerant of people who just want to glide along to retirement in their well-established grooves.

One of his special extra jobs was as buyer of non-food in Waitrose, followed by a stint as its temporary merchandise director for seven months in 1957, when he worked out the best way to set out the merchandise in a self-service supermarket, a task he described as the most exhausting he'd ever had. He was well ahead of his time. In a letter to him, Bernard Miller said that, until Mahon had applied his mind to it, the previous Waitrose management had 'had little conception of how to run a self-service business and of the volume of trade that can be achieved in the food trade.' In practice it wasn't until Carter arrived that his prediction began to be fulfilled. There was a period in the late 1950s when Bernard Miller in fact contemplated Mahon as his successor – he felt he needed someone of about that age – but Mahon's health broke down and he died before he'd reached fifty. In his Gazette obituary Miller recalled his 'penetrating and wide-ranging mind, combined with great human sympathy and a puckish sense of humour, which made him a delightful companion and colleague.'

## Selling, and Max Baker

In early 1955 Spedan had, at Bernard Miller's request, persuaded Max Baker as selling director to concentrate on improving the overall John Lewis selling operation, and making it less variable. Miller wrote to Max to tell him that he felt the selling operation had lagged behind buying in efficiency for years. In 1951 Miller and May had taken a long hard-nosed look at the department store portfolio, and concluded that the worst performers were those below a certain size. Partly these were relics of the SPS purchase, while some had been acquired opportunistically, and sometimes unwisely, after the war. They took the decision to sell these smaller branches in the quieter towns like Gloucester, Stroud, Eastbourne and Tunbridge Wells, helping to fund a policy of larger shops restricted to heavily populated centres. They reckoned that the central buying structure could support up to a maximum of twenty to twenty-five branches. More than that would be too great a strain, with the manual analysis tools available in those pre-computing days. Computers (barely out of the lab at Manchester University) were still massive engines stuffed full of valves – behemoths based on Turing's ideas and von Neumann's internal architecture. It was by no means apparent that computing would indeed *have* any application in commerce beyond, perhaps, streamlining some accounting functions – if cost and size ever came down.

It seemed clear, too, that smaller shops that tried to carry the range of departments of a John Lewis or a Peter Jones would always be out-competed by the increasing swarms of multiples. The rise of the chain store in the 1920s and 1930s had been temporarily checked by wartime and post-war rationing, which led to the scarcer goods being allocated disproportionately to larger stores. But between 1950 and 1957 UK department stores saw their proportion of the nation's trade drop from 10.2% to 8.8%, a trend even more pronounced in the United States, where the comparable figures were 9.0% to 6.5%. May and Baker were not slow to see the writing on the wall; the problem was how to stem the losses. Was the department store in fact a dinosaur about to be made extinct by economic climate change? Greater taxation had led to a shift in disposable income since the war from the more wealthy, who tended to shop in department stores, to the less well-off, who frequented multiples. Between 1946 and 1958 Marks & Spencer's profit went from £3m to £17m, in a period when the Partnership's only went up from £0.4m to £1.2m. It's salutary to note that in 1959 the British Woolworths (fifty years before its collapse) had profits of well over £30m before the Partnership's had reached £2m.

The sluggish performance of the John Lewis department stores after the war was aggravated by other factors. One of the reasons Spedan was so sore about the inability to get John Lewis Oxford Street rebuilt was that multiples were able to build and rebuild their smaller outlets in the many more locations available to them. Moreover, in the 1950s big city centres were becoming increasingly choked with traffic, and parking was much more difficult. Trade, too, was moving gradually away from traditional Partnership strengths like furniture, soft furnishings, clothing and fabrics, and national branded goods were beginning to dominate. Department stores everywhere lost ground in fashions, being slow to pick up on the new teenage market, though in truth fashion was always the Partnership's least satisfactory area – it was said that they sold clothes, not fashions... Worse, they were losing out in other new areas like radio, TV and domestic electrical appliances, where the trade was dominated by the new chains springing up. Frankly, too, most of the John Lewis shops were old and tired.

It did look to some as though the Partnership was going to go down with the other department store battleships, but after the tribulations of 1952 it did begin to hold steady, helped by two purchases of larger shops in big city centres. In 1953 it bought Bainbridges of Newcastle, the shop in which Emerson Muschamp Bainbridge had been the first to tally takings by department. It was still run as something of a private fiefdom by his great grandson George Bainbridge, who had married the daughter of the great Newcastle rival Fenwick in a big society wedding in 1934. (In fact, the Partnership's major problem was to delicately unpick the quiet cartel agreement by which Fenwick and Bainbridge had divvied up the Newcastle trade: 'Fenwick for Fashion, Bainbridge for Furnishing. The families had always been close, ever since the heads of both companies had been elders of the same Methodist chapel.) In Spedan's last year Heelas of Reading was bought to replace AH Bull, the smaller shop it had there. In that year of 1955 Max Baker and his colleagues started to formulate a plan to bring more consistency to newly acquired department stores with internal layouts and fixturing that were highly variable, be it from history, local preference, or building shape. Once they had at long last the go-ahead to rebuild Oxford Street and redesign its interior, they pored over the options – eventually dismissing one which included a hotel – and came up with a plan that they submitted to a firm of experienced store designers in New York for a second opinion. The US designers changed very little, and the Oxford Street pattern became a template for the other department stores whenever a redesign was necessary and possible.

Baker described this store design philosophy to a conference in Berlin in 1957. Ensure that your store's 'personality' and target customers are reflected throughout the shop. Start with a forecast of the trade you expect to get in each department, and its degree of sensitivity to positioning. Get the ground floor right first: trade diminishes as you go higher. Locate departments with a high transaction rate, particularly if they're distinctive like John Lewis's haberdashery, where they can draw traffic through the shop. Cluster together departments whose products customers tend to buy on the same shopping trip. Place round the walls departments that need high fixtures or merit a wall-to-ceiling display of the range, like plain carpets or coloured towels. Make sure that departments that need natural light get it. Size a department's area according to the amount of stock it needs on the selling floor, to keep stockroom visits to a minimum, and keep those stockrooms close. Don't bury important profit-generating departments in a traffic backwater. Help customers to see as much of the assortment as possible from key vantage points, and make it easy for them to move around the shop. Get the main and subsidiary 'arteries' of customer-flow right, and above all stick to a rectangular plan – don't be seduced by zigzags or wavy passages. It may look dull and regimented, but it works.

Planning a new shop, or a rebuild like Oxford Street was thus a multivariable problem that suited the bright minds the Partnership attracted. But, said Baker finally, avoid being seduced by a satisfying plan. What may look perfect from above, mapped out on a table, can turn out to be disastrous in practice. He cited an instance of a recent ground floor replan done on diagonal lines, which looked fine from above, and even from a half-landing on an open staircase, but it was a failure and had to be expensively reconfigured. 'The way out of a maze can be easily seen from the air, but the people in it are lost.' Derek Rawlings spent much of his life as an MD moving from branch to branch, reconstructing or resiting them as they went. One of them was at Newcastle, where he'd had the sensitive job of following the last of the Bainbridges at his retirement in 1974 Rawlings had worked under Stanley Carter at Oxford Street in 1959, so there was little he didn't know about shop reorganisation. So difficult did it seem to him to get department managers (particularly women, he said with cheerful bluntness) to visualise their future departments that he raided the toy department to get

Lego building blocks and assemble a model. Then they could get at least some sense of a 3-D image and get down on their hands and knees to 'walk' themselves through it. It seems obvious now, but it wasn't then: you were supposed to be able to read architects' drawings.

In early 1939, shortly after they'd both signed a lifelong contract with Spedan, Michael Watkins had suggested that Max Baker would be his ideal successor as director of trading. Spedan disagreed; it took Max till 1959 to get there. In a letter welcoming him back after war service – Spedan was forced to badger the Chancellor Stafford Cripps to release him, so valuable had he become – Spedan had described him as a rarity in having an equable temper, 'a very rare and valuable combination in a man with such excellent powers of work and drive'. Max well understood Spedan's virtues and foibles. Late in his career he winnowed out some of Spedan's best advice on trading from his copious writings and assembled it in a slim volume packed with pithy quotes. *Retail Trading* was the Partnership's 'little green book', at the time of Chairman Mao's little red one. Along with Spedan's *Fairer Shares* and *Partnership For All*, a numbered copy was given to everyone in the Partnership who reached an elevated management level, strictly a loan to be returned on retirement. After Max retired in 1967, and well into his eighties, he used to run intensive week-long courses at Longstock on Spedan and his trading principles. He was not an especially good public speaker, but a compelling conversationalist who could and did go on late into the night. Anyone about to be a department store MD for the first time, such as the high-powered civil servants Stuart Hampson and David Young recruited in the early 1980s, would attest to his intellect and stamina. Young described Max as brilliant, and several up-and-coming young MDs, who arrived wondering what this wizened old man from a bygone age could possibly tell them, found themselves getting quieter as the week progressed, and left with a new respect and a determination to put things new-learnt into practice. Thus was the continuity and consistency maintained – a clear line through Max Baker and Stanley Carter, theory and practice, ran down from Spedan to the leaders of both John Lewis and Waitrose in 2010. Baker's successor as director of trading described him like this:

> He had the great gift of encouragement. His appreciation of success made one feel ten feet tall and his patient unravelling of a problem without a fluster or a tremor left one with confidence and a clearer view … He could be stubborn, a nice English word balancing uncertainly between vice and virtue … He was one of those rare people blessed with an exceptional mind and ability who contrive to balance high seriousness of purpose and steam-rolling efficiency, almost as relentless and sometimes as unforgiving as the tides, with the greatest good humour and an infectious enjoyment of life.

## Consolidation

Consolidation sounds a boring word, but it's just what the Partnership needed when Miller took over. We've seen how buying and selling were put on a sound and coherent footing, but until the return of the Oxford Street shop to full power in the early 1960s the Partnership's finances were still comparatively precarious. Like a swan on a lake labouring to get clear of the water, it took a long time to take off, but it got really airborne by the mid-1960s. In 1967 the annual Bonus reached a dizzying 18%, not reached since Peter Jones' heyday forty years before. Sales were double what they had been in 1958, but pre-tax profit had gone up by a factor of six, despite what seemed at the time a turbulent decade for retailers. (Then came the Seventies…) It included big increases of corporate taxation after a balance of payments crisis, the 'SET' tax on employment which hit retailers especially hard, and devaluation of the pound. The finances were still, as Spedan had specified, in two pairs of hands. For much of the period Paul May combined the deputy chairmanship with a day job as finance director, while his 'critical side' opposite number as financial adviser was Muriel Ward Jackson. With two people on the same patch, this twinning arrangement could have led to unpleasant infighting, but in the Partnership at this time it rarely did. If so, Miller came down hard on it.

One of Spedan's last recruits, Ward-Jackson was a pre-war Oxford graduate of impressive intellect and considerable courage, yet without the usual First. 'I enjoyed myself too much. Unlike little Jimmy Wilson.' Interviewer looks blank. 'Harold Wilson to you. He was determined to get a First, and he did, so the only extra-curricular activity he had was posting round circulars for the Liberal Party.' More puzzlement – he'd been a *Labour* prime minister. 'Oh yes, he was a Liberal then, but he soon saw they were dead on their feet.' As a senior civil servant after the war she had successfully challenged the outdated rule that women couldn't marry and still stay in post, and led a successful campaign for equal pay and conditions in the civil service. She had retained her maiden name, and entered the Partnership as Miss Jenkins, outfacing Spedan, who had objected to her 'masquerading as unmarried'. She was stubborn and feared no one. Spedan's ideas had so inspired her that she was prepared to forgo her civil service pension after twenty years to join him – if you left the civil service before retirement you got no pension, an iniquitous rule even she hadn't been able to alter. (Her successor as finance director, John Sadler, had to give his up as well.) When Spedan offered her a job she phoned her old Oxford contemporary Elizabeth Barling, then chief registrar. 'How would the natives receive news of an outsider? There was a profound silence at the other end. But long-distance swimmers like me know that, as long as your head is above it, it doesn't matter how deep the water is.' It was said that at one-to-one meetings she would take no notes, but that such was her memory she could produce the perfect summary out of her head.

## Paul May

Paul May was Miller's number two – loyal, calm, diplomatic, far-sighted: in Miller's words 'a delightful companion with a wry sense of humour', a modest man with 'a conspicuous unconcern with status and the trappings of office'. Unlike Spedan's other close lieutenants he had stayed away from the 'Odney dachas', as his son Stephen put it, when he was exploiting his silk knowledge as head of parachute supply in the war. His rapid postwar promotion catapulted him to the job of financial adviser in 1950, and on through the troubled early years of that decade when, as he said on retirement: 'I did jolly nearly leave, but when it came to the point I was too much hooked on the whole thing and couldn't leave the Partnership and the other chaps.' He had an independent mind and was particularly good at standing up to Spedan under fire that would make others shrivel. Apart from his financial acumen and sheer steadiness, as research and expansion director through most of the 1960s he was responsible for two decisive statements of direction. The first was his continued championing of Waitrose when others, especially Miller, were still inclined to sell. The other was an early recognition of the power of computing to speed up and improve the information available, especially to buyers.

May was clear that the first priority when computers arrived for commercial application was to improve sales and profits and not, as other businesses were doing, to focus largely on cutting costs through replacing clerical functions. The first computer's arrival coincided with the decision to improve the department store distribution chain by building a massive warehouse outside London at one of the postwar 'New Towns', Stevenage. The two projects were closely connected – it was through the doors of the new Stevenage warehouse that the first computer was trundled in 1962 – and one of its first jobs was to help manage the flow of orders and stock between buyers and branches. By 1970 it was providing stock, sales and forecast information to buyers for both department stores and Waitrose. Better forecasts meant better sales, and the improved efficiency of the supply chain and these new computer systems were key – and usually unremarked – constituents of the growth of the John Lewis profit-to-sales ratio in the late 1960s. The computer's influence would grow rapidly in the 1970s, but it was Paul May's clear-sighted direction of its development that got the Partnership on a sales-generating and profit-building track.

## Summing Up the Miller Era

A business is successful if it can make substantial sales and increase them year on year. But that's no good unless your profit is increasing at the same rate, and preferably faster. That gives you a measure of a business's *real* effectiveness, the profit-to-sales ratio. In Spedan's last year of 1955 it was 4.8%

– profits were £1.3m on sales of just under £28m. This led to an annual Bonus of 8%, paid entirely in shares. In Miller's last year, seventeen years later, the profit-to-sales ratio was 8.7%, nearly double, earned from profits of £15m on sales of £172m. (At that point inflation had started to rocket, so the sales and profit were in real terms up 3.3 times and 6 times respectively.) The annual Bonus was 18%, now paid entirely in cash.

There is nowadays an alternative measure of performance: return on invested capital (ROIC), but the historical figures are not calculable. There is no doubt, though, that the capital was pretty carefully husbanded. As we saw at the start of this chapter, no new department stores were built, so there was in fact slightly *less* selling space. The capital went into moving shops to new sites (in Southampton and Sheffield), and into apparently mundane infrastructure projects – warehousing, the first computers, and a steady replacement of old fixtures and fittings. And money was by no means lashed out on shop appearance. Stan Withers, who had been there in Reading when the AH Bull business was incorporated into the larger Heelas premises, was asked what he felt the main difference was fifty years ago. 'Fixtures,' he said. 'We had to go on for years with scruffy old fixturing. Only John Lewis got new stuff. But look at the shops now.'

And Partners' working lives? In 1955 provincial shops were largely open five and a half days a week, including a midweek half-day and all day Saturday. Because trade on Mondays was relatively light, and in some towns pressure was growing to end or vary the mandatory midweek half-day, the Partnership experimented with a five-day trading week, Tuesday to Saturday, closed Sunday and Monday. Its success at Southampton in the early 1960s led to its adoption everywhere outside central London by 1966, thus giving staff two consecutive days of rest, a real rarity in retailing. That tidying up of the week had distinct advantages to the business as well as to the ordinary shop assistant. An associated measure, which would on the face of it adversely affect the bottom line, was increased holidays. Spedan's successors shared his conviction that everybody, not just department managers and above, would work better if they had four weeks' holiday instead of three. In 1965 it happened in John Lewis Oxford Street, where the day-in-day-out pressure was considerable. Four branches followed the next year, but then it stuck. Several branch councils were unhappy with the hold-up, but Bernard Miller patiently explained that new government limits to improvements in pay and benefits, introduced in the wake of the sterling's devaluation in late 1967, would prevent its extension. But by 1970 all Partners outside Central London had both their five-day week and their four-week holiday.

'Core business' is an over-used and sometimes misused expression these days, but Miller and his team consciously cropped the Partnership back to its essentials. Most of the miscellaneous factories acquired in the 1930s were closed, as was Spedan's ill-fated overseas venture into a small retail chain in South Africa, and only an old-established cloth-printing factory in Cumbria was bought. Miller was self-effacing by Spedan's standards, but extremely tough and single-minded. And he was determined to maintain the Partnership's special character. There might have been a temptation to cut back on amenities, but in fact Miller seized the opportunity to buy a decrepit crenellated castle, a romantic Victorian conceit built on a ruined Elizabethan base. It was on the nature reserve island of Brownsea in Poole Harbour off the South coast, an island shared with red squirrels, peacocks, rare wildfowl and waders, the naturalists who sought them, and over twenty species of mosquito, which thrived in the stagnant pools. The mosquitoes haunted the castle, though to its first Partnership visitor, Captain Cooper, an ex-navy officer, anything would be an improvement on the Japanese prisoner-of-war camps he'd managed to survive. While Bernard Miller addressed Bournemouth and Poole councils to convince the sceptical local burghers that the Partnership would genuinely turn it into a holiday home and not a brothel, Cooper set about the restorations. He called in old naval chums for advice and expertise and heavy moving equipment: there were trees growing through the outbuildings and wartime installations to dismantle. He summoned a mosquito expert from the Natural History Museum, who identified only five biters from among the Brownsea horde. Five biting species out of twenty-six that is, with a million representatives each. Remove the standing water and they'll go, he said, and persuaded the doubting Dorset naturalists who leased the island that the birdlife wouldn't suffer. The first Partner holidaymakers arrived in the summer of 1962, using the castle boat that plied to and from Poole Harbour twice a day. The Castle had its own beach. One of the first visitors was from Newcastle. 'What did you do all day?' 'Swam, walked.' 'And when the weather was bad?' 'Started to tunnel.' The Castle's visual similarity to the German prisoner of war camp at Colditz ensured its early reputation, but it soon became a heavily subsidised holiday destination that was over-subscribed and had to be balloted for.

In 1961 Miller decided that the centenary of John Lewis in Oxford Street should be marked by a piece of public sculpture, so he instigated a competition. He liked none of the entries enough, so he gave the commission to Barbara Hepworth, who came up with an abstract design which was intended to convey the twin figures of Capital and Labour in combination, connected by the slender but strong wires that represent the virtues which hold the Partnership together. At the head of the chapter – and at the corner of Oxford and Holles streets today – you can see the result. It cost £7,000, the equivalent of a little over £100,000 today, a sum he wouldn't have dreamt of spending had he not felt the Partnership had at last turned the corner.

In 1964 at the combined celebrations for the centenary of John Lewis's little shop, and the fiftieth anniversary of Spedan's arrival at Peter Jones, Bernard Miller summed up his first years as Chairman:

> Perhaps the real significance of these ten years has been that the system of Partnership has shown that in all essentials it was soundly conceived and has needed no fundamental change, and that it can and does work without its founder.
>
> In the Partnership's journalism ... I myself have been not merely willing but anxious to give full explanation upon anything which seems to give rise to doubt or disquiet ... I do so not only because the constitution requires it, but it is a necessary part of the atmosphere of the whole Partnership ... It is an atmosphere in which people do speak their minds freely and do expect to be answered back, in which there is no obsequious deference to higher authority, but nevertheless a sense of the discipline that every large team must have. Newcomers have frequently commented upon this general friendliness, and for me it has always been something I value very highly.

Trevor Fry, the 'Bevin Boy' Spedan had recruited, was a buyer in this period, and met the top brass because he was an expert photographer and took most of the portrait photographs for the Gazette. Of Bernard Miller he added:

> He was a good sport too. I used to photograph those early revues, you know, after the war. He was in them – looked superb as a baby in a large pram being wheeled on stage. Spedan sat in the front row and laughed along with everyone. They helped avoid the danger of the Partnership taking itself too seriously, which it was inclined to, probably still is. Laughter's very healthy.

Miller had also appeared as Buttons in a glorious blonde wig to impersonate a new head of intelligence, and played the lead in *You Never Can Tell*. Like Spedan, Miller supported the revues, and though they disappeared in the 1960s one was devised to mark his retirement in 1971. Five years after he retired he summed up his time in the Partnership, which crystallised into four distinct stages:

> The first, from 1927 to 1939 was for me a time of youthful zest and energy spilling over in all directions; nothing was too zany to look into and everything was possible. This was followed by the grey days of 1939 to 1952, full of worries, personal tragedies among senior Partners and always new trials round the corner. From 1952 to 1960 was a period of real progress, but with the question-mark over all – would we get it right? Then, from 1960 onwards, the way ahead was clear and the Partnership went ahead steadily and continues to do so.

He finished his Partnership career as Sir Bernard Miller. He had been knighted in 1967 for his services to retailing, suitably enough in the year in which the Bonus reached 18% for the first time since 1929. While

Partnership Chairman, he was on the Council for Industrial Design for nine years and a member of the Monopolies Commission for most of the 1960s. He retired in the year he was seventy, then went on for another seventeen years at Southampton University, initially as its Treasurer and finishing as its Pro-Chancellor at the age of eighty-six. His robust health, which had kept him going through the tribulations of the war period, enabled him to live till ninety-eight. With no apparent loss of mental sharpness either: in his nineties, on one of his occasional visits to a Partnership function, he found the then finance director David Young in the lift. 'He pinned me to the wall with a detailed question about the Exchange Rate Mechanism, the linkage between the pound and the euro, and gave me a grilling.'

CHAPTER 16

# Peter Lewis and a Bonus Bonanza

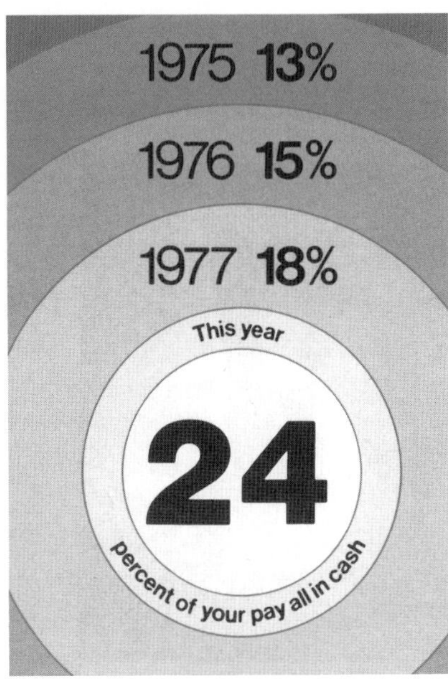


Peter Lewis, and the Gazette illustration of the record Bonus distributed in 1979 (and again in 1987 and 1988).

The *Financial Times* said last week that the atmosphere inside the Partnership, generated by profit sharing and so on, 'not only cramps the style of managers with an authoritarian frame of mind but can hamper decision-making and expansion. If over the last twenty-five years the British economy had enjoyed half the Partnership's growth in sales, profitability or employment, what a country we should be!

PETER LEWIS, IN HIS ANNUAL CHAIRMAN'S SPEECH TO THE PARTNERSHIP COUNCIL, MAY 1986

In the Partnership the next Chairman is nominated by his predecessor towards the end of his term: there has never yet been a modern 'nomination committee' approach. As we've seen, Spedan had eventually settled on Bernard Miller after much heart-searching, once he was convinced that his son Edward didn't want the job. Although Spedan appeared to hope Edward might change his mind, it was soon apparent this wouldn't happen. It looked as though the Chairmanship had left the Lewis family for good, because the only other possibility, Oswald Lewis's son Peter, virtually the same age as his cousin Edward, had like his father opted for the Law. After a spell doing National Service in the Coldstream Guards, Peter had read History at Oxford before studying Law, and was called to the Bar in 1956. Three successful years later he was contemplating his next move and trying to choose between two attractive alternatives, both in the Law. His default long-term aim, though it wasn't something that often crossed his mind, was to be a judge.

He was discussing these options with a friend who at one point said, 'Have you never contemplated going into the family business? Well, of course, you're too old now for that.' Peter Lewis was twenty-nine, and this suggestion that he was too old rankled. He had decided the Law would suit him well; his grandfather's business was long out of the family, and he had not really considered the Partnership. But now he did, and somewhat to his surprise a short time later in the summer of 1959 he found himself as a management trainee at John Lewis. His father, incidentally, proud of his success in the Law, described it as 'a lamentable decision'. By the end of the year he was managing the stationery department on the ground floor in Oxford Street. The Partnership didn't treat him (or anyone) with kid gloves: the run-up to Christmas was pretty hectic, and in stationery it was something of a baptism of fire. That was in the Stanley Carter days, a year before the shop was fully re-opened, and Peter Lewis recalls that when he first started there 'the whole of the south-west corner was a hole in the ground.' Derek Rawlings was then a merchandise manager, and remembers with some relish an early encounter: 'There was quite a crush in the department, and I found him in his office. I said I thought he would be more use at the moment serving customers than doing his paperwork.'

The following August Peter Lewis became the buyer for stationery, where he stayed for the best part of three years prior to a two-year stint in the general inspectorate, examining various parts of the business. In 1965 he went to join Max Baker's small central trading team to oversee buying, and two years later, when Max retired, he took over from him as trading director for the whole of John Lewis. That was quite a rapid rise to the top of the John Lewis tree, but nobody felt that his family tree had anything to do with it. It was achieved purely on merit. He was clear-sighted, with a forensic intelligence and a keen eye for the logical flaws in an argument – as many Partnership directors and Gazette letter writers would later discover – and he stuck to the principles he decided were important. He was tall, even taller than Spedan, with startlingly bushy and expressive eyebrows. But unlike Spedan's his prose was clear, spare and direct. By June 1969, ten years after Peter joined the business, Bernard Miller had seen enough to be convinced of his successor, and he took over three years later, in October 1972. In Miller's view: 'The Partnership has been as lucky as I have in getting him as Chairman, and as lucky as I have been in not having a difficult choice to make.'

Peter Lewis said he took over a first-class management team, and that was important against the background of a disturbed and divided country. The 1970s was a period of economic stress and conflict, not least because, as he said at his first Partnership council dinner:

> It is no disrespect to the leaders of the CBI or some of our trade unions to point out that they represent companies and organisations that have outgrown the traditional methods available for their public examination and, in the last resort, their control. Many of them have grown increasingly impervious to contemporary means of criticism.

In the Partnership the forum for public examination was the Gazette, and woe betide a director who didn't respond properly to criticism in its letter column. There was plenty to write about. The decade was disfigured by strikes, power cuts, student revolts, an imposed three-day week, and the fear of IRA bombings. And a rash of bomb hoaxes. In 1974 the MD of John Lewis Oxford Street, in the immediate aftermath of the devastating Harrods bomb, was hoaxed out of over £50,000 in blackmail money. (Bill Melly, the genial brother of the jazz musician, smelt a rat and avoided a hoax around the same time when he was general manager of Pratts of Streatham.) Moreover, there was rapid inflation of a kind rarely seen in Britain for such a sustained period. By Peter Lewis's last year as Chairman, inflation had devalued the currency by more than a factor of six from the year he'd started. So one pound in 1972 was worth barely 16p in 1992. It was hard to keep a grip on a company's finances when annual inflation peaked at 24%, as it did in 1975. In the first seven years of Peter Lewis's Chairmanship annual inflation averaged over 16%, and businesses had to manage through a period of interference by successive governments desperate to curtail the wage-price spiral. Fortunately, the Partnership had strong systems of financial control, and from 1971 to 1987 it had another formidably intelligent finance director, John Sadler, again an Oxford First. Sadler was a former civil servant who spent three years in the branches before becoming Muriel Ward Jackson's deputy in 1969 and succeeding her in 1971. Any project brought to the board by a trading MD would undergo scrutiny the twin searchlights of

Lewis and Sadler. Supplicants soon learnt that a case had to be absolutely logical and error-free before it would pass muster.

## Growth – the Legg Legacy

Not that the Partnership battened down the hatches against the economic turbulence and eschewed rapid growth. It continued the Miller period doctrine of creating department stores large enough to dominate a catchment area, rather like mediaeval castles, and there was now more money available for expansion. Although the Partnership remained decidedly risk-averse and most of its leaders were conservative, opportunities for new stores were out there, as were openings for extensions or relocations to existing city-centre shops. And in Harry Legg, the man who arrived with Kinghams and had been services director, it had someone who was not at all bothered by risk. He had the ability to play a long hard game, as he often had to in a spell of seventeen years as research and expansion director. During the twenty-year Peter Lewis period the number of department stores increased from sixteen (plus four smaller shops, soon disposed of) to twenty-two, but the total selling space doubled. Despite being a champion of city-centre trading, John Lewis opened its first ever shop in a custom-built out-of-town shopping centre off the North Circular Road on London's outskirts. Brent Cross was panned by a sceptical press but loved by shoppers: the reaction has been the same for almost all such large developments since. New shops were opened in Edinburgh, Milton Keynes – in a genuine green field site – Peterborough, and in Kingston. All had long gestation periods, but Kingston was an exhausting twenty-year long haul which tested Legg's resolve and his powers of persuasion – both outside and inside the Partnership.

An experiment with a restricted 'Furnishing and Leisure' range was opened outside High Wycombe, visible from the M40 motorway between London and Oxford. It had no fashions because of a trading restriction imposed by the local council. There were doubts about whether it would succeed there, and – daringly for the Partnership – it was built quickly as a 'shed'. But the car park was full by midday throughout the first week, and on Saturday the M40 was gridlocked and had to be closed, so popular was the concept. Peter Lewis told the Partnership council:

> For quite a time our researchers and thinkers demurred at halving our department store assortment, fearing that it would diminish both footfall and profit. But High Wycombe is encouraging. The assortment, over its limited range of departments, is genuinely very powerful.

So there were more like it? No. The view that the Partnership should stick with its well-tried 'full-line' department store model prevailed. There were arguments, then and later, that with the payback period for a new store being so long, there should be more experimentation with a smaller format: you could have more sites, get them up and running and paying back more quickly. It wasn't until 2009 that such a smaller store was opened: in Poole on the south coast. Meanwhile back in the 1980s existing stores were acquired and converted to the Partnership pattern in Bristol, Norwich, Aberdeen and Welwyn. The old shops in Nottingham, Newcastle and Watford were relocated, more or less within sight of the originals. Heelas in Reading, a store existing in an agglomeration of old buildings – with as a result over forty different levels – was essentially rebuilt on the spot in a complicated six-year manoeuvre before emerging with a new configuration, like a butterfly from a long-dormant chrysalis. The old Robert Sayle shop took many years to redesign and reconstruct to the satisfaction of conservative Cambridge; Legg once said wryly to Ian Bassett, an elected board member: 'We think ahead a hundred years and imagine it's a long time. In Cambridge colleges they think a thousand.' The long-serving Bassett said that the Robert Sayle revamp came up at his first board meeting and at his last, over twenty years apart. Four shops in the London suburbs were closed, in Hampstead and Islington in the north, Brixton and Streatham in the south. Trade had become stagnant and rebuilding and re-siting were impossible, though the North London pair were reopened as large Waitrose shops, instantly successful.

For most of the period from 1969 to 1986 Harry Legg presided over this development, a risk-taker in a cautious business. He was urbane, guarded and steely and had a trademark enigmatic smile: 'He may sit here silent, but he has not been asleep', said Peter Lewis to the Partnership council in that last year of 1986. 'The diet he has fed his colleagues since I have been Chairman may not excite the *Financial Times* but it has sometimes scared the pants off us.' At the 1982 council dinner the guest speaker was the head of the development corporation with whom Legg had been negotiating over the opening of the new Peterborough John Lewis. He painted this picture of Legg in action:

> He's a man dedicated to the Partnership's interests and most assiduous in fostering them, a man of great urbanity, charm, good humour and personal kindness – except when you're negotiating with him. The urbanity and the charm remain – but you can say goodbye to the kindness! After you have negotiated, you feel bereft, stripped, excoriated and even bloodless. He tells you that you drive a hard bargain, that he has had to make far too many concessions, that he doubts the council will agree with all that he has given away – and that you are the most skilful negotiator he has ever met.

His negotiating skill was apparent inside the Partnership as well; the son of a builder, he had trained as a barrister but switched career. He persuaded his colleagues of the merits of several projects many had doubts about: notably, and most notoriously, a new shop in Kingston-upon-Thames, south west of London. Kingston was a project which spent much of its early life in intensive care, with a priest hovering to administer the last rites. It faced onto the Thames so it needed elaborate anti-flooding precautions, it had major structural problems, it had a wondrous but expensive glass roof from Germany – and, of all things, by the end it had a four-lane road tunnelling right through the middle of it. But Legg and his doctors kept resuscitating it, though the costs escalated inexorably, and the project became a long-running battle between risk and caution, development and finance – Harry Legg and John Sadler – which carried on into several board meetings. The final board meeting was one of the few that came to a vote, and the project went ahead after a long debate and a narrow vote in favour. One of the witnesses to the saga was Ian Bassett, a systems analyst whose thoughtful council contributions had got him re-elected to the board every year for the best part of twenty years. He said that board consensus was so normal that intractable arguments in that period were uncommon, and a vote at the end of a debate was even rarer. Bassett lived near Kingston, so had a particular interest, and he went to an early public inquiry. The local council had selected the John Lewis scheme from among a number of competing proposals, including one from Debenhams, who then challenged the legality of its decision. Bassett recalls:

> Harry Legg was masterly on his feet, very calm. He was being cross-examined by the Debenhams barrister when at one point he flourished the FT, which had reported on poor annual results which had just come out, unfortunately for them. 'Which of these two businesses would you prefer, Debenhams or John Lewis?' he said. He demolished the opposition. What was absolutely typical of Legg was that he'd produced some documents about the John Lewis scheme for the Inquiry, which had far more in them than I'd ever seen so far, and I was a John Lewis board member, for goodness' sake. He was so secretive, his secretary asked me for them back! For a long time there was a three-way impasse over money, between Kingston Borough Council, Ken Livingston at the GLC and Maggie Thatcher the Prime Minister. Ken was in favour, so naturally she was against. But the biggest problem was congestion. Kingston's traffic was a disaster, and we simply wouldn't put a shop there until it was sorted. In the end someone came up with this idea to put a relief road diagonally through the middle of the site. It was bizarre, but it worked.
>
> Peter Lewis was immaculate as a board chairman for the Kingston debates. There were several, and they got very tense, but he never gave you a clue what outcome he wanted. He was clearly concerned that he had his key directors disagreeing, with views sincerely but strongly held, though it never got nasty. The worst I remember it got was when Harry once said 'Where do you want to put the money then? National Savings? We're a trading organisation, for goodness' sake.'

The issue in the end was whether the Partnership was ever going to get a payback. To John Sadler the figures were absolutely clear, and he still holds the view nearly thirty years later – it never would. To him it was the Partnership's Concorde. But Peter Lewis had a longer perspective than most; after all, the year he retired was nearly 130 years after his grandfather had opened his Oxford Street shop. He spoke to the Partnership council in 1986, still four years before Kingston eventually opened, on buying a department store in Aberdeen when the North Sea oil boom was at its peak. He had been distinctly lukewarm about Aberdeen, but the board wasn't, despite the sudden drop in the oil price. He told the council:

> Towards the end of the negotiations the price of oil clattered through the floor. That does not disturb us for the long term. Our calculations are for twenty-five years but our hopes are set on a hundred.

At intervals the demise of the department store format was regularly forecast. Peter Lewis and his directors had no such doubts. Other groups may have been ailing, but the Partnership stuck to its Never Knowingly Undersold philosophy, still offering a full-range department store. Peter Lewis was unrepentant about avoiding experimentation. He told the Partnership council in 1973 – discussing trading stamps, credit cards, advertising, overseas expeditions, food retailers building larger shops and selling more non-food – 'We have been outside the main whirlpools of activity. I do not regret this in retrospect.' Nor in prospect either: note the word 'whirlpool', with its implication of being sucked in and unable to escape. Whenever the Partnership opened in a new area it could guarantee its reputation would precede it, despite the long aversion to the siren song of advertising. One weakness, as we've seen, was that the gestation period for a full-size department store could run into many years. Nevertheless, there was a distinct advantage in having a business that could set its sights on the long-term without worrying about its share price, or appeasing the stock market and its commentators. The name John Lewis rarely appeared in the business pages, and that's the way they liked it. Most criticism came from inside the business, particularly during the strike-bound 1970s.

## Surviving the Turbulent Seventies

The Partnership's elaborate internal process for settling grievances enabled it to avoid almost entirely the strikes that were besetting industry in the 1970s, though in truth retailing, with comparatively weak unions, was not in the forefront of the battle. The Partnership had just two brief brushes with strikes, and they were instructive. Although workers on the selling floor and in offices were not members of a union, most of the drivers belonged, as did some of the workers in 'service buildings'. These were local warehouses for each department store. Their introduction, which had taken place over the previous twenty years, was designed to streamline the arrival and departure of stock, and to provide buffer stock space between the shop and the national distribution centre at Stevenage. They freed up more selling space in the shop, and helped to avoid the artery-clogging corridors of overflow stock that restricted its movement behind the scenes in the run-up to Christmas. A disadvantage, though, was that the service buildings couldn't be sited close to city-centre shops, and this led them to becoming islands, away from the all-for-one culture of the selling floor under the continuous eye of the shop's management and the registrar. The workforce there was often mostly or partly unionised, their managers typically more rough-and-ready than those running the host shop. This led to two successive problems during 1975 at Speke, the service building for George Henry Lee in Liverpool, where most – but not all – were members of the Transport and General Workers Union ( TGWU).

In the January a number of drivers were suspended for apparent abuse of a somewhat generous incentive scheme which had been operating without overt trouble for several years. But it had led to some dubious practices, including some drivers clocking off well after completing a day's work so they could get enough hours to qualify. When four people at Speke were suspended for alleged irregularities in claims for overtime pay, it led to a walk-out. As they had more than five years' service, the four suspended Partners had the right of appeal to the Partners' counsellor, who set off for Liverpool and ended by recommending that three should be reinstated with a warning and the fourth, the service manager, should be demoted. That settled the immediate issue, which had been complicated by the local TGWU shop steward trying to introduce at Speke a national agreement that didn't actually apply to retailing. The action lasted four days and led to an emergency branch council meeting condemning it, followed by a furious fusillade of critical letters in the Gazette. Most were from Partners far away, shielded from the complexity of operating in a partly-unionised unit. The difference in reaction of fellow-workers to a strike was completely different from those bigger disputes going on in the country at large. In the Partnership it was 'How dare you? Get back to work before you damage our – *our* – business. And you people who (we pay to) run our business, get your act together.' Indeed the Stevenage delivery drivers, not short of a militant or two themselves, drove through the picket line and themselves threatened to strike if the Speke miscreants weren't sacked.

Clearly this dispute led to continuing bad feeling, because in July a driver who was a TGWU member refused to go out when assigned to work with a non-member he disliked. Until that point, the local management had been able to avoid such a pairing, but in a holiday period it wasn't possible. The driver continued to refuse after a warning, was suspended, and fifteen other Speke Partners walked out, about a fifth of the workforce. Twelve days later, after refusing to give a written undertaking that they would observe their rules of engagement, they were sacked. Some of them then picketed the front of the shop, abusing and jostling shop workers trying to get into work. The local TGWU official was sensible enough to dissociate the union from the action, and eventually persuaded them to sign up to an assurance that he'd written on their behalf, whereupon they were taken back. The much-liked Liverpool MD Brendan Henry then had a difficult time defending his decision to reinstate them at a further emergency branch council meeting, from councillors unhappy about what they saw as a climb-down in face of union militancy, and in particular that he'd made the decision without asking their opinion first. He wasn't obliged to, and was probably wise not to, so high was feeling running against the strikers. A further barrage of Gazette letters rained down, the outrage focusing on the behaviour of the pickets. If we'd done anything like that ourselves, said the Partners who wrote, it would have led to immediate dismissal.

I've dwelt on this issue because it was virtually the only time the Partnership suffered an industrial dispute in the 1970s, or indeed since. The Partnership escaped the disruptive dramas being played out across the country, a country whose Prime Minister, Ted Heath, had been toppled the previous March. He'd gone to the polls following a crippling national miners' strike, the second in three years. He asked the nation the question Who Governs Britain? Next day he knew the answer: it wasn't him, but Harold Wilson with an unworkable overall majority of just three. The Partnership's grievance procedures were carefully documented, and worked well enough when cranked into action, but were intended for 'men of goodwill on all sides', and understandably couldn't cope with instant flare-ups. Two years later, an unexpected and entirely different flashpoint occurred at the Stevenage distribution centre in February 1977. Between October and December the warehouse had taken in and moved out a huge volume of stock in the Christmas run-up. Excellent Christmas and January Clearance sales figures, reported as usual the following week in the Gazette, led the hard-pressed Partners there to expect a bumper Bonus. But sales aren't the same as profits, nor are weight and volume, and much of the merchandise the Stevenage warehousemen had been humping around was big stuff like televisions and washing machines – heavy, expensive, but not very profitable in an area where, because competitive pricing was so strong at the time, Never Knowingly Undersold kept the margin down. The Gazette's year-on-year comparison figures were exceptionally high, but so was the underlying inflation.

When a Bonus of 15% was announced, much less than ill-informed rumours had suggested, there was a wave of disgruntlement and a section of the Stevenage staff walked out for twenty-four hours. The majority at Stevenage decided to work on, using their branch councillors – this time sympathetic, if not with the walk-out – to pass a motion that 'many Partners felt that the Bonus should have been higher'. Three other councils, though their branches didn't resort to industrial action, also publicly expressed their disappointment. The Partnership council, in a regular meeting already scheduled for the following Monday, took the emergency proposal from Stevenage, which simply asked the Chairman to 'take note'. After a long and measured debate it was defeated by 69 votes to 32, but it was a wake-up call to the board and Peter Lewis, whose annual caution in his Bonus forecasts had come to be disregarded. 'They always say that, don't they? The Bonus is always bigger than they forecast.' Well, this year it wasn't, and it's a telling reminder of how much expectations had grown in twenty years. In 1959 the Bonus had reached double figures for the first time since the early 1930s. Since then it had always been over 10%, and three times it had touched 18%. Partners were relying on it, and often spending it before it arrived – hence the ructions. The strength of feeling surprised the board, including its five elected members, but government pay restrictions, in a period when inflation had averaged over 20% for each of the last two years, had left everyone feeling worse off. It's hard in an era of much lower inflation to remember – or imagine – what it's like when the price of butter is constantly moving up. Those in shops knew all too well, for in those days every item, from butter to towels, had an individual price label on it, and they were always being changed. The Partnership's ticket factory was working flat out.

In fact, the board meeting deciding that year's Bonus had led to more discussion than usual, and to unusually heated argument. Bassett said:

> Contrary to what you might expect, it was often the elected members who were more conservative in their Bonus preference. In this case, I remember, Eric Greenhalgh and Dorothy Barrett [then department stores director of trading and chief registrar] were clearly both well aware of how hard the branches had worked. There were only one or two percentage points in it, but we couldn't get the usual consensus. John Sadler [finance director] presented the figures and the options as usual. Peter Lewis never pressed his own view on the Bonus, and the discussion went on for so long that he called a break. Afterwards we got quickly to the more conservative figure. I think we thought we'd done a good job, but we certainly weren't prepared for the fall-out.

Peter Lewis and the board weren't going to get caught like that again. They recognised that there was a gap between the way they presented the figures and how much the ordinary Partner, and indeed their councillor representatives, understood of them. It had been traditional to decide the Bonus immediately after the end of the trading year, which typically in retail was the end of January: after Christmas and the subsequent sales period. But that meant they were basing the decision on estimated figures, and of course when shop and warehouse workers in the front line were still often pretty exhausted from the last two months' battle. The following year the board decided to postpone the Bonus decision and announcement by a month to the end of February, and to present the annual results visually in an arresting glossy colour insert (in a Gazette then still black and white). Other companies were doing it, but the Partnership had fallen behind. Partners could now see graphically – that, for example, while *sales* had more than doubled in five years from £209m to £437m, the *profit* figure with inflation removed was almost exactly what it had been in 1973. Indeed, although the business had been piloted shrewdly through the see-sawing Seventies, its underlying profit-to-sales ratio had even dropped slightly from its historic peak in 1972 – a level never subsequently achieved (see the graph on p. 316).

Nevertheless, for that trading year of 1977, the annual Bonus reached 18% again, and the next year it reached a hitherto unimaginable 24%. This was the start of an extraordinary and unprecedented run in which the figure averaged 20% over the eleven years from 1978 to 1988. By any measure that was outstanding. In two consecutive years, in 1986 and 1987, it reached 24% again. Even though some Partners felt increasingly uneasy that so much was being distributed when more might go into developing the business, the board was adamant that it would plough back no more than it felt necessary, and distribute the remainder once it had kept the pension fund topped up. If the board wasn't receiving spending proposals from the trading directors, then its constitution required it to distribute the residual profits.

And the Partners were happy. Occasionally in letters, and in questioning after the Chairman's annual set-piece report and speech to the council, issues would be raised about policy (proposing a chain of smaller non-food shops, or trying advertising) and progress with this or that. But the pressure was mild, the answers as clear and as open as they could be, and the Partnership's continuing success, marked by its steadily increasing annual Bonus, left the vast majority of its members in a state of contentment. Most people felt that their pay could be higher, but, after an awkward period of a government-enforced pay freeze that lasted from 1975 to 1977, that regular high Bonus was a marvellous annual tonic. Partners had indeed never had it so good.

The sustained level of the Bonus was an annual confirmation that Spedan's experiment was now an undoubted success. Nobody outside took much notice of this, and it wasn't in Peter Lewis's nature to tell the world. If people wanted to find out about the curious organisation, and perhaps to emulate it, they were received with the utmost warmth and given every help. But that's as far as it went. Interestingly, the only faint whiff of a public disagreement with his predecessor that entered the pages of the Gazette was at a Partnership council dinner in 1979, the year the Bonus reached 24%. Bernard Miller had been several years retired, but his two sons Peter and Michael were both directors of the business and he remained keenly interested. In a typically courteous speech at the dinner he ventured: 'The Partnership is not yet widely known for the outstanding example of a successful industrial democracy that it is, and … should perhaps turn outward rather more than it has in the past.' To which Peter Lewis replied with equal courtesy: 'As some of you will know, that is not my view.' A councillor that year tried him out: 'Surely the experiment is over. Should we not now publish the results?' He responded by saying it was important to avoid vainglorious gestures. And there it rested, and if the FT didn't get it, well, it didn't matter much.

## 1978 to 1988 – Why So Successful?

As we've seen, the department store business expanded steadily and with only occasional upheaval throughout Peter Lewis's twenty years as Chairman. In the same period the number of Waitrose branches more than doubled, having just topped 100 when he retired. In real terms John Lewis sales increased by a little less than half, but Waitrose's went up by three times. While at the start of the period Waitrose had only half the amount of sales that the department stores were making, by 1992 their sales were almost identical. This meant that because much of the sales increase during the period was in food, which traditionally had a much smaller profit margin, Waitrose profits in 1992 were only 60% of department stores. Not until 1990 did Waitrose profits exceed half of John Lewis's (and in 1993 they plunged below half again). So the effect of the substantial Waitrose sales increase was to dilute the Partnership's overall profitability, just as Bernard Miller had foreseen in 1964. And yet the Partnership was able to keep the Bonus, from 1978 to 1988 anyway, averaging 20%. How? There are many reasons, but it's a combination of two main factors: improved efficiency, and the ability to hold hard to a five-day trading week in department stores.

A key factor in controlling costs and improving sales lay in the way computers were employed. Paul May's 1960s directive that the computer should be used primarily to improve information for buyers and branches had an important impact. When in 1968 Ian Anderson left Waitrose to take over the Partnership's rapidly growing computing, buyers already had information on the rate at which stock left the Stevenage warehouse, but they had no actual sales figures. Nobody in retail did back then – that would only happen after the application of a barcoded ticket to every product sold. But Anderson had been a buyer himself and knew that accurate sales figures were the real prize. He became the prime mover in UK retail in promoting what became known as EPOS, electronics at point-of-sale. In 1970 cash registers that punched sales figures into computer-readable paper tape were trialled in the hardware department in Oxford Street, a buyership where early experiments with automatic sales forecasting had already started. Assistants had to laboriously key in the stock number. However, before long IBM and NCR were offering competing EPOS systems which allowed sales to be 'transmitted' electronically at the end of the day. NCR's was ready first and was installed throughout Peter Jones and the new opening at Brent Cross, but had no way of capturing the stock number. However, IBM's had a more complete system that included a wand that could read tickets or labels on the merchandise, with the stock number embedded in a magnetic strip. This was a huge advance, years before the barcode-based systems that are now used everywhere. The system was trialled in Holloway and Newcastle before being extended throughout John Lewis by the end of the 1970s. The information encoded was not yet a 'universal' product code, applied to the goods by every manufacturer as it is today, but had to be produced by the shop itself as the goods came in. However, this extra work was overwhelmingly compensated for by the discipline it introduced and the accurate sales information available to buyers. None of the rival department stores had it for at least ten years, and this gave the business a priceless competitive edge. The right stock was more than ever getting to the right place at the right time.

By the time he moved on in 1977 to be the overall John Lewis MD (then still called the director of trading), Anderson had built up a strong computer department. He had done so largely by following the firm Partnership tradition and employing almost exclusively new graduates in the computer department, where they got excellent home-grown training. Peter Lewis, although he could certainly see the crucial benefit of accurate product sales information, was innately a computer sceptic. Given the rapidly growing expense of computer departments everywhere, and the increasing tendency elsewhere of major projects to go spectacularly wrong, he was clear that it needed close supervision. As a consequence he ran a special quarterly computer policy committee expressly to vet all applications for expense on computing. He feared a galloping inflation of costs, especially as the computer's acolytes seemed to be asking every couple of years for the newer, faster mainframe model that IBM kept producing. These were the days before computing ubiquity – no company had anything but massive 'mainframe' computers, impenetrable to all but the priestly caste who understood them. The PC hadn't been invented, 'real-time' computing via screens was in its infancy, and the John Lewis computer was housed near the BT Tower in central London in a basement full of IBM's big blue boxes. The discipline instilled by Peter Lewis's caution largely prevented the Partnership succumbing to the rash of big computer project failures. Despite this, and perhaps because of it, the development of computing in the Partnership in his era was a keystone of its improved efficiency, an irony that at the time was lost on those who battled to get their projects through.

## Waitrose – Small is Beautiful

Oddly, because the universal product code (UPC) system had been instituted originally for food in the USA, Waitrose would have to wait years for accurate information about how much of each product it had sold. Despite that, it did manage to develop one of the very first and most effective automatic ordering systems in supermarkets, for stock coming from the Bracknell warehouse. That was about half the total – the remainder came direct from suppliers. The system helped to reduce the counting and reordering effort in the shops, where keeping the cost of labour down was an ever-present problem. Whereas the John Lewis department stores tended to be much larger than the opposition, and had real economies of scale helped by a powerful central buying organisation, Waitrose was a much smaller player in an industry increasingly dominated at this time by big supermarket groups like Sainsbury's, Tesco and Safeway, a trio which Asda joined by the end of the 1980s. And it was smaller not just in total numbers – it had little more than 2% of the total food market in the 1970s – but in the size of its shops. From smaller shops you couldn't chisel out as much profit either, unless your range was smaller. The range in Waitrose, though, was very often wider than in shops twice the size. This was because, after rationalising the rather random collection of shops it had at the start of the Carter period of the 1960s, it had settled into a specific niche. And to a large extent this was by making a virtue of necessity. So, paradoxically, while for Partnership department stores Big was Best, for Waitrose at that time Small was Beautiful.

From 1977 to 1991 the Waitrose MD was John Foster – affable, philosophical, engagingly argumentative, and a retailer through and through. He had worked, of course, in a number of the department stores, including a formative spell as a merchandise manager at John Lewis Oxford Street under Stanley Carter. There he picked up a mass of experience – and an inexhaustible supply of anecdotes. He ran three department stores in turn and followed Patrick Mahon as the buying director for fashions in 1972. Like Carter before him he was plucked out to run Waitrose. Unfamiliarity with food retailing fazed him no more than it had Carter, and he brought Carter's trading principles and enjoyment of food with him, if not his driven nature and obsession for detail. In particular he held fast to Carter's – and through him the original John Lewis's – views on assortment width. A determination to preserve and extend a wide assortment was his hallmark, coupled with a steady extension into fresh food and service counters, which had largely been removed in the rush to self-service. Peter Falconer, the Waitrose buying director we met in Chapter 14, needed no encouragement to extend his buyers' ranges, and there was an increasing desire to hunt out and help the smaller suppliers who couldn't come up with the volume that the big competitors demanded. At a time when the balance of power was shifting to the huge supermarket chains, Waitrose was still trying to nurture the suppliers that could give its range a distinction. Peter Lewis reflected in 1988:

> The obsession with the new-found technique of self-service and the emphasis on price above all else led to a remarkable deterioration in other elements of retail service – no fresh foods of certain kinds, poor fresh fruit, no patisserie, poor bread, no fresh fish, no butchering of meat: all retrograde steps from the customer's point of view. The best supermarkets have been putting that right, and none faster than Waitrose.

The steady increase in ranges appealed to the person Waitrose was now more consciously targeting, what market research jargon termed the ABC1 customer. In layman's language, the well-off. Increasingly, new stores were sited where a high proportion of households fell into that ABC1 category, which essentially meant those typically with 'more money than time' and with discretionary money to spend on food – and who in particular really liked their food. Waitrose was now appealing to the discerning foodie. Foster, whose watchword was 'polish the difference', was keen to avoid becoming too much like the competition, increasingly monolithic. Sainsbury, Tesco, Safeway and Asda, building shops that were larger and larger, tended by contrast to appeal to those with tight budgets and growing families: customers who were more concerned with cost and convenience. Although a lot easier than the search for the massive sites needed for department stores, hunting for places to build new supermarkets was a highly competitive business. There was a self-fulfilling prophecy taking place. For a given potential site, the amount of money you were prepared to bid depended on the sales you thought you could achieve. Sainsbury's and Tesco (nowadays we'd list them the other way round) could command more for the bigger sites. Waitrose had to be content – and in this period was content – to pick up smaller sites, often with a less-than-ideal shape that forced building compromises. They were often very profitable, though the drawback was that they often lost sales heavily if one of the competition's big guns opened in the vicinity.

This small-size Waitrose suited Lewis and Foster, who both disliked the huge supermarkets that competitors were building, with their acreage of shelving, long aisles and impersonal service. 'Shops on a human scale' was John Foster's mantra. Moreover, not least because of a decision that no shop would be more than a day's return journey for a driver from its single central warehouse in Bracknell, Waitrose outlets were congregated largely in the Home Counties. The branches were solely in a triangle bordered by the English Channel and the rivers Trent and Severn, typically in affluent towns like Henley and Beaconsfield. Even those in the Midlands were small, and few and far between. Not until the 1990s was one built on the Trent and one a few miles beyond the Severn (in Monmouth, barely in Wales). There weren't even any in Devon. Wales and the industrial north were *terra incognita*, and as for Scotland, well, you could whistle. Pained Partnership councillors from the North, unable to buy food on discount as their southern colleagues often could, would occasionally gripe at Peter Lewis at his annual Q&A session, but would get nowhere.

Peter Lewis was entirely happy that Waitrose growth was slow and steady, with three or four new branches a year. He was delighted with its success, naturally, especially at the end of his period in charge, when in 1990–2 Waitrose profit was for the first time more than half that of John Lewis, which was struggling in a retailing slowdown. People could put off buying a new three-piece suite but had to keep buying food, and Waitrose – as in 2008 and 2009 – stayed pretty well insulated from recession. So it had its uses as an adjunct to the core department store business, but an adjunct it still remained. The 'corporate' directors, trained solely in department stores, largely ignored it. So did a Partnership council disproportionately dominated by John Lewis Partners. One Waitrose director said: 'Down in Bracknell, for us it was a bad news, good news story. The bad news was that the centre wasn't interested in Waitrose. The good news was that the centre wasn't interested in Waitrose.' In Waitrose itself people may have chafed at the slowness of change, indeed it was a typical complaint that several of its innovations were spotted and picked up by competitors, then rolled out to all their – many more – shops before Waitrose itself had got them halfway out. But its competition was far tougher than that faced by the department stores (in the 1980s anyway), so Waitrose was always pushing the borders of what the Partnership's leaders were comfortable with. Waitrose felt it was in a war against better-equipped enemies, while John Lewis was running a contented peacetime operation. When Peter Lewis appointed David Felwick, then managing director of John Lewis Welwyn, to be selling director at Waitrose at the start of 1987, he enjoined him, only half joking, to 'sort out those cowboys at Waitrose'. Felwick was soon seen riding hard and swinging a lasso with even more gusto than his new colleagues.

## Trading Hours

If you were to tell a young person about shop hours back in 1985 in a regional John Lewis department store like, say, Cole Brothers of Sheffield, the reaction would be amazement. It opened only five days a week. The store would have been closed on both Sunday and Monday, it traded a single late night until eight o'clock, on Saturday it closed at six and on the rest of the week at half past five. Hours were regulated by local councils, often with a fixed half-day closing which varied from place to place. If you wanted to change the rules in a town, you often had to club together with other retailers to persuade the local council. That happened in the Miller era when the Partnership decided to cut the week to five days from five and a half, with shops shut on Mondays everywhere outside central London. Sunday shopping was banned by law, except in Scotland, although as the 1980s progressed increasing numbers of

English shops were able to open on a Sunday because local councils wouldn't prosecute them. Thus in 1985 John Lewis regional shops usually opened just forty-six hours a week. London was different, but only in the Brent Cross shopping centre (open 10 a.m. to 8 p.m. every weekday) did a John Lewis shop open more than fifty hours. Both John Lewis Oxford Street and Peter Jones opened on Monday but closed at lunchtime on Saturday. What, you say? Closed on a Saturday afternoon, when Oxford Street is solid with shoppers? You're joking? No – 'our' customers didn't shop on a Saturday afternoon. It didn't stop them trying. David Young, the finance director who succeeded John Sadler, said that when he did a stint as MD of Peter Jones one of the most difficult jobs was getting the customers out and the doors shut at lunchtime on Saturday. Now it has all changed. All John Lewis shops open every day, like everyone else. By 2010 regional John Lewis opening hours have gone up from forty-six to between sixty-two and seventy-four hours, depending on location – up by 35–60%. Its Oxford Street trading hours have gone up by almost 50%. Waitrose had also been closing on Mondays – as many food shops used to do on the grounds that it was washday and families would eat Sunday joint leftovers – but by 1985 it was open fifty-six hours. By 2010 it was trading in the range seventy-four to eighty-six hours, and in its new smaller 'convenience' shops as high as ninety-four.

Clearly, if you're open nearly seventy hours a week you need almost two complete sets of staff. If you traded for forty-six hours, as regional Partnership department stores did for most of the Peter Lewis era, this allowed you either to have decidedly lower staff costs – and in retailing they form a high proportion of total variable costs – or to get more people onto the selling floor to provide better service. Or a combination of the two. Partners could have two-day weekends, Sunday and Monday, and work a five-day week. The Partnership could trade for as few as forty-six hours a week with two successive days closed because at that time its regular customers knew their local store was closed on a Monday, so didn't try to shop then. People could shop on one late night if they worked in the daytime, and everyone knew when it was. Nobody shopped on a Sunday because you couldn't: everyone recognised that Sunday was special. It's true that there was some irritation from customers in new-built John Lewis stores that they couldn't shop on a Monday or on more evenings. But if John Lewis could rack up sufficient profit – and its aim was and is to generate 'enough' profit, not the maximum possible – to pay its Partners approaching 20% in Bonus every year, why should it change? There was occasional reference in the press to the Partnership as a business that looked after itself more than its customers, but customers voted with their feet, and their feet kept coming through the doors. No problem.

## Sunday Trading

No problem, until the 1980s, when Sunday trading began to rear its head. In 1979 a National Consumer Council survey reported that two-thirds of people were opposed to Sunday trading, and indeed any increase in trading hours at all. By November 1982, three years into the new Margaret Thatcher government, a MORI poll indicated that the figures had abruptly reversed, and that month Peter Lewis explored the issues at length in his speech to the Partnership council dinner. Nevertheless, a Private Member's Bill in Parliament the following February to remove all restrictions on shopping hours was defeated by 205 votes to 106. The issue wouldn't go away, however, and in November 1984 the Auld report proposed the abandoning of shopping hours regulation. In his next speech to the council Peter Lewis set out to explain the dilemma. He was worried because he recognised that people would flock to shop on Sunday, but knew that the Partnership would simply be cannibalising its own trade and would have to bear the cost. He feared that the quality of British life would suffer, and not just for people in shops forced to work on Sundays.

He listed what he called the three myths that proponents of Sunday trading used: that it would generate higher retail activity and hence improve the economy; it would lower prices; it would reduce unemployment. He thought all three were unlikely, but that they were arguments 'all highly attractive to the public and to any politician whose wishes outpace his thought' – classic Peter Lewis, whose view of politicians was rarely complimentary. He concluded that five-day trading, Tuesday to Saturday, had been 'magnificently successful', but that if the competition opened on Sunday the Partnership would have no choice but to follow suit. In May 1985 the Commons passed a motion recommending deregulation by 304 votes to 184, and Peter Lewis told Partners to expect government legislation in 1986. Nothing, though, was forthcoming: some Tory grandees were clearly cautioning that there might be a backlash from the conservative (and Conservative) Sunday-worshipping shires.

In 1989 the Shopping Hours Reform Council (SHRC) was formed. None of its major officers, noted Peter Lewis, knew anything about retailing. 'They don't listen to the British Retailing Consortium, and a minister comes down from the Home Office to bless the SHRC and condemn all other faiths.' The debate rumbled on. Nothing more was brought to parliament, but many large shops, including most of Waitrose's major competitors, began to trade on Sunday, flouting a law that they reckoned wouldn't be enforced. Waitrose began to leak customers. Those who ten years before would have sniffed at going to the downmarket Tesco they remembered from the 'pile it high, sell it cheap' Jack Cohen days found their cars driving them there on a Sunday for a pint of milk, and discovered that the business had been transformed under his successors. In 1991 Peter Lewis was pressed at the Partnership council to take a lead against the SHRC, but demurred: 'The Partnership is not a lobbying organisation.' However, the Partnership increasingly gave substantial help to the Keep Sunday Special campaign, and lobbied MPs extensively, and put its then general inspector, Paul May's son Stephen, on the case. Later in the year, in telling Partners that they would not break the law by opening on Sundays in the run-up to Christmas, as virtually everyone else was now doing, Peter Lewis described the current situation as 'a disgrace to the Home Office'. Then – in a rare act more typical of Spedan – he published a letter he had written to Home Secretary Kenneth Baker that began: 'It's hard to frame our question without sounding sarcastic.' He made little attempt to avoid sarcasm, naturally, and printed Baker's reply with the comment: 'The Home Secretary has not answered the question, nor made any attempt to do so.' Well, he was a politician. Peter Lewis wasn't: he was a man of the Law, and one with a strict morality, and the whole mess offended him.

Illegal Sunday trading was hurting the Partnership, and at the beginning of the 1990s there was a major recession. Some of the natives started to get restless in the Gazette. Is it right, for instance, for us still to close on Mondays outside London? In the previous twenty years the only concession to those who wanted to increase hours had been in 1985, with a little extra late-night trading. Throughout 1991 and 1992 in the Gazette the new MD of John Lewis, Brian O'Callaghan, was defending the five-day trading status quo, often against aggrieved Partners from a Waitrose business which traded six days and in 1991 was at last contributing substantially to the Partnership's profit. 'Unlike you, we open when people want to shop,' said one. O'Callaghan was adamant – and quite right – in asserting that one of the reasons that John Lewis department stores had been so successful was that service from its experienced and knowledgeable assistants was so much better than at its competitors. Dilute the staffing by opening on Mondays, and costs would inevitably increase sharply and service slide. That was indisputable, whereas the increased trade on Mondays was distinctly uncertain.

## Twenty Years On

How did the average Partner view the Peter Lewis years? Although the Bonus fell rapidly in the recession of his last three years, it had still averaged 17%, (a sixth of Partners' pay), across his whole two decades. By the time of his departure, too, Partners were better off in other ways. Everyone, not just managers, had been given five weeks' annual holiday after three years. Shopping discount in department stores had been increased from 20% to 25% after one year of service – and in Waitrose from 10% to 12%. And, in a move that marked the Partnership out from every other large company, in 1979 Peter Lewis announced a 'long leave' scheme to commemorate the fiftieth anniversary of Spedan's 1929 Settlement. Partners would be entitled to take a six-month break on full pay after age fifty if they'd been in the business twenty-five years. Many had. Staff turnover is notoriously high in retail, and although at John Lewis it is lower than most, it's still high among the young. But once you'd been in the Partnership for a while, 'an umbilical cord starts to grow, and it's increasingly difficult to leave.' So there were many who qualified. The buyer Peter Yaghmourian was one of the first. He used his life-savings for a round-the-world trip which so enthused him that the first thing he did on return was to ask the pensions manager how soon he could afford to retire. His director Ian Anderson was far from happy at this, and Peter Lewis was prevailed upon to prevent directors and senior managers from taking the break until six months before they retired. They were arguably among those who would have benefited most from the break, but commercial caution won out. It often did. Nevertheless long leave was regarded by many inside the business as Peter Lewis's greatest legacy to the Partnership, enabling low-paid Partners to do things and go places they'd never have been able to, and inspiring them to do more on retirement.

At the beginning of 1993 Peter Lewis, having presided until 1990 over an astonishing period of unbroken success, handed over smoothly to a new Chairman, Stuart Hampson, who said of him at his accession:

> Peter Lewis may not be an expansionist, but the Partnership has not stood still ... The savaging of any trace of weak thinking may have been painful at the time, but it has kept a management style which requires clarity of forethought as a safeguard against precipitate and unwise action.

Delicately put. Unfortunately, Peter Lewis retired at a time when the Bonus had gone from 22% via 17%, 12% and 9% to 8% in his final year. He had always warned that the Bonus would dive sooner or later, and it was a pity that it had to happen in his final years. Looked at over the whole twenty years, by any measure his tenure had been highly successful, but his successor would have several growing problems to grapple with. The trading hours pot was being vigorously stirred and coming nicely to the boil: a Sunday trading bill was at last in the offing. The recession continued, and, in a Waitrose group increasingly criticised for being behind the times and coming under severe pressure from the Sunday traders, profits were about to tumble. An investment banker even informally put together a case for Waitrose to be 'floated', sold off. The new Chairman would begin with in-tray stacked high, and rising. He was one of a cadre of former civil servants recruited in the early 1980s who would run the Partnership through into the next century. Like everyone else, they had all started on the selling floor.

CHAPTER 17

# Leading Sacred Cows to Slaughter

**Left to right, Sir Stuart Hampson, David Young, David Felwick and Brian O'Callaghan.**

We need to do better ... Are we a sufficiently 'can do' organisation? Every time we find ourselves saying 'no' or 'can't do' we need to be asking why ... 'It's not Partnership' should not be an excuse for failing to pursue new ideas vigorously ... We all think the Partnership is special, but the competition does not share our enthusiasm.

STUART HAMPSON, ADDRESS TO THE PARTNERSHIP COUNCIL, MAY 1993

At the beginning of the decade, Waitrose had been losing direction. It had hung on to the sacred cows of outdated policy in the belief that its customers had accepted them because Waitrose was 'special'... Fortunately many of its sacred cows had been slaughtered.

TREVOR ELLIOTT, A WAITROSE COUNCILLOR,
SPEAKING IN THE 'FLOTATION' DEBATE, SEPTEMBER 1999

Soon after the start of the 1980s, the Partnership's personnel director Stephen May had been concerned at the shortage of strong leadership candidates coming through in the next generation. May placed a small advert in the *Sunday Times* for 'senior learners'. The ad picked up three high-powered civil servants, Oxbridge graduates all in some way dissatisfied with the service, and a fourth arrived a few years later. An RAF officer in the middle of a promising career wrote in out of the blue and joined them. All five were prepared to shift to an unknown horse in mid-career stream, and all began with the usual selling floor immersion. They became the men who would steer the Partnership through the 1990s.

## Learning on the Selling Floor

Stuart Hampson in fact had a retailing childhood, for his mother ran the little family draper's in Oldham. (His father had died when Stuart was four.) As a boy he'd gone with her to Manchester on buying visits. By the time he joined the Partnership he had worked for several government ministers of different political colour, from Roy Hattersley to John Biffen, and ended in Lord Rayner's team charged by Mrs Thatcher with improving the efficiency of the civil service. David Young had worked for three defence ministers, ending with William Rodgers, and finished that career as head of the MOD's budgetary division. He chose the Partnership in spite of being tempted by Rodgers' suggestion that he manage the new breakaway Social Democratic Party (SDP), started by the so-called Gang of Four, which included the ex-Partner Roy Jenkins. Ken Temple had started as a diplomat, worked for Nicholas Ridley in the 1979 Thatcher government, then found himself on diplomatic missions to the Falklands both before and after the war. Another new entrant with a Falklands link soon joined them. David Felwick was a career RAF officer whose last job had been chairing jointly with an army brigadier a staff college review of the Falklands War. He turned down an offer of a prestigious job as Serjeant-at-Arms at the House of Commons. Five years later Ian Alexander joined them from the DHSS, where he had been helping implement pension reforms – he'd come to the right place for those.

What these men had in common was that they were prepared to slog it out on the selling floor, and that they really enjoyed the work there. They speak of the expertise and kindness of their first department and section managers. Being on their feet selling all day, smiling heroically at awkward customers, they soon knew what it was like to be a Partnership foot soldier. Hampson started out selling pyjamas at John Lewis in Oxford Street. Young, Temple and Felwick began on the selling floor in Peter Jones. The brigadier who had just chaired that Falklands review with David Felwick was perplexed to find him up a ladder in the basement of Peter Jones unscrewing a chandelier. Some of the customers of Peter Jones in particular were notoriously demanding or eccentric, often both. Felwick politely offered to help two dragons touring the fairy grotto (as its lighting department was popularly known). 'Help? You want to *help*? Usually in Peter Jones you have to lie on the floor and kick your legs in the air before anyone will serve you.' David Young was recognised in the shop by a startled ex-Navy man. 'What are you doing here, Sir?' 'It's me who calls you Sir, now,' was the wry response. They all went through the mill of section manager and department manager, and on to managing a branch. Promotion wasn't automatic – others fell by the wayside – but by 1993 Hampson, who had replaced Harry Legg as research and expansion director, was the new Chairman; Young was deputy chairman and finance director, his job since replacing Sadler in 1987; Felwick was MD of Waitrose; and Temple was a Waitrose director and would later be chief registrar. Of those in the top four Partnership jobs in the 1990s only Brian O'Callaghan, running department stores, had joined before 1982. He'd been a retailer since leaving school, and the others had all learnt from his outstanding shopkeeping skills when they had been running shops in the mid-1980s. Outsiders they may have been, but by 1993 they had ten years' experience. Moreover they firmly bought into the Partnership ethos, and they brought a change of style.

Bernard Miller and Peter Lewis had been private people who had cultivated a certain detachment, and were Chairmen who tended to observe from above the day-to-day fray. The Partnership's board, with its five elected members, was not a body which discussed strategy – it simply debated and usually agreed (and rarely voted on) the proposals brought to it. The Partnership's directors had been left to get on with it, meeting monthly under the chairmanship of the *deputy* chairman, not the Chairman. There was little formal debate about strategy. Although the Chairman remained powerful, and could effectively veto almost anything if he chose, he didn't discuss overall planning. Peter Lewis had left it to individual directors, who were, though, *very* clear on his views, and on what would pass muster. By contrast Stuart Hampson and David Young had been at university in the 1960s in a new age of openness and individual freedom. Hampson wanted a closer engagement and more debate, and began by taking over chairmanship of the monthly meeting himself, while continuing to allow the trading MDs freedom of action. John Lewis's organisation didn't change, and it continued to have an MD with a very small central team. But Hampson increased Waitrose's independence by turning its 'managing committee' into a proper board, although the central purse strings remained tight. Waitrose was in fact the major problem that he, Young and Felwick confronted when he took over in early 1993.

## Waking Up Waitrose

The days of easy profits in the 1980s had gone. The Bonus had dropped from 22% to 8% in four years. The recession was biting hard, with high interest rates, a housing market crash, and the notorious Black Wednesday, when £27billion of reserves was spent by the Treasury in a vain attempt to prop up sterling. In 1993, Stuart Hampson's first year as Chairman, Waitrose profits fell to a ten-year low in real terms, and in a single year its percentage of the John Lewis profit figure halved, from 60% to 30%. Twenty years earlier, in Peter Lewis's first year, Waitrose sales had been well under half of John Lewis's. Now they were virtually level, but its profit margin had declined in recent years. David Felwick had taken over in 1991, and was determined to do something about what he considered to be a shameful lack of investment in technology: 'I had as much computer power at home as I found in a Waitrose branch.' The computers were almost entirely in the centre, and the groundbreaking advances in computing of the 1970s hadn't been followed up: to Felwick it was all too slow and over-centralised. And the glaring omission was at the 'point of sale'. All the big competitors were scanning items at the checkout and collecting sales data. Why not Waitrose?

Both Peter Lewis and the Waitrose MD John Foster had been unconvinced by the claims of the scanning technology being embraced by its competitors in the 1980s. A major underlying problem was the size of Waitrose branches. An average of 13,000 square feet of selling space was about half that of Tesco or Sainsbury or Asda. The financial argument for introducing scanning was much more clear-cut in bigger supermarkets with their economies of scale. Throughout the 1980s the Partnership's caution had prevailed. To overhaul and equip 100 branches with scanning and to get all the own-brand products repackaged to incorporate a barcode would cost £20m. About that there was no argument, but you could dispute the 'soft' benefits till the cows came home: the speed through the checkouts, the labour savings, the benefits of accurate sales data. Those cows were a long time returning. When the first pilot was reluctantly agreed, Peter Lewis asked how long it had been since the first proposal for such a scheme had been rejected. 'Seven years.' 'We've saved seven years, then.' When Tony Davies, branch manager at Waitrose Caversham, showed Peter Lewis and his wife Deborah the new set-up and took them through the checkout, Lewis said that it didn't seem any faster. Deborah from behind him silently mouthed: 'Oh yes it is.'

That epitomises the struggle to modernise Waitrose, before Felwick took over with the encouragement of Hampson. The business had started to look old-fashioned, new competitors were opening at a rapid rate – in 1993 more than 60% of its branches suffered new competition – and sales were bleeding away to the illegal Sunday traders at an estimated £1m a week. Moreover, Waitrose was starting to haemorrhage loyal customers *all* the time, not just on Sundays. But at least when Hampson took over as Chairman the Sunday Trading issue would soon be resolved one way or the other. The Partnership was now actively supporting the Keep Sunday Special (KSS) campaign – which was trying to prevent Sunday trading entirely – against twin opponents: the total deregulators and the compromisers, the SHRC (Shopping Hours Reform Council). About the SHRC Peter Lewis had been scathing: 'You can't compromise between two extremes.' KSS had a boost at the start of 1993 when the European Court ruled that Sunday trading was indeed illegal, an opportunity for Hampson to write tart letters to John Major, Margaret Thatcher's successor. With a Bill in the offing they were unavailing: Major was clearly going to take no action. That summer the Home Secretary, Ken Clarke, proposed a three-option Bill: total, partial or zero deregulation. In December each was debated and voted on in turn in a single sitting. Total deregulation was defeated by 404 votes to 174. The no-change motion then lost narrowly, 304 to 286. That motion was supported by ninety Conservatives and opposed by sixty-nine Labour members – any ten of those Labour voters would have swung it against Sunday trading. Limited deregulation, allowing large shops to open a maximum of six hours, was then passed by 333 to 258. Not the answer the Partnership wanted, but at least it was finally settled.

David Felwick's natural ebullience had been fraying at the edges at the forced inactivity. He had at last persuaded the Board to commit substantial sums to a makeover of the business, incorporating scanning, but it couldn't happen overnight. He was confronted by unhelpful stories like one in the *Independent* that speculated: 'Partnership directors have become increasingly concerned about Waitrose, which faces an alarming rise in its capital investment bill this year in a bid to stem the fall in underlying sales and profits.' There was another in the *Sunday Times* which forthrightly advised the Partnership's leaders to be rid of Waitrose. One of the trade magazines took up the cry. They were going to do nothing of the sort, but that didn't help Felwick in his attempts to improve Waitrose morale. Letters to the Gazette complaining about the articles were met by the rumbustious general editor, Hugh McPherson, who replied: 'In dealing with journalists we can but give the facts. God must supply the understanding. Clearly, on this occasion, He has not been bountiful.' McPherson was an ex-journalist who knew well that, whatever you said, journalists would write what they wanted to. Bernard Weatherill, the retiring Speaker of the Commons, reflected the Partnership's sour view when he told the council at its annual dinner that the modern Press operated by the dictum: 'Make it brief, make it juicy, and make it up.'

But with Sunday now a legal trading day, at least Felwick could launch a trial of Sunday opening. It was soon as popular as he'd anticipated, and its costs not as high as he'd feared. Meanwhile, a long trial of a new scanning system allowed Waitrose to plan its rollout to every branch meticulously, coupling it with a major store makeover. In the same 1993–5 period an increasingly messy distribution chain, based on one Waitrose-run centre at Bracknell and eight specialist distributors, was streamlined down to two Regional Distribution Centres (RDCs) at Bracknell and a new centre run by the contractor Hays at Milton Keynes. Each centre distributed virtually every class of merchandise to half the branches in new vehicles with compartments of differing temperatures, much more efficiently than hitherto. By early 1995 David Felwick's infectious laugh was back. Scanning was rolled out, sales were up, the supply chain was slicker. A sure sign they were into a new era was that Waitrose had started winning industry prizes, led by its team of wine experts under Julian Brind, and that it had begun to advertise. Until then the Partnership didn't enter competitions, and it didn't advertise. But that lofty detachment was too ascetic a view for the times, and pressure to change was building. In two years Waitrose had experienced the most change in its history. Can do? They could, and did. One by one the sacred cows were taken off to slaughter, and another one was being led from its stall.

## Advertising? Marketing?!

Advertising for years had been the big Partnership no-no, and for very sound reasons. You can start, but you can't stop, and you can't measure your success. Estimate it, go on gut feel, sure, but calculate it? No. As Lord Leverhulme said: 'I know that 50% of my advertising is wasted. The trouble is I don't know which half.' Spedan's successors were calculators and not risk-takers. Spedan had tried it, as he'd tried everything, and had been at pains over the years to point out that he wasn't against it *per se*. In fact he'd advertised on and off in the early 1920s, including on the front page of the *Daily Mail*. But he was soon convinced advertising didn't achieve enough to justify the continuing expense. The Partnership's attitude to public relations in the 1990s can be summed up by the appointment of the former television documentary maker Helen Dickinson as its first professional PR officer in 1995. She was parked out of the way in Bracknell:

> I was put in a corridor on the fifth floor, with a broken desk, a malfunctioning computer, a secretary in Victoria, and a phone that didn't work after 5.30. I reported the phone because I thought it was faulty. They were worried about me: 'Is everything all right at home?' Why would I need a phone to call out of office hours? But my bacon was saved by the BSE crisis. I had journalists ringing day and night that first week. I thought – what have I done? But joining the Partnership was the best thing I ever did. Later, when I went to work in Victoria in 2000, my predecessor told me she kept her phone in a drawer with the answerphone on, so that she could listen to it later and decide how to respond. On my first day I overheard someone saying: 'We prefer not to promote our products – word of mouth is better.' Next Christmas one buyer told me flatly: 'I will not be forced into promoting my products.'

As the Millennium approached, in a world where consumers were bombarded from every angle, it became clear that word of mouth simply wasn't enough – for Waitrose anyway. So in a business where advertising had been a dirty word, and marketing a completely unknown one, Felwick started cautiously. The first agency wasn't engaged until 1995, and advertising began on a very small scale. It wasn't until early 1998 that the M word first appeared on the card, with the appointment of the first marketing director. To many Partners in the wider business, inured to advertising-aversion, this was the first surprise. Marketing, really? The second, frankly, was that a man with marketing instincts could be found within the business, and running a department store at that: Mark Price.

For Mark Price, the son of a grocer from Crewe, it was his archaeology degree and enthusiasm for golf that had got him to Tyrrell & Green in Southampton in 1982 for his first Partnership job. He had pondered the offers – like many others he had them from both Marks & Spencer and John Lewis – and tipping the scales in the Partnership's favour were a golfing society and a sailing club. In Southampton he could play golf on the Leckford course (he had a handicap of 2), sail, and dive on the *Mary Rose* – the ship that had turned turtle and sunk in the Solent in front of Henry VIII – then being excavated before being raised from the seabed. Price's personality and approach were clear from the outset. Beryl Meredith, a retired selling assistant from Tyrrell & Green who had started at fourteen in the war, paid 12s 6d a week, recalled him as 'a lot of fun – we had some good laughs'. Her friend Beryl Cook from accounts, another fourteen-year-old starter, frowned. 'Fine for you, but whenever we had a till discrepancy he would wave it away as too small to worry about.' Price: 'In those days a penny difference and you were in the dock.' Beryl Cook remembers chasing discrepancies of a farthing.

Price learnt his shopkeeping from Brian O'Callaghan at Southampton, worked his way up the ladder and round the country, and in 1995 became MD of a new John Lewis at Cheadle, outside Manchester, which had long been a desired destination for the business. His imaginative approach there, both to merchandising and in engaging with his Partners, marked him out as a buccaneer. For all his piratical instincts, though, he was shrewd enough to operate within the confines of John Lewis's closely-defined trading methods. Though he sailed close to the wind from time to time, he was strongly supported by Brian O'Callaghan, who recognised his abilities. By then the overall John Lewis MD, O'Callaghan was increasingly and erroneously regarded as being against innovation. He wasn't, but it had to be on his terms, and Price knew where to stop. Mostly.

Price started as Waitrose marketing director early in 1998. By the end of the year his first campaign had picked up awards for both best advertisement by a retailer and best press advertisement. Stylish and understated, with a modest spend by industry standards, the spare images of trawling, of sunflowers and of a picnic managed to convey just the right message. You could almost sense relief in the advertising world that the Partnership, through Waitrose, had at last come in from the cold. At exactly the same time David Felwick received an award from *The Grocer* for outstanding achievement which, together with a continuous string of prizes for the wine buyers, brought a halo effect. Felwick and Price were both naturally flamboyant figures, toned down for certain by a long absorption of Partnership values, but conspicuous entrepreneurs in a business where these had been lacking for some time. The atmosphere in Waitrose was now decidedly upbeat. Felwick's 'can do' injunction to take risks had eventually overcome those who had grown up with caution. The mood was exemplified by the two-day annual Waitrose managers' meetings at the Belfry golf club, orchestrated with élan by Felwick's successor as selling director, Alistair McKay, a former RAF pilot. The Felwick/McKay 'Rafia' encouraged a work-hard-play-hard mentality, and after joining in – leading – a late night's drinking and singing at the end of the conference they would be seen teeing up on the golf course a couple of hours later. McKay was still flying jet trainers, and would take up all-comers on a Sunday, loop-the-loop a couple of times to test their mettle, and inspect opposition car parks from the air to see how their trade was doing. As one branch manager said: 'You sensed he'd bomb them if he could get away with it.'

## John Lewis in the Nineties

Morale was way up in Waitrose in the Nineties, although in 1997 its profit had peaked at £74m and was starting to drop again: down to £61m in 1998. The equivalent figures for John Lewis were a massive £197m in 1997, easily the highest ever in real terms, and still at £164m in 1998. Thus John Lewis provided the bulk of a Bonus which reached 20% for two years running. It was an outstanding achievement, and to the John Lewis MD Brian O'Callaghan it proved that his long and careful stewardship was working, and he would need cast-iron evidence if he were to change anything. The John Lewis recovery from the low point of 1991 was spectacular. Throughout the decade O'Callaghan concentrated on improving and standardising the look and layout of every department store, helped by the shrewd and empathetic successor to Robin and Lucienne Day as design coordinator: Douglas Cooper. O'Callaghan emphasised a simple and effective approach to merchandising, close to the principles Max Baker had espoused in the 1950s. Stick with a rectilinear layout, with blocks of fixtures no more than three deep positioned on what he called a 'merchandise mat', with promotional material at the front. Use the height of a back wall, but don't position anything else higher than the height of a washing line. And as for fixturing, don't let it dominate the merchandise. 'The best fixture is the one you don't see, and if the product's right you can sell it off a table.' He was renowned throughout the business for his fixation with straight lines. Beryl Meredith was at the end of her career when O'Callaghan arrived in Southampton:

> Everything had to be in straight lines. Everything. It got to the stage when I took a two-foot rule around with me to make sure everything lined up. At home one day my husband asked me what I was doing. I'd been unconsciously making sure everything on the dresser was lined up. It got to you like that.

In 2010, ten years after his retirement from the Partnership, O'Callaghan still had an intense interest in retailing and a sharp eye for anything that strayed from his exacting standards. He could be persuaded to try something new, but you had to convince him with results. Jill Little, who in 2010 was the John Lewis overall merchandise director, was able to do that as manager of the trend department in John Lewis Oxford Street in the mid 1970s, when Brian O'Callaghan was its general manager. At that time 'trend' was hardly a word you'd associate with the Partnership's fashions. Jill Little saw no reason why she shouldn't clothe the mannequins the way customers dressed, including mini-skirts. No, said Brian, concerned about good taste. Give me a week, said Jill, and the leap in sales proved her right. Later she put a balloon down the front of a mannequin's maternity dress – innocuous enough now but not quite the thing in the staid John Lewis of the 1970s. O'Callaghan enjoyed a reputation for shopkeeping as strong as his old mentor, Stanley Carter. He inspired a similar fear and awe, too, but without the rages. Many of his shop managing directors still hold him in high regard, even if they found his branch visits discomfiting. David Felwick, who was the menswear manager in the Southampton shop when O'Callaghan was its MD, clashed with him occasionally then, and often later, when he was running Waitrose and O'Callaghan John Lewis. They may not have seen eye to eye, but Felwick pays tribute to the enormous amount he learnt from him.

But at the end of the 1990s, although Felwick's Waitrose was making less than 40% of the profit of O'Callaghan's John Lewis, morale seemed high in Waitrose and low in John Lewis. On the bald figures it seems perverse in retrospect, but increasingly through the 1990s O'Callaghan found himself under internal pressure. Nobody in an equivalent job among his competitors had to respond to criticism in a company journal as he did, an average of a letter a week. When he'd been promoted from selling director to the top job, he made the decision not to have a replacement, and he chose to answer almost all the letters himself: he was a soloist. Gazette letters and questioners at the Partnership council were increasingly complaining. There had always been – and still are – grumbles about tight staffing on the selling floor and low pay rates, but there was now something else, an insistent demand from below for change. It seemed to many of those working in department stores that they were under more pressure than ever because staffing levels were kept low (as indeed they were in competitors). A somewhat cheerless atmosphere prevailed: visits from the centre were awaited with acute anxiety rather than pleasure. As one MD of a regional branch said: 'They were inspection without inspiration.'

It was a seesaw effect. As Waitrose rose up at one end of the morale seesaw, John Lewis went down at the other. As Waitrose seemed to be out there trying everything, John Lewis appeared to be hunkering down, defending its trading principles. It had undoubtedly been successful, but the world was changing – should the department stores not change with it? People began to ask the question in various forms with increasing persistence. A BBC documentary of 1995 on John Lewis, *Modern Times*, had rather wilfully dwelt on its eccentricity, and deliberately set up comparisons with the earlier comedy series *Are You Being Served*, leading a reviewer to describe it as 'Grace Brothers without the laughs'. They opted to focus on Peter Jones and its 'dog log', which recorded the calling cards that customers' dogs – still then allowed into the shop – had left behind, and chose to film its MD and Stuart Hampson from a low angle behind imposing desks. They also showed a lot of selling floor Partners who were passionate about the Partnership – and a few who weren't. *Their* passion would soon be unexpectedly roused.

It all came to a head at the end of the 1990s, when with no enemy in sight the Partnership was ambushed. Everything seemed fine. In 1998, as well as the awards for Waitrose had come a knighthood for Stuart Hampson for services to retailing. The Partnership was opening up, continuing in his words 'to shed its Trappist tendencies'. Later in the year came a windfall of over £30m, the result of a retrospective court action against the Inland Revenue about overpayment of VAT. Anticipating the fiftieth anniversary of the so-called Second Settlement of 1950, Hampson set aside £5m from it for a Golden Jubilee fund to allow Partners to spend six months full- or part-time engaging in work for a charity. With the previous Bonus level at 22% – the next would come in at 19% – he and the Partnership were riding high. The Bristol department store had been relocated to Cribbs Causeway, a new shopping centre next to the M5, giving access at last to South Wales, and was opening for four hours on Sunday (though not the maximum six, and still no Mondays). The other new out-of-town store at Cheadle was a clear success. Shops were being planned for another new centre in a huge chalk quarry at Bluewater near the M25 in Kent, and one in the very middle of Glasgow. The old Southampton shop was about to be relocated to a new Dockside development. At his Partnership council address in May 1998 Hampson announced an expensive but essential major renovation at Peter Jones, now a listed building, sixty years after its construction. (The listing had the special designation of II*, which means you can barely change anything.) In among the questions, keen but good-humoured, was one about a mischievous *Daily Telegraph* article of 23 May that had suggested that a 'sell-off' of the Partnership might net each Partner over £100,000. Hampson was irked:

> I have to say it was one of the silliest stories that I have read for a long time and gross irresponsibility on the part of *The Daily Telegraph*, when, after consulting our press office and being told very firmly that demutualisation was not a starter, none the less the journalist ... put together a series of totally meaningless figures to demonstrate his point ... It is a non-starter – a totally unacceptable idea for us even to contemplate.

With that, he kicked it firmly into touch and high into the crowd. A year later, however, it was booted back, and some of the crowd rushed onto the pitch after it.

## The Flotation Furore

Nobody in the higher echelons of the Partnership had given it much further thought. There had been a rash of Building Society 'demutualisations', which delivered something for nothing to ordinary citizens who had stashed money away for safe-keeping and a modest annual interest. But the Partnership couldn't be unpicked, could it? Surely Spedan had tied it up good and proper at the High Court, and it would be a wait of twenty-one years after the death of the Queen – whose mother was then still soldiering on at ninety-nine – before it could be questioned, challenged or most probably simply renewed. However, in the spring of 1999 a few letters started to appear in the Gazette, replied to with diminishing patience by chief registrar Ken Temple. He certainly knew his way round the Partnership labyrinth, because he'd spent much of the previous year rewriting Spedan's constitution, simplifying it into modern language and removing anachronisms. In June a letter suggested a referendum on the question of a sell-off. 'But', said Temple, 'it's not ours to sell.' That only prompted: 'The *Gazette* states gloriously on the back page, "The business belongs to those who work in it", so why does he say it's not ours to sell?' Many companies had just been floated, reminded another, who 'didn't hear any complaints from Goldman Sachs secretaries who would be picking up an average of £120,000 the next year'. The cases were simply not comparable, but try telling that to a shop assistant on £10,000 a year. Temple did try, but instead of saying, 'Oh sorry, how silly of me', the assistant wrote another letter, and so did others. Temple was answering all these at the same time as a sheaf of letters on the redraft of the constitution, and conspiracy theorists started to link the two. Was the rewrite a Machiavellian plot to stave off a sell-off? New letter writers kept stirring.

The plot thickened, the pot simmered through July 1999 and then boiled over on the last day of the month. Stuart Hampson, trying to cool things down by explaining the issue to the Press, was misquoted in *The Daily Express* as saying that the Partnership could be sold off if a majority of Partners wanted it. But, by then going on to say he 'didn't detect any groundswell of feeling in favour of selling the business', he invited one: 'Sir Stuart should lunch in the dining room at our branch – the talk is of nothing else.' One key issue that emerged was this: did the Partners really own the business or not? Many were accustomed to tell their friends that they did – 'it's *our* business, that's what makes us different' – but they soon realised they didn't, not exactly. It was owned by a Trust on their behalf. The difference may sound pedantic, but it was important in this highly charged debate. Hampson was appalled and alarmed at the turn of events, and on 14 August wrote a forthright article under the banner headline:

## THE PARTNERSHIP IS NOT FOR SALE

It was too late. One of the problems was that in the Partnership, when anyone can query anything, the Chairman had at intervals to answer questions publicly about his pay. To someone on or about the minimum wage, the amount the Chairman takes home as his share of the annual Bonus – or indeed his annual increase – makes their own pay look derisory. In other businesses the difference between top pay and bottom pay by now was absolutely huge, fuelled by the sell-offs of the past few years. That gap was far bigger than in the Partnership, where since Spedan's time it had been governed by a multiple, enshrined in the constitution. There was, and still is, a maximum that any Partner can be paid. Indeed, Peter Lewis, when inflation had been high in the 1970s, had for a time been so reluctant to increase his own pay that rates for his top managers were slipping behind the market, and that was well before top salaries in industry started to go stratospheric. In 2010, after years of competitors' share options and disproportionate bonuses for their directors, they still lag behind. Rightly, most Partners would assert, from bottom to top of the business.

In the same 1999 Gazette issue as Hampson's 'Not for Sale' article there were forty-three letters on flotation, among them some loyalists leading a belated fightback. It looked as though there might potentially be a dangerous split between management Partners who bought into the Partnership's ideals, and those still then called, demeaningly, 'rank and file', who weren't at all interested. And, as nineteenth-century property owners said when opposing votes for everyone (male): there are more of them than us, so they're bound to vote for revolution. It came to a head when Paul Fineman, a Partnership councillor from Peter Jones, tabled a question for the September meeting asking: 'How does the management intend to obtain Partners' views on the matter of demutualisation? Will it consider a referendum?' Hampson wrote to branch and Partnership councillors in advance of the meeting to say that, while he and the trust board would not countenance 'demutualisation', he welcomed the opportunity to see the Partnership's democracy in action through discussion in (he hoped) the more sober setting of the councils, rather than the fevered letter column of The Gazette. The Partnership council's debate went ahead despite an ill-advised attempt by one of the three trustees, who were elected from within the council, to have the question ruled invalid. But he was put firmly in his place by one of the other two, pointing out Spedan's wording in the original constitution aiming 'at extreme freedom of speech'. They got it.

What emerged at the councils was an absolute determination to defend the Partnership, but out poured a long list of possible explanations for the reaction from the shop selling floor and the warehouse picking floor that had so unnerved managers. The support for a sell-off had largely seemed to come from department stores. It hadn't helped either that, after several years of steadfast refusal by John Lewis to take credit cards (Waitrose had long been accepting them), radio and TV interviews had revealed that they could be used in shops from the following month. Partners were told the day before the council meeting, although the decision had in fact been made four months earlier. Logical, perhaps, because you didn't want to announce it publicly before you could start it, lest you lose sales. But: 'Typical. Once again I have to rely on Breakfast TV to find out what is going on in the Partnership.' 'Have they learnt nothing?' councillors asked. With the previous week's Gazette carrying Hampson's report of a 22% drop in trading profit for the first half year, all the recurring criticisms were ready to spill out: top-down communications, staff levels, stock levels, lack of career structure, tense managers passing down the stress and paying lip-service to the democracy. Systems lagged behind those of competitors: one Newcastle Partner had struck a chord by suggesting that if the Partnership were sold the new management would get rid of half the paperwork so the assistant could get back to serving the customer again. (He didn't add: and shed half the Partners too, and most of the benefits.) By contrast, Waitrose was praised for its 1990s overhaul. The message was clear and it was all summed up by the councillor Roger Fearn in unusually picturesque language:

> Partners felt trapped, and all of a sudden £100,000 had poked its nose out of the newspapers. First of all, it had fondled people. Then it had started to seduce them. Suddenly £100,000 became a meal ticket from a life of misery.

## Why Had it Happened?

Not misery, of course, but not the Partnership's vaunted 'happiness' either, down on the selling floor. The council overwhelmingly rejected any idea of flotation, but it served up a long wish-list. The Partnership's management shouldn't have been surprised. Ten years earlier almost to the day there had been a debate provoked by another Peter Jones councillor, John Winter, who had begun the session with Macaulay's ringing words: 'The voice of great events is proclaiming to us – reform if you would preserve.' Winter spoke of 'discontent and bewilderment, cynicism and boredom', which led to a not dissimilar debate to that of 1999, but not a single follow-up question in The Gazette. That 1989 'Winter of Discontent' seemed to have been followed by a Spring of Content. The nettle patch that Winter had revealed was noted but neglected. Then, at the beginning of 1996, Stephen May had been asked by Hampson to consider the Partnership's structure, to look for any weaknesses, and come up with ideas for change. May and Ken Temple spent months taking soundings, interviewing thirty-five directors, middle managers and registrars (but nobody at a lower level, note). May concluded in a 51-page, 189-paragraph report that the only thing fundamentally wrong was *attitude*. The Partnership was falling short of its ideals in the way some of its managers treated people, and its democracy was misfiring. May cited one interviewee stressing the old truth: 'The Partnership is only as good as your department manager is prepared to make it', and went on to add: 'This needs emphasising because the Partnership's culture militates against grasping nettles in this way.' The May tour of the nettle patch was titled *Tomorrow's Partnership*, and in it he confessed to feeling out of touch in a business of 37,000 Partners:

> Somehow I feel we should know, better than I do now, how different Partnership units are rated (how many start marks they would justify out of 10) for such things as management courtesy, thoughtfulness and friendliness, effectiveness of the branch council, reaction to management responses to Gazette/Chronicle letters, quality of correspondence (particularly disciplinary) sent to Partners, and so on.

May went to look at other companies that employed attitude surveys – the Partnership had never felt the need to – but concluded artfully: 'If we set about addressing areas of concern without waiting to be told and, if we do so successfully, we will come better out of a published survey than we would now.' He went on to suggest that the Partnership should undertake an attitude survey in two to three years, because the one certainty would be 'that management cannot delude itself that things are better than they really are', as perhaps they had done 'to a degree in the past'. That was the point. Hampson wrote to managing directors at the end of 1996 enjoining them to heed the messages in the report and take action, though in reply to a Gazette letter writer who had 'heard rumours of a Happiness memo', he said merely that he'd reminded all principal directors of its importance:

> It is a key feature of our business that we also score our success in the sense of Partners' pleasure from coming to work, satisfaction from their contribution to the business and fulfilment in terms of their personal capabilities and aspirations. The memorandum did not call for any specific action, as it was merely a repetition of well-established Partnership principles.

'Merely a repetition.' And how was the business to 'score its success' if it didn't measure something, anything? It's clear that there was some resistance in the management camp. There was a view: 'It would be a distraction, and it wouldn't tell us anything we don't know anyway – like everyone thinks they're paid badly.' As a consequence Hampson still didn't press the case until 2003, after the third of a series of annual two-day meetings he'd started for 100 or so of the more senior managers. These meetings were a Hampson innovation, and their impact on the old buttoned-up Partnership was immediate. Jill Little, then the buying director of fashions, had a stream of concerned visitors asking her advice on what was meant by 'smart casual'. The meetings loosened the stiffly formal atmosphere, led to some more radical voices being heard, and actually got people from John Lewis and Waitrose talking to each other. (Were they a single species after all? asked one.) The 2003 meeting was held, daringly, in Paris, where two outside speakers talked about the crucial importance in their own companies of employee and customer surveys. One was from Unipart, the other from Nationwide, the only major building society to resist the rush to demutualise into a bank (and a strong survivor of the 2008 banking meltdown as a consequence). This demonstration of the value of surveys, from a company that wasn't in common ownership but held similar values, led Hampson to initiate the first survey of Partners' attitudes in 2004. He summarised the results in the Gazette and to the Partnership council that autumn.

## The First Survey

They were chastening. First, the overall response rate was unexpectedly low: 69% may be acceptable for a general election but not for a co-owned business, the Chairman felt. Second, while there was a gratifying response to questions on customer service, working together and feeling good about the Partnership as a place to shop, the overall result wasn't good. Among the worst were responses on the following four issues: 'My pay is fair; We have enough Partners to get the job done; I get a buzz from working here; Our admin processes are straightforward.' That wasn't entirely unexpected, but down close to the bottom was 'Our democratic bodies are effective'. For that to get the fourth worst result from forty-six questions was pretty dreadful for a business that prided itself on its level of democratic engagement.

There was also clear evidence that the behaviour of some managers was far from ideal. This all prompted a further analysis, which returned to Bernard Miller's old conclusion that a third of Partners understand the Partnership and are engaged in it; a third understand it but aren't engaged; a third appear to neither know nor care. Fifty years later the pseudo-scientific outcome, with jargon invented for the occasion in the modern style, labelled 32.9% as Champions, 33.4% as either Bystanders (understanding without engagement) or Loose Cannons (engagement without understanding), and 33.7% as Weak Links – those who neither knew nor cared. On the face of it a closer fit to Miller's three thirds could hardly be imagined, but of course the 31% who hadn't bothered to respond were also Weak Links, so the figures in fact were no better than a quarter, a quarter, a half.

For Hampson this outcome was disturbing, but at least it gave him some pointers to putting it right, as did the free-form comments that the survey encouraged. The result was a 2005 initiative called PBOP – Powered by our Principles – which set out to provide in simple language a set of behaviours that Partners, managers and the business as a whole could work by. The six tenets of its prescription for good citizenship stated that Partners should: be honest; give respect; recognise others; show enterprise; work together; achieve more. In order to provide the right environment the Partnership's management would provide a set of employment conditions, each of which mapped onto the six above. It undertook to:

Maintain a climate of transparency and trust.
Guarantee a fulfilling working environment.
Ensure a fair reward for all.
Give Partners the freedom to use their talents.
Provide a sense of common purpose.
Recognise and celebrate exceptional achievement.

Motherhood and Apple Pie? They were certainly an improvement on some modern business 'mission statements', couched in language way off the obfuscation scale. It was hardly Good Citizenship rocket science, and some older and retired Partners scoffed – for goodness' sake, we know all that, we just do it. But as many people on the ground asserted, up to and including Peter Lewis's son Patrick, appointed Partners' counsellor in 2009, it gave Partners and their managers a 'language' to employ. It cut both ways, and the Partnerships' leaders weren't exempt from pointed criticism in the Gazette if any action, for instance in dealing with the increasing number of redundancies after 2000, was deemed to transgress one of these six tenets. Over the next five years the Partnership survey was gradually refined, and the results got better. Because, moreover, they were analysed by branch and department, it meant that the survey results in a manager's area of responsibility became a part of their annual appraisal process, to add to the usual comparison of this year's financial outcome to the previous year's. Thus there was a shift in emphasis, and the democracy's poor showing led to a serious reappraisal of its make-up, to be explored in Chapter 20.

The 1990s, then, was the decade of overhaul and recovery for Waitrose, and a time when John Lewis clung fast to its trading principles, but alongside both was a blithe neglect of the feelings of the ordinary Partner that led to the internal ructions of 1999. The following ten years saw more time and attention lavished on the Partner than had occurred since, perhaps, Spedan's early days at Peter Jones – and yet it saw more redundancies than any other previous decade. It also saw a major upheaval in John Lewis. Many Partners, if not all, said that its 1990s success had been bought at the price of a refusal to recognise that the world was moving on and that John Lewis was in danger of being left behind. At the end of 1999 the flotation furore had died down, but profits were more than 20% below the peak of 1997, and the prospects weren't good. Competition was getting far stronger and more aggressive, not least on Sundays, and most John Lewis department stores were still trading only on five days a week. New Internet traders were starting to threaten, on price and convenience if not on personal service. Things would have to change, but how, how much, and how fast?

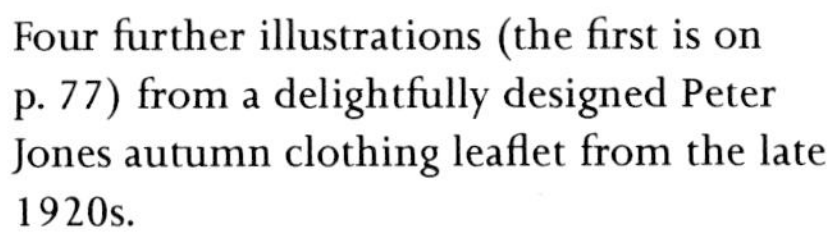

Four further illustrations (the first is on p. 77) from a delightfully designed Peter Jones autumn clothing leaflet from the late 1920s.
TOP LEFT: The leaflet's front cover, with the old Peter Jones behind.

ABOVE LEFT: A pre-Partnership Waitrose advertising leaflet from the 1930s.
ABOVE RIGHT: A Waitrose brown paper bag of the period.
BELOW: A colour chart of John Lewis's dyed Japanese silks, like a paint colour card today.

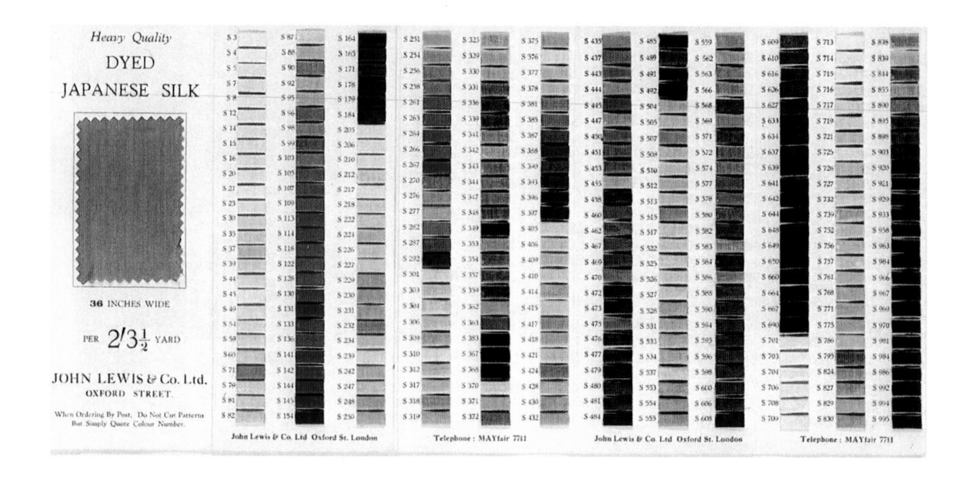

ABOVE: The John Lewis 'castle' on Brownsea Island.
LEFT: The Partnership hotel at Ambleside, centre right, on the northern shore of Lake Windermere.
BELOW LEFT: The Longstock water garden.
BELOW RIGHT: A map of the Test Valley, showing Leckford Abbas and Longstock House.

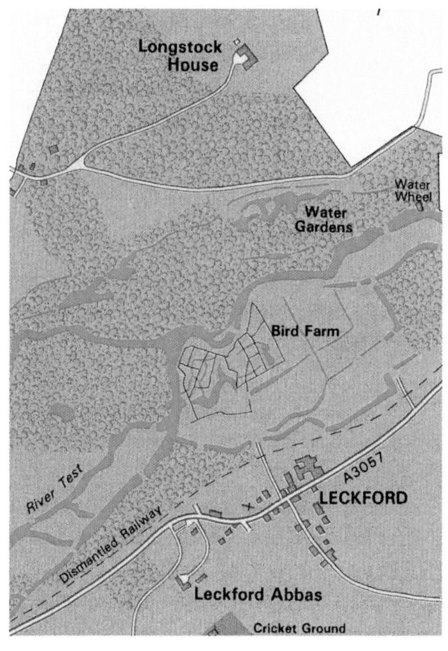

ABOVE: The music society orchestra and choir in 1999.
RIGHT: A flower border at Odney.
BELOW LEFT: Athletics medal winners in 1996.
BOTTOM RIGHT: A sailing club yacht in 2009.

## Waitrose packaging, and early television advertising

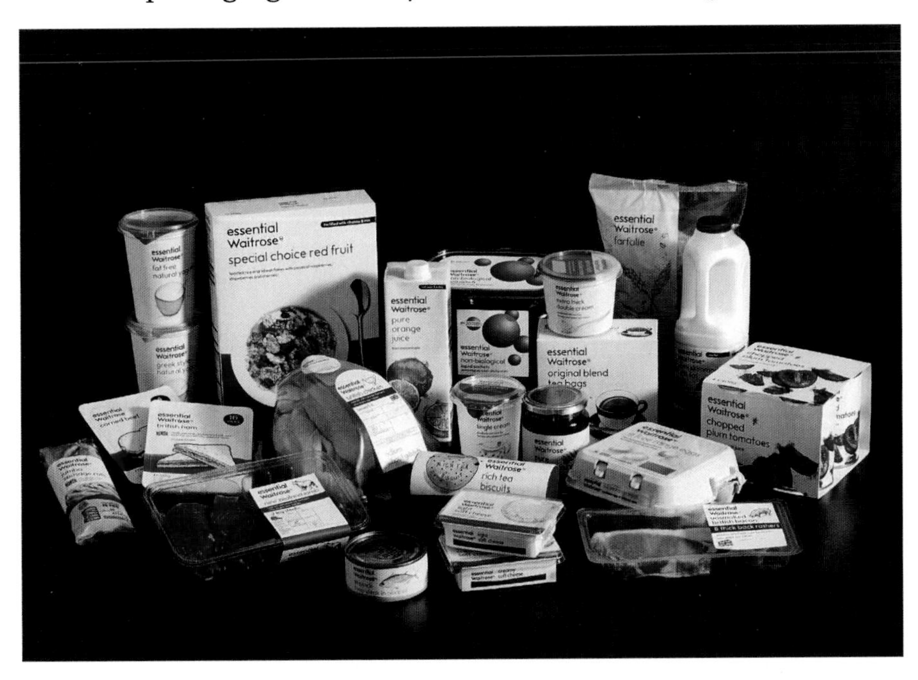


ABOVE: The Essentials range that bolstered its performance in the 2009 recession.
BELOW LEFT: Waitrose cooks' ingredients range.
BELOW RIGHT: Two stills from its early TV ads.

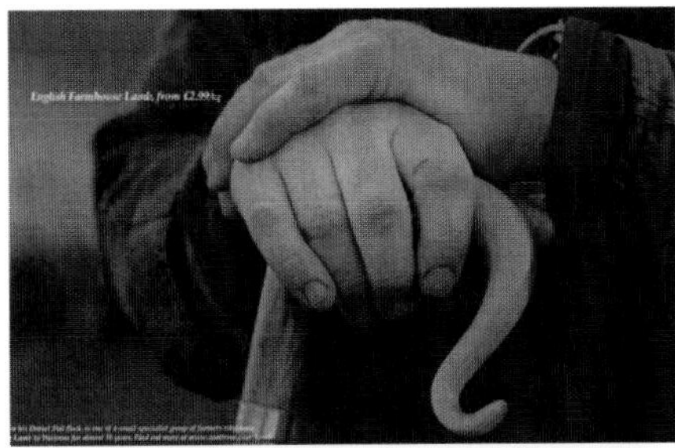

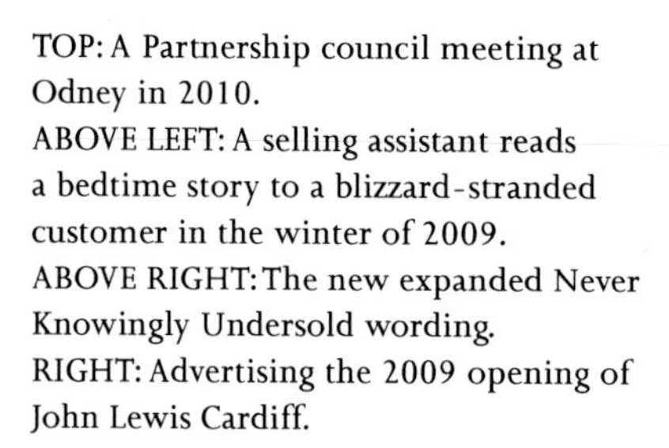

TOP: A Partnership council meeting at Odney in 2010.
ABOVE LEFT: A selling assistant reads a bedtime story to a blizzard-stranded customer in the winter of 2009.
ABOVE RIGHT: The new expanded Never Knowingly Undersold wording.
RIGHT: Advertising the 2009 opening of John Lewis Cardiff.

# Things to Come? (1)

TOP: The shopping mall in Dubai where Waitrose opened in 2008.
ABOVE LEFT: A Waitrose iPhone application.
ABOVE RIGHT: Inside a new Waitrose 'convenience' shop in Oxted.
LEFT: A pineapple picker from Ghana, from a Waitrose Foundation farm.

# Things to Come? (2)

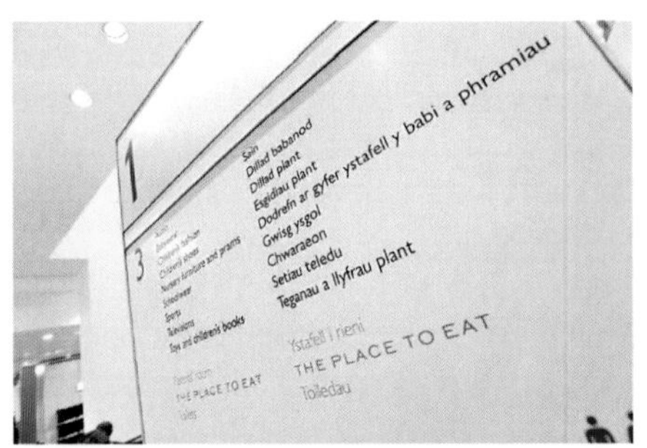

ABOVE LEFT: A John Lewis Direct screen from its online fashions initiative of 2009.
ABOVE RIGHT: A dual language sign at John Lewis Cardiff.
RIGHT: The first John Lewis at Home, at Poole.
BELOW: A still from a ninety second cradle-to-grave TV advert in May 2010 that evoked an unexpectedly emotional response in viewers.

CHAPTER 18

# Into the Internet Age

Charlie Mayfield, left, made Chairman in 2007, brokered the deals that led to the purchase of Buy.com and the arrangement with Ocado. Mark Price, right, appointed Waitrose MD the same year, had been the first to see the power of the Internet. His 'Chubby Grocer' blog identity is entirely appropriate.

In bad times, where should the line be drawn against eating up capital? It was too good an opportunity to miss. People who run a business must do what any really plucky, clear-headed, far-sighted individual would do.

SPEDAN LEWIS IN THE GAZETTE OF 3 FEBRUARY 1940, ANNOUNCING THE PURCHASE OF SUBURBAN AND PROVINCIAL STORES

Finance director David Young and the Partnership's three IT directors watched the end of the twentieth century from the Partnership computer bunker in Central London. Although the Millennium came in with a whimper for their and the world's computer systems, it brought a major upheaval for John Lewis. At the end of 1999, John Lewis MD Brian O'Callaghan agreed to take early retirement from the Partnership, and he left in January 2000. Questioned by councillors on his Partnership council report in March 1999, O'Callaghan had painstakingly defended everything that could be bowled at him – credit cards, Sunday trading, the Internet, advertising, trousers for female shop assistants. A cricket enthusiast, he was like some embattled England captain wearily seeing off another set of West Indian fast bowlers. At the height of the flotation debate that summer he suffered a bombardment: Gazette letter after Gazette letter. Typical was one that contrasted 'one side of the business that is winning awards left, right and centre for its innovation and senior management and marketing strategy, and the other, an increasingly stale business...' In vain, in his patient reply, did he quote from a report from the previous issue of the retailing consultancy *Verdict*:

> The John Lewis Partnership is the number one store group in this sector, and is as good as any retailer in the UK. It manages this by being authoritative in its product offer, having high levels of customer service and competitive pricing ... Only by consistently meeting, and exceeding, customer needs, does John Lewis achieve its success.

Indeed, he left with John Lewis profits still well over twice those of Waitrose, from virtually the same level of sales. But the conclusion of Stuart Hampson was that the business in 1999 was fit for the past decade and not for the next. Brian O'Callaghan, schooled by Stanley Carter at Waitrose in the late 1960s, had been running John Lewis since 1989, and was its selling director for five years before that. Hampson decided a new approach was needed. He chose someone very different.

## Mayhew takes over John Lewis

Luke Mayhew, open and approachable, and looking disconcertingly like the impressionist Rory Bremner mimicking Paddy Ashdown, took over John Lewis. Yet another Oxford graduate, with a later master's degree in organisational behaviour – he would witness a fascinating specimen of that – Mayhew had been recruited from British Airways in 1992. After five months in china and glass at Peter Jones, which, he said, transformed the way he worked, he had succeeded Stuart Hampson as research and expansion director. He told a meeting early on: 'An old BA colleague asked me what *exactly* that meant in a company that did hardly any of either.' In the Partnership's Millennium revue in the year 2000, the first since Bernard Miller's send-off in 1971, O'Callaghan's reluctance for change had made him the perfect subject of Bird and Fortune interviews, rigorously defending an entrenched position. By contrast Mayhew had been satirised as Luke Shopwalker, being told by the ageing Obi Miller that he sensed 'a terrible weakening of the Force'.

To strengthen his force, Mayhew brought in Gareth Thomas and Andy Street, who had been running the two new motorway-side shops: Cribbs Causeway, the relocated Bristol store, and Bluewater, the one in the Kent chalk-pit. (They were two of the four full department stores previously prepared by Mayhew as research and expansion director. Two more, the Southampton relocation and a shop in Solihull, the first Partnership department store anywhere in the West Midlands, would open in the next eighteen months.) Thomas and Street would look after selling and the supply chain, and the new Mayhew team started a root-and-branch review of every aspect of the department store business. In a benign questioning session at the Partnership council in March 2000, Mayhew was able to announce a popular concession – that female selling staff would be able at last to wear trousers – while the team went off to tackle the tougher issues. One of them became clear when he asked an advertising agency to say what John Lewis would be like if it were a person. The answer was a moustached man of fifty – but looking older – in grey flannels and blazer, who is a member of the parish council. (Only the *parish* council?)

Mayhew's team looked at organisational structure, merchandising, marketing, the supply chain, trading hours, personnel and the shops' fabric itself. We couldn't afford, said Mayhew, to go on sweating tired old assets. The performance of the older city-centre shops didn't match the newer ones in out-of-town shopping centres. They probably never would in the new twenty-first century, but we could at least freshen them up, including a major overhaul of the Oxford Street shop itself. Dudley Cloake remembers the realisation after Mayhew reported back on his initial findings to Hampson's monthly meeting of directors. 'It was clear that it would be a long haul. It was a relief, really, that we knew what we had to tackle.' Cloake, the man who nearly thirty years before had battled to bring the infant automated Bracknell warehouse into the world, had become the Partnership's personnel director in the reorganisation sparked by Mayhew's appointment as John Lewis MD. He replaced Ian Alexander, who was appointed development director with a remit to review the Partnership's overall strategy, and to examine new business opportunities. Alexander took under his wing one of the last people he'd recruited in his old job, Charlie Mayfield, to head up a small new business development group. While Mayhew's team set out on the long grind to refresh and streamline the John Lewis business, Mayfield looked at how the Partnership might better exploit the Internet, where online trading was starting a Darwinian explosion – into strange new life forms and many gory deaths.

Unusually for the Partnership's 'senior learners', Charlie Mayfield hadn't moved on to university straight after school. Instead, after Sandhurst and a career as a Guards officer, he had done an MBA at Cranfield before going into a pharmaceutical company and a consultancy. Although he didn't receive the usual total-immersion Partnership baptism, his three weeks in menswear at Heelas of Reading certainly left him far from dry. What startled him was the quantity of paperwork and the backwardness of the systems. There were as yet no computer terminals on the selling floor, for example. In particular the supply chain seemed bloated and lumberingly slow. The Reading shop was served by its own vast distribution centre nearby at Theale (castigated in an earlier generation by John Sadler for being expensively over the top). But in addition it had substantial in-store stockrooms, and stock was moved from supplier to Stevenage, Stevenage to Theale, Theale to stockroom, and finally out onto the selling floor, with paperwork to be completed at every stage. Mayfield spent hours with an old part-timer preparing suits to be transferred to another branch because they weren't selling, only to unload a stack of identical merchandise a few days later. Shirts from French Connection came in boxed and had to be removed and put on hangers for the fixtures, still looking creased from the box. There was a French Connection outlet in Reading, so he checked how their shirts arrived, and found that they came in already on hangers, looking immaculate.

Why hadn't John Lewis done the same? Their buyers, often with a large number of suppliers to deal with, many operating in a small way, couldn't be as tightly in control of the supply chain as were many of the multiples, who had begun to use their leverage with suppliers to define exactly how merchandise was to be packed and delivered. Supermarkets were also doing this with a proliferation of own-brand products, and Waitrose was no exception. Had John Lewis learnt from their experience? No. Was there an eager cross-fertilisation of ideas across the two businesses? No. This appears in retrospect an inexplicable and culpable failure to exploit any synergy between the two: they rarely spoke to each other. Thus this extended and *laissez-faire* supply chain meant an extra cost per item which could be substantial. Furthermore it didn't contribute to a buyer's crucial mark-up figure, which could look artificially rosy. The buyers felt they were doing fine, and the intricacies of the supply chain were someone else's problem. While Mayhew and his team started to tackle that and other thorny questions, Mayfield went back to the head office in Victoria, at just the time the iridescent dot.com bubble was about to burst.

## Exploiting the Internet in Waitrose

Seasoned observers of the Partnership, like old Partners within it, expected John Lewis to be slow to catch on to the Internet. It was bound to be off the pace, wasn't it? But Alexander and Mayfield knew that, if Internet trading took off, John Lewis customers were among those most likely to be attracted by it. It was clear from early exploiters that you could sell more cheaply online, particularly if you didn't bother with the kind of guarantees that John Lewis provided. Not only would the Never Knowingly Undersold slogan come under pressure from simple (and sometimes misleading) price-comparison sites, but a good many John Lewis customers would buy off the Internet from others. In the late 1990s Jeff Bezos' creation Amazon had shown what could happen to book prices and to retail booksellers. Much of the merchandise John Lewis carried could be sold in the same way by online competitors. This was dangerous. Amazon also exhibited a bizarre new model – a business could make huge annual losses and yet still have a stock market valuation the size of a small planet.

While its management was considering how John Lewis should exploit the Internet, an unexpected opportunity arose for Waitrose. Waitrose had used the acquisition of a venerable wines mail-order business, Findlater Mackie Todd, as a platform for online selling, moving on to flowers. But there were still doubts about delivering food to the home. OK, you could set up online shopping lists for customers, but how could you possibly make such an operation pay? Waitrose like other grocers had delivered to middle-class homes before the war, but that service was long gone, wiped out by the introduction of self-service to a burgeoning car-owning middle class. Now customers had effectively been engineered into the supply chain as a working part of it themselves, saving the supermarkets effort and money. Although some fresh-food service counters had returned, customers still selected most of what they bought, took it to a checkout – indeed were now sometimes scanning it and paying for it themselves with no human contact – then taking it to the boot of the car and driving it home with no concern to maintain the 'cool chain'. If the supermarket were to deliver it, the integrity of that cool chain would become the supermarket's responsibility. Refrigerated vehicles would be costly, as would the drivers, the pickers, the warehousing – and early experience had shown that customers tended to order bulky non-food items, which were low margin. They still wanted to inspect and select the higher margin fresh food themselves, and they didn't trust anyone else to do it. High cost, low margin – at first the food home delivery case didn't stack up at all. It was a non-starter, surely? True, but...

If a supermarket did deliver food to the home, there were two models. In the first, you built a central distribution centre, one which had to be as big as a normal food warehouse but organised completely differently, because you were picking individual items for customers, not cases for a supermarket. It was hugely expensive to build, and not cheap to run until you could crank the volume up, but you could service a wide area and take a lot of money – eventually. However, in 2000 the jury was still out on home shopping for food, and Waitrose certainly wasn't going to propose such an expensive option. The cheap test-the-water alternative was to pick and deliver from existing shops, as Tesco had begun to do. The set-up cost was low, but you could deal with little more than 200 orders a week. However, you could trial that method quickly and cheaply, and Waitrose had done so as soon as the competitors started. David Felwick and Mark Price – who was by then running the selling operation as well as marketing – realised quickly that the typical Waitrose time-poor-cash-rich customers would be readily seduced away by the competition. Price was an Internet enthusiast who had pushed ahead with an early home-grown Internet service provider, Waitrose.com, a not-for-profit 'ISP' which gave its profits to a set of charities. His IT team went on to develop a service called 'Waitrose Deliver' as their store-based trial.

At that point Mayfield heard of an intriguing start-up company called LMS (Last Mile Solutions), begun by some young Goldman Sachs money-makers who employed a couple of experienced Marks & Spencer food men. They were convinced that home shopping for food was going to succeed, and were prepared to venture a clever solution based on the big central warehouse model, the one with the high start-up cost. After several months of planning and discussion the Partnership invested £40m, a 40% stake in Ocado, the trade name LMS would employ. The crucial meeting that agreed it was understandably a long and tricky one. A strong proponent was the finance director David Young, who subsequently rode shotgun for the Partnership on the Ocado board for several years. One key issue was the risk of handing over the Waitrose reputation to a company of non-retailers. Another was that in future they might turn from co-operators into competitors. But in the end the decision was unanimous, and the traditionally risk-averse Partnership had committed itself and a large amount of money in a highly speculative investment in home shopping for food. A time-limited trading agreement meant that Ocado would deliver only Waitrose products, in an initial catchment area within about fifty miles of the first distribution centre, a little north of London at Hatfield. One key benefit was that Ocado could tackle the long-standing problem of poor Waitrose representation in Central London. Further warehouses were planned for the north, another attraction for Waitrose, which still had no shop beyond the Trent, so northern customers – and Partners – could at last see what all the fuss was about. Ocado recruited the head of the software team that had built Waitrose Deliver, developed sophisticated systems and distribution methods, and began to expand rapidly. Thus before long Waitrose food was being delivered by *two* home shopping services, both of which began to win awards. There were awards for everything by now, and the Partnership was no longer such a shrinking violet.

## John Lewis Takes the Plunge

While Waitrose now effectively had two embryonic online selling operations, John Lewis was still a long way behind, starting a low-cost low-key experiment of its own. It was still well off the pace. In the spring of 2001 a four-man team had launched a limited experiment called John Lewis Now (to distinguish it from the shops, said someone, which were called John Lewis Yesterday). But it would take a long time to scale it up... unless a ripe plum fell into their laps. It did. Around the time the John Lewis Now experiment began, Buy.com, an Internet seller of non-food in the US with a volume of trade second only – if by a distance – to Amazon, decided to open in the UK. It brought over the parent company's online 'fulfilment' software package, linked up with a pick-and-pack distribution specialist in Birmingham, and recruited a team of people in London. But it was overstretched financially and badly in need of a rescue, and Mayfield, who knew the Buy.com MD Murray Hennessy, seized the opportunity. Here was a chance to gain crucial time in the race to become what had begun to be called a 'bricks'n'clicks', and later a 'multi-channel' retailer. Mayfield and Hennessy came to a tentative agreement that John Lewis would acquire Buy.com, and Mayfield rapidly assembled a board paper. But this was taking place at just the time it was clear that the dot.com bubble had truly burst. In the US the Internet retailer Boo.com had gone bankrupt the previous May after spending the best part of $200m in six months. While the Buy.com negotiations were taking place eToys crashed, its share price descending from its high of $80 to a few cents.

Thus the potential acquisition came to the board at a time when Internet trading was looking very flaky, and more money was being lost (by many investors) than fortunes made (by a few individuals – see under venture capitalism, effects of). Luke Mayhew feared the danger was too great at a time when there was a huge amount on the John Lewis plate. Moreover, the John Lewis profits were being sapped because Peter Jones was in the middle of its £100m makeover, and the shops in Nottingham and Edinburgh were temporarily less profitable because they were being overhauled too. Part of the issue about online retailing in a very young industry was the level of customer service, which at that time ranged from tolerable to dreadful. John Lewis was highly regarded for service – and for putting right mistakes without fuss – and there was a distinct reputational risk if it went in too fast. If they were to bail out Buy.com, moreover, they'd have to take over the costs of the operation. That included a seventy-man team with future built-in bonuses due – if the business survived. Mayhew's team had a big enough job to revitalise the main John Lewis business; the Internet was important, but a distraction now. There were issues, too, about how well these maverick Internet boys would integrate with 'Partnership values'. The Buy.com managers had all bought ties to wear when John Lewis people turned up at their premises, but...

Hampson's board turned it down. Mayfield was desperately disappointed, but before the weekend was up he decided to get Murray Hennessy and Mayhew together in a last attempt to save the deal – and to save Buy.com, which was forty-eight hours away from insolvency. Curiously, Mayhew hadn't yet met Hennessy – another example of how compartmentalised the Partnership was at this time – so his caution was even more understandable. In the event they hit it off, Mayhew changed his mind, the reconvened board agreed on it and emergency money was found to stave off the rapidly looming collapse. A few days later the Gazette cover showed the Buy.com management team – beaming, as well they might – and the business was relaunched as John Lewis Direct a few months later in October 2001. It was a rush by John Lewis timescales (if not for the Internet) but not a panic: get it right, and get it in for Christmas. Eight years later, by the autumn of 2009, John Lewis Direct sales had outstripped those of John Lewis Oxford Street (itself more than double the size of any other JL shop) and its profit margin had clawed its way up to the average. In fact it was a major contributor to the resilient way John Lewis weathered the financial crisis that started in 2008.

This combined move to multi-channel retailing by Waitrose and John Lewis didn't happen without a continuous jangling of nerves. The costs were inevitably heavily front-loaded – you had to spend vast sums before you got a payback. In this new world that wasn't entirely the point. If an Internet start-up traded successfully it could float, or 'go to IPO', meaning to put an 'Initial Public Offering' of shares to the stock exchange. Most Partners, to whom stock market jargon was entirely foreign, had to ask what that meant, and when they knew were no happier. Each year the Partnership invested more in Ocado to retain a substantial – though reducing – stake in the business. By 2009, although its contribution had reached over £120m, its stake was below 30%. Each year Partners looked at each other as the figures emerged, hoping the investment was safe and that Ocado would go into profit. While the Amazon model had proved that you could lose money hand-over-fist each year and yet stay on course for world domination, it was still pretty unnerving when it was happening in your own business – and one you effectively *owned*, of course. Every £10m pumped into Ocado each year was the equivalent of around one percentage point of Bonus. At the outset, in 2001 and 2002, without the Ocado investment the Bonus could in theory have been 3% higher than its 9% and 10% respectively, and Buy.com was an added strain. But Hampson and Young were convinced they'd got it right, and that they had to keep their nerve. Gazette letter-writers and Council questioners expressed alarm and puzzlement at intervals. That was their right – and indeed responsibility – in a genuinely co-owned business, but at no time did the hubbub reach the crescendo of the late 1990s. The Bonus, which had slumped from 22% to 9% between 1997 and 2001, inched its way steadily up till it reached 18% for 2006, Hampson's last year.

## Transforming John Lewis

While the Internet decisions in retrospect look vital, at the time it seemed to many of the directors a distraction, a worry about something that might not happen. For Luke Mayhew the main task was the transformation of the whole of John Lewis, and he knew it would be a painful and lengthy transition. His detractors would soon start calling him Luke Mayhem, but it had to be done. What kept customers returning to a Partnership department store was the service, the reasonable price and the wide assortment. Shop assistants did an excellent job once the merchandise arrived on the selling floor, which was immaculately organised. But getting it all there was the problem. A Partnership department store had long operated on the basis that, carrying up to 500,000 separate items – for comparison Marks & Spencer sold about a quarter of that number and Waitrose had about 25,000 – you needed a massive central warehouse, a local 'service building', and lots of stockroom space in the shop. Although for over twenty years products had carried computer-generated price tickets, largely printed and applied in the branch, getting stock from supplier to fixture was still a long and labour-intensive chain, as Mayfield wasn't the first to recognise. Moreover, with that huge number of products the value of the stock tied up in the business was considerable. And, in retail jargon, the 'stock-turn' was not good by the standards of the industry. Since the rapid development of computer systems in the 1970s, in contrast to Waitrose in the 1990s, there had been little progress with computerised support systems in John Lewis, and there were simply too many people in the branches in 'selling-support' roles. The ratio of selling staff to non-selling was bad, about 50:50, whereas in competitors' shops it was more like 75:25. That had to change. It's instructive that when Peter Lewis's son Patrick joined Mayhew's team in early 2002 it was with the title of 'project director, simplification'. A lot needed not just simplifying, but re-engineering.

At that point, six months after the rising of John Lewis Direct from the ashes of Buy.com, Murray Hennessy was made the first marketing director with a brief to look at the John Lewis 'brand' and its advertising, and the tough and experienced fashions buying director Jill Little became merchandise director. At last John Lewis had been granted an independent board, equivalent to the one that had run Waitrose for many years. The arrival of a strong marketeer in Hennessy (even though he left within two years to run Avis Europe) led to the kind of national advertising push that Mark Price had introduced at Waitrose, and also to the end of the original local store names. Although ever since the stores had been acquired by the Partnership they had traded as, for example BAINBRIDGES, *a branch of the John Lewis Partnership*, few customers knew them by anything other than the local name. Some might have been vaguely aware that it was part of John Lewis, but far fewer than had been fondly imagined back at head office. So when in 2003 eleven branches still trading under their original names changed to John Lewis, many customers commiserated with the assistants on being 'taken over'. QED... As recently as 1996 Stuart Hampson had answered a question on the subject with: 'I am in no doubt that we would cause considerable offence in Liverpool if we expunged George Henry Lee, and Sheffield if Cole Brothers went.' But the world was changing, so all those resonant local names had to go. With one exception – Peter Jones.

## Overhauling Peter Jones and Oxford Street

Looked at in terms of turnover, Peter Jones was little more than a John Lewis department store with sales somewhat greater than average. Crabtree's 1930s Peter Jones building was over sixty years old, and its electrics in particular were getting beyond repair. After years of battling with the restrictions imposed by its 'Grade II* listed' status, acquired for better or worse in 1969, and faced with a stubborn landlord, the Partnership had in 1998 at last committed to a project to give it a complete and overdue overhaul. This was a scheme tinged with sentiment and a sense of history. The Partnership had been faced with two unpalatable options: to refurbish it, or to close it down completely and sell it. There was no viable halfway house, and from a strictly financial viewpoint to close it was the only sensible course. That's what other companies would doubtless have done – not the Partnership. In the event the project was fiendishly complicated and was to shut down much of the building for five years. Its cost had increased to over £100m since the plan had first been tabled, and by the time the conversion was over, the John Lewis name change had already taken place. Trade had inevitably fallen severely in those five years, though loyal Peter Jones customers – and, let's be clear, most saw themselves as customers of *Peter Jones*, not John Lewis – had traipsed round to a cut-down 'PJ2' shop in Draycott Avenue, half a mile away from the shop. This held the Peter Jones 'home' merchandise for the duration. (Its success prompted a thought – would a similar cut-down format succeed elsewhere? The idea was parked, as it always had been.)

Peter Jones, the birthplace of the Partnership, as the plaque over the Cadogan Gardens entrance still proclaims, catered largely to a particular kind of customer. In another era we'd call them a 'superior class' of customer – and, as Oxford Street Partners had always been wont to say, they were served by some, a minority, who saw themselves as a superior class of shop assistant. They might no longer have had local buyers selecting special ranges for Peter Jones, but they were still different. Beverley Aspinall, the Peter Jones MD heading the rebuild project full-time, had come from running the more prosaic department store in Peterborough. She knew what to expect, though it manifested itself in odd ways. She was taken aback, then amused, to find that the average price of a fitted kitchen bought in Peter Jones was distinctly lower than one sold in Peterborough. 'It dawned on me that customers were buying for their servants. They weren't going to use it themselves. So any basic kitchen would do.' Peter Jones cast a certain magic on people who worked there, and certainly on those who ran it. In 2005, when the Peter Jones rebuild was at last over, there was still enough of the old Thespian spirit to mount an 'Up the King's Road' revue at the Royal Court Theatre, across Sloane Square. This was partly a thank you from the Royal Court, which the Partnership had supported financially from 1955 to 1962, despite its own tribulations. Indeed, typically, Spedan had wanted to buy it in 1943, only to be dissuaded because bomb damage had weakened its foundations. As well as the revue, the American composer of film scores, Carl Davis, an account customer there since 1960, was commissioned to write a piece in celebration of Peter Jones, performed that September. After the rebuild, Aspinall herself could see no job within the Partnership to match Peter Jones, so she was delighted to be able to take her unusual range of experience to Fortnum & Mason, where she became MD and oversaw its 300$^{th}$ anniversary refurbishment in 2007.

Peter Jones also cast its magic spell on the man charged with running John Lewis Oxford Street when it too was given an expensive (£65m) facelift a few years later: Noel Saunders. It is no surprise to hear that Saunders began his Partnership career at Peter Jones in 1977, at the age of nineteen. But unlike all his predecessors, he began *right* at the bottom, on the cash desk in its Partners' dining room (and don't say staff canteen). One of ten children, he'd come from Ireland to London after his father died when he was just fourteen, and had done a variety of jobs before he wandered in to buy a present. He read the words above the Peter Jones portal: 'Here is Partnership on the scale of modern industry', and was intrigued. 'What do I do to get a job here?' he asked an assistant, who sent him upstairs to the staff office. There he blarneyed, bemused but amused the staff manager, who gave him the only job going, at the lowest wage in the shop. With that, he calculated, it would take him six months to save up to join his brothers in Australia. In 1982, still in Peter Jones and now a section manager on the selling floor, he met the then MD Philip Morgan for his five-year review. Back then it was still considered an important rite of passage – get through it and you could, and did, consider yourself a Partner for life. Morgan said 'Can you see yourself here for the rest of your working life?' 'Oh, no, I'm still planning on Australia.' Morgan paused: 'I don't think so.'

Noel never did go. In 2005 he arrived back in London after running Liverpool, Cheadle and Bluewater, where as MD he brought in seven-day trading. He took over John Lewis Oxford Street in the week after the 7 July

London tube and bus bombings, and so badly hit was trade in London that the second half-year forecast had to be revised down, from £250 to £245m. That still seemed highly optimistic, but they took £255m. The refurbishment programme began with the boilers – shades of Peter Jones in 1914 when Spedan arrived – and went right through the shop. When the work began the sales target was £300m in ten years: it was met in half that time. When Mayhew had taken over in 2000 a councillor from the Oxford Street selling floor challenged him to improve the branch: 'It looks dull, it looks dingy, it looks tired.' Derek Rawlings, the shop's MD in the 1980s, returned recently to walk the branch with Noel Saunders. He stopped at the Oxford Street/Holles Street corner entrance and recalled his first arrival at the shop as a merchandise manager in 1959, a year before the long post-war rebuild was finally complete:

> Stanley Carter had just got in some new counters. Walnut, with glass tops. We thought they looked superb. But the combination of them with the old suspended lighting made it all rather gloomy. Of course we didn't think that then – all our competitors' shops were the same. But look at the lighting now – it's an Aladdin's Cave.

## Buying and the Assortment – Flair v Process

Although freshening up the branches that weren't new, relocated or rebuilt was important, it was the product assortment and how it got to the branch that was the first priority. In the Partnership the buyer had always been King (though was much more likely now to be Queen – male buyers were outnumbered by over two to one). One of Spedan's earliest tenets was that if you found a good buyer you should leave him or her alone, and he was adamant that you should rarely change the merchandise group they bought. It was experience of the trade and its suppliers that was crucial. Review the buyers annually, yes, install tough financial constraints to prevent a natural tendency to overspend, but give them their heads and allow them their foibles. It's their unfettered flair that will make your profit. The other priority was the assortment. If you're going to achieve authority in a range, make sure that you have enough colours and sizes and styles and price variety to satisfy your most demanding customer. What you lose on increased markdowns you'll win back by persuading the customer to try your shop before any other. And don't just strip it down to the winners. Spedan used this example in a memo to his future wife Beatrice Hunter soon after she joined, when she was the Peter Jones boot buyer:

> Fifty patterns of promenade shoes, each of them reasonably well chosen and tolerable value, will tend to sell far more of the twelve most successful models than those twelve alone would do.

These policies were a tremendous strength, but by 2000 many felt that it had led to an assortment that was often *too* wide where it didn't need to be, and bought by buyers who perhaps needed more supervision. There was a lack of consistency across the assortments. At the start of 2004 Luke Mayhew and Jill Little launched a project to analyse the John Lewis assortment in its entirety. Hitherto the Partnership had been extremely guarded about using consultants – they borrow your watch, then tell you the time, as one old sceptic put it – but now they brought in Bain, a consultancy Murray Hennessy had worked for. Consultants, from the US? Don't we know how to run a department store group after all this time? Well, yes and no. Bain started by interviewing 6,000 customers, a massive sample, something John Lewis had never done before. 'We're astute, our model has passed the test of time, and we know what our customers want,' had been the old reflex.

The customer analysis revealed that, although John Lewis had the best customer satisfaction rating, it was only marginally above Marks & Spencer, Next and IKEA. Importantly, John Lewis was vulnerable particularly when stock availability was poor. It was all very well having a theoretically wide assortment across the board, but if it led to shortages customers would shop at multiples or specialists that had a smaller range but were more likely to have the item in stock. It made more sense to decide which merchandise categories were crucial (most important to customers, and of most value to John Lewis), keep the assortment wider there, and restrict it sensibly elsewhere. Moreover, you should concentrate on target groups of customers, those who were called in the prevailing market research jargon Shopping Enthusiasts, Service Seekers and Solution Demanders. That led the joint Bain/John Lewis team to construct what they considered a more consistent style and price architecture, a more contemporary style, and more authoritative own brands. There wasn't enough consistency on 'entry' price, the lowest price in any range, and that led John Lewis to be regarded as expensive, for all its assertion that it was Never Knowingly Undersold. In the shops there was a need to promote products more boldly, especially nationally advertised brands, and to provide more self-selection. The John Lewis store signature was, like its culture, understated, but sometimes at the expense of visibility. Customers' eyes needed more help.

That, then, was the assortment itself sorted and, although it took a long time to happen everywhere, from 2004 onwards buyers had more explicit and restrictive guidelines to operate by than they'd ever had before. What's more, they were to do it with newly reorganised teams. In the rest of the retail world most buying team members held specialised responsibilities. Some focused on the assortment itself, on choosing, sourcing and pricing the product. Others, the 'merchandisers', took it on from there, deciding which shops it should be sold in, how it should be packaged and passed through the supply chain. In a John Lewis buying team before 2005 responsibilities weren't split in that way: each 'assistant buyer' tended to do everything for a particular subset of the assortment. In the autumn of 2004 all the buying teams were called together for a presentation and told that in future they'd specialise – either do the 'product' bit or the 'merchandising' bit for a larger assortment subset. Two months later the buying team members each had their 'assessment day', a process that unnerved many assistant buyers, some of whom had been doing the same job, differing only occasionally in the merchandise, for over twenty years. While they recognised the need for the change, they found it a painful and somewhat demeaning day of testing and interview, and for some it meant a tough readjustment. The buyers themselves saw less direct change in their roles, although many found it hard to adjust to a job in which they felt hemmed in by 'process', after they'd had so much more freedom of approach. 'Yes, we had to do it', said one, 'but we lost something on the way. You can still exercise flair, but there are so many boxes to tick that some buyers just cave in and lose their initiative. It was such a major change after years of almost total freedom.' The problem, of course, was that it couldn't be done gradually.

## The John Lewis Supply Chain

In the year 2000, to distribute its half a million products John Lewis was still hugely reliant on its cavernous warehouse at Stevenage. When this had opened in 1962 much stock still went directly from supplier to shop; now hardly any of it did. John Lewis had been able to rely on Stevenage and its national network of service buildings near the shops until after 2000, when it added central warehouse space further north at Milton Keynes and Northampton. But, as John Lewis Direct started to expand at a rapid rate from small beginnings, it was clear that this would need more and very different space. Ocado had built at Hatfield a highly-mechanised warehouse for picking 'singles'. If you were running a warehouse to deliver to shops, the merchandise (apart from the big or awkward stuff like furniture) arrived in cases, which you stacked and put away on pallet boards. Each night as orders came in you retrieved the pallets and 'picked' the right number of cases for branches up and down the country. But home delivery is different. You have to break down the cases, either on arrival or departure, and send them out either via a 'hub' location for onward despatch, or direct to the home via a national carrier. The whole process is much more costly. John Lewis Direct had begun using the same national distributor at Redditch in the Midlands that Buy.com had employed, but it was such a critical component that they decided to bring it in-house. Luke Mayhew and his then supply chain director Andy Street began to plan the replacement.

Dino Rocos, who had begun, pony-tailed and cowboy-booted, as a Christmas temp in Peter Jones in 1977, had by 2004 run nearly all its various distribution operations. One of them was at Park Royal, a distribution centre for the London shops, recently adapted to include a 'garment sortation' operation to solve the problem with the shirts that Mayfield had confronted in his first week. Rocos was charged with commissioning and introducing a new warehouse to distribute smaller articles, those that would fit into a stackable 'bin', including most of the products that would go direct to the customer. In early 2008 they were ready to go on a £45m project, and at that stage prospects for expansion were such that Stevenage would remain open. 'Ten in Ten', ten shops in ten years, and full-size department stores at that, had been the ambitious expansion aim. The day Lehman Brothers collapsed that September, Andy Street, now John Lewis MD, sat with the papers in a coffee shop. 'I thought: what the hell are we going to do?' One thing was soon clear – by the end of the year the global recession had blasted those plans away. Developers could no longer raise the money to fund the building projects, be they out-of-town shopping centre or town centre reconstruction. So, after Leicester, the relocation of the Liverpool shop, and finally Cardiff in 2009, the planned John Lewis expansion was abruptly halted. The new distribution centre at Magna Park on the outskirts of Milton Keynes (which is arguably nothing *but* outskirts) would be ready to open in June 2009, and in that February the Partners at Stevenage were told that their warehouse would close. There were 319 of them, with an average of nearly twenty years in the Partnership, and although some moved the thirty miles to Milton Keynes most – not all – of the others were happy to take their redundancy money. (The redundancy question is a tricky one for the Partnership, a co-owned business, and it's something we'll look at later.)

Magna Park opened not a moment too soon. John Lewis Direct was closing in on £400m of annual sales, and in the Christmas run-up Redditch began to sink under the weight of its orders, over 30,000 a day at peak. Rocos had expected to be worrying about Magna Park's first Christmas, but for the fortnight up to 23 December he and the squads of Partners bussed in to Redditch managed to keep it operating. The new highly automated warehouse at Magna – nearly forty years on from Bracknell's troubled launch – by contrast worked like a dream. Through 2010 it increasingly took over the John Lewis Direct operation. These supply chain stories rarely see the light of day. Retailers tend to regard distribution as a necessary evil, a cost to the business rather than a 'core competence'. They don't any more. In the new world of delivery direct to the customer's home, and of 'Just in Time' delivery to the shop – only a few hours away from 'Just too Late' – its efficiency and accuracy are even more vital. A malfunction, an unexpected peak, a fuel shortage, and you're staring at a disaster.

More crucial now too is a supply chain's flexibility. For years John Lewis needed a delivery operation to satisfy a flotilla of department stores, its battleships. With ten more planned in 2007 that didn't seem likely to change.

But the following year's financial crisis did a demolition job on the 'full-line department store' as the sole John Lewis operating model. In a move that was a surprise to almost everyone, they opened a much smaller shop in Poole in Dorset, calling it John Lewis at Home. A few people in the Partnership had over the years thought that the difficulty of finding sites for full-size department stores suggested a smaller operating model, selling the 'core' John Lewis ranges. It's no surprise that Spedan had thought of it. He'd said in 1944, answering a Brains Trust question in the Gazette, that: 'Department stores will have to supplement their buying power by selling some goods from many little shops as well as from fewer big ones.' Sites a third of the size would surely be easier to find, and so John Lewis could infill the gaps by positioning destroyers between their big battleships. They would cost less to build, in both time and money. But successive Chairmen and John Lewis managing directors were so wedded to the full-line store mentality – it works, damn it, and we understand it – that the idea never got to the slipway. Nevertheless, in 2008 Andy Street persuaded the Partnership board to try a cut-down John Lewis shop selling home furnishings and technology in Poole, where a site had been found. Journalists questioned the business's sanity in starting a new format in the depths of a severe recession, but there were precedents. In early 1940, anticipating criticism after buying the fifteen SPS stores, Spedan had made the comment quoted at the head of the chapter, arguing that at tough times you should do what 'any plucky, clear-headed, far-sighted individual would do'.

With the dearth of larger sites, this new direction was made viable and attractive through the focus on 'multi-channel' retailing. You don't have to strive to keep all of a huge assortment in stock. With enough products now available online on John Lewis Direct, a small shop with a limited range could open a window on the whole assortment. Click 'n' Collect was the somewhat ugly name for this idea. Customers could choose to order online, or in the shop, for delivery to home – via the local service building, a John Lewis 'hub' network already in place – or for collection at their local shop. Shop collection is a win-win for customers who work all day and would prefer to collect the order, and for John Lewis who'd like people coming into the shop, please, to buy something else. Cardiff and Poole both opened in the pivotal year of 2009, and by the autumn of 2010 there would be three more on the Poole model, with its 40–50,000 square feet of selling space against Cardiff's 170,000, four times the size. Cardiff, built with massive stockroom space, is perhaps the last launched on the old battleship plan, Poole the first of the new sleek destroyers, full of electronic guidance systems… Perhaps.

## The Rise and Rise of Waitrose

In 1999, John Lewis took just under £2 billion of sales. Waitrose was only £42m behind them – but still behind. The profits, though, were starkly different: John Lewis made £150m and Waitrose only £64m. But that was Waitrose's low-water mark. The following year Waitrose hit David Felwick's long-standing '£2 billion by 2000' sales target, overtaking John Lewis. The year after that their profits were practically identical. In 2003 Waitrose profits were the higher of the two for the first time, and they have been ever since. So how was it that this little chain of ten shops, bought by Spedan Lewis in 1937, seventy odd years later had surpassed its big brother in both sales and profit? The first half of 2009 was the nadir of John Lewis's fortunes as the house market dried up – its profit is highly dependent on people furnishing new homes – and it plunged. In that six-month period 80% of the Partnership's profit was achieved by Waitrose, though the balance began to be redressed as John Lewis came back to spectacular effect later in 2009 and into 2010.

Whenever talk – idle or serious – of selling Waitrose arose over the years, the wiser heads had counselled caution: our food business may be struggling, but even if they haven't enough spare money for new clothes or furniture the middle classes will always want feeding, and feeding well. Waitrose was undoubtedly more expensive than its competition, however loudly trumpeted were the shopping basket tests and the price matching. So the trick was to keep the offer attractive, the range wide, and innovation coming in those areas more food-conscious customers aspired to. It also simply had to expand faster. Although little Waitrose punched way above its weight, it wouldn't get really weighty unless it moved out of its Wessex heartland. As we've seen, it only acquired sites for new branches little by little. Felwick increased the size of new shops, and indeed in 1994 pioneered a new 'food with JL products' format called Food and Home, but there were only three of these by the year 2000. Organic growth wasn't enough, but fortunately the new century brought a restructuring in the UK food industry. In 2000 Waitrose was able to pick up eleven Somerfield branches, the first time it had grown by acquisition for fifty years. It didn't extend the group northwards yet, but it gave Waitrose practice in shop conversion, and 3000 Somerfield employees became enthusiastic new Partners once they'd overcome the shock of different and tighter disciplines. When Felwick moved to Victoria as deputy chairman in 2001, keen to reform what he saw as a top-heavy central management, he was replaced as MD by the young buying director Steven Esom, recruited, like his long-serving predecessor Peter Falconer, from Sainsbury's.

Esom had already rationalised the supplier base, and extended a series of policies which particularly attracted liberal-minded food lovers. Waitrose had initially been equivocal about organic food, wondering whether this was just an expensive passing fad, but it started to lead the industry when customers showed they liked organic and were prepared to pay the premium. The same approach was taken to sustainably-sourced food. In the late 1980s Waitrose had begun a partnership with Welsh sheep farmers, led by Philip Morgan, the man whose departure to raise sheep – more docile than Waitrose branch managers – had brought Felwick to Waitrose. Morgan had thrown up his retail career and become a hill-farmer on a large scale. That model of farming cooperation was exploited further by the enterprising meat buyer, Richard Sadler, and eventually by all the Waitrose buyers, who continued to be respected across the industry. This was in contrast to those in some of the larger supermarket chains, who were widely accused of exploiting farmers and other suppliers. Dairy farmers were a particularly endangered species, buffeted by BSE and foot-and-mouth crises, and Sadler started a 'Select Milk' scheme, paying dairy farmers a premium if they joined and accepted stringent standards. Waitrose's farming credentials were strengthened further when it took over the Leckford Estate, an odd relic of Spedan's time that was still under the Chairman's aegis. With an eclectic mix of apples, mushrooms, poultry and dairy cattle on 4,000 acres on either side of the pretty River Test in Hampshire, it helped to establish the Waitrose position as a supermarket retailer with a human face. Human to its farmers as well as its customers.

That was all very well, but Waitrose needed to grow bigger and to expand beyond the Severn and Trent, and into Scotland. It did so by capitalising on monopoly rules when Safeway collapsed in the UK. Morrisons acquired the Safeway stores and was happy to divest some to Waitrose rather than to its larger and more direct competitors. Morrisons and Waitrose had competed at first only in Newark, where they'd coexisted, catering largely to different customers. In 2004 Waitrose bought nineteen of the Safeway/Morrisons, ten outside the limited area in which it then traded. That led to an accelerated rate of growth that gave it over 200 shops by 2009, including eighteen as a spin-off from the Co-op's takeover of Somerfield. In fact in the single year of 2009 it opened or converted twenty-five branches, exactly the same number Waitrose had in total when Stanley Carter had taken over that undistinguished little business in 1967. In 2007 Mark Price had become managing director, and he widened the scope of the expansion, moving into smaller 'convenience' shops, even tinier outlets in motorway service stations, and began a cross-selling arrangement with Boots the Chemist in 2010. By then Waitrose was also in Dubai and Bahrain, in a tie-up with Fine Fare Food Market, and had extended its arrangement with Ocado until 2020. All this led to increased buying power, enabling Waitrose to strike better deals with suppliers. Waitrose had always suffered in comparison with much larger competitors able to achieve a better margin. By the beginning of 2010, Waitrose annual sales were over £4.5 billion, half as much again as those of John Lewis. They'd come a long way, and were no longer stopping to admire the scenery.

## Stuart Hampson Bows Out

Towards the end of 2006, in a year when the Bonus had been 15% – and looked as if it would beat that comfortably for the year in progress – Stuart Hampson announced his retirement. Spedan had gone at seventy, Bernard Miller at sixty-eight, Peter Lewis at sixty-four. In the Partnership, the Chairman 'nominated' – in effect decided – his own successor, each of them handing over to a prince they had already anointed: to a man appointed deputy chairman some time earlier, and widely regarded as next Chairman even before any announcement. Hampson was younger: he decided to go at sixty, the standard retirement age at that time for Partnership managers. The only problem was that this time the succession wasn't clear cut. The current deputy chairman was Alistair McKay, the Waitrose ex-RAF pilot, who was close to retirement himself. He was a stopgap, appointed after Ian Alexander, the incumbent, had died suddenly in November 2005. Alexander had not been unwell and it was a huge shock to his colleagues, and particularly to Hampson. The genuine sense of grief and dislocation wasn't on the same scale as the series of illnesses and deaths that affected Spedan so much after World War II, but it was still a severe jolt.

The four possible candidates for the Chairmanship were all about the same age, late thirties to mid-forties. Luke Mayhew was older, but he had left at the end of 2004 when it became clear that he wasn't in the frame for the succession. His last day as MD was Christmas Eve, and he spent it cheerily packing china and glass in Peter Jones, where he'd started and been much liked. Mayhew was able to go out with an award for John Lewis as the best European multi-channel retailer, just two years on from his change of heart over Buy.com. He had, as the incoming John Lewis MD Charlie Mayfield stressed at the first opportunity, done the hard grind to equip the business for the trading conditions of the new century, and when he left the recovery was only just beginning. Mayhew took up other chairmanships, and in 2010 had become the Chairman of the British Retail Consortium, as David Felwick had done before him. That left the comparative newcomers (comparative in Partnership terms, anyway) Charlie Mayfield and Steven Esom, and the longer-serving Andy Street and Mark Price, who had both joined John Lewis straight from university. Mayfield and Esom headed John Lewis and Waitrose respectively, Street was then the Partnership's personnel director and at that point Price had moved temporarily from Waitrose to be the overall development director.

Thus in late 2006 Hampson had four strong candidates to take over in the following February. Aware of the looming problem, a long time earlier he had carefully defined the selection process, which included consultation with board members individually. Other companies had a nominations committee, usually chaired by a non-executive director. The Partnership now had two non-executive board directors, but they were newly in post, and not a little perplexed by what now happened. As a result of Hampson's soundings, the front-runners emerged as Mayfield and Street, and each had his adherents. Hampson settled on Mayfield and told the board his decision. Some members of the board didn't agree and began a debate in the meeting, something quite unprecedented, but Hampson was not going to change his mind. Unfortunately, a leak to the press over the following weekend alluded to a 'contest', and so Hampson's announcement in the next Gazette, the Christmas issue, came after everyone already knew.

It was all thoroughly unsatisfactory, not least because in an open organisation with a weekly journal it all took place in the glare of publicity, and it all seemed to come very much at the last minute. Some older and retired Partners were distinctly unhappy. But after a brief flurry of dismayed letters to the Gazette (with one suggesting that Mayfield's first task should be to engage a plumber), the business settled back down. Stuart Hampson was able to bow out of a strong, energetic and more forward-looking Partnership, with pre-tax profits up by a quarter and above £300m for the first time, and the Bonus back up to 18%. At Odney that month, reported under the headline Keep the Humanity, he told 150 senior managers that he was impressed by the change in management style he'd seen in his fourteen years as Chairman. They combined professionalism with 'approachability, decisiveness and a relaxed manner', he told them. He had the additional pleasure of seeing John Lewis made Retailer of the Year by *Retail Week* magazine, and of receiving the same journal's award for his own outstanding contribution to retail.

Nothing could better convey the change in the Partnership's position in the retail world in his time. From a determination to remain in the background, avoiding publicity and deliberately not seeking accolades, it was winning awards wherever you looked. At the same time the Partnership topped the list in *Which?* magazine's table of customer service, voted for by over 10,000 on its online panel, with Waitrose scoring 81, John Lewis 80, and the next highest scoring 70. The retail specialists *Verdict* ranked them the other way round, so internal honour was satisfied. Of course, as grizzled veterans were inclined to mutter, you couldn't move for awards these days, but it was a measure of the business's appeal to its customers, the ones who voted with their money or their feet. The Partnership might still have a profit-to-sales ratio, and a return on invested capital, worse than its top competitors, but is that really so important, provided it yields sufficient profit to safeguard its future and those of its *de facto* owners, the 70,000 Partners? And the expression 'sufficient' profit, not maximum, is what's on the card, enshrined in the constitution.

What is it about the Partnership, John Lewis and Waitrose both, that makes it so attractive to customers? Is it simply the fact that it's a co-owned business, in which the Partners, its front-line troops, treat customers as they themselves are treated? Is that really so significant – or is it just that it's a well-run business operating on ancient and simple retailing principles, unchanged since 1864? Does the Partnership method of calling managers to account hamper or help, slow it down perhaps, but make sure it goes in the right direction? Does the fact that the share price is not under constant scrutiny enable it to avoid knee-jerk measures when times are bad, so that it can take the long view? Can it keep its Partners contented and modernise in ways that do not lead inevitably to redundancies? If not, how do you square redundancy, saying goodbye to someone of fifty after twenty-five years of faithful service, with the idea of a business owned by a trust on behalf of all its workers? In the two final chapters we'll stand back and examine the Partnership from two angles, comparing it in 2010 with the business Spedan Lewis retired from in 1955. Chapter 19 considers the Partnership purely as a retail organisation, while Chapter 20 will look at it as an industrial democracy, unique for its size in the UK. Can the Partnership survive and thrive in the rest of the twenty-first century, especially at the start of its second decade when the country faces an economic future as uncertain at any time since World War II?

CHAPTER 19

# The Partnership as a Retailer

**The futuristic angular aspect of John Lewis Cardiff, opened in 2009, and the 'Georgian' Waitrose built in Bath.**

The Partnership aims to make sufficient profit from its trading operations to sustain its commercial vitality, to finance its continued development, to distribute a share of those profits each year to its members, and to enable it to undertake other activities consistent with its ultimate purpose.

The Partnership aims to deal honestly with its customers and secure their loyalty and trust by providing outstanding choice, value and service.

EXTRACT FROM THE 2009 REVISED
JOHN LEWIS PARTNERSHIP CONSTITUTION

What distinguishes the Partnership in the minds of many is the unique structure and 'democratic' character. Two retail businesses dating from 1864 and 1904 have been brought together into this peculiar organisation. The vast majority of retailers from that period have become extinct, evolved into something very different, or have been swallowed up into a conglomerate bearing neither their name, nor indeed much relationship to the original business. Why has the John Lewis Partnership survived? In essence it's because of Spedan Lewis's three big ideas, though the first one was originally his father's:

1 The principles of genuine customer **service**, excellent **value** for the customer, scrupulous **honesty**, and a wide **assortment**. Four highly effective principles in combination, but by the time Spedan got inside the workings of his father's shop in Oxford Street he decided that they could be made to operate far better. He improved the way they functioned, gradually put detailed arrangements in place to ensure they did, but he didn't alter the principles themselves. A tinkerer by inclination, these he left well alone.

2 The conviction that his employees would be more productive if they owned a stake in the business, and his consequent single-minded drive to make it happen. This did indeed create a shop culture where his father's trading principles could flourish. What's more, he managed to evolve a method of running a retail enterprise by and for its employees that survived into the twenty-first century, much against the odds. It survived his own tendency to profligacy – both of ideas and of money – and came through the inevitable repeated market turbulence. That was exemplified most starkly by the war: its destruction, and the long-drawn-out aftermath.

3 His appreciation early on that a retail business should be run by intelligent, educated people. He inspired the best to join, and stay, and in the end to bring his vision into reality. (Indeed often better than he had managed to do himself.) Daily contact with strong minds, amid a system of checks and balances, prevented him from being too over-ambitious. Spedan presented an authoritarian figure, but he was a curious mixture of intellectual arrogance and humility. Many dominating personalities in positions of power fail because they instinctively surround themselves with pliant subordinates: yes-men. Spedan succeeded because he didn't. They were in awe of the man, certainly, but that didn't stop them disagreeing with him forcefully when they had to. They were not yes-men, but yes-Spedan-but-men.

## The Retailer 1 – Customer Service

In this chapter I want to examine those trading principles, and consider how they have stood the test of time. Service, value, honesty, assortment. Have they been able to withstand the pressures of a world mightily different from the one that Spedan inherited? How much has retailing really changed? What is unchanging is a customer walking into a shop – though that may nowadays be a 'shop' entered via a keyboard at home – and looking for something to buy. At the heart of retailing is still that moment when an assistant says 'Can I help you, Madam?' There may be fewer such moments now, as self-service dominates in food shops and increases inexorably in department stores and non-food multiples, but that personal interaction is still vital. *Which?* and the retailing journals all focus in their annual awardfests on customer service. We might have reservations about these orgies of self-congratulation (whose turn is it this year?) but award ceremonies do year after year hand out best-service gongs to both John Lewis and Waitrose. Service remains vitally important, and the Partnership is still better than most.

A hundred years ago, when Gordon Selfridge arrived in London, the immaculate shopwalker guarded his fortress's closed entrance, eyed you up and down to establish whether you were likely to be a paying customer, then escorted you to your destination department. That sense a customer had of being carefully controlled took a long time to go, and many without a middle-class self-confidence found department stores forbidding places. 'Service' was provided on the shop's own terms. Only in the 1950s were the managing director and department managers of a John Lewis shop allowed to dispense with morning dress. It's fair to say that Peter Jones still carried a little of that atmosphere until late in the twentieth century – the sense that you had to dress up to shop there – and Waitrose didn't entirely escape that charge, either. But by the 1960s the aim was firmly to put customers at their ease, as well as to ensure good personal service from knowledgeable assistants.

How important is that personal service now? If you ask any retired Partnership selling assistants what they think of a John Lewis department store now, you realise what they're going to say. Take the trio in their eighties who had joined Tyrrell & Green in the war soon after their fourteenth birthdays, working in a dowdy relocated shop after the bombing, and paid 12s 6d a week (apart from the apprentice tailor and cutter, who got just 6s 9d). They weren't allowed, incidentally, even to *speak* to customers till they were sixteen. Now they think the new John Lewis at West Quay is wonderful: looks so lovely, bright new fixtures, beautifully lit, all that tempting merchandise on display. They're resolutely loyal to the old Partnership which still pays their pension and improves it each year in line with inflation. But, they say wistfully, it's so difficult to find an assistant sometimes when you want one. They're from a generation brought up on personal service and a selling floor with assistants – well, they were ten a penny. Not quite that cheap, but their 12s 6d equates to a weekly wage of £25 today, and they'd have given most of it to their mothers to swell the housekeeping.

Customers' expectations have shifted. Many who have grown up with self-service feel uncomfortable with a looming presence, over-eager to help. And of course the inexorable and overdue post-war rise in pay for selling assistants made the balancing of selling floor staff numbers and the quality of service a real competitive issue. Those John Lewis trading principles in combination make a hard taskmaster. You can keep high levels of staff on the selling floor, but against strong competition you can only stay profitable by raising prices. The Partnership's Never Knowingly Undersold slogan simply won't let that happen. So, like everyone else, John Lewis has been finding ways of reducing staff levels, despite its traditional reluctance as a co-owned business to make anybody – Partners, co-owners – redundant. Staffing reductions have been managed more gradually than with the competition, helped by the traditional high staff turnover rate in retail which brings 'natural wastage' into play, even though fewer leave John Lewis each year than is the case in other shops.

In the post-2000 period John Lewis decided that the approach to customers by selling staff needed refining and making more consistent: staff have to be able to deal with customers with different wants, so assistants may need to be assiduous or inconspicuous as occasion demands. The strategy called simply ABC was introduced – acknowledge, build, close. In the old days 'close' would have meant the same assistant ringing up the purchases at the cash register. Now it's not so easy. To reduce staff and improve efficiency, the tills, once dotted strategically around the selling floor, have been grouped together into fewer banks of three or four, with a single queuing system. But this specialisation brings a potential problem. 'OK, now where do I pay?' asked the long-retired Derek Rawlings rhetorically as he stood with the John Lewis Oxford Street managing director Noel Saunders. 'It's not obvious from the fixture I've just selected something from. And what if I want to ask someone a question about what I've bought? The cashiers at the payment point don't have the product knowledge.' At which moment an assistant appeared and saved the day and the blushes. The skilful deployment of knowledgeable selling floor staff, minute by minute, is more important than ever.

That illustrates the other customer service issue for John Lewis posed by its trading principles. Until well into the twenty-first century it carried an assortment of 500,000 lines. There weren't half a million in each branch – perhaps three-quarters of that – but the Oxford Street shop carried nearly all of them. If you want to be regarded as providing the best service, then your assistants must have knowledge of most of the products on their part of the floor, so that they can genuinely help a customer with a query. Up until the 1990s, with trading only five days a week outside London, that wasn't too hard. But now, in a want-it-now age, with seven-day trading and more part-time staff spread more thinly, that product knowledge is inevitably diluted. Have there been fewer assistants on the selling floor as a consequence? Yes, but it's arguably still better than the competition. Is that product knowledge diluted? Yes, of course, although the reduction in the assortment from 2005 onwards has certainly helped the assistant, as has more online product information on the selling floor. But if customers keep giving you their votes in surveys and with their purses, you've probably pitched it about right. That, surely, is the measure.

## The Retailer 2 – Value

Chapter 15 explained how Spedan's Never Knowingly Undersold slogan came into being. The principle was maintained, monitored and enforced in much the same way for eighty years after its introduction in 1925, with the same – if a gradually widening – limit on distance. The Internet, however, caused the policy a stack of problems. Those who began Internet trading early were able to cut costs to way below those of John Lewis, and of every other traditional retailer. Moreover, they were not location-limited. Like mail-order companies, who weren't seen as a threat, they could post the article from anywhere, and not necessarily in the UK. That was a real headache. If the policy was not suspended with reference to online retailers the Partnership would increasingly lose money; if they made the exception, the policy could be criticised as a sham. 'Never Knowingly Undersold... but only in a Real Shop?' But it was soon clear that as Internet trading became more popular – and especially to John Lewis's traditional customers – to maintain parity with the lowest Internet price would be suicidal. How then to call attention to John Lewis's 'value proposition'?

Typically, Internet comparison sites incorporate into their tabulation neither quality nor service – service both during and after the sale, such as guarantees. If you take these into account, on for example televisions, the John Lewis overall offer is usually decidedly better than its online competitors. John Lewis decided to stress its customer service and product quality in all its advertising, and eventually to extend the slogan formally to read: 'Never Knowingly Undersold on Quality, Price and Service.' If you'd walked round a John Lewis shop in autumn 2009 you'd have seen the window posters constantly reiterating this adapted Value slogan. In April 2010 a television marketing campaign began to reinforce the message. In launching it, Craig Inglis, head of brand communications – one of the titles that the new advertising age sprouted in John Lewis – said: 'For a long time Never Knowingly Undersold has been perceived as just a price promise.' (Indeed, for that's exactly what it was.) 'We believe it's more than that: it's about the value we offer our customers, about the quality of the products we sell, and the added value customers receive with the service our Partners offer.' At the same time, John Lewis increased the reward it paid its own staff for reporting an undersale to £3 an item from £2, where it had stayed for many years. The number of shop assistants who use their lunch hours to augment their income in this way had dropped considerably in the last thirty years. In any case the first line of defence is increasingly the Internet itself, because most companies now post many of their prices there. John Lewis shops still nevertheless enforce a local undersale policy, often having to move fast when a nearby competitor launches a price-cutting event.

So John Lewis today is using the slogan not just to communicate the price commitment, but to stress the service message too. And it incorporates quality. Now, to beat competitors on quality was never Spedan's intention. A reasonable quality standard, yes – the Partnership wouldn't sell you stuff that fell apart, and it would soon drop any suppliers providing shoddy goods. But he clearly recognised that customers' wants varied. Some needed durability, something they wouldn't replace till it wore out in thirty years. Others sought something stylish and contemporary, accepting that it would go out of fashion in a few years. So 'quality' in the slogan means 'quality at that price'. The new extended slogan, by deliberately combining price with quality in an overall 'value' message is clearly aimed at combating those who simply compare on price. That had always left John Lewis vulnerable to the issue of 'entry price', the lowest price in a range. You will not, true, be able to buy the same £6.99 John Lewis mug any cheaper elsewhere, but if you want an ordinary mug for a daughter's bedsit you'll go to Tesco or IKEA and buy one for £1.99. So hand-in-hand with the Never Knowingly Undersold extension came a determination to make sure that customers could no longer affirm that John Lewis is too expensive *in spite* of its slogan, as many do. By 2010 the entry-point issue had been tackled – at last, some said, and at the risk of diluting profit – by introducing an inexpensive good quality 'Value' range in simple designs.

## 'Value' in Waitrose

Waitrose, by contrast, has had many years of experience of dealing with the value issue for food. When Waitrose came into the Partnership fold in 1937 there were attempts to apply the Never Knowingly Undersold principle. But they foundered. The profit margins on most food items, and certainly anything tinned or boxed or frozen, are considerably lower than that for the products John Lewis sells. If Waitrose offered Never Knowingly Undersold on food its shops would have to match the lowest price of all of its nearby competitors combined, and it would go bust. None of the competitors has ever done it. They indulge in occasional very public price wars, but when the smoke clears after the propaganda bombardment they have suffered very little damage. There are massive headline reductions on the products that a customer is most likely to know the price of, while the prices of items not classed as 'everyday' sneak upwards, off the customer's radar. Without there being formal collusion between the major supermarket food chains – from which I exclude Waitrose, which despite its recent expansion still has only 4% of the British food market – there is acceptance that a long-lasting price-war would damage them all. And, for all the criticism that the big supermarkets attract, the food offer available in the UK is a vast improvement on fifty years ago on every single measure – except the volume of packaging landfill.

The Waitrose response to the knotty value question was to run the classic 'shopping basket' tests. For years a comparatively small number of common products was checked regularly against competitors' prices by the Partnership's Intelligence department, and – lo and behold – Waitrose came out very close in total price to the opposition. But because the chosen products didn't change frequently, the buyer made sure prices stayed competitive. When *Which?*, or more frequently a newspaper (with all the rigour that word conjures up) ran a shopping basket comparison in the 1970s or 1980s, Waitrose often came out poorly. It expostulated in response about quality, and about comparing the wrong lines, and about increasing the items in the shopping basket, but until David Felwick conjured up a Waitrose-specific slogan in the 1990s nobody really attempted to link quality to price. 'Altogether Better Value' did the job up to a point, soon amplified by Mark Price with the adage for TV advertising of 'Quality Food, Honestly Priced'. The word 'honestly' there is the key one. 'Look', it says, 'we may not be as cheap as the others, but we go for quality, for sustainable sourcing, for milk from high-quality farms, for only line-caught fish, for pigs reared outdoors, for eggs only from chickens that aren't pecking each other in misery. We encourage African farmers with help in forming co-operatives, we don't drive our British farmers into the ground. But all this comes at a price, just a little extra. Are you prepared to pay it?'

Indeed they are prepared to pay for it, as long as the price difference isn't too great. When Mark Price took over as managing director of Waitrose in 2007 he recognised that, although many of its traditional customers were buying more and more each year, they were a gradually diminishing proportion of the population. Too many, when they shopped in Waitrose at all, used it for 'treats'. To counteract this, he and his new buying director Richard Hodgson began to plan a 'Waitrose Essentials' range. Hodgson said bluntly in the Gazette in September 2009: 'Some of our prices are too high.' Hodgson's was the first Yorkshire voice heard in the Waitrose shires and suburbs, a man from Asda, whereas every predecessor since the 1960s had been from Sainsbury's. The

Essentials range launched in early 2009 rebadged and repriced a set of existing own-brand products, adding some new ones, and was an instant success. Price acknowledges he was fortunate that the new range coincided with 2009's deep recession, but lucky generals have been in demand since Napoleon, and he is nothing if not intensely commercial. In addition Waitrose not only made sure they matched the major competitors' price on key branded lines, but they flagged the fact on the shelves. (Begging the obvious question: what about all these other *unflagged* lines?) The outcome, after a slight profit dip in 2008 following its most successful ever year in 2007, was a Waitrose profit increase to a new peak of £268m in 2009. Certainly there had been twenty-five new branches, certainly the recession affected food purchases far less than other products, but Waitrose outperformed competitors in the traditional measure of 'like for like' sales. When the 2008 financial crisis struck, the expectation of many was that its profits might well plummet as customers retreated to the cheap discounters. Far from it.

## The Retailer 3 – Honesty

A retired Waitrose branch manager, a Stanley Carter veteran, ambled down the aisle of his local Waitrose late in 2009 and pointed to the profusion of 'price-match' and, particularly, price-reduction tickets. 'That's what it used to be like before Stanley got here. He got rid of them all. "Don't bombard the customer with messages," he said. "Let them see the stock and they'll make their own minds up."' The policy of not showering the customers with messages even extended to aisle signage, so well after 1990 new customers had no signs above Waitrose aisles to show them what was where. It took until the Felwick era for these to be put up, and for a gingerly start to be made to extending promotions – 20% off, 3-for-2 and so on. There had existed a very strong moral principle that you didn't try to confuse the customer about value, and constant promotions blurred the picture. That didn't stop the competition, of course, and the seemingly interminable slash-and-burn price-cut message they sent helped to make Waitrose – whose pristine shops *looked* expensive – seem even dearer than it actually was. Waitrose simply couldn't afford to sit atop a moral mountain watching others take their customers. Now, as the old branch manager observed, promotion tickets are everywhere. What particularly troubled him was the 'reduction' policy:

> They put stuff on sale now, I reckon, at an inflated price so they can reduce it in a fortnight to a sensible price and claim it's a third off. Look at those cherries. They've been 'half price' for weeks ... But then everyone's doing it – can we afford not to? You know what it reminds me of – green shield stamps forty years ago. Remember those? Shops issued higher and higher multiples. We wouldn't touch them.

The Partnership's Constitution enshrines honesty towards its customers as a key principle: 'The Partnership must deal honestly, fairly, courteously and promptly with customers.' The 'Honesty' component of Old John Lewis's trading principles was born out of his distaste for some of the sharp practices he saw when he was an apprentice. Until the law changed in 1968, for example, retailers would advertise something at 50% off when it had never been on sale at the higher price. John Lewis would never do that. 'Honesty' for Wallace Waite meant a refusal to indulge in the tricks still going on in the 1930s – thinning the butter, adulterating tea and flour, 'bouncing' the scales – that cheated the customer. Spedan likewise ensured that his Partnership was founded on strict standards of probity. In his insistence on honesty in business he followed his father, of whom he said:

> He never allowed any sort of deceit or trickery at the expense of any of his customers or any of his suppliers. Somewhat perhaps as a consequence of his fastidiously high standards of probity, he aimed always at extreme promptitude of payment.

Spedan was determined that his business should continue to be as honest with suppliers as it was with customers. Treat fairly, pay promptly. The Waitrose cultivation of farmers has its roots in that attitude, and has been maintained to this day. This wasn't particularly because of a notion of 'fairness' on Spedan's part, but of clear business sense, both in pricing and in relationships with suppliers:

> A really first-rate buyer will never lose sight of the fact that one must live and let live: one must let live those whose life one thinks that one may possibly have some reason for desiring at a future time. It may be unwise to buy very hard … I may give him more, even much more, than the lowest price he would accept … and hope that the bread that I have cast thus upon the waters will return to me satisfactorily.

> A buyer must be incorruptible. He must be insusceptible to flattery and proof against every kind of present, from a crude offer of money, at one end of the scale, to the gradual and delicate establishment of private relations, with a good deal of hospitality, at the other.

The Partnership has continued to be adamant in its refusal to allow buyers, or anyone else, to profit from a supplier's eagerness to grease palms. Decline such a gift, it insists in its rules, unless you cannot reasonably and without embarrassment refuse it or return it to the donor, in which case it goes into the Partnership's sizeable charity pot. Originally such gifts went to the 'committee for claims', which helped Partners in need; now they go to those responsible for involvement with the local community. Some new arrivals were and are startled by the rigid application of this rule, and so are suppliers. Hospitality is also treated in this way. The rules say: 'A Partner may only accept hospitality from someone with whom he has a business relationship if it is modest and if refusal would risk offence or disadvantage to the Partnership.' The Partner is expected to return the hospitality in kind to ensure that there's no build-up of obligation, conscious or unconscious, towards the supplier. And suppliers attempting bribery do it only once.

## The Retailer 4 – Assortment

His father's adamant view that the width of assortment was even more important than rigorous price-matching startled Spedan at first, but he soon recognised its wisdom, as long as it was sensibly applied. The classic case in Old John's time was his determination to carry ribbons, which many department store competitors didn't stock, in every colour under the sun. On analysis, most of those ribbons would probably have been losing money, and the few that were profitable might not be selling enough to compensate. That wasn't the point. If a Victorian customer had a shopping list that included ribbons as well as more expensive items, she was likely to get everything from you rather than go somewhere else. John Foster, trained in Oxford Street by Stanley Carter, who illustrated the point by using the word 'cornucopia' of a good assortment, understood this well. In the early 1980s, when Waitrose MD, Foster introduced patisserie service counters. The initial experiment showed that in themselves they were often unprofitable, but the shop's total sales and profit went up – and even more so if you baked bread on the premises so you could, for once, attract customers' noses as well as their eyes.

We've seen how in the last decade John Lewis decided its assortment had got too wide. Another problem with assortment width is that if it's unbridled it can lead to an 'embarrassment of riches' bafflement for a customer. If you walk down a supermarket aisle, how many products can you actually see on the top shelf if you're five foot tall, or on the bottom if you're six foot? In a business that encourages assortment width, and judges a buyer on his mark-up and not on his wastage, as used to be the case in Waitrose, the buyer will tend to steadily increase the number of lines on his assortment. Especially if, in Waitrose's case, you're battling with competitors who are much bigger than you. Studies in the 1990s showed that, in an over-full assortment of, say, jams, you can increase sales by about 10% if you remove that same percentage of products. The art comes from realising when your selection is over-full, and from making sure that you don't simply exclude the slowest sellers. Have you too many sizes? Have you too many different makes of (say) strawberry jam? It may be that you do better by eliminating one of those rather than taking out the only ginger-with-rhubarb jam. Even if the removed strawberry jam sells better than the less popular combination jam, customers can easily find another to switch to. Take out a distinctive product that's someone's favourite and you irritate them more. Equally, take out the slow-selling small packs of tea or cereals, and you upset the loyal 'grey' customers, those who live alone and don't want to stuff the shelves in their little kitchens with big packs that last months.

This issue of width versus distinction became apparent in John Lewis. In the previous chapter I described how the John Lewis assortment was comprehensively reviewed in 2004–5 with the help of outside consultants, a resort to outside expertise which still reduces some of retired Partners to apoplexy. How does it look now, a few years later? Andy Street, the John Lewis MD in 2010, was the Partnership's personnel director at the time of the assortment overhaul, so can look back at it objectively. In his view it was essential, and the issue was consistency: each buyership might have a slightly different target group of customers, and their price structures could vary. There are now much clearer guidelines for buyers. A more important point is that, while an individual department in a specific branch used to have a theoretical assortment of, say 5,000 lines, in reality it didn't *on the selling floor*. If the customer saw, say, only 4,250, because the shop was out of stock of 750 at any one time, that's the *actual* assortment size. In fact, it might only have been 'out of stock' of half of those 750, but the other half were still stuck in a congested stockroom or the local service building. If customers can't see them, they're not there. In food shops, and in many multiple non-food chains with a much more restricted assortment than John Lewis, there is central direction of what product goes where in each shop. Thus Waitrose Belgravia has a precisely defined shelf layout that's different from the Waitrose in Glasgow. Every product has its exact place, so you can *see* whether it's out of stock. In a department store that level of precise control is much more difficult, though it's improving. So it's hard to achieve the same level of efficiency.

Which is worse for a customer, to be told, 'We don't sell it', or 'We do but we're out of stock'? The John Lewis approach since 2004 has been to improve markedly on the availability of what it chooses to sell, and there's no doubt this has been successful. At the same time the total assortment has been 'edited' down to a more manageable size, so that the right ranges in each department can be stocked to suit the target customer – those Shopping Enthusiasts, Service Seekers, and Solution Demanders – primarily but not exclusively. Have they got it right? Andy Street and his merchandise director Jill Little, who drove the change through in the first place, concede that it's impossible to get it right and keep it right. Both say that the retail world is changing far too fast these days to be able to look at a range and say, 'Good, we've got that right, we can leave it for a while.' The whole point is to strive constantly to compare the assortment with the competition, and to make sure that in no area that John Lewis wishes to dominate does it cede the lead, and that in areas of less importance the assortment doesn't look too weak. That speed of change is cited as the reason that buyers rarely nowadays stay with the same merchandise longer than five years, where a generation ago some had been buying the same assortment for over twenty.

One specific department divided people in John Lewis after 2005: toiletries. In every John Lewis the perfumery department sits on the ground floor near a main entrance, where Gordon Selfridge first planted his a hundred years ago. It's sold by brand everywhere, and the perfumery companies staff it with their own personnel (a historical anomaly, and the only place in the shop where products are sold by non-Partners). Perfumery is a traditional impulse buy. In the year 2000 John Lewis shops also carried a wide range of toiletries, the sort of thing that you would find at Boots the Chemist or Superdrug. It sold well, but at a price – the Never Knowingly Undersold promise meant that John Lewis had to match the lowest of the specialists' prices all the time. So its profitability was low. But, said its defenders, it provides 'footfall', bringing a lot of people into the shop in the lunch hour and after work on a weekday. By 2010 that wide toiletry assortment had virtually vanished. 'Ridiculous – it's been annihilated,' say some old hands, with distinct vehemence. So what do the present traders think, department store MDs who have been running branches throughout the last ten years? Do they rue its passing? No. Noel Saunders at Oxford Street was quite clear. 'Footfall? Yes. In the shop and out again.' You have to put it on the ground floor close to the entrance, otherwise people won't bother. The classic positioning of an important 'destination' department is somewhere not *too* far away from the entrance, but which brings customers past other areas where they might stop and buy *en route*. You can't do that with toiletries – they simply won't bother when they can walk into the inevitable branch of a chemist chain round the corner, and find it quickly. The old hands are not persuaded, but the present John Lewis MDs are. Not that they all feel the overall assortment's right. 'It never can be', says one. 'The important thing is that the buyers listen to us.' Do they? Pause. 'Yes and no. They do their best, but to be honest, some of them don't get here to the selling floor enough. We used to see buyers here much more often.' I asked an experienced buyer. 'I agree. In fact we're making a concerted effort this year to get the team into the branches more. We used to, true. But it was a more leisurely time then. There's so much pressure now.'

Whenever you take a snapshot of a business, as this book is doing in 2010, it's in transition. The assortment certainly is, and always will be. Is it near enough right at present? Andy Street is clear that it remains a constant challenge, and not least because of the huge growth, current and potential, of Internet trading. John Lewis Direct has an assortment now of over

100,000 products, some of which aren't sold in John Lewis shops at all. This 'multi-channel' retailing will have an impact on the business's current and future direction. For now, as with everything else, it's the customer who tells you if you've got it right, and you have to look at the results. In March 2008 the Partnership delivered an annual Bonus of 20% for 2007, with John Lewis making a profit of just under £200m. Then into a clear blue sky came a black pall, the aftermath of the volcanic banking collapse of late 2008. The virtual standstill of the UK housing market affected John Lewis severely: profits fell to £146m in 2008 and the Bonus dropped to 13%. In the first four trading months of 2009 – February to May – John Lewis department stores ran at an overall loss. Many retailers folded. How would the Partnership cope with such a deep and probably long-drawn-out recession? Could a co-owned business move decisively enough to halt the slump that was affecting everybody? Does its 'democracy' slow it down, make it reluctant to take unpopular decisions? Has it been able to adapt and yet still stay true to Spedan's vision?

CHAPTER 20

# The Partnership as a Co-owned Business

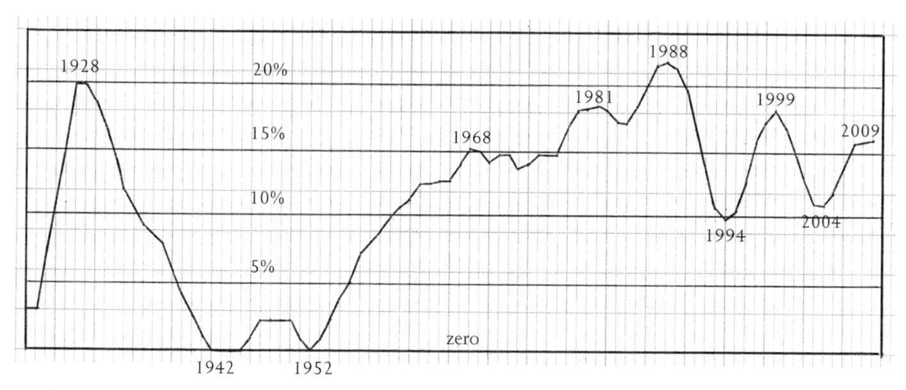


The movement in annual bonus percentage for the years from 1919 to 2009. In order to avoid it looking unreadably spiky, for each year it shows the average for the previous five. Note the lean years before and after the war, and the long steady climb from 1953 to 1988.

> The advantage of your Partnership is the freedom from the City's distraction, so one needn't dance or twitch a muscle to its music. This advantage leaves you free to do the other foolish things you're so fond of.
>
> PETER LEWIS AT THE PARTNERSHIP COUNCIL DINNER IN 2000, QUOTING A FRIEND WHO HAD SPENT HIS WORKING LIFE IN THE CITY

> Is the Partnership damaging instead of improving the relations of managers and managed? Is it in these times of much overtime and business pressure more akin than it has been in the past to the relationships in most businesses run by limited companies?
>
> SPEDAN LEWIS, MUSING IN REPLY TO A GAZETTE LETTER OF COMPLAINT, 5 NOVEMBER 1921

The Partnership's ultimate purpose is the happiness of all its members, through their worthwhile and satisfying employment in a successful business. Because the Partnership is owned in trust for its members, they share the responsibilities of ownership as well as its rewards – **profit**, **knowledge** and **power**.

That is the stated purpose of the John Lewis Partnership, the first paragraph of its published principles. The Partnership pays its employees an annual Bonus which has averaged 16% in the fifty years to 2009, the equivalent of over eight weeks' pay. It still, almost uniquely among UK companies in 2010, gives them a non-contributory final-salary pension. It allows them a say in the running of the company through five Partnership board members, chosen by a democratically elected representative council. It allows *anyone* to question its decisions in a weekly journal, and the responsible director *must* reply. On top of all that it subsidises a range of amenities that in themselves are pretty much unequalled in UK businesses. It remains a co-owned enterprise, a 'Partnership on the scale of modern industry', as the words above the entrance of Peter Jones stress, though it would now be more accurate to say it's an industrial democracy on a scale far larger than most modern industries now remaining in the UK. So how does it work?

The Partnership's ownership structure is very different from that of the ordinary company. This chapter explores how it differs, how it works, and examines whether it makes a real difference to its business success. A sceptic should ask: so what? In the final analysis, what all people want is to earn what they think is a fair wage, to have a reasonably agreeable place to work, to feel secure in a job that doesn't drive them mad with frustration or boredom, and to be able to put away enough for retirement. To most of them, the sceptic might say, it doesn't matter a fig whether the company is a private one, a public plc, or a part of the government, as long as it ticks those boxes. The ordinary employee arguably has no particular interest in the 'benefits of ownership' which Spedan defined, very early on, as the sharing of profit, knowledge and power (although he always called profit 'gain'). We'll look at each of these in turn, starting with profit. The first and most important thing to recognise is that no part of the profit goes to a shareholder outside the business. The shareholders are the Partners, over 70,000 of them in 2010. The stakeholders are regarded as the Partners and the customers, as these stated precepts indicate. Note the reference to 'sufficient' profit in the paragraph below:

The Partnership should make sufficient **Profit** to sustain our commercial vitality and distinctive character, allow continued development and distribute a share of profits each year consistent with Partners' reasonable expectations.

> **Partners** should gain personal satisfaction by being members of a co-owned enterprise in which they have worthwhile, secure and fulfilling employment and confidence in the way the Partnership conducts its business.
>
> The Partnership should recruit and retain loyal **Customers** through their continued trust and confidence in our reputation for value, choice, service and honesty and for behaving as good citizens.

## Profit – Pay Policy, from Floor to Ceiling

Before we start by looking at the Partnership's uses of profit, we should examine its pay policy. This is what today's constitution says:

> The Partnership sets its pay rates to attract and retain high calibre people. Each Partner is paid the local market rate for satisfactory performance and as much above that as can be justified by better performance.

That definition from the outset was subject to two caveats; a minimum and a maximum wage. The maximum was what Spedan defined as 'a handsome professional wage', such as he envisaged for a successful doctor or lawyer. Below that he would pay managers and managed alike the market rate – the rate at which they could be recruited and retained – right down to the bottom. But that lowest pay would not necessarily be decided by the market. In Peter Jones, when he took it over, the market rate for shop assistants was, he thought, completely inadequate, and in his view the first use of the profit of his co-owned business was to improve it. He said:

> What is to become of this [profit]? In the first place it will provide a decent minimum wage, no matter how much more cheaply equivalent performance may happen to be available in the conditions of the modern world. A business that cannot give a decent living to every worker whose services it really needs should not exist at all.

Thus from the outset the first use of profit was to create a 'decent' standard of life for everyone in the business. Spedan, though not religious, is likely to have been influenced by the encyclical Rerum Novarum, issued in 1891 by Pope Leo XIII, which had shaped Liberal thinking. Entitled 'The Rights and Duties of Capital and Labour', it proposed a minimum living wage to mitigate the worst effects of capitalism, and to stave off encroaching communism, two of Spedan's principal concerns. Later, in his Fairer Shares, Spedan used the expression 'living wage', which in the early Partnership was interpreted over the years in various ways. Until the government provided family allowances, the Partnership's minimum was a graded scale based on age, sex and the number of dependent children, set above the statutory retail wages council minimum. It was constantly adjusted, especially during World War II, and it was of key importance. Later it lapsed as a formal instrument, and in fact when in 1998 the new Labour government introduced a minimum wage for everyone there were a few Partners outside London who had slipped below it. In 2010 the UK national minimum wage stood at £5.80 an hour, £4.83 for those aged eighteen to twenty-one. (The modern living-wage campaign urges a figure some 20% higher.)

What is unique is the explicit definition in the Partnership's constitution of a *maximum* wage. It was originally defined by Spedan as whichever was the lower of two calculations: twenty-five times the wage of a London selling assistant with four children, or the equivalent of £5,000 a year in 1900, both expressed *after* tax. The tax rate then was tiny in modern terms, only 7.5%, whereas in 2010 the top rate is 50%. In the Partnership the statutory maximum is now simply expressed as seventy-five times the average basic pay of non-management Partners *before* tax. In the Partnership today that top figure comes out as just under £1m before tax, including pension entitlement. Spedan's original £5,000 in 1900 is equivalent to around £900,000 today before tax. Unless you're a banker or business leader, on the face of it seventy-five seems an unjustifiably large multiplier, but in today's world it's typical. The actual multiplier on basic pay for the top 100 UK companies is eighty-one (though the figures don't compare exactly because that's the top divided by the average of *all* the firm's employees, which is higher). It has been rising inexorably: only as recently as 2000 that figure was 'only' forty-seven. However, with the Partnership, what you see is what you get. In other companies the top earners get share 'options' and special bonuses which pay out very substantial sums if the company is successful – and often very large sums even if it isn't. While most Partners recognise this, and accept that it has no option but to pay its top people the market rate, every year there is a trickle of critical Gazette letters, usually after a tight pay review such as 2009 and 2010. The problem for the Partnership, over the years since Peter Lewis eventually allowed his own salary to rise to let those in the next tier get something near *their* market rate, is how at the top level to provide a package near 'a market rate that will attract and retain good people', when at the very top the market seems out of control. As a consequence there's an anxiety that large salaries attract those who don't share the Partnership's values. In one senior Partner's opinion:

> Frankly, we don't want the kind of people who are only going to join us if the pay rate is so huge. We don't want just good people, we want *good* people, those who really do share our values. Do we really try hard enough to test that when we recruit them? Look at the number of highly-paid recruits since 2000 who have already left. I think not.

The rules state: 'The Partnership seeks to recruit only those who share its values.' The current MD of John Lewis, Andy Street, a Partner since he left university in 1986, made his own view clear in the 2010 TV film *Inside John Lewis*, and spoke perhaps for his senior colleagues. 'I could earn a lot more, but I put it to you that this is a more fulfilling job.' Mark Price, his opposite number at Waitrose, another one who joined the Partnership from university, rejected the prospect of running a rival supermarket group in early 2010, at a total figure much more substantial than his Partnership pay.

## The Uses of Profit – Partnership Bonus

When Spedan started his annual Bonus scheme in 1920 he decided that it should be paid to everyone at the same percentage of their annual pay. In *Fairer Shares* he said that it should be paid in proportion to the contribution that the Partner provided to the business. The best approximation of that, he reckoned, was their pay. That is what was incorporated in the 1929 Trust settlement. At intervals people have questioned whether a person's pay, set as it is by the market rate, is indeed a fair equivalent of the amount of the contribution provided by each Partner. Some say that if you examine it logically it doesn't really stand up to scrutiny – how do you compare the contribution provided by someone in a loss-making department store, or a department within one, with someone in a hugely successful one? And does the *market rate* operate on the principle of comparative contribution? No, it's to do with the demand for certain skills and their comparative scarcity. Spedan decided simply that it was the best approximation available, and in practice every alternative, all the way down to paying everyone an equal sum, can be similarly demolished. Anyway, even if someone could come up with a better measure, the calculation appears to be locked up in the Trust settlement, so, as every Gazette letter reply has emphasised, that's that. (Note, however, that in 1934 Spedan chose to distribute a 9% bonus only to those earning under £400 pa – an experiment he did not repeat.)

At the head of the chapter is a graph of the Bonus payouts every year since 1920. Until 1965 it was paid entirely in shares, which many people cashed immediately even though they were worth less than their face value. In 1965 the Finance Act made shares an inefficient way of distributing profit, so for the next four years it was paid in a mixture of shares and cash, and thereafter it has been entirely in cash. That was much more welcome to low-paid Partners, who often needed the money straight away. For many years the Partnership lobbied to make the Bonus tax-deductible – it is taxed twice, once on the business's declared profit, once when the Partner receives it, and the Partnership reckons there should be an incentive for employee-owned businesses. That lobbying was eventually successful in that it could be deemed 'profit-related pay' when the Conservative government of 1986 introduced the concept to encourage employee share ownership, up to an effective tax-free maximum of £4,000. The rules required the then finance director, David Young, to declare a percentage before the final year's results were known, so he was obliged to estimate low to be on the safe side. Nevertheless, for a period, the average Partner benefited by an extra sum of about 20–25% of the Bonus. The outgoing 1997 Conservative government then withdrew the profit-related pay scheme, although in 2007 a scheme was devised to save tax on that part of the Bonus that a Partner is prepared to lock away for five years, up to a maximum of £4,500 each year.

## The Uses of Profit – Pensions

Unlike almost every single company in Britain the Partnership has not withdrawn its non-contributory final salary pension scheme. That is remarkable. In the post-war period it became increasingly necessary for businesses to have a pension scheme as part of their recruitment package. That is no longer needed, and yet the Partnership continues with a generous non-contributory system, and it bends over backwards to be fair. Moreover, there is generous free life insurance if a Partner dies in harness, and a half-pension for widows. This, they contend, is absolutely right for a business owned by its employees, one that has a genuine sense of community. Indeed it continues to make its amenities available to that retired Partner community, mounts special outings and dinners for them, and provides shopping discount as long as the Partner lives. We have seen in Chapter 11 how it all began when Spedan started a non-contributory pension scheme in 1941. He had been reluctant at first, but after a few years was writing that he wished he'd started it sooner and paid more into it in the 1930s rather than distribute so much as Bonus. The advantage he saw was that, in the long drawn-out trading difficulties after the war when it wasn't possible to pay a Bonus, he could at least point to the pension fund as providing a future benefit for Partners to help stave off the very real fear of an impoverished retirement. And the actual running cost to the Partnership was very low at first – the fund only had to pay out when Partners retired. It was also, and still is, a tax-efficient way of distributing profit.

Until 1975 the pension paid out was based on *total* earnings throughout a Partner's career. That made the pension value extremely vulnerable to the prevalent high rates of inflation, so the scheme was altered to a final salary one. Hence for example after thirty-five years a Partner earning £12,000 at retirement (after the value of the state pension had been subtracted) would then get an annual pension of 35/60, i.e. £7,000, revalued upward at frequent intervals to combat inflation. That revaluation now takes place annually. Part-timers were not originally included, but gradually brought into the scheme so that by 1994 everyone was in, irrespective of how many hours they worked. The minimum qualifying age for a pension was originally set at thirty-five for men and thirty for women. From 1975 this was progressively reduced to the earlier of age of twenty-two or four years' experience. In 2003, with pensions costs increasing because of extended life expectancy, the minimum age was lowered and replaced by an increased qualifying period for new entrants. Originally Partners only got a pension if they'd worked fifteen years in the business. This had been gradually reduced to two years by 1988 before going up to five again in 2003. Since 1979 widows and widowers of Partners have been paid a half pension. It's noteworthy that whenever the scheme has been improved it has been applied retrospectively, so retired Partners can benefit from improvements.

The problem for any pension fund is the rapidly improving life expectancy at age sixty-five, which went from an average 11.6 years to 17.5 between 1911 and 2001, an increase of over 50%. Not only does it continue to rise, but the Partnership's early concentration on occupational health – it had residential nurses from the early 1930s – and its ban on smoking at work, means that its retired Partners will tend to live longer still. The most rapid rate of improvement took place between 1925 and 1945, and this so-called 'cohort' effect means that actuarial estimates made twenty years ago turned out to be distinctly low, everywhere in the UK.

The John Lewis pension fund, like almost every other, was hit by the sharp reductions in share values after the 2008 financial crisis, and funding it will remain a thorny issue. At the start of 2009 the Partnership decided, as well as the usual annual contribution from profit, to transfer to the fund its notional investment in Ocado (£127m). In July 2010 the fund profited from Ocado's flotation, and sold about half its holdings for just over £100m, while retaining shares worth a little less than that. As long as the Partnership continues to be successful it can keep ahead of the curve, but any downturn means that pension fund contributions eat into the Bonus. Between 1998 and 2008 the annual contribution to the pension fund went up from £48m to £98m, a rise of 55% in a period of comparatively low inflation. If it had stayed the same in real terms, the 2008 Bonus would have been 17% not 13%, all other things being equal. In that period the annual pension fund contribution averaged 75% of Bonus. Forty years earlier the ratio was 55%. Not as large an increase as you might have imagined, but still a relentless one. That's why other businesses have scrapped their final-salary pension schemes, essentially by diktat – and usually with the stakeholders' (the shareholders') enthusiastic support. But this is the Partnership, its stakeholders are its Partners, and any and every proposal on pension arrangements goes to the Partnership Council for debate and decision.

## The Uses of Profit – Amenities

The Partnership rules say that it will provide amenities that will 'promote happiness, a sense of community and the Partnership's reputation'. Many large companies used to provide amenities for their employees. It was a typical Victorian ideal to give opportunities for healthy play and polite entertainment. Major retailers did this well before the Partnership began; old John Lewis certainly didn't, but in the late nineteenth century many department stores and other businesses took up this practice. So did the civil service and the armed forces, and they still do up to a point, so senior newcomers from those public services had no difficulty in accepting that the Partnership spends a considerable amount of money and attention on amenities. But the extent to which public companies make this provision began to dwindle in the late twentieth century, and the Partnership is alone in the scale and range of subsidised facilities for its employees. Often those who join now, especially those schooled in companies who have been through one or more draconian cost-cutting exercises, find it surprising. Some regard it as old-fashioned and paternalistic, and a waste of money: it's a 'Partnership value' they don't instinctively share.

Spedan was certainly paternalistic when it came to giving his Partners opportunities to play together. He was an enthusiastic sportsman, if not a very good one, but, as we have seen, funded a sports club for the Oxford Street employees out of his own pocket well before he went to Peter Jones in 1914. He was motivated by a desire to give his father's employees the chance to do things their station in life and lack of money wouldn't ordinarily allow them. He genuinely grieved at the loss of his first sports club for Peter Jones at Grove Farm in Harrow when plummeting trade forced him to sell it in 1921. Spedan rediscovered his zest for a country estate when his money worries receded in the later 1920s. We have seen in Chapter 8 how he came to start the Odney Club in 1927, close to the Thames at the pretty village of Cookham in Berkshire. It was a rural estate thirty miles from Peter Jones, and in the early days he had grandiose schemes for it. They had to be reined back, but he designed and built a water garden there, as he would do more famously at Longstock, he reconfigured the estate with a cricket ground, tennis courts (though decidedly fewer than the fifty he envisaged in the late 1930s), football and hockey pitches, and a squash court. He had wanted a zoo there, which led to some Gazette opposition, and to start his own form of Glyndebourne.

One of Spedan's later regrets was that he was unable to develop at Odney a fascinating scheme he devised during the war, to set up a residential college, for which typically he drew up plans that were magnificently over the top. He was strongly influenced by AD Lindsay's *The Modern Democratic State* – he marked ninety paragraphs in his own copy – and the radical educational ideas of Richard Livingstone and George Cadbury. The unusual Danish 'folk high schools' particularly attracted him, and he decided that Odney would be the perfect setting for a college for Partners – most having left school at fourteen or fifteen – who wished to better their education. Education in the broadest sense: he brought in a working potter, John Bew, set him up there, and recruited teachers. In 1948 Joyce Smith was a shop assistant, one of seventeen who spent two six-week terms there in January and February, July and August – two of the coldest and the hottest periods on record – at the charming old Dial House in Cookham, on the top of a hill overlooking the Thames. Later she described how they were taught English language and literature, economics and current affairs by three resident tutors. They were professionally coached in tennis, boxing, and (of all things) fencing. They lived in, were docked £1 (about a third of their wages) were given candlelit dinners at a single immense table with a different guest each night, took out boats on the river, and lived a life of sublime pleasure. It was, for a brief moment, a tiny replica of Oxbridge college life.

But it folded at the end of that year. The Partnership was struggling and there was simply not enough money to pay for it. The warden had to retire through ill-health, the pottery was unable to make ends meet and, a major psychological blow, John Bew vanished and was found drowned some months later. Odney continued at a low ebb for some time after that, until the Partnership's financial resurgence of the 1960s. By then, although Partners from the further-flung branches could and did have annual holidays at Odney, it was largely seen as a benefit available only to those from London and the Home Counties, and, frankly, as overly middle-class. So too was Leckford, from where Spedan had moved across the Test valley to Longstock in 1945, leaving his old home Leckford Abbas and a holiday camp (no, do not think Butlins) available for Partners. As the number of Partners rose, pressure mounted for a northern holiday centre, and a hotel with a hostel attached was acquired in 1978 at Ambleside on Lake Windermere. In 2009, defying both the recession and those who thought the Partnership was losing its zest for providing affordable holidays, the Partnership bought an activity centre in Wales at Lake Bala. Although provoking a sigh from those north of the Scottish border (where's ours?) it became instantly popular with the first energetic families who went sailing, kayaking, canoeing, climbing, windsurfing or mountain biking there.

The Partnership has not lapsed from Spedan's oft-repeated principle that if it's worth doing something for Partners it's worth doing it properly – better not do it at all than skimp. Although Odney, for example, was allowed to run down somewhat for two periods, the 1950s and the 1980s, it has been refurbished comprehensively, most recently after 1995, when its houses were transformed from large functional buildings with shared facilities to hotels with en-suite bathrooms. They retain, though, that country house feel, dotted around a charming estate where the grounds are still beautifully and expensively groomed under its loving head gardener Uel McGowan. McGowan arrived in the year of the great storm of October 1987, and wept when he saw that one of the great cedars had come down. The modern Odney is a place that expresses Spedan's original intentions better than ever. One of the subtle and important shifts in the Partnership's progression from its somewhat formal and punctilious post-war period is the kind of people who stay at its amenity centres. The majority of the accents are regional, and nearly 60% of those who stayed in 2007, the year of a major amenity review, earned below £15,000 a year.

Few companies now do anything remotely similar. To stay at the main holiday centres in 2010 cost a Partner £38.50 full board a night, and a family of four with two children under 16 was paying just £113.50. Originally the charges were staggered depending on income, but the cost structure has been simplified. The full board cost in an equivalent hotel would be around four to five times as much – even a non-Partner guest pays only £77 full board – and the Partnership subsidises its holiday centres by over £3m a year, a little under 1% of its profit. That's not all: total amenity subsidies are considerably larger, and include those for clubs and societies. Anyone with enough local support can seek a subsidy and start up a club. The world has altered hugely from the 1930s, with television the relaxation of choice and Sunday trading sharply reducing the opportunities for group participation in sport, in particular. Nevertheless each John Lewis department store still employs a benefits coordinator to organise trips and events. Although Sunday trading has wiped out many inter-branch tournaments – twenty-four branches participated in an annual cricket knockout tournament as recently as 1995, but now there are only two teams left – a resurgence is being attempted through a Partners in Sport initiative, tied to the 2012 Olympics. Still going strong, though, are two societies that have weathered every storm: the sailing club and the music society.

The Partnership's sailing club was for years funded out of the Chairman's own budget, so wasn't subject to scrutiny. That left it open to charges of elitism. It's true that the backwaters of the south coast provided a natural haven for the retired naval officers populating the middle reaches of the Partnership after the war. But anyone could sail, and did, for very little cost. Managers and selling assistants alike set out from their shops on Friday nights to take the train to the coast for a weekend trip across the channel. The sailing club is now treated just like any other society with its budget managed by the Partnership council. The Chairman also traditionally has involvement in the music society, which was fostered in the 1930s among others by Enid Locket (née Rosser) when she was the young legal adviser, and later by 'Paddy' Palmer, who was recruited as the Partnership's social secretary when she was the leader of the Boyd Neel orchestra. Between 1950 and 1964 the music society gave many little-known operas their UK premiere, and one was commissioned by Bernard Miller in 1957, although after the 1990s the operas proved too difficult to mount, and especially to rehearse. In the 1990s interest was rekindled when Stuart Hampson began to use its orchestra and choir at customer events. It now has a full-time conductor, Manvinder Rattan, a trained musician who had started in the Partnership on the selling floor. As the music society's standards improved it undoubtedly helped to attract graduates who sang or played an instrument. It can now muster a thirty-piece orchestra with only a little stiffening from professionals, and runs two choirs. One choir has an audition requirement for entry, and it is good enough to win competitions; the other is a people's choir in the modern style, and puts on concerts several times a year. Beverley Aspinall, who left to run Fortnum & Mason in 2005 after completing the massive Peter Jones overhaul, was asked whether she missed anything about the Partnership. She confessed: 'I haven't picked up the oboe since I left. Playing in an orchestra was such a pleasure, and my managers were always very good about giving me the time.'

I have dwelt on the amenities at length – and there's a range of further subsidies for things like shopping discount, meals, adult learning and special bursaries – because it is in the amenities, say many involved current and retired Partners, that the Partnership's special quality resides: the sense of family. And that community continues into retirement, for retired Partners have a central support network, and retirement coordinators in each John Lewis shop. Some loyal retired Partners worry that the sense of community will be eroded as the world changes, as businesses become more ruthless, and the Partnership is obliged to tighten every belt another notch. They fear that new arrivals from outside don't really 'get it', particularly the expensive 'soft' benefits under the amenity banner. They worry that when the finance people get the scent of that fat subsidy in their nostrils they'll be on the hunt. Odney? How much is that estate worth alone? It's true that the amenity centres in particular are under increasingly close observation to ensure that they're not too lax, and that they exploit opportunities to offset their costs. They do feel the hounds' hot breath at times. But there is no doubt that the Partnership's current leaders are as devoted to the ideal as any of their predecessors. And, many argue, it pays to be like that. It adds considerably to the attractions of the recruitment package. It's not only Mark Price, knowing little about its ideals, who joined the Partnership because it had golf courses and a sailing club. Spedan's paternalism can be faulted, even mocked, but he used the 'family' metaphor often and with reason. That sense of family, of community, has been maintained against the grain of British business culture.

## Knowledge – The Gazette and Chronicles

As we've seen, Spedan began his Gazette in Peter Jones in the first year after World War I, and soon sold it at 2d a copy, a quarter of its cost. Two pence may seem little to fork out now, but that was thirty pence in today's money to a household earning the equivalent of about £100 a week, where that two pence would pay for a subsidised lunch. In a single department store of a few hundred people there weren't at first that many who wanted to write something week after week, and the author of *The Young Visiters* was a rarity. Spedan filled much of it himself, spicing up the letter column whenever he felt a topic needed airing, giving him the chance to demolish his own Aunt Sally sallies. Soon he was asking his new Partners if they wanted to keep it; half said no, not really, it's waste of time and money. He carried on, and, despite gaps in the early years for a few weeks at a time when he went on holiday, it gradually settled into a regular weekly rhythm and format, although it went through editors pretty fast. The longest-serving, Barbara Thomas, editor from 1954 to 1976, survived Spedan's last two years as Chairman:

> Very early I learned that the editor is a fool, and furthermore that the editor couldn't possibly win. If I omitted a comma that was in the original copy I was not only a fool but an illiterate fool. If, on the other hand, I refrained from inserting a comma that hadn't been there but that, on second thoughts, the Chairman had decided there should have been, I was not only taking the Partnership's money under false pretences, I had the mental capacity of one of the more retarded of the Mesozoic lizards. But… I don't think he ever called anyone a dinosaur that he didn't really like.

By the time the first new branches arrived in 1934 it had become a solid routine journal of Partnership record, appearing every Friday morning with the results of the previous week's trade, always compared with the week before and the equivalent week the previous year. Every Partnership council meeting was reported verbatim, as in Hansard. It summarised almost every major meeting, from the Partnership board downwards, and to this day shows the Partnership's results weekly. No other large business does anything remotely similar. To augment the Gazette Spedan began local journals he called Chronicles. They were more cheaply produced, with the local registrar acting as Editor. Chronicles were originally more widely read than the Gazette. Photographs started to appear before the war, and in 1985 the Gazette began to employ colour for the first time. But it was still in essence the same publication until well into the 1990s, when the journalist and broadcaster Paul Burden took over in 1999 as part of his role as communications director, then called the general editor.

Until that point it had remained somewhat austere, with pages full of print, articles written in an educated style suitable for a reader of the broadsheets, which most Partners in branches certainly weren't. Burden introduced a larger-format Gazette, full of photographs; it looked terrific but ran into opposition because of its size. People were used to reading it in groups with their coffee and pastry in Partnership dining rooms at Friday morning break, and the new Gazette was unwieldy and got in the way. The morning and afternoon breaks were enshrined in the rules for office workers as well as for tired selling floor Partners, and only recently have office workers been allowed to take a drink back to their desks. (Spedan's view had been that a break was necessary to refresh you, so you did better work rather than more.) Burden was concerned, too, to exhibit the Partnership to the world, and it became focused much more towards outside journalists in the 1990s. As a consequence it became more outward-looking and less parochial. But Partners wanted to hear about their own doings – Steven Forfar, who arrived as its editor in 2004, said that for many issues there wasn't a single photo of a working Partner – and one of Burden's last acts before retiring was to return it to a smaller format.

The Gazette has since gone back to being more explicitly for Partners, with a subset of articles about the business extracted and offered to the press in the weekly e-zine (how the new terminology trips lightly off the tongue). Despite its availability online, the readership of the paper Gazette remains at about 50–60%, with the local Chronicles selling a little more. The most frequent current criticism is that it is somehow dumbed down, and that there's a tendency in this PR-dominated age to put on a gloss, to 'spin', to tell good-news stories. That may be inevitable, given the times. One unreconstructed Old Partner (cf. Old Labour) said:

> Now it's simply full of how well everything's going. Every face is a smiling face. You get a set of happy touchy-feely articles, often surrounding several pages of letters of complaint. There is no verbatim record of council meetings any more, which is a disgrace, just a summary, and the trading comments are full of the usual banalities...

Those 'weekly trading comments' have always been dreaded by generations of trading directors – another ordinary trading week, same as the last, so what the hell can I say this time? They differ these days by being mercifully shorter and by being relentlessly upbeat. The verbatim records were read only by councillors themselves and a few ardent democrats, who would argue, and still do, that a Hansard-like record is crucial to a functioning democracy – nothing can be rewritten after the event. But bad news is not disguised, and the six-monthly results are always analysed honestly. The tough year of 2009 was a case in point, when John Lewis actually made a loss in the first four trading months of the year – as the John Lewis MD Andy Street pointed out in the Gazette. He was no less candid in the *Inside John Lewis* film:

> In the first six months of 2009 profits were down 49% on the same period in 2008. That wasn't unexpected – we budgeted for a loss of £12m and made a *profit* of £18m. Our operating model is too costly for the first half and for the recession. As costs rise and sales drop there's a pincer movement.

## Knowledge – Anonymous Letters

A reader of the modern Gazette would often find a stark contrast between the good-news stories in the bulk of the journal, and the usually forthright criticism in the letters column. There has always been a corrective against internal good-news spin in the Partnership, and it remains one of Spedan's most effective ideas: the anonymous letter column, and the rules that surround it, which ensure that any letter that isn't clearly offensive or personally defamatory *must* be published. There is no censoring of unpalatable questions and comments. Letters come in from young trainees and retired directors alike. In what other business would the directors have to answer armour-piercing missiles from retired intellectual giants in their eighties, sometimes week after week? Successive Chairmen have refused to relax the stringent rules of engagement, even though the toughest questions often come to them. The 'appropriate authority' must answer the letter within three weeks. And they must make a good job of the reply, or letter writers will start to hound them in the following weeks. Many have learnt the hard way that you don't fail to answer a question, you don't belittle the questioner, you don't wrap the answer in complexities – you'll only have to undo it a couple of weeks later. The best approach is a wry self-deprecation, ideally with a touch of humour if you can be *sure* it's not misunderstood. A witty brevity is best if you can get away with it. In 2009 the Waitrose MD Mark Price was under attack for starting his own Internet blog. His harmless 'Chubby Grocer' pieces were seized on as evidence of overweening pride inappropriate to a member of a co-owned business, one that doesn't do self-promotion. Eventually a supporter wrote in with a letter saying here's a man whose heart and soul have been in the business, he's being successful, leave him alone. Price's reply was 'Thanks Mum'.

While many Gazette letters do lead to changes for the better, the benefit of a healthy anonymous letter column is unseen: a dog that doesn't bark in the night. The engagingly eccentric Warren Gilchrist, the last of the great ex-naval characters, was for many years deputy to the personnel director Stephen May. Gilchrist once took a proposal to him for some change in the personnel rules. In the Partnership these changes are dangerous, because even if they benefit the majority there's always someone who will pipe up and complain, and the personnel director usually gets to answer more Gazette letters than anyone else. May was doubtful of the benefit of Gilchrist's projected change, and wrote him the kind of tricky letter that he thought the change would prompt. 'Respond to that.' Gilchrist did; the reply passed muster, and the change went ahead. It's this threat of the Gazette letter which makes Partnership managers – usually – consider changes with extreme care if they think they'll affect people adversely. We all know of the hasty, poorly communicated office move that leaves everyone fuming. In the Partnership you'd be lampooned in the press, and you know it, so such things as office, department or whole branch moves have been meticulously planned over the years. Surely, an outsider says, that simply slows you down in a fast-moving world like retail. To which the experienced Partnership manager would reply: 'We'd rather be a bit later but with everyone pulling together, than quicker but with stragglers or people who don't buy in.'

## Power

The Partnership is run under the auspices of what it calls its 'three governing authorities' – the Chairman, the Partnership board and the Partnership council. The Chairman appoints the executive and carries responsibility for its performance. The executive consists of the MD and appointed directors of both John Lewis and Waitrose, and a corporate management providing common services. The Partners are represented in this governing apparatus as follows:

1 Through five elected directors of the Partnership board. The other directors are the Chairman, a deputy, five directors that the Chairman appoints from the executive, and, since 2006, two non-executive directors from outside the Partnership. In 2007 Charlie Mayfield appointed for the first time one of the non-executive directors as deputy chairman. So the original twelve members became a nominal fourteen, but in practice thirteen. In 2010 the finance director, one of the non-executive directors and two of the elected directors were women.

2 By the Partnership council, who now elect their five members of the Partnership board every three years, which is when the council's members themselves are elected. Its numbers have fluctuated over the years but have recently been cropped back to seventy: two from corporate management, twenty-nine from John Lewis and thirty-nine from Waitrose. That reflects the weight of numbers in Waitrose nowadays: until an overhaul in 2006 there was a bias towards John Lewis, and before the 1980s a further bias towards John Lewis Oxford Street. Waitrose had its own subsidiary council, but only recently does John Lewis as a whole have one (though every department store had its own local council).

## Power – the Board

After Spedan retired in 1955, his democratic apparatus was left largely unchanged for many years. Different generations looked at it, committees reported back, and there was fiddling with the mechanics but no great engine redesign. The only major change for fifty years, between 1955 and 2005, was Bernard Miller's decision to change his appointees to the Partnership board. When Spedan had decided to have elected board members in 1946, the five he appointed were not members of the executive, as you might expect, but the so-called 'critical side' en bloc. They were the Partners' counsellor, the chief registrar, the financial adviser, the internal auditor, and the general inspector. To redress the balance, the then Partnership council simply elected the key members of the executive. Thus, most peculiarly to modern eyes, it was those who piloted the business who were the *elected* members, while the appointed members were the critical side, the Watchers. This arrangement worked up to a point – it had all the key people on the board, after all – but in 1969 Bernard Miller decided to switch to a more rational approach. This led to a typical board composition of Chairman, deputy, John Lewis and Waitrose MDs, finance director, personnel director and general inspector, with the Council usually choosing the Partners' counsellor and chief registrar as two of its five elected members. That left only three elected members who weren't senior Partnership worthies. Although these two were from the critical side and hence notionally independent, and certainly helpful to the other elected members, it led to an imbalance.

What was it like to be one of the three remaining elected board members? They were likely to be middle management (though, rarely, some selling floor Partners were elected) with often stressful full-time jobs, who had to read board papers every other Sunday with follow-ups on some Wednesday evenings. Board meetings took place on alternate Thursday mornings outside holiday periods. This split was emphasised on one occasion in the Stuart Hampson era when a lengthy board meeting was adjourned over lunch, which was taken by three of the elected members together in the ordinary Partners' dining room at the Victoria head office, while the others went off unthinkingly to the small separate Chairman's dining room. In a business that prides itself on its democratic character that seems perversely elitist, and the sense of exclusion was not lost on the three. Subsequently Stuart Hampson closed down the separate dining room.

The elected board members often stay for many years. The systems analyst Ian Bassett, as we've seen, clocked up more than twenty years. Other long servers in the same period were the trenchantly witty buyer, John Stott, and the Waitrose operations manager, David Ramsey. All these were graduates. One current long-standing elected member, though, is Ann Buckley, who began as an 'A' level temp on the checkouts at Waitrose Harpenden, emphasising that you can still get to the board despite a lack of further (formal…) education. Recently a former Waitrose meat buyer, David Jones, a massive figure who looks as though he comes from a long line of family butchers, was on the board for a lengthy spell before moving over to the democratic side permanently, and in 2010 becoming president of the Partnership council. They all found it difficult to acquire confidence at first among the intellectual big hitters around them on the board, but gradually gained it. Some felt under intense – if usually unstated – pressure to agree to a board proposal. Once, when they baulked at the imminent closure of a specialist unit, they were read the riot act – but they got their way, and the unit is still open some years later.

> There's a tendency to play the 'greater-minds-than-you' card if one raises an objection to a course of action that's clearly been agreed by all the appointed board members in advance. That's when you get put under psychological pressure, and you just have to persist. You must tell yourself that you've been elected by your fellow Partners to represent them and you're damn well going to do it. Obviously the person bringing the proposal has put a lot of time and effort into it, and doesn't want to lose face, so it's understandable if they get a bit tight-lipped. If you ask them, of course, they all agree with the system in principle, but not always in the particular. Sometimes as well they don't like it if you stray outside what they think of as the prescribed area under discussion. It's fair to say though that in the last couple of years it has felt much more open.

There is general agreement among the newer elected members that the arrival of the two non-executive directors made a real difference to their self-confidence. The non-execs have no qualms over asking about anything, and that emboldens the elected directors to do the same. And what further helps them to feel more equal nowadays is that they are given far more background information as a matter of course – as indeed are Partnership councillors.

## Power – the Councils

After Charlie Mayfield became Chairman in 2007 he stressed the importance of the councils in holding him and the John Lewis and Waitrose managements to account on behalf of Partners. He wanted to instil more of an adult:adult relationship between management and council. Had the Partnership achieved its targets? If not, why not – and in the 2008–9 recession there were many targets to miss. To do that he gave them an unprecedented volume of information on targets and strategy; his predecessors had been much more guarded. Partnership councillors form special-interest groups to analyse and discuss them: co-ownership, customer, Partner and profit. In 2010 the Partnership and divisional councils had been reduced to four meetings a year, usually one or two days in January, March, July and September. In March the annual results are presented, analysed and questioned. The Partnership trading year runs from January end to January end, thus catching the most recent Christmas and New Year trade. The half-year's results are discussed similarly in September. The Waitrose MD presents his results at the Waitrose council, the John Lewis MD at the John Lewis council, and the Chairman the combined results at the Partnership council. At each meeting the respective executive directors answer questions for as long as there are any; a Chairman's questioning usually takes around two hours, and he can be asked about anything within or outside his results report. That has been traditional since Bernard Miller began the practice after a review of the democracy in 1969. But council meetings have changed markedly from his time, when they were formal debating chambers, discussing and voting on proposals brought by directors or individual councillors. Now there are few formal proposals, a more relaxed and informal approach, and more reporting back by special-interest groups. In June 2010, for example, there were some heartfelt opinions expressed on 'what it felt like to be an ordinary Partner' in an extended recession, a tough period of fewer pay rises and fear of redundancy.

In individual John Lewis branches, each of whose full-line department stores would employ an average of eight or nine hundred Partners, there are two forums for discussion. One is branch-wide, the other for each department, of which there are usually between twenty and thirty (much fewer than there used to be). These forums in 2007 replaced the original branch council, modelled on the Partnership council, and what was called the C for C, the committee for communication. The reasons for the change may seem esoteric to many readers, but the replacement of the latter in particular caused some disquiet. The C for C was born out of Spedan's idea that the ordinary selling assistant, the one at the bottom of the heap, had no voice at all in any organisation. Initially Spedan ran the meetings himself, which must have been pretty intimidating, but he soon withdrew, and the meetings came to be chaired by an independent Partner from outside the shop, guaranteeing confidentiality. This chairman discussed any problems raised, and wrote a report to the local department store MD, and all such reports went to the Partnership's Chairman. He made it clear to local John Lewis MDs that he expected anything they flagged as an issue to be sorted out. This became another useful safety valve. (In Waitrose branches, incidentally, averaging about 150 Partners, a big majority of whom were part-time, there used to be no formal local democracy. There is now Partner Voice, similar to the John Lewis forum but smaller, which also began in 2007.)

When the John Lewis branch councils and the C for C were replaced by branch and department forums, neither chaired by an independent Partner, this caused some alarm. Most of those involved at both ends of the scale do think the current system is an improvement on the old, which was getting tired and perfunctory. But some don't agree, and in 2010 there were several Gazette questioners perturbed that there was now no meeting without a manager present. One letter was typical: 'In the old C for C I could say what I liked without fear or favour. Now it depends entirely on whether I trust my manager.' That was Spedan's point. And the branch councils used to be consulted whenever there was a need for a change of trading hours, operating like the old works council in a traditional unionised business. That didn't mean they always won. In 1997, for example, the High Wycombe branch council voted against Sunday trading. It came back with a small improvement in working conditions and was passed, if only by 18 votes to 14. That year the Edinburgh branch council voted against its MD's recommendation to open for the Clearance sale a day earlier than usual. Brian O'Callaghan took it to the whole Partnership council, which reversed the decision by 71 to 43. They decided – by no means unanimously, you'll note – that a local branch, sharing equally as it did in the profits of the whole business, shouldn't be able to have it easier than everyone else. The most tricky instance came in the next decade, when Luke Mayhew wanted to extend opening from five to six to seven days. That would affect everyone's working hours and contracts, incorporating Sunday as optional. All of the change proposals went separately through each branch council. The first was Welwyn, which voted it through only by 16 to 13. No other branch got that close a result. At Nottingham, with the branch in the middle of an extensive refurbishment, the MD Simon Fowler delayed the change and went straight from five to seven days, and got it through – plus the name change from Jessops to John Lewis – after a long debate and a secret ballot.

At intervals throughout its history the Partnership council has been criticised for being sheepish, a compliant tool of management, though it usually reasserts itself at intervals. This is a typical Gazette letter, from back in 1939:

> It is very difficult for the outsider to believe that the members of your council are elected by yourselves. One might be excused for thinking they were elected for their dumbness, actual and metaphorical, by a cunning and far-sighted management, so that lambs might be led to the slaughter with scarcely a bleat... The verbatim reports of your council meetings are chiefly remarkable for their anaemia.

Though it doesn't happen often, the council can and does kick against a director's advice or recommendation. That's what happened in 1987 with 'open' annual reporting of performance. Until then the annual report was discussed with Partners by their managers, but the contents not revealed, unless a manager chose to read it out. A groundswell of feeling emerged that it should be open, despite the risks, pointed out to them at length by Stephen May, then Director of Personnel. After a vigorous debate the council agreed with a proposal from an Edinburgh councillor to make reporting open, and Peter Lewis ultimately accepted the argument. A good example of a local equivalent was when the Peter Jones council voted to allow male selling assistants to wear short-sleeved shirts on hot summer days. Opposed at first as a dangerous slackening of standards of dress, it was soon adopted throughout John Lewis. The best councils have been those with independent-minded mavericks prepared to represent a cause, but because it's rare for there to be burning issues – the various safety valves mean the Partnership management isn't stupid and usually gets it right – it's easy for the council to acquiesce to virtually every management proposal.

## Redundancy in a Co-owned Enterprise

The council was tested in 2010 when it became apparent that a change to 'benefits in retirement' made in 2007 had left one particular group of Partners disadvantaged when the national statutory minimum age for retiring on pension went up from 50 to 55. This touched a nerve when some of those worst affected were made redundant between the ages of 50 and 55, after over fifteen years' service in the Partnership, having arrived at a time when they felt that, unless their performance fell away alarmingly, they had that 'job for life'. Now they'd lose as well the lifetime benefits in retirement they'd expected – shopping discount, Odney membership, the use of clubs and societies. They felt they were being expelled from their tribe. What particularly stung these long-serving loyal Partners was that their loss of benefits occurred at just the time that the shopping discount rules were being relaxed for new recruits. When a councillor highlighted the benefits issue in one of the new 'special-interest' groups into which the Partnership council is divided, he was persuaded not to bring it up as a proposal. Because it wasn't raised, a number of unhappy Gazette letters resulted, accusing the council of being craven. As a consequence the council did decide to re-examine it – anonymous letters can still do the trick.

In the 2010 television series *Inside John Lewis*, the then director of retail operations Gareth Thomas said bluntly: 'The model we operate is unsustainable. It's as stark as that.' It wasn't the Partnership model he meant, but the degree of over-manning in John Lewis. In essence there had been a reluctance to tackle the duplication of effort across the department stores. There was always an innate conviction in John Lewis that 'the local branch knows its customers best', so work was still performed in each shop that could sensibly be done centrally. For that reason, while the selling floor operation received much attention throughout the 1980s and 1990s, behind the scenes it didn't, despite the electronic age making a local presence less of a necessity. Eventually, functions like credit management and shop maintenance were outsourced, and in 2010 it was the branches' help-desk operations that were the prime cost-saving target of a 'branch of the future' initiative. Not outsourced abroad as typically happens in other businesses, but transferred to a new operation in Scotland – where they claim with reason that the most understandable English is spoken – and set up as a new Partnership operation.

When competitive pressure leads it to consider redundancies, the co-owned Partnership always has a struggle between business sense and compassion, as it should. The problem is that delays in taking tough decisions can both slow a recovery and shovel the personnel consequences under the carpet, where they fester. This is one of the toughest issues for a co-owned business. It can no longer manage, as it did when the London suburban branches in Streatham and Brixton were closed, and those in Hampstead and Holloway converted to much smaller Waitroses, to find homes for virtually everyone displaced. As recently as 1996 Stuart Hampson was able to say: 'When Partners reach their five-year review we tell them that the Partnership will go to extraordinary lengths to enable them to remain in the business for the rest of their working lives. In the 1990s that is an amazing promise for a business to make.' That promise was simply unsustainable and, what's more, led Partners to imagine they had a job for life, an expectation that led to much heartache when they discovered they didn't have one, after all, or at least not the same one. The Partnership's constitution now says that Partners with over five years' service 'will be encouraged to develop their skills so they may continue in the Partnership for all their working lives'. It bends over backwards to try to find another job for, or retrain, a displaced long-serving Partner, but outside London it's difficult to do so with department stores widely dispersed.

## The Partners' Counsellor and Registrars, Last of the 'Critical Side'

Finally, I return to examine briefly this critical side construct, so elaborately established by Spedan. It consisted of Partners' counsellor and chief registrar, whose jobs have now been combined. There was an internal auditor, a watchdog on financial probity corresponding to the external auditor required by company law. The fourth was a financial adviser, whose remit was to 'observe and assist' the finance director: a prospect most modern finance directors would find extremely irksome. The fifth was the 'general inspector'. If the Partners' counsellor acted as an ombudsman on behalf of the Partnership and the Partners, the general inspector did the same for the business as a retailer. For many years his job included a rolling programme of inspections of department stores, production units and buyerships. With the increased independence granted to Waitrose and John Lewis that degree of separate scrutiny has gone. Gradually the formal critical side was whittled away. By the 1970s the financial adviser role had sensibly been embedded in the normal John Lewis and Waitrose management structures, and was eventually called what it by then was, a divisional finance director. The internal auditor was relocated inside the finance directorate. The general inspector's job diminished, became part-time and eventually lapsed.

The lubrication in the Partnership's democratic machinery at ground level has historically been supplied by the registrar. The title and the concept are troubling to the newcomer and the outsider. The role was invented by Spedan in the 1930s to act as a local ombudsman, to make sure that the management of the shop – far away from London – stuck to the Partnership's principles and treated individual Partners fairly. At the outset they were almost always professional women in their middle years, single or divorced and hence independent and able to move over the country – they were supposed to change branch every five years or so to avoid becoming too close to the local management. Over the years they became responsible for holding all the personal files, a job usually carried out by the staff function in other businesses, which meant they knew every Partner and their background. The best registrars were a vital component of the fair and smooth running of a branch. They reported in to a chief registrar, often an independent-minded woman who took no prisoners, unlikely to be cowed by top management, and responsible directly to the Chairman. But by the 1990s, although it had been evident long before, it was clear that there was far too much duplication of work. The local staff office took over the personal files and the admin, and the registrars were free to take on more branches. In 2010 there were thirty-five registrars covering over 70,000 Partners, a ratio of one to 2,000, and there is some concern that this dilution, which doesn't allow there to be one on the ground in each department store, resulted in a lessening of their influence, although each has a full-time resident assistant registrar in place. 'We never see a registrar these days', said one department store MD. Many of his more independent predecessors, of course, would have been only too happy with that. Now individual registrars report not to a chief registrar, whose post has lapsed, but to the Partners' counsellor.

The Partners' counsellor is the final piece in this seemingly complicated democratic jigsaw. Reporting directly to the Chairman, he – and it has always been a man – has typically been a trusted senior Partner of long-standing, a strong devotee of the Partnership, and one with an affinity for Partners and an understanding of what makes them tick. He is an overall Partnership ombudsman. Anyone who has been dismissed can appeal to the Partners' counsellor, who will examine the case. There are very few reinstatements, but on occasion changes in working practice may result, or more often a quiet word to an MD or local manager. In 2009, after an investigation into the role of the diminished critical side, Charlie Mayfield made a break with tradition by appointing a younger man as Partners' Counsellor, Patrick Lewis. As Spedan's great nephew and Peter Lewis's son, he had the Partnership in his DNA, but he was a trader through and through. He began in the Partnership at the age of twenty-nine, coming from Procter & Gamble, and worked his way through local department store management before joining Luke Mayhew's management team in 2002 in a series of jobs that included the supply chain and selling operations.

## Spedan's Legacy

Patrick Lewis today carries the responsibility for making sure that Spedan's Partnership keeps its principles alive in a world very different, but just as challenging, as when Spedan took over Peter Jones in 1914. What would Spedan make of today's Partnership? He would certainly recognise it. He would probably argue intensely about each of the changes that had been made to his structure, but he would acknowledge that his followers had their hearts and heads in the right place. He would be gratified by the Partnership's subsequent success and probably envious of it, while recognising it as a tribute to his foresight. Spedan would perhaps be amazed – publicly diffident but secretly pleased – that in 2002 he was voted the UK's most admired businessman, ahead of Andrew Carnegie and Joseph Rowntree (a decade earlier and few would have known who Spedan was). He would probably be surprised that the Partnership had still managed to maintain its principles and the strength of its democracy, despite a size that would seem to him colossal. Some retired Partners indeed think it's too big to be sustained, but that certainly doesn't apply within each shop, where staff numbers have in fact shrunk. As ever, for each Partner it's their immediate manager's attitude and behaviour that embodies the Partnership.

I suspect Spedan would be most exercised about two things. First, he would be appalled that the gap between rich and poor in Britain had grown so wide since his death, and especially in the last thirty years. As *The Spirit Level*, the 2009 book by Richard Wilkinson and Kate Pickett, has convincingly shown, the more unequal nations have the worst record according to every measure of a society's health. That is almost certainly true of businesses as well. Second, Spedan would remain severely disappointed that very few other enterprises had followed his lead to try a form of employee ownership. None of any size did in his lifetime, but it's fair to say that when he retired in 1955 the jury was still out on his experiment. That jury returned its verdict long ago. Is the next decade the time for a change in the way businesses are formed and run? Can the Partnership model be replicated?

POSTSCRIPT

# And Now for Something Completely Different?

New Partners at the opening of John Lewis Cardiff in September 2009. Despite the recession, they all received a Bonus of 15% of their pay the following March.

We should have a society far healthier and for almost everyone far happier if the national income were divided very much less unequally.

SPEDAN LEWIS, *FAIRER SHARES*, 1954

I care for riches, to make gifts to friends, or lead a sick man back to health with ease and plenty. Else small aid is wealth for daily gladness; once a man be done with hunger, rich and poor are all as one.

FROM EURIPIDES' *ELECTRA*, C 400 BC, QUOTED BY RICHARD WILKINSON AND KATE PICKETT IN *THE SPIRIT LEVEL – WHY EQUALITY IS BETTER FOR EVERYONE*, 2009

We have a once in a lifetime chance to renew our idea of what a company is for.

WILLIAM DAVIES, FROM *REINVENTING THE FIRM*, 2009

> Even today, fifty-seven years after Spedan Lewis first formed his ideas, they run against the grain for most businessmen. It is taken for granted in British industry that employees do not have the same rights within the business as they are commonly given by the political system outside. They are not expected to vote for their leaders, they rarely have highly developed systems for complaining about the leadership and making suggestions to it, and there is not even the notional assumption that leadership in the business world should in the last resort be referred to the approval of the workforce. The ultimate sanction rests theoretically, and very occasionally in practice, with the shareholders. And yet there is no interest in a company's health quite so obvious or overpowering as that of the people who work for it.

That quote came from an article in *Management Today* over forty years ago, and things have if anything got worse. This book is published on the second anniversary of the collapse of Lehman Brothers, when the world's biggest bankruptcy plunged the financial markets into freefall, with more than £50 billion wiped off the FTSE 100 index in a single day. The banking crisis illustrated the flaws in a financial culture that put 'shareholder value' at its centre but without any genuine accountability – the shareholders became the victims of a system that supposedly put them in charge. They were the sufferers, as British taxpayers would be for a long time afterwards. Moreover, shareholders had done nothing to prevent the spectacular increase in pay levels at the top of industry, and a consequent vast growth in inequality.

In *The Spirit Level* in 2009 Richard Wilkinson and Kate Pickett illustrated the effects of that inequality on the health of society. Most northern European countries, and Japan, with high tax rates and a culture of communal care, score well on the ten measures of a healthy society that the book examines, such as life expectancy, childhood mortality and drug-taking rates. The United Kingdom scores badly, and the United States worst of all. But it wasn't always so in the UK. During World War II, in real terms middle-class salaries went down by about 10% and working-class salaries up by a similar margin, and universal rationing contributed to a comprehensive levelling effect – and to a sense of 'we're all sharing the pain together'. Those health measures improved, as they continued to do after the war through a better diet, the arrival of the National Health Service, increased taxation rates for high earners, and improved levels of education. That improvement then slowed, going abruptly into reverse in the 1980s and thereafter. Despite its positive side – businesses were freed up from restrictions, tax rates were reduced, the country's growth rates improved, most people were *materially* better off – societal health measures in the 1980s began to deteriorate. Between 1979 and 1999 inequality increased in the UK faster than in any other industrialised country outside the former Soviet Union. In 1986 the poorer half of the population owned over 10% of the UK's wealth; now they own just 1% of it.

Does it have to be like this? Can labour not employ capital, instead of the other way round? The John Lewis Partnership is a 'co-operative society of producers' with over 70,000 members. It has survived and grown because of a combination of strong trading principles and an ownership structure that gives *all* its employees a share in its success. Because of that, it has been able to maintain a distinct internal culture, with a degree of communal feeling rare in the business world. Moreover, it cannot be taken over by corporate raiders. Its stakeholders are its employees, its customers, and to a certain extent its suppliers, not a set of anonymous shareholders. Its customers are largely uninterested in the unusual structure, and judge it by its ability to give them what they want. It has its flaws, it has at times been complacent, defiantly insular, and occasionally arrogant, but it keeps on thriving. For the trading year 2009–10, one of the toughest recent periods for retailing, it delivered for every employee a Bonus of 15% of annual salary. John Lewis recovered from a dire start to 2009, and by the middle of 2010 was putting on a sales increase of more than 10% above 2008. For Waitrose the figure was nearly 20%: it had barely missed a beat during the recession. So Spedan's concept does work for the Partnership he created. Can it work for other enterprises?

After years of indifference from politicians the Partnership increasingly became the subject of scrutiny, particularly in the year before the 2010 UK general election, when the 'John Lewis model' was held up as a fairer way of doing business. But can it be replicated? There are two crucial components: its ownership and capital structure, and its internal democracy. The second is not difficult, though it requires care, determination and goodwill on all sides. The first really is the awkward part.

The John Lewis Partnership exists because it was transferred to all of its employees, its Partners, by its owner. It was to all intents and purposes in 1929 a private company. That made the process easier. In 1920 Spedan Lewis had been able to turn Peter Jones, a public company, into his embryonic Partnership, thanks to an ingenious plan, a persuasive personality and a group of shareholders who he dazzled out of their objections. There seems little possibility of any sizeable public company today going through a similar process. In the UK only private companies have been able to move to a form of employee ownership, and a comparatively small number at that. The typical circumstance is when a self-made man who has constructed a successful business decides to dispose of it. He has no family he wants to pass it on to. But he doesn't feel the need to make as much as he possibly can from the sale: he cares more about the loyal workforce he has built up over many years than he does about whether he walks away with £20m, say, rather than £5m. He has a set of values that aren't often visible in the hustling entrepreneur. If it were easy to do, it's fair to say, probably more enterprises would transfer in that way. Most self-made businessmen don't *want* their business to be asset-stripped after their departure, its employees made redundant – but what can they do? Interestingly, despite the dominance of public companies, it's striking that over 30% of the country's GDP is generated by family-owned enterprises. Moreover, nearly a third of business failures have been identified as victims of problems with succession. This provides plenty of candidates for employee ownership.

The answer is to transfer ownership into an 'employee benefit trust', rather as Spedan did. According to a tracking mechanism set up in 1992, listed (hence not including John Lewis) employee-owned companies have out-performed the FTSE by an average of 10% each year. Every study shows that it is the participation of and consultation with the employee-owners that is responsible for this improvement – shared ownership alone is not enough. There has certainly been a steady expansion in employee-owned companies, and, as William Davies's 2009 Demos publication *Reinventing the Firm* confirms, any comparison shows that they can stand up to and out-perform traditionally organised businesses. However, none is on anything like the scale of the Partnership, which in 2010 was by some distance the largest privately owned business in Britain, and they take considerable will and effort – and selflessness on the part of the owners – to set up. The largest employee-owned manufacturing company is the Baxi group, which was given to its employees by its owner Philip Baxendale in 1983. In the year 2000 the Baxi Partnership was formed to give advice and a financial kick-start to companies wishing to move to employee ownership, and in the following decade it helped over twenty to do so. That's despite the removal in 2003 of tax advantages designed to help their formation. (Why? Because other companies were using them for tax avoidance dodges.)

Before the May 2010 UK election there was much talk by every political party about the 'John Lewis model'. This doesn't seem to mean structuring companies differently, but employing a form of internal democracy. In local government the Labour-controlled Lambeth Council in February 2010 grandly announced its intent to become the first to use a type of consultation similar to John Lewis's in local government, to become the first 'co-operative' council. It remains to be seen whether it was anything more than a riposte to Tory-controlled Barnet council's 'budget airline' approach of asking its citizens to pay extra for specific services. In the health service several NHS trusts are looking at forms of employee consultation, if not ownership. One interesting enterprise is Circle Healthcare, a company that is 50.1% owned by investors and 49.9% by the Circle Partnership, which belongs to everyone who works in its clinical services. We can hope that successes in local government and the NHS will spread, despite the 2010 government's aim of diminishing the power of such NHS trusts and giving more control to general practitioners. One encouraging sign came in August, when the Cabinet Office minister Francis Maude announced that twelve organisations would take part in a 'Pathfinder' mutuals project. The Partnership will be helping several of them.

In 2005 Waitrose began a foundation to fund and encourage South African farmers to form co-operative farms. It rapidly found fertile soil and local enthusiasm for the model, and it has already begun in Kenya and Ghana. (It's an interesting paradox that this kind of local participation seems to transplant more successfully than Western-style democracy...) The British could benefit from looking abroad at many long-running co-operative success stories. One is the massive Mondragon enterprise in the Basque region of Spain, started after the war by an idealistic young priest. Its influence and philosophy have spread across Basque society. It now employs nearly 100,000, and its retail arm has sales the same size of the Partnership's.

So do we, as Davies suggests, have a 'once in a lifetime' chance to renew our idea of what a company is for? It won't be easy. In its election manifesto of 1979 the Labour party included the words 'Industrial democracy is an idea whose time has come...' We got nothing of the sort, of course. The problem has always been, as Spedan found once the UK's politics became polarised between Conservative and Labour, that neither party is doctrinally attuned to employee ownership. One espoused the model of the unfettered market, the other supported state ownership, and both were at worst hostile to, and at best uninterested in, employee ownership models. We must hope that with a UK coalition government from the spring of 2010, and much talk of 'fairness' in our society in future, there will be an upsurge of interest and active support for employee ownership in business, and employee participation in state-run organisations. Then perhaps Spedan's idea will start to take root in other soils – a seed that has been waiting to germinate for a hundred years.

# Major Sources and Acknowledgements

## Major Sources

This is a summary of the book's principal sources; detailed footnotes are available for researchers on the book's website: www.spedanspartnership.co.uk. The Partnership is fortunate in having a substantial and well-kept archive, maintained for over thirty years by Lorna Poole after its original founding by Rosalind Hadden, and continued from 1996 by Poole's successor Judy Faraday and her assistant Linda Moroney. Without the unstinting support of the archivists this book would simply not have been possible.

After 1918 the main sources of information are the annual Gazette volumes, each often containing over 1000 pages, which, from the early 1920s when it settled as a weekly magazine of record, contains all fifty-two Gazettes. Until 2003 they were exceptionally well indexed, so although the amount of information is daunting they can be scanned in less time than you might imagine. Those covering World War II in particular give an intriguing and undoubtedly unique insight into a company's day-to-day response to war. Until 1955, moreover, Spedan's ideas are constantly expressed and explored in its pages. At other times I must say that without the lively anonymous letter column the Gazette volumes can be an unmatched antidote to insomnia. That column, of course, was and still is a good guide to what many ordinary Partners are thinking.

## Chapters 1, 2 and 4

John Lewis's early life has been researched by others, notably Kenneth Hudson in an unpublished document, but recent advances in the availability of the early censuses online have filled in some of the gaps. John Lewis, orphaned at seven in 1843, said hardly anything to his own family about his early life. Notable is the Partnership story, promulgated unwittingly by Spedan himself, that John was brought up by a kindly aunt named Ann Speed, the name reversed to give 'Spedan'. The census records show that the aunt in question was undoubtedly his mother's eldest sister Christian, a conclusion that John's grandson Peter Lewis had reached in his own research. I'm most grateful to him for sharing information about the life of his grandfather's family, and for correcting a number of my errors. Much of the information about John comes from Spedan, largely in his *Partnership For All*, and from the reminiscences of Albert Sherring and Alice Cook published in the Gazette.

## Chapter 3

Daily life in the Victorian and Edwardian department store is vividly depicted in HG Wells' semi-autobiographical *Kipps*. Wells was a lifelong supporter of measures to improve shopworkers' lives, as was his friend Philip Hoffman, the shop assistants' union organiser on whose autobiography *They Also Serve* I also draw. Hoffman catalogues the grim conditions, particularly in hostels, and the fight to improve them – if not to the extent that Spedan did at Peter Jones. Robert Bichan, another whose reminiscences appeared in the Gazette, one who started as Hoffman did in a store in Holborn, describes the process of 'cribbing' for a new job. For the growth of the department store in the late nineteenth and early twentieth centuries, and especially the arrival of Gordon Selfridge, a good source is Bill Lancaster's *The Department Store, a Social History*, as is a book published in June 2010, Claire Masset's *Department Stores*. For its Victorian beginnings, read Alison Adburgham's *Shops and Shopping 1800–1914*.

## Chapter 5

The years at Peter Jones during World War I when Spedan was testing out his ideas informally are described from different perspectives by Robert Bichan and by Spedan himself. Bichan's first-hand experiences on the shop floor and behind the scenes show exactly what Spedan was up against in the 'near-derelict' Peter Jones, and how Spedan set about improving the shop and instilling his principles. Bichan is invaluable because he's an articulate fighter for fairness who never becomes a management figure, so maintains that perspective. He begins a tradition of sturdy democrats (especially at Peter Jones) who won't be fobbed off, a necessary corrective to the understandable tendency, in a co-owned business as much as any other, to focus on sales and profit and let the democracy take care of itself.

## Chapters 6 to 8

From this point onwards the Gazette comes more into play, particularly in 1918–20 when Spedan explores his ideas and engages with his staff – 'Partners' from 1920 – in a public debate. The most detailed information on the Oxford Street strike comes from the daily newspapers, which were full of it, from Kenneth Hudson's account, and from Philip Hoffman, who dwelt on it at length is his autobiography. One must be wary of bias, of course – in any account – but Hoffman proves himself an open and likeable reporter throughout the book. His reluctant admiration for John Lewis, his intransigent opponent, is telling, as are his later comments commending Wallace Waite for his empathy with grocery workers. Back at Peter Jones, Spedan's employment of women is examined at length in Judy Faraday's MPhil thesis *A Kind of Superior Hobby*, which looks at women managers in the Partnership between 1918 and 1950. To add to Spedan's own reminiscences, Albert Sherring, Stanley Carter and Bernard Miller all wrote at various times in the Gazette about the excitement of the 1930s when, as Miller said, 'nothing was too zany to look into and anything was possible'. William Crabtree and his wife Sylvia, a former chief registrar, wrote about the commissioning and building of the new Peter Jones, as did Charles Reilly, his professor at the Liverpool School of Architecture, who rode shotgun on the project, in his *Scaffolding in the Sky*. Andrew Marr's *The Making of Modern Britain* is a racy background to the first forty years of the twentieth century.

## Chapter 9

The prime source for Wallace Waite's early years is his daughter Monica Freeman, interviewed by Lorna Poole when she was archivist. Life in a grocer's between the wars was recalled in the Gazette by two Waitrose veterans, Harold Tobias and Harold Tickner, who began in 1923 and 1928 respectively. Tobias was still working part-time in Waitrose in the 1970s, long after formal retirement, and is remembered by more than one branch manager today. Michael Winstanley's *The Shopkeeper's World 1830–1914* has a fascinating section on early grocers (learn why they kept hedgehogs...). Philip Hoffman is the source for 'the doughty Daniel' Waite's active support for grocery wages boards and for improving working conditions in the trade. Stanley Carter's trenchant views on Spedan's decision to buy Waitrose – which he still held despite becoming a reforming MD there – were published in a fascinating Gazette article in 1995, when he was in his eighties.

## Chapters 10 to 12

In this period the Gazette is the prime informant, and the only problem is what to leave out. The letter relating events on the night of the Oxford Street fire was an accidental find: I'd never heard of it before and no third-hand description could possibly match its immediacy. There's nobody still alive to talk to today who had been in the building at the time of the fire. But from 1940 onwards personal reminiscences do start to arrive. I had already interviewed Paul Roake at his Somerset home before I twigged that he was the Quaker referred to in the conscientious objector debate of 1940. (Roake was over ninety, although he wasn't the oldest person I interviewed: a woman who at fifteen had travelled from Newcastle to Watford for a job at Trewins, where she lived in the hostel.) On an early visit to Newcastle to interview four retired Bainbridges department managers I was surprised to discover that one of them, Robert Owen, had been a London boy who not only watched the fire in Oxford Street but also subsequently worked at the shop with Edward Lewis in hardware. Trevor Fry, the Partnership buyer (and official photographer), whose *Spectator* article about life as a Bevin Boy had typically attracted Spedan's attention, gave Judy Faraday a long and engaging recorded interview in 2002. Eric Pearce remembered the Korean War crisis, and was eloquent in his admiration of Patrick Mahon and Stanley Carter.

Max Baker's compilation of Spedan's advice on retailing, *Retail Trading*, is of course invaluable, not least because it saved me a sanity-threatening trawl through his 39,396 memoranda in the archive, all painstakingly indexed. Although it only starts from the 1930s, *John Spedan Lewis, 1885–1963*, brings together a range of warts-and-all personal memories of his later years, notably from Bernard Miller, Max Baker and Paul May. Written by Hugh McPherson, it draws on research by Rosalind Hadden, the first archivist and at that point the Gazette editor. One of the most sympathetic summaries of Spedan's life appears in Carol Kennedy's *Merchant Princes*, which looks at the development of the Partnership alongside that of the Sainsbury and Cadbury businesses. David Kynaston's exhaustive *Austerity Britain, 1945–51* and *Family Britain*

1951–7 give the background to a tough period for the Partnership. As it recovered, it barely seemed to notice the changes described by Jenny Diski's *The Sixties (Big Ideas)* – (a period during which the former Partners Roy Jenkins, Eddie Shackleton and George Brown were part of the government).

## Chapters 13 to 14

The Partnership archive contains a number of personal files of important retired Partners who are no longer alive. It's a far from complete collection, so it's pot luck who turns up, but they give an excellent feel for Partners' working lives at every level. Fortunately the files of both Wallace Waite and Stanley Carter are there, and they underpin Chapters 13 and 14. Carter's file provided a detailed record of his working life from 1929, when he started as a sixteen-year-old selling assistant in the silk room, to his retirement in 1973 as Waitrose MD. It also gave an insight into how Bernard Miller as Chairman dealt with his occasionally unruly buccaneer, with a shrewd mixture of support and encouragement, the occasional shot across the bows, and the promise of a rich prize if he succeeded. Of Carter the personal recollections came thick and fast, from Stan Withers at Heelas in the 1950s, via John Foster, Derek Saward, Derek Rawlings, Philip Morgan, Peter Falconer, Dudley Cloake and the late, much-lamented Richard March, to the many young Waitrose managers, since retired, to whom he was an inspiration. And one not so young: Bill Anderson, pushing ninety and still working – over seventy years after he started in a grocer's before the war. It was he who converted the first Waitrose shop to self-service in 1951.

## Chapters 15 to 20

The sources for these chapters are almost entirely the Gazette and masses of personal testimony from interviews. Helpful sources are Gazette articles by Bernard Miller and Max Baker. I'm particularly grateful to Brian O'Callaghan for copies of Max Baker's Berlin conference paper of 1957 and his reflections on department store layout and design. They were essentially the same as O'Callaghan's own, which he expounded as we walked the Bluewater selling floor ten years after his retirement. Just as absorbing was a tour of the Oxford Street shop with its former MD Derek Rawlings and Noel Saunders, the current MD, exactly fifty years after Rawlings first arrived there as a merchandise manager under Carter. Steven May reminisced about his father Paul, while Peter Yaghmourian and the glove expert Mabel Hammett were two of many who brought to life the very different world of department store buying that operated between the middle and end of the twentieth century. Mary Cooper filled me in on the resuscitation of Brownsea Castle, augmenting her husband's lively written account. The 1968 academic analysis of the Partnership's system of government by Flanders, Pomeranz and Woodward, *An Experiment in Industrial Democracy*, which seemed to sink without trace, is more useful than its reputation within the Partnership might suggest. Of many books about the period, Andrew Marr takes the century's story on with *A History of Modern Britain*, while the minefield of the 1970s, through which the Partnership carefully navigated its way, is recreated in Andy Beckett's *When the Lights Went Out* (which, dear reader, they did). Richard Vinen's *Thatcher's Britain* does the same for the following decade. For an exploration of the effects of the Thatcher transformation, read Will Hutton's *The State We're In*, Robert Peston's recent *Who Runs Britain?* and Wilkinson and Pickett's *The Spirit Level*. Finally, William Davies's booklet for Demos, *Reinventing the Firm*, examines whether a Partnership-style organisation for businesses is possible and how it might be achieved.

## Acknowledgements

My thanks go to a panel of readers from both inside and outside the Partnership. Judy Faraday, never too busy to stop and answer yet another arcane query, has probably forgotten more about the Partnership than I'll ever know. Her support has been immense. The librarian's acuity of Peter Allen has been enormously helpful. They, Dudley Cloake, Tessa Murray, Sheelagh Neuling and James Wyper read and constructively criticised it all as it progressed, as did Jessica Cox, Gary Hird, Robert Horley, Patrick McNeill and Vanessa Pawsey for sections of it. Dudley Cloake, concerned at the loss of word-of-mouth history in the Partnership, is the one who encouraged me to write it. I'm indebted to him and to Charlie Mayfield, who agreed that now was the right time for such a book. My thanks too to my wife Angela Cox, and to Peter and Patrick Lewis, who read it when complete. I owe most once again to the rigorous but sensitive editing of Sheelagh Neuling, and to Ros Horton of Cambridge Editorial and the designer Paul Barrett for piloting it through its final stages. There will be far fewer errors and infelicities as a consequence, though those that remain will most certainly be down to me. Knowing the long and undimmed memories of many Partners, as I do, I trust that they will be eagerly pointed out...

It's the memories of the people I interviewed, usually in person but occasionally by phone, and their continued interest in the Partnership, combined with those Partners whose reminiscences have been published in the Gazette over the years, which – I hope – have prevented the story being too dry and impersonal. It was gratifying, but not unexpected, that only one person declined to talk to me, and that was for understandable reasons. They were without exception open and honest, and my apologies to those whose stories didn't make the final cut. Here are the people I spoke to. My thanks to them all:

Derek Addy, Reyn Agard, Johnny Aisher, Bill Anderson, Beverley (Bolton) Aspinall, David Barclay, Dorothy Barrett, Ian Bassett, Jeremy Bate, Kevin Berry, Bill Bishop, Mike Bourke, Julian Brind, Anne Buckley, June Card, Brian Carroll, Sally Carruthers, Marisa Cassoni, Russell Cattell, Judith Cave, Lawrence Chapman, Margaret (Watkins) Childs, Stan Chung, Neil Clarke, Dudley Cloake, Beryl Cook, Geoff Cook, Douglas Cooper, Mary Cooper, Wally Crouch, Janet Cundall, Caroline Dilke, Susan Dole, Stephen Drei, Florence Dwyer, David Erdal, John Fagan, Guy Fairbank, Peter Falconer, David Felwick, Des Fitzgerald, Leslie Fletcher, Brian Forbes Turner, Steven Forfar, John Foster, Simon Fowler, Andy Gay, Warren Gilchrist, Eric Greenhalgh, David Gumm, Pamela and Robin Gunn, Joan Hall, Mabel Hammett, Sir Stuart Hampson, Charles Hawes, Richard Hodgson, Malcolm Holloway Vine, Sally Hudson, Arthur Hughes,

Russell Husband, David K Jones, David St J Jones, Jerry Kelliher, Tracy Killen, Carole Lee, Patrick Lewis, Peter Lewis, Jill Little, Bill Lunt, Liz Mahon, Richard March, Stephen May, Charlie Mayfield, Luke Mayhew, Alistair McKay, Alastair McKerlie, Angela Megson, Bill Melly, Beryl Meredith, Michael Miller, Dee Monaghan, Philip Morgan, Tessa Murray, Robert Owen, Tony Paine, Lucy Parks, Gordon Parris, John Pass, Eric Pearce, June Pilar Martin, Mark Price, Alan Rabin, David Ramsey, Derek Rawlings, Bill Redmond, Mark Richardson, Brian Riley, Paul Roake, Dino Rocos, Ken Roe, Ann Rush, Simon Russell, Brian Ryder, Joan Sadler, John Sadler, Noel Saunders, Derek Saward, Andrew Slater, Joyce Smith, Rosemary Smith, Tony Solomons, David Stevens, Tony Stoller, John Stott, Andy Street, Evelyn Strouts, Ken Temple, Christine Theophilus, Ray Thomson, Mary Vizoso, Muriel Ward Jackson (in 1999), Phil Waters, Rosie Watts, Ron Whitley, Irene Whitty, David Wilson, Helen Wilson, Stan Withers, Peter Yaghmourian, David Young.

## Partnership Leaders Since 1960

### Chairman

Bernard Miller 1955–72
Peter Lewis 1972–93
Stuart Hampson 1993–2007
Charlie Mayfield 2007–

### Finance director

*[No single post until 1969]*
Muriel Ward Jackson 1969–71
John Sadler 1971–87
David Young 1987-2001
Ian Alexander 2001–5
Marisa Cassoni 2006–

### John Lewis MD

Max Baker 1960–7
Peter Lewis 1967–72
Eric Greenhalgh 1972–7
Ian Anderson 1977–90
Brian O'Callaghan 1990–2000
Luke Mayhew 2000–5
Charlie Mayfield 2005–7
Andy Street 2007–

### Waitrose MD

George Walton 1961–7
Stanley Carter 1967–73
Charles Hawes 1973–7
John Foster 1977–91
David Felwick 1991–2002
Steven Esom 2002–7
Mark Price 2007–

# Glossary of Partnership and Retailing Terms

**ABC1** A classification of households used by planners, which runs broadly from A (most disposable income) to E (least). A is classified as 'higher managerial and professional', B as 'intermediate managerial and professional', and C1 as 'supervisory, clerical and junior managerial'.

**Apprenticeship** A method of contracting a young employee to a master for a fixed period of years. It was the standard method of employment in retail, lasting three or five years, but gradually fell into disuse in the early twentieth century.

**Assistant buyer** In the Partnership until 2005 the assistant buyer ran the buyer's office, often becoming an expert on a single group of merchandise over many years. Often starting their careers as shop assistants, they were only rarely promoted to buyer. After that date buying office roles were split and became more specialised.

**Assortment** The set of products sold in a shop, or in a department within it. Assortment 'width' is a measure of the number of products in a range.

**Bainbridge** The original name of John Lewis Newcastle, begun by Emerson Muschamp Bainbridge in 1838 and bought by the Partnership in 1953.

**Barcodes** A machine-readable code containing (usually) the product number and price of an item for sale, either attached to it or displayed on the shelf-edge. In the UK John Lewis was the earliest major adopter in the late 1970s, many years before the competition. Then the information was encoded in a magnetic stripe with a JL-specific stock number, well before the UK adopted the standard UPC (universal product code). That's encoded nowadays in vertical parallel lines of different thicknesses. Waitrose was one of the last supermarket groups to adopt such 'scanning' technology, in the early 1990s.

**Blocking silk** Fabric arrives in shops nowadays wrapped around cardboard rolls. Originally silk used to come wrapped around wooden boards, from which it was unrolled for customers. 'Blocking' was the tricky job of rewrapping it so as to avoid kinks or creases.

**Branch council** One of the two local institutions within John Lewis department stores responsible for local consultation and management accountability until 2007, when it was replaced by the (very similar) branch 'forum'. Each of the 20–40 departments elected a member to the council, which was attended by the shop's MD and its registrar. It usually met six times a year, under a president elected by its members. It would, for example, discuss and vote on any proposed change to shop trading hours and working conditions.

**Branch forum** The branch forum replaced the branch council in 2007.

**Branch manager (BM)** The manager of a Waitrose food shop.

**BRC** The British Retail Consortium is the retail trade association for UK retailers. It was formed in 1992 after a merger between the British Retailers' Association (which the Partnership had left over the Sunday trading issue) and the Retail Consortium.

**Brownsea Castle** A castle on Brownsea Island, leased to the Partnership in 1962 by the National Trust as a holiday centre for the Partnership. The island, in Poole Harbour, also contains a wildlife reserve run by the Dorset Naturalist Trust on behalf of several billion mosquitoes. The castle was originally a blockhouse built by Henry VIII. In 1907 Robert Baden Powell ran his first scout camp there, and at the same period the radio pioneer Marconi experimented in a room in its tower.

**Buy.com** A Californian online retailer which began in 1997 selling electronics. Its struggling UK arm was bought by John Lewis in 2001 and converted into John Lewis Direct. Buy.com has subsequently reopened in the UK.

**Buyer, Buyership** Originally in all department stores the 'buyer' both selected and bought a range of merchandise, and ran the department that sold it. That still happens in single stores like Harrods today. In the 1930s John Lewis centralised all its buying in London, and gave selling responsibilities to a 'department manager', the DM. The merchandise selected and bought by a buyer is known as a buyership.

**Chief registrar** The person to whom registrars reported from 1938 until 2005, when the post lapsed and registrars reported to the Partners' counsellor.

**Chronicle** The local weekly journal, the Gazette equivalent for a department store, for Waitrose, and any other organisational unit sufficiently large to merit one.

**Clearance** The John Lewis word for its half-yearly sale. Spedan Lewis wanted to draw the distinction between his shops and others, which reduced prices across the board. His policy was to sell at competitive prices all year round, whereas sales had, in his words, 'a reputation for trickery'. So the twice-yearly 'Clearance' was originally used only to 'clear' slow-selling stock. That gradually changed, and in the John Lewis Clearance there is much less perceptible difference from competitors' sales.

**Clearings** The service building for Peter Jones opened in the 1930s.

**Cole Brothers** The original name of John Lewis Sheffield, opened as a silk mercery by the brothers John, Thomas and Skelton Cole in 1847, and bought by the Partnership as part of SPS in 1940.

**Commission** Selling assistants in a department store used to receive a commission on their sales, from the buyer/manager to the lowest-paid assistant. It was pernicious, because it led to intense rivalry, and there was a clear selling floor pecking order: the top assistants appropriated the best customers. Spedan began by abolishing it in Peter Jones, then was persuaded to reintroduce it, but on a fairer basis in which a department's sales were split across its employees. Buyers' commission, however, remained after their selling responsibilities were removed. The rules changed many times before it was finally abolished after World War II.

**Committee for claims** An internal charitable body, set up to help Partners suffering cases of hardship, made in the form of a grant or a loan. It has now been replaced by a financial assistance committee.

**Committee for communication** The first democratic body set up by Spedan Lewis, exclusively for 'rank and file' staff, experimentally at first at Oxford Street, then formally after he took over Peter Jones. In its original form he chaired it himself, no other managers were present, and it operated as a forum for airing and dealing with low-level grievances. Before long it was chaired by an independent person who reported to the Partners' counsellor. Reports were always sent to the Partnership's Chairman. It was replaced in 2007 by the department forum in department stores and Partner Voice in Waitrose.

**Constitution** The 'Articles of the Constitution' were first published in the 1920s, then refined constantly before the 1950 settlement. They are the Partnership's principles, rules and regulations; the current version is available from www.johnlewispartnership.co.uk.

**Council president** The chairman of the Partnership (and formerly branch) council, elected by its members, now at three-yearly intervals.

**Counting house** In a department store, what we would now call an Accounts department.

**Credit manager** The person responsible for dealing with all credit customers, an extremely important job in the early Peter Jones – 80% of its trade was credit. For many years the Partnership had its own charge card which carried no interest charge or financial penalty for late payment (though you were soon chased).

**Crêpe-de-Chine** and **Cretonne** Fabrics: a fine gauzy silk, and a heavy printed cotton.

**Critical side** See p. 137 and 291. A set of five 'shadow' directors: Spedan Lewis's early form of 'corporate governance' before the expression was coined.

**Date coding** See p. 177. A system requiring packaging to show the date by which a product in a supermarket must be sold and/or consumed. The open date coding of products in the UK did not begin until the late 1960s.

**Deferred pay** See p. 114. An arrangement whereby Partners could defer a proportion of their pay to help it survive the war, obviating the need for pay cuts and reducing the number of redundancies. Pay levels were restored before the end of the war, and the backlog repaid at 5% pa interest.

**Department (local) forum** The department-level discussion forum in John Lewis department stores, introduced in 2007 to replace the committee for communication. Each of the 20–30 departments holds them, at monthly intervals.

**Department manager (DM)** The manager of part of the selling area of a department store. They reported directly to the shop's MD, and had anything from 20 to 80 people reporting to them. Originally there were between around 30 and 50 departments in a typical John Lewis shop. Now there are far fewer – John Lewis Oxford Street had 25 in 2010 – because the span of their control has widened, not because there are fewer merchandise ranges.

**Draper** Originally a cloth merchant, the term expanded to include made-up clothing and fabrics of all kinds. In the late 19th century many department store owners still tended to call themselves drapers even though they were selling much else.

**East 'house'** The part of John Lewis acquired from TJ Harries in 1929 on the Oxford Circus side of Holles Street, until being sold off when the west 'house' was fully reopened in 1960. There was a separate MD for each building.

**Elected director** One of five directors elected to the Partnership board every three years by the Partnership council.

**Founder** The name used to describe Spedan Lewis in the Partnership after his retirement.

**Gazette** The weekly Partnership journal, first published in 1918 to print the previous week's results, a letter column, plus news and articles about the Partnership. It is now also available to current and retired Partners online.

**Gazette letters** The Gazette must publish every letter sent to it unless it's defamatory, with a reply if appropriate within three weeks from the director or manager responsible. Letter writers may remain anonymous if they choose.

**General decrease** The temporary across-the-board pay reduction that was imposed three times: in 1931, 1938 and 1952.

**General inspector** A director reporting to the Chairman with a free-wheeling role investigating any aspect of the Partnership's trading activity. The post was made obsolete in 2007.

**George Henry Lee** The original name of John Lewis Liverpool, started as a straw bonnet shop by George Boswell Lee in 1853 and bought by the Partnership as part of SPS in 1940. In 1962 the Liverpool business of Bon Marché, begun in 1878, was acquired and merged with it.

**Golden Jubilee Trust** A charitable trust set up by Sir Stuart Hampson while Chairman in 2000 to commemorate the fiftieth anniversary of Spedan Lewis's second and final 'settlement'. It allows working Partners to take time off to work full- or part-time for a charity for up to six months. An average of forty Partners participate each year.

**Haberdashery** Articles used in sewing, such as ribbons, cotton reels, buttons and needles.

**Half-day closing** In the UK there used to be local bye-laws requiring shops in a given area to close on one specific afternoon a week.

**Heelas** The original name of John Lewis Reading, opened in 1854 by John and Daniel Heelas. It was bought by the Partnership in 1953, replacing another Reading shop, AH Bull, acquired in 1940 with SPS.

**Hostels** Hostels were often provided by Victorian drapers to house their unmarried staff. Begun usually with the best of intentions, some became notorious at the end of the nineteenth and beginning of the twentieth centuries for their poor conditions and restrictive rules. They could be above the shop or nearby: that for Peter Jones was above it, while John Lewis's was in Weymouth Street.

**Indenture** A copy of a legal contract drawn up for (in this case) an apprenticeship. The 'dent' part of the word refers to the fact that it appeared 'toothed', because the two copies, for master and apprentice, were cut in zigzag fashion to prevent forgery.

***Inside John Lewis*** A three-part series made about John Lewis by the BBC and broadcast in 2010.

**Intelligence** The Partnership department set up to check competitors' prices, among other things. In 2010 it was dissolved, and its role split and moved under John Lewis and Waitrose.

**Jessops** The original name of John Lewis Nottingham. Opened in 1804 by John Townsend, its sole owner became Zebedee Jessop in 1866. It was bought by the Partnership in 1933.

**John Lewis Direct** The direct selling arm of John Lewis, created following the acquisition of the UK branch of Buy.com in 2001, and replacing the short-lived John Lewis Now. Also known as johnlewis.com.

**John Lewis Furnishing and Leisure** The department store close to the M40 motorway in High Wycombe with a restricted range, lacking clothing. Although highly successful it hasn't been replicated. Now called 'Home and Leisure'.

**John Lewis Home** A small department store with the limited range its name implies. The first was opened in Poole in 2009.

**Knight and Lee** The original name of John Lewis Southsea, begun in 1831 by the 'laceman' William Wink and bought in 1887 by Jesse Knight and Edward Lee. It was acquired by the Partnership in 1934.

**Learner** The name given by Spedan Lewis to graduate recruits when he began to experiment with them in the 1920s. They were paid much more than ordinary selling assistants, and he paid the difference from his own budget.

**Leckford Estate** The substantial estate that includes the village of Leckford on the River Test in Hampshire that Spedan Lewis bought in the late 1920s. He lived there in Leckford Abbas (now a Partnership hotel) before moving across the valley to Longstock in 1945. He started a separate Partnership there for a spell, improved the primitive housing, and introduced advanced mechanisation to the farm. Leckford Camp was created there as an outdoor holiday centre and is still in use. Spedan constructed a golf course and a cricket pitch.

**Long leave** A scheme introduced in 1979 by Peter Lewis to mark the fiftieth anniversary of the settlement of 1929. It provides a six-month break on full pay for any Partner who has completed twenty five years' service.

**Longstock** The estate and village on the opposite side of the River Test to which Spedan Lewis moved in 1945. He bequeathed Longstock House to the Partnership for the use of its Chairman in perpetuity. It is now used as a hotel by senior Partners, and for strategy meetings. On the estate Spedan designed a water garden, which now has worldwide renown. It took ten years to create – all the work had to be done by hand because the soil is waterlogged.

**Marking-off** The area of a shop where goods arrived from a supplier or central warehouse, where they were checked against a delivery note and had tickets attached.

**Maximum wage** See p. 273. A limit on the maximum pay any Partner can receive, defined in the Partnership's constitution.

**MD** Managing director. Either the head of a specific John Lewis department store, or of the whole of John Lewis or Waitrose. These latter posts used to be known as directors of trading, or trading directors.

**Mercer** A merchant who trades in fabrics. John Lewis described himself as a silk mercer in his census entries, although the term was already slipping out of use.

**Merchandiser/ing** Overworked words which mean different things in different businesses, and have changed over time. Merchandising is the art of presenting and promoting products for sale in a shop. The word merchandiser has come to mean the person who, working in a central office, ensures that products are on sale in the right place and in the right quantities. In John Lewis this was part of the assistant buyer's job until 2005. In Waitrose the job is more concerned with deciding shelf layouts in shops. A merchandise *manager* in a John Lewis department store was responsible for merchandise layout for a part of the shop – a complete floor, for example, in John Lewis. Almost every potential department store MD would have a spell as a merchandise manager. A central merchandise *adviser*, or CMA, was responsible in John Lewis for ensuring buyers didn't overspend their 'purchase ration'.

**Modern Times** A one-part BBC TV documentary about John Lewis broadcast in 1995.

**Never Knowingly Undersold** See pp. 184 and 262. The expression coined by Spedan Lewis in 1925 to convey a price promise. It meant that the Partnership would reduce its price if a nearby competitor was found to be selling an identical item more cheaply.

**Non-selling** All the jobs in a shop that do not involve contact with the customer on the selling floor.

**Ocado** An independent company founded in 2002 which delivers Waitrose products to the home from a central warehouse. The Partnership initially took a 40% stake, though it had dropped below 30% by 2010, when Ocado 'floated'. By this time its holding had been transferred to the pension fund.

**Odney club** See pp. 93 and 278. A hotel, leisure and later training centre complex for Partners on a country estate bordering the Thames at Cookham in Berkshire.

**Operations manager** In Waitrose, a regional manager responsible for a number of branches.

**Partner** Anyone employed on a permanent contract by the John Lewis Partnership, whether part-time or full-time.

**Partners' counsellor** The person with responsibility for safeguarding the Partnership's constitution. In the words of the constitution he 'seeks to ensure that the Partnership is true to its principles and compassionate to individual Partners, and... has responsibility for the independence, health and effectiveness of the Partnership's elected representative bodies.'

**Partnership Boards** The Partnership's Board now has the Chairman, five appointed members, five elected, and two non-execs. The John Lewis and Waitrose boards don't have elected members.

**Partnership Bonus** (formerly Partnership Benefit) The share of the annual profit that the board decides each year should be distributed to Partners. See the graph at the head of Chapter 20. Each Partner gets a cash bonus in March as a percentage of their total pay in the previous trading year, end January to end January.

**Partnership council** Originally the 'staff council' at Peter Jones from 1920, and the 'central council' until it was renamed when the subsidiary John Lewis council was formed. In 2010 it had seventy elected members who could vote, plus a small number of members appointed by the Chairman who may not vote. Various elected councillors serve on four special-interest groups (co-ownership, customer, Partner and profit), and on three committees (pensions, financial assistance and community investment).

**PartnerVoice** The local democracy in a Waitrose branch. Each section (there are usually 10–15) elects a member.

**PBOP** Powered By Our Principles – see p. 235. A 'behaviour' template created in 2005 which set out how Partners should behave towards each other and the Partnership, and vice-versa.

**Piece goods** Fabrics sold in standard lengths.

**Profit-to-sales ratio** Profit divided by sales, a simple measure of a retail business's trading efficiency. See ROIC.

**Provisions** Items that used to arrive at a grocer's in bulk, like flour, tea and salt, and were made up into individual packets on the premises.

**Radius agreement** A clause in a contract expressly forbidding an employee from leaving to work for a competitor within a certain distance of the shop.

**Rank and File** An expression meaning any Partner in a job with no management responsibility. It persisted until 2000, when it was replaced by the more prosaic but inoffensive 'non-management' Partner.

**Registrar** A post independent of management invented in the 1930s by Spedan Lewis for each department store to safeguard Partners' welfare and the Partnership's constitution, and ensure that its principles and policies are correctly applied.

**Robert Sayle** The original name of John Lewis Cambridge, opened by Sayle in 1840 and bought by the Partnership as part of SPS in 1940.

**ROIC** Return On Invested Capital. A measure of a business's profitability in relation to the money invested in it.

**Sales ledgers** The department that used to record sales by department.

**Selling floor** The area of a department store where products are sold.

**Service building** A warehouse designed to service a single department store, providing buffer space between the supplier (or central warehouse) and the shop. The first in the Partnership was known as 'Clearings' in Draycott Avenue, Chelsea, to service Peter Jones.

**Settlement 'in trust'** The legal arrangements by which Spedan Lewis sold his business in trust to the Partnership he had formed at Peter Jones. The first, in 1929 (see p. 78) set out the terms of the transfer, and the mechanism by which the Partnership would repay the debt over future years. Spedan in fact never took back all the money he was owed. The second settlement of 1950 (see p. 143) finalised the process. The settlement was called 'irrevocable'. The wording stated in fact that it could not be altered until 'twenty-one years after the death of the last surviving grandchild of Edward VII then living, in 1929'. In 2010 two were still alive, Queen Elizabeth II and her cousin Lord Harewood. It seems safe for a while yet...

**Shares** In the Partnership the annual bonus was issued in share 'promises' from 1920 until 1929, in shares from 1929 to 1965, in a mixture of shares and cash between 1965 and 1969, and in cash ever since. Spedan Lewis issued them as 'promises' initially, so they could not be traded on the stock exchange and cause conflict with his father. After his father's death the share promises were turned into genuine tradable shares, though they were usually worth less than their face value. Unlike the shares in other businesses, they had no voting rights, but delivered a regular 7½% dividend on the 1st of June and December each year.

**Shopwalker** The man who supervised customers in a department of a Victorian department store, and effectively controlled access to it. Although Selfridges didn't use them when Gordon Selfridge opened his shop in 1909, they persisted in many places until the 1930s.

**Silk room** The 'long' silk room (see Plate 5), positioned where the original shop stood, was regarded as the heart of the old John Lewis before it was bombed, and every senior Learner spent a spell of training there.

**SPS** Suburban and Provincial Stores, bought by the Partnership for £30,000 from Gordon Selfridge in early 1940. It consisted of fifteen shops with a combined turnover of £3.3 million. Only the businesses in Liverpool, Sheffield, Cambridge and Watford remained within the Partnership in 2010.

**Stock turn** The number of times a year at which stock of an item or range 'turns over' – a stock turn of four means that stock is held on average for thirteen weeks before it's sold.

**Stockroom** The area in a department store reserved for back-up stock for a particular department. Ideally sited next to it, they were often at some distance from the department.

**Suffragettes/gists** Campaigners for votes for women, who called themselves Suffragists. Suffragettes was a derogatory term coined by a newspaper, which stuck, to their irritation.

**Superintendent** The chief salesman in a department of a John Lewis shop until the 1930s.

**Trustees** The trustees of the constitution are three Partners, elected by the Partnership Council every three years, who are responsible for deciding the detailed operation of the Partnership's democracy. They also hold between them sixty of the hundred voting shares in the John Lewis Partnership, and consequently have the theoretical power to unseat the Chairman if the Partnership Council passes a 'Resolution upon the Constitution' to unseat him.

**Tyrrell & Green** The original name of John Lewis Southampton, opened in 1897 by Reginald Tyrrell and William Green and acquired by the Partnership in 1934.

**Utility clothing** In 1941 Michael Watkins was seconded to the government (though he continued as the Partnership's trading director) to create a national civilian clothing industry. 'Utility' clothing, essentially his idea, was the outcome, followed by utility furniture in 1942. Watkins was knighted for his services (as Sir Metford Watkins) in 1945.

**Wages councils** Wages councils were set up as 'Trades Boards' in 1909, in industries such as retail where sweated labour was endemic and there was poor union representation. They set minimum wages but gradually drifted into disuse – not least because of trade union opposition – and were abolished in 1993. (The UK national minimum wage across all industry was established in 1999. The 'living wage' movement begun in 2001 recommends a minimum acceptable living wage for an individual or family, one higher than the formal minimum wage.)

**Waitrose Deliver** The home shopping service provided from some Waitrose shops. Ocado is a separately-owned business that delivers Waitrose products from a central warehouse.

**Waitrose Food and Home** A larger Waitrose format that sells an unusually wide range of non-food, including a 'Home' assortment from John Lewis. The first was at Southend in 1995. There are now five, the largest at Canary Wharf in London.

**Wastage** See p. 167. Losses of stock through theft or damage, or by exceeding a sell-by date.

**West 'house'** The name given after 1929 to the original John Lewis block to the west of Holles Street (where the current building now stands). At that point the east block came into the Partnership when it acquired the business of TJ Harries.

# Money Values

February 1971 brought an end to what was called LSD. Not the hallucinogenic drug, though it had similar effects on some, but the system of currency that had been employed in England for much of the previous 1000 years.

This is how the system worked. Like today's decimal currency it had a pound (**£**) and a penny – but a Latin **d** (for denarius) not an English **p** – but the relationship between them was different. Now we have 100 pence to a pound, although it was originally 240. That apparently odd number was a combination with a third unit, the shilling. There were 12 pence in a shilling, and 20 shillings in a pound. A price, for example 3 pounds, 7 shillings and 11 pence, would be written as £3 7s 11d, or £3-7-11, or £3.7.11. In this book I shall use the first format throughout – £3 7s 11d. The arithmetic involved in dealing with these units was tricky enough, as anyone born before about 1960 will recall, but was even worse if a value included fractions of a penny. The halfpenny, pronounced ha'p'nny, was ½d, and the farthing was ¼d. If you'd like to imagine what life was like for a shop assistant, try calculating the cost of two and three-quarter yards of material at 3s 4¼d a yard.

In today's currency £3 7s 11d was between £3.39 and £3.40. However, because of the effects of inflation I would discourage you from doing that mental calculation. Although for much of the early period of our story the inflation rate was relatively stable, at the time of decimalisation it was rising rapidly. Thus £1 on Decimalisation Day, which was 19 February 1971, is now worth over £10. I append simple tables so that you can do the calculation yourself. These are derived from historical government all-items price indices and, rather than a massive year-by-year translation table, I've provided a series of way-points, and I've set the start at 1914, the year Spedan took over Peter Jones. However, because the value of the £ in 1864 was almost exactly the same as its value in 1914, close to one hundredth of its value now, for the first five chapters you can simply multiply a figure by 100 and take a bit off. In fact I've done many of them in the text, but not all.

| Year | Value of £1 | Year | Value of £1 | Year | Value of £1 |
|---|---|---|---|---|---|
| 1864 | 0.91 | 1926 | 1.89 | 1970 | 7.46 |
| 1870 | 0.97 | 1934 | 1.61 | 1975 | 13.76 |
| 1900 | 0.94 | 1939 | 1.77 | 1980 | 26.91 |
| 1910 | 0.98 | 1945 | 2.67 | 1990 | 50.77 |
| 1914 | 1.00 | 1952 | 4.01 | 2000 | 68.55 |
| 1919 | 2.23 | 1960 | 5.01 | 2010 | c. 88.00 |

# Partnership Performance History

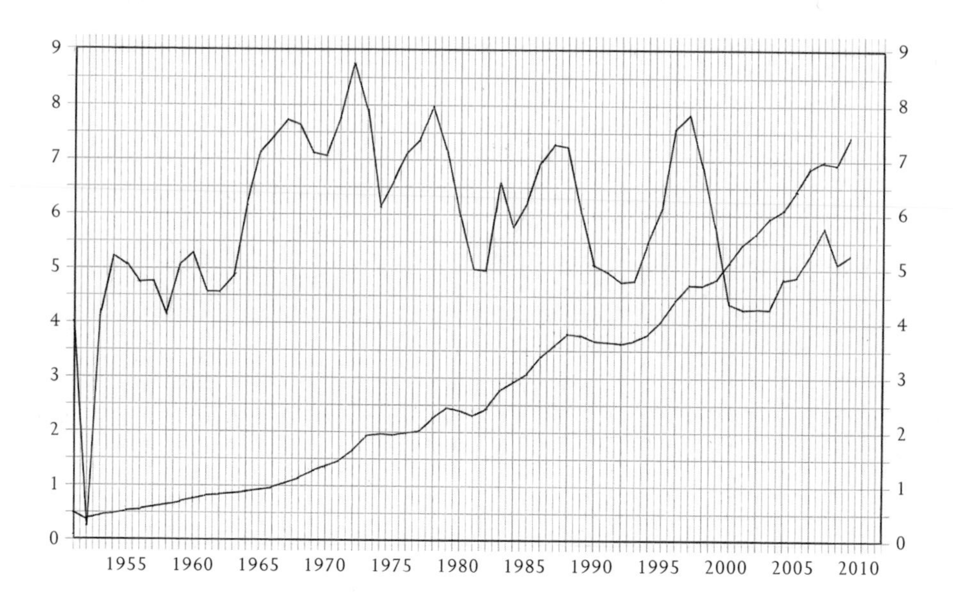


A composite graph showing the progression of two measures over time. The smoother line shows Partnership sales to 2009, from a start point of 1951, which is the first year for which profit figures are available. The sales are at 2009 prices, so inflation – a factor of nearly 24 – has been stripped out, and the vertical scale runs from zero to £9 billion. The spikier graph shows profit as a percentage of sales each year. Note the terrible initial plunge in 1952, a steadying, then a dramatic rise from 1963 as the Oxford St shop rises from the ashes, to peaks in 1968, 1972 (8.74%) and 1978. In real terms sales rose by a factor of four from 1959–79. There were two further peaks in 1987 and 1997; sales increased by a factor of three from 1979 to 2009. Note the low profit period from 2000–3, coinciding with increased trading hours in John Lewis and a higher proportion of sales for Waitrose, and how comparatively minor was the dip in the 2008–9 recession. Compare this with the Bonus progression graph on p. 271.

# Map of Oxford St, 1940

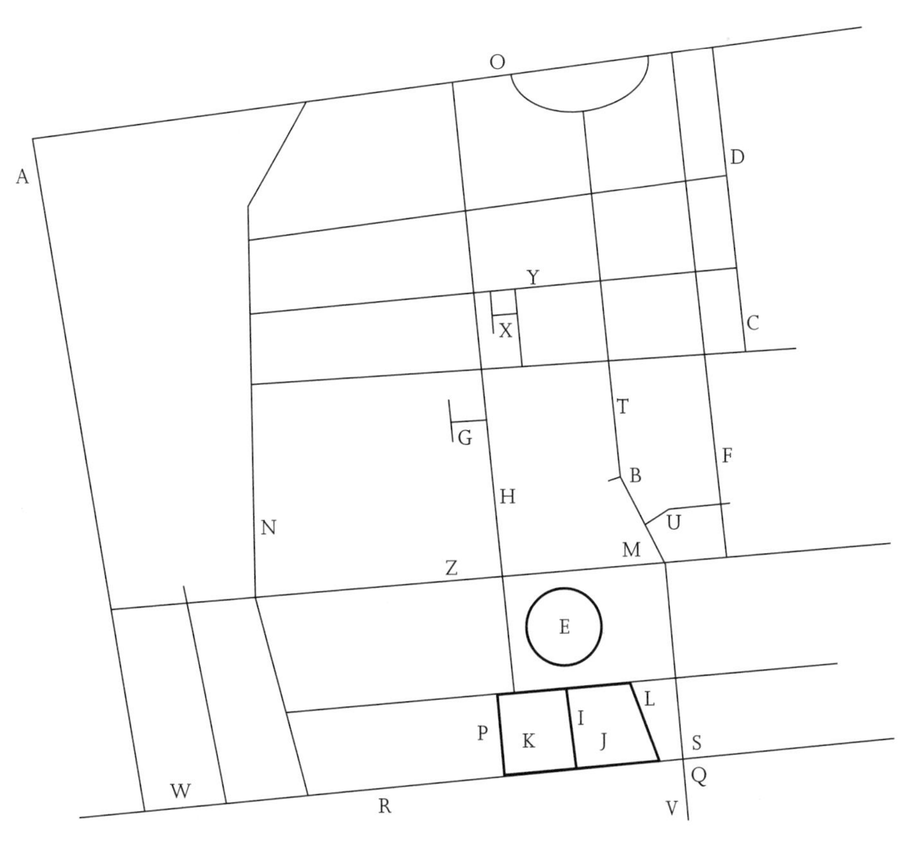


| | | | | | |
|---|---|---|---|---|---|
| A | Baker St | J | John Lewis east house | S | Peter Robinson |
| B | BBC | K | John Lewis west house | T | Portland Place |
| C | Bolsover St | L | John Princes St | U | Queen's Hall |
| D | Chadwickham House | M | Langham Hotel | V | Regent St |
| E | Cavendish Square | N | Marylebone High St | W | Selfridges |
| F | Gt Portland St | O | Marylebone Rd | X | Weymouth Mews |
| G | Harley Place | P | Old Cavendish St | Y | Weymouth St |
| H | Harley St | Q | Oxford Circus station | Z | Wigmore St |
| I | Holles St | R | Oxford St | | |

Map showing the area north of Oxford St in 1940. The Langham Hotel and the Queen's Hall (birthplace of the Proms) were hit the night before John Lewis was, but the BBC was unscathed. The first hostel was in Weymouth St and the stables in Weymouth Mews. A second (1913) hostel was Chadwickham House, where everyone assembled the morning after the fire. John Lewis originally lived near the O, at 1 Marylebone Rd, then moved to 7 Harley Place. Oswald, when he moved out of Spedan Tower, lived where the A marks the top of Baker St.

# Timeline

| Year | Event |
|---|---|
| **1836** | John Lewis born in Shepton Mallet |
| **1856** | John Lewis in London working for Peter Robinson |
| **1864** | John Lewis opens a shop in Oxford St |
| **1884** | John Lewis marries Eliza Baker |
| **1885** | Spedan Lewis born |
| **1887** | Oswald Lewis born |
| **1896** | Major rebuild of the now much bigger John Lewis shop |
| **1903** | John Lewis in prison for contempt |
| **1904** | Spedan joins the business (given a quarter share in 1906) |
| **1905** | Oswald joins the business (given a quarter share in 1908) |
| | John Lewis buys Peter Jones |
| **1909** | Oswald leaves the business |
| **1910** | Spedan finalises his Partnership plan |
| **1911** | John Lewis 'loses' a libel case with his landlord |
| **1914** | Spedan chairman of PJ but must still work at Oxford St |
| **1916** | Spedan swaps his quarter share of JL for sole control of PJ |
| | Oswald returns to JL |
| **1918** | The first Gazette |
| **1919** | The first council meeting |
| **1920** | The Partnership begins: everyone at PJ is a Partner, first profit sharing |
| | JL staff strike over pay and conditions |
| **1921–2** | PJ in acute financial difficulty; no Bonus until 1924–5 |
| **1923** | Spedan marries Beatrice Hunter |
| **1924** | John Lewis injects cash into PJ |
| **1925** | First use of the Never Knowingly Undersold slogan |
| **1925–9** | Four successive years with a Bonus of 20% or above |
| **1926** | Spedan buys Oswald's share of the John Lewis business |
| | Michael Watkins joins the Partnership |
| **1927** | The Odney club formed; Bernard Miller joins the Partnership |
| **1928** | John Lewis dies and Spedan combines the businesses |
| | First Partnership constitution published |
| | Spedan acquires TJ Harries in Oxford St, which becomes the 'east' house |
| **1929** | Formation of the Partnership after signing of the first trust settlement |
| **1931** | Pay cut for all but the lowest paid |
| **1933–4** | Four department stores acquired |
| **1934** | Last double-figure Bonus for 26 years |
| **1935** | Bonus of 9%, only given to those earning £400 or less |
| **1936** | DH Evans acquired to complete the 'west' house |
| **1937** | New Peter Jones building completed |
| | Waitrose bought – ten shops with sales of £167,000 |
| **1938** | Pay cut |
| **1939** | 'Deferred' pay introduced at the outbreak of war |

| | |
|---|---|
| **1940** | SPS chain of fifteen shops bought |
| | John Lewis Oxford St, Knight & Lee and Tyrrell & Green bombed |
| **1941** | Non-contributory pension scheme introduced |
| **1945** | Five elected board members introduced |
| **1946** | First Bonus for nine years |
| **1947** | First branch Chronicles published |
| **1948** | *Partnership For All* published |
| **1949** | Branches opened in South Africa (closed 1954) |
| **1950** | Second trust settlement |
| | Oswald Lewis returns to the business part-time |
| **1952** | Pay cut |
| **1953** | Acquisition of Bainbridges and Heelas |
| | Beatrice Lewis dies |
| **1954** | *Fairer Shares* published |
| **1955** | Spedan retires, succeeded by Bernard Miller |
| | First purpose-built Waitrose supermarket opened |
| **1960** | Oxford St rebuild complete |
| **1962** | Stevenage warehouse opens for department stores |
| | Oswald Lewis retires |
| **1963** | Spedan dies |
| **1964** | Five-day working week begins in John Lewis |
| **1965** | First part-cash Bonus |
| | Brownsea Castle opens as a holiday centre |
| **1970** | First wholly cash Bonus |
| **1972** | Peter Lewis succeeds Bernard Miller as Chairman |
| | Bracknell head office and warehouse opens fully for Waitrose |
| **1974–9** | Electronic POS systems installed throughout John Lewis |
| **1976** | First shopping centre John Lewis in Brent Cross |
| **1978** | Bonus reaches 20% for the first time since 1929 |
| | Ambleside Park hotel purchased |
| **1979** | Six months long leave introduced after 25 years' service |
| **1984** | Five weeks' holiday for everyone after three years |
| **1988** | John Lewis High Wycombe opens with a restricted range |
| **1992** | 100th Waitrose opens |
| **1993** | Stuart Hampson succeeds Peter Lewis as Chairman |
| **1993–5** | Scanning installed throughout Waitrose and supply chain reorganised |
| **1994** | Sunday trading legal, and begins in Waitrose |
| | First Waitrose Food & Home |
| **1999** | Demutualisation debate |
| **2000** | Golden Jubilee fund set up |
| | Waitrose sales pass John Lewis for the first time |
| **2001** | Buy.com acquired and becomes John Lewis Direct |
| **2002** | Ocado begins distributing Waitrose products |
| **2004** | Seven day trading begins in John Lewis; first Partnership survey |
| **2005** | Waitrose Foundation formed in South Africa |
| **2007** | Charlie Mayfield succeeds Stuart Hampson as Chairman |
| **2009** | John Lewis Home opens in Poole |
| | Bala Lake amenity centre opened |

# Illustration List and Explanation

## Chapter Headings and within the text



## Photos from 1870–1939, between pages 76 and 77

Many of these images, of course, are taken from old newspapers and books, so their quality ranges from poor to awful – but they still carry an atmosphere.

1. Top left: A John Lewis letterhead of 1877. Note that in Oxford Street he still only has the original premises, though he has two unattached shops in Holles Street. Top right: A delivery horse and van, reputed to be 'the best turned-out in London', outside the Weymouth Mews stables. Right: John Lewis's house 'Spedan Tower' in Hampstead; the house was named Spedan before his son was. Below: Oxford Street in the 1890s. The original shop is between the N and the L of John Lewis.

2. Some early shop cartoons. Above: Closing time. Note the disparity in times. A busker outside is singing: '...never shall be slaves'. Right: Rarely were seats supplied for shop assistants before (and sometimes after) the Shop Hours Act of 1899. Here a sympathetic customer is handing hers over to the pale assistant behind the counter. Below left: Hostel life. Not all hostels provided a bath, and many not even hot water. Below right: Aristocratic assistants. A notice reads: 'Customers, please do not annoy the assistants'. Spedan Lewis recruited aristocratic *ladies* rather than men.

3. Above left: Robert Bichan, a shop assistant who started at Peter Jones in 1915 and became a staunch admirer – but council adversary – of Spedan. Above right: The immaculate Philip Hoffman, in normal shop assistant's clothing. An orphan like John Lewis, he became an organiser of the shop assistants' union and a campaigner for better conditions. He particularly admired Wallace Waite. Left: A crammed Harrods window photographed the day before Selfridges opened in 1909. Below: An elegant Selfridges window the same day – compare and contrast. John Lewis's windows would have been like Harrods' at this time.

4. Above left: Spedan's younger brother Oswald in 1906, dressed for work at the shop. Above right: Spedan in an olive grove in Menton in 1907. He had a lifelong fascination with wildlife, at one point keeping lynxes in a cage that abutted his tennis court, which somewhat disconcerted Bernard Miller. A pet gibbon once crossed the River Test from Leckford, alarming the owner of Longstock House – which Spedan later bought (the two events are not thought to be connected...). Right: Spedan and Oswald, now with his moustache, in a John Lewis cricket team in 1907. Below: Grove Farm, Spedan's much-loved home and sports ground in Harrow until a financial crisis forced him to sell it.

5. Above: the 'Long Silk Room' at John Lewis, the heart of the pre-war shop. Left: Eliza Lewis in middle age: she had a hard time maintaining a placid household. Below left: The front page of the *Daily Mirror* on 8 March 1911; Lord Howard de Walden leans languidly as he gives evidence in his libel case against John Lewis, in front of the Lord Chief Justice, seated on the right. Below right: The poster that caused the trouble, on the corner of Oxford Street and Holles Street. John Lewis was spoiling for a fight, and you can quite see the reason de Walden's sued for libel.

6. The newspapers followed the 1920 strike at John Lewis avidly, and supported the strikers. Top: A meeting of the strike committee. Standing is Hilda Canham, who inadvertently became the strike leader. Left: A set of three photos, deliberately juxtaposed by the *Daily Mail*, showing the dour John Lewis flanked by two cheery strikers, Hilda Canham and Bobbie Stirling. By the end John Lewis was smiling, his strikers sacked but eagerly snapped up by other department stores. Right: Strikers outside the theatre to which Sibyl Thorndike had invited them for a free performance of her new play *The Showroom*. Bottom: Strikers leave Morley Hall after voting to continue their action.

7. Above left: Beatrice with the three Lewis children: John Hunter, Jill and Edward. Above right: Spedan and Beatrice (hidden) with the children. Both photographs were taken not long before the tragedy of John Hunter Lewis's sudden death from meningitis at the age of eight. Left: John Lewis was reconciled with Spedan by the time he married Beatrice Hunter in 1923. Here they are with John Hunter as a baby. Below: The old Peter Jones from the far side of Sloane Square in its mid-1920s heyday. The words Peter Jones have now replaced Star and Garter...

8. Top left: Harvesting on the Leckford estate in the 1930s. Spedan invested much of his own money in mechanisation, and in improving the farmworkers' living and working conditions. He began a separate Partnership there. Above right: The inside of Waitrose Gerrards Cross in the 1930s, showing the spacious interior and seats for customers. Left: The unexpected thrills of domestic life between the wars. Below: A Christmas 1913 advert for Waitrose, which 'for quality at competitive prices has no equal'. Longer than the Spedan's original Never Knowingly Undersold, but close to its modern extended version.

## Photos from 1940 to 2010, between pages 152 and 153

9. Above: A panoramic view of Oxford Street showing the devastation to the original 'west house' after the fire on the night of 18 September 1940, still burning late the following day. On the right is the Holles Street junction. Right: Pedestrians in Oxford Street soon after part of the east house reopened. Below left: The devastation in the basement in the aftermath. A lidless cash box was retrieved with coins fused to the metal. Below right: Partners at a table with potential customers outside the burnt-out shop.

10. Above: A Partnership council meeting of 1948 with Michael Watkins in the chair. He was Spedan's right-hand man and a probable successor, but, already ill at this point, he would die aged 50 in 1950. Left: In 1951 the newly-appointed deputy chairman Bernard Miller and his wife Jessica see Spedan off on a trip to South Africa, during the ill-starred venture to open shops there. Below left: Spedan inspects a new yacht in 1955, bought for the sailing club despite the Partnership's fragile financial position. Below right: Spedan returning from the West Indies in April 1955 (brooding on a future in retirement?).

11. The complicated rebuilding of the Oxford Street shop, reduced back to the 'west house', which took from 1955 until 1960. Above: The single storey shop at the Holles Street junction, with its commendably short-lived lettering. Right: Later, an old London bus passes the west house with the reconstruction further advanced. Below left: A man with a barrow and a man with a plan: clearing rubble from the site, a temporary 'hangar' behind. Below right: When Peter Lewis joined the business in 1959 part of the site was still a hole in the ground.

12. Above left: John Bew with his staff outside the Odney pottery, around 1950. Right: Spedan's astounding plan for Odney, drawn up before the war. There was

to be an education centre, accommodation, and a mere fifty tennis courts. Getting planning permission for that in Cookham today would be tricky... Below right: The Partnership Ball was a tradition that straitened circumstances didn't stop. This is the packed dance floor at the Royal Albert Hall in 1956. Below left: A dramatic photo of the fire that destroyed Robert Sayle of Peterborough in 1956.

13. The post-war Waitrose. Above: The first custom-built supermarket, built on the site of a gents' outfitters in Streatham, exciting massive interest before its 1955 opening (just a fortnight before Spedan retired). Self-service began the revival of a Waitrose that had been nearly sold off several times. Left: A grocery interior before self-service, at the Leigh-on-Sea shop in 1951, still with its counters and chairs for customers, the cashier's booth at the end, and tins, tins everywhere. Below left: The interior of an early Waitrose converted to self-service. Note the free-standing fixtures, placed diagonally. Below: The kind of display Stanley Carter banished when he arrived in 1967, at the cavernous Slough Waitrose, a refurbished cinema. Note again the restrained wallpaper.

14. The revues, often directed by Spedan's wife Beatrice, were a feature of pre- and post-war Partnership life (though there is sadly no photo of Bernard Miller being wheeled in a pram, or in a glamorous blonde wig in the 1937 revue). Above, right and below left are scenes from the 1954 revue, which have the advantage of showing the selling floor and office dress then current. Bottom right: The year 2000 saw *Never Knowingly Understood*, a revival after a gap of twenty-nine years. Here four 1930s farm labourers sit in a Leckford pub asking: 'What has Spedan Lewis ever done for us?' (yes, but *apart* from the Bonus, the pension, the rent-free cottages, the...)

15. Above left: Bernard Miller commissioned Barbara Hepworth to create a sculpture for the Holles Street corner. Here she is in 1963 underneath it before – above right – it is hoisted into place. It weighs twenty tons, and it depicts the figures of Capital and Labour, connected by wires representing the virtues that bind the Partnership together. Below left: In place – see also the photo on p. 182. Below centre: The old JLP symbol, no longer used. Below right: An early advert for John Lewis TV and radio, providing a five-year maintenance contract even then.

## Partnership People, between pages 152 and 153

16. Some key figures from the late 1930s. Above: Michael Watkins, shown here, in one of the few parts of John Lewis to escape the blaze, after his appointment to the Board of Trade in 1941. There he introduced Utility clothing and furniture, for which he was knighted (as Sir Metford Watkins) while continuing as overall John Lewis MD. Watkins had been a public school maths master before being invited to join the Partnership, as had – right – Hugh Alexander, the British chess champion. Alexander held several top jobs before being called up to work at the secret Bletchley Park code-breaking centre, where he ran Hut 8 after the computer pioneer Alan Turing. He returned to the Partnership after the war but left to head the crypotography unit at GCHQ. Below left: Sebastian Earl. Oddly, the Partnership has

no photo apart from this in his university rowing VIII. He was responsible for integrating the new 'SPS' stores during the war. He exhausted himself in that period, recovered, and went to run Selfridges. Bottom right: Old grocers meet up in 1963. Wallace Waite front centre, with among others Harold Tobias and Harold Tickner, whose reminiscences are in Chapter 9.

17. Top left: The last of the Newcastle Bainbridge dynasty, the passionate hunting man George Bainbridge, posing at his retirement beneath the portrait of its founder Emerson Muschamp Bainbridge, one of the first to record store takings by 'department'. Above right: Two 'Bevin Boys', in front of the winding gear of the Kent coalmine which Fry (left) wrote about in the *Spectator* as an eighteen-year-old. With him is the playwright Peter Shaffer. Fry became a buyer and the Partnership's photographer. Right: the reforming Home Secretary, and later Chancellor, Roy Jenkins, part-time Partnership financial adviser for several years until the Labour election victory of 1964. Below: Two great post-war Partnership minds, Muriel Ward Jackson and Max Baker, still debating long after retirement, at Odney in 1987. Baker distilled Spedan's retailing advice into a 'little green book', once loaned (not given) to every senior Partner.

18. Major figures from the 1970s and 80s, a period of great stability at the top in the Peter Lewis era. Top left: Ian Anderson, responsible for the Partnership's computing in its expansion period of 1968 to 1977, who drove through the crucial early adoption of point-of-sale technology in John Lewis, before becoming its MD from 1977 to 1990. Top right: John Foster, who ran several department stores, became the John Lewis director of buying for fashions, then headed Waitrose as its MD from 1977 until 1991. Bottom left: Harry Legg, the research and expansion director 1969–86. Bottom right: John Sadler, the finance director from 1971 to 1987, and deputy chairman 1985–90. It's fair to say that he and Legg occasionally did not see eye to eye...

19. For a spell in the early 1980s the Gazette verbatim reports of Partnership council meetings, great slabs of print that ran to several pages, were enlivened by caricatures of its leading players. Here are six. Top left: Ian Bassett, a systems analyst who served as one of the five elected board members for virtually twenty years. Top right: Harry Tossell, a salt-of-the-earth councillor from Peter Jones, and another elected board member. Middle right: David Ramsey, a Waitrose operations manager, and another long-serving board member. Bottom left: David Stevens, who joined John Lewis from school and became a long-serving board member and finally Partners' counsellor. Bottom centre: John Stott, a buyer blessed with a shrewd wit, who was another long-serving elected board member. Bottom right: John James, the Brent Cross accountant, a councillor who crossed swords with some of his MDs.

20. Top: Another of Peter Lewis's long-serving team, Stephen May, with his father Paul. Stephen was personnel director from 1978 to 1992. His father, a silk buyer before the war, did several vital jobs afterwards, and was Bernard Miller's right-hand man as deputy chairman from 1955 to 1970. He played a key role in deciding how the first computers should be used. Below left: Dudley Cloake, who between 1987

and 2003 was successively the Partnership's computing director, Partners' counsellor, and personnel director. Below centre: Ken Temple, chief registrar between 1994 and 2003. Below right: Ian Alexander, personnel director from 1995 to 2000, was development director in the crucial early days of Internet exploitation, and both finance director and deputy chairman when he died suddenly in 2005.

21. Top: Over sixty years of Stredders. Terry, a driver at Peter Jones, who followed his father onto the Partnership council. His father had first become a councillor in 1934. Left: David Jones, a board member for several years, was Partnership council president in 2010. In that year he returned to Waitrose, where he'd begun, as its supply chain director. Below left: Anne Buckley, who started at school as a part-timer on the checkouts at Waitrose Harpenden, and eventually became a councillor and elected board member. Below right: Noel Saunders started on the cash desk in the Peter Jones Partners' dining room, He ultimately became MD of John Lewis Oxford Street, where he piloted through the shop's transformation in the first decade of this century.

22. Four of the Partnership's appointed board members in 2010. Top left: Marisa Cassoni, the first Partnership finance director to have previously worked in that capacity outside the Partnership, and the first with a science degree. Wary after experience of 'testosterone-fuelled' retailers elsewhere, she spoke of her surprise on arrival: 'They looked me in the eye, and actually *listened* to me.' Top right: David Barclay, one of the first two external non-executive directors on the board, appointed deputy chairman in 2007. Bottom left: Andy Street, appointed John Lewis MD in 2007, who had been in the Partnership since university. Bottom right: Patrick Lewis, son of Peter Lewis and thus great-grandson of John, who became Partners' counsellor in 2009.

## Colour Photos from 1925 to 2010, between pages 236 and 237

23. Although the Partnership rarely used to advertise in national newspapers, it did put out promotional material. Here are four further illustrations – another was on page 77 – from a delightfully designed Peter Jones autumn clothing leaflet from the late 1920s. Top left is the leaflet's front cover, with the old Peter Jones behind. Note in all of them the lifestyle references in the background. Nothing could better illustrate the shift of customers from the 'butlers and servants' of Belgravia to the house owners themselves.

24. Top left: A Waitrose advertising leaflet from the 1930s, before the Partnership took it over. Note the 'Buy from the Empire' instruction, a constant theme of Wallace Waite, who championed Empire produce and was awarded the CBE for it. Top right: Advertising on a Waitrose paper bag that further underlined the message. Brown paper bags may not have been 'bags for life', but they were constantly reused in a period where nothing useful was thrown away. Below: A colour chart of John Lewis's dyed Japanese silks, like a paint colour card today. There are 312 distinct shades. Note the blacks and near-blacks – not quite as many as for Victorian mourning fifty years earlier perhaps, but still a healthy choice...

25. Above: An aerial photograph of the John Lewis 'castle' on Brownsea Island, which it shares with the Dorset Naturalists' Trust. Left: The Partnership hotel at Ambleside, centre right of the photo, on the northern shore of Lake Windermere. Bottom left: The famous water garden that Spedan designed at Longstock in Hampshire. The area was so marshy that all the earth-moving had to be done by hand. Bottom right: A map of the Test Valley, showing Leckford Abbas at the foot and Longstock House at the top. Spedan moved across the meandering river to Longstock House after the war. His bird farm no longer exists, and the agricultural estate is now owned by Waitrose.

26. Above: A music society orchestra and choir performing for a Christmas concert at St John's Smith Square in 1999. Below left: Spedan fostered and heavily subsidised sporting activities right from the outset. Despite the difficulties in coordinating events, caused by Sunday trading and shift working, the tradition continues, with an initiative linked to the 2012 Olympics. Here are athletics medal winners from 1996. Right: A flower border at Odney. Bottom right: The strong sailing club tradition continues, too – a yacht at a regatta in 2009.

27. Top: Much of Waitrose's success during the deep 2009 recession could be attributed to the timely arrival of its Essentials range. Below left: Since the 1970s Waitrose has spent considerable time and attention on own-label packaging design. Here are some typical items from its Cooks' Ingredients range. Below right: Full-scale advertising was slow to come to the Partnership. Waitrose dipped the first toe in the water. Above: a characteristically spare early advertisement for Waitrose English lamb, with the focus on the shepherd's crook and calloused hands rather than the product. Below: A still from its TV ad for South African wines, once again typically concentrating on the people who produce it.

28. Top: A Partnership council meeting at Odney in 2010. Compared with the old days (see Plate 10, sixty years earlier) there's now more reading and discussion, less formal debating. Above left: Many customers were stranded in the High Wycombe area by a blizzard before Christmas 2009. The John Lewis shop put up nearly a hundred for the night. Here a selling assistant reads a bedtime story. Above right: A simple label for its new Value range of low-priced products, emphasising the new expanded Never Knowingly Undersold wording. Below right: Advertising the opening of John Lewis Cardiff, entirely in Welsh.

29. Things to Come? (1) Above: The unfamiliar architecture of a shopping mall in Dubai, where Waitrose opened in 2008. Waitrose has further expansion plans in the United Arab Emirates. Above left: Waitrose on the move – an iPhone 'app' launched in the summer of 2010. Above right: The delicatessen department at Waitrose Oxted, a new 'convenience' store, a tricky format to make profitable. It's ironic that Waitrose is now opening shops the same size as those it was closing in the 1960s... but of course they're very different. Left: A pineapple picker from Ghana, the latest country where the new Waitrose Foundation has kick-started co-operative farming enterprises.

30. Things to Come? (2) Above left: part of a John Lewis Direct screen, from the new online fashion initiative launched in September 2009. Note '1940s Glamour' – a far cry from the days when John Lewis sold 'clothes, not fashions'. Above right: Practice in foreign languages – for future expansion? A dual language sign in John Lewis Cardiff, a gentle introduction. Right: The first John Lewis at Home, at Poole. Below: A still from a May 2010 TV advert, which followed a woman from birth to old age in ninety seconds. What would Spedan and his advertising-averse team think of a world where a John Lewis TV ad cost nearly 4% of the previous year's trading profit, and received emotional responses, national headlines and countless plays on YouTube?

# Picture Acknowledgements and Text Permissions

All photos are the copyright of the John Lewis Partnership except where indicated below. I'd like especially to pay tribute to Trevor Fry, who took virtually all the photographs of Partnership people between 1960 and 1990. Many thanks to Judy Faraday and Linda Moroney at its archive, and Howard Malone of the Gazette.

Mark Mackenzie pages 258, 294, Pl. 29–30 and back cover; Jeff Hopkins Pl. 22, Pl. 28–9, David Townend Pl. 21–2; Adrian Lyon Pl. 27; Roy Riley Pl. 26; Daily Mirror pages 31, 64 and Pl. 5; Daily Mail Pl. 6 and Pl. 9; Margaret Childs Pl. 16; Peter Lewis page 1 and Pl. 5; Keith Morris page 25; Map on page 9 by Kenneth Hudson; Map on page 25 by John Flower; Cartoons on Pl. 2 by permission of Punch Ltd: www.punch.co.uk.

All quotations are by permission of the John Lewis Partnership except where indicated below.

AP Watt Ltd for extracts from *Kipps* by HG Wells. Reproduced by permission of AP Watt Ltd on behalf of the Literary Executors of the Estate of HG Wells.

In some instances we have been unable to trace the owners of copyright material and we would appreciate any information that would enable us to do so.

# Index of People

# Index of Places, Shops and Businesses

# Index of Topics

Peter Jones